PSYCHOLOGY AND SEXUAL ORIENTATION

PSYCHOLOGY AND SEXUAL ORIENTATION

Coming to Terms

Janis S. Bohan

Routledge
New York and London

Published in 1996 by
Routledge
29 West 35th Street
New York, NY 10001

Published in Great Britain by
Routledge
11 New Fetter Lane
London EC4P 4EE

Copyright © 1996 by Routledge

Printed in the United States of America on acid-free paper.

Library of Congress Cataloging-in-Publication Data

Cataloging-in-Publication Data may be obtained by writing
the Library of Congress.

Dedicated to my family, Ann at its heart,

and to Colorado's Lesbian/Gay/Bisexual Family . . .

frightened
courageous
wounded
resilient
sharing light and love

CONTENTS

Preface and Acknowledgments   *ix*

Glossary   *xi*

Introduction: Coming to Terms   *1*

Part I: Conceptual Frameworks

1. The (Uncertain) Meaning of Sexual Orientation   *13*

2. Heterosexuality, Gender, and Heterosexism/Homophobia   *31*

Part II: Lesbian/Gay/Bisexual Identity

3. The Question of Causation:
   Origins of Sexual Orientation   *63*

4. Lesbian, Gay, and Bisexual Identity:
   Stigma Management, Identity Formation, and Coming Out   *92*

5. Diversity and Lesbian/Gay/Bisexual Identity:
   Intersecting Identities, Multiple Oppression   *122*

6. Lifespan Development and Lesbian/Gay/Bisexual Identity   *140*

Part III: Lesbian/Gay/Bisexual Relationships

7. Lesbian/Gay/Bisexual Families: Partners and Children   *177*

8. Lesbian/Gay/Bisexual Communities   *205*

Conclusion: Coming to Terms   22

References   237

Index   259

PREFACE AND ACKNOWLEDGMENTS

THIS BOOK IS THE DIRECT OUTCOME of my own personal odyssey over the past few years. When Colorado voters passed the now-infamous Amendment 2 in November 1992—an amendment to the state constitution that rescinded existing gay rights legislation and prohibited the passage of new ordinances— the direction of my personal and professional life changed dramatically. Teaching at a public, four-year college in Colorado, I found myself in a unique position to respond in a positive and constructive manner to an event that was fundamentally negative and destructive. I developed a course in the psychology of sexual orientation, with the hope that access to correct and affirmative information would facilitate attitude change and, at the same time, provide validation for gay, lesbian, and bisexual students. I have now been teaching the course for two years and have been moved by that experience to write this book.

At present, there is no appropriate text available that addresses the range of topics covered in the course, and I have found that too much class time is spent on efforts to cover extensive material and too little on other experiences that might enhance students' understanding—discussion, exercises, guest speakers, films, and so forth. A primary aim of this book therefore is to provide such a text. The book is informed not only by my extensive reading over recent years but also by my experience teaching this course. That experience has taught me a great deal about where students' interests and questions lie, as well as which approach to the material serves the dual aim of validating the experience of lesbian, gay, and bisexual students while educating others.

In addition, as I have become increasingly involved in this subject area, I have come to realize that there are many, many people who are interested in knowing more about the experience of lesbian, gay, and bisexual individuals, but who have no readily available resource for gaining that knowledge.

x   Included among these people are bisexual, gay, and lesbian individuals themselves, whose lives are notably absent from typical curricula, and who therefore
have had no opportunity to explore the now-vast literature about their own and
their peers' experience. Also included are those who have friends, family, or
acquaintances who are gay, lesbian, or bisexual; those who have an interest in
the subject for professional reasons, such as therapists, counselors, social workers, and teachers; and others whose interest stems from a simple wish to
understand human experience. The book is geared to these people, as well.
Although it relies on a large scholarly literature, the tone and level are intended
to make it accessible and pleasurable reading for those who want to understand. Those who have more academic interests will find extensive references
that suggest directions for further reading.

I am also grateful to Philip Rappaport, who was the psychology editor when
I decided to list the book with Routledge. He was inspiring and helpful, and
convinced me that the book was important when I was still unsure. In his
absence, Jonathan Korzen has been both supportive and encouraging, and I
appreciate his commitment to the book. Margaret Buttenheim provided a very
affirming and very constructive review of the book in its last stages, reaffirm-
ing its value and suggesting some useful directions for change.

As is true of all efforts of this magnitude, I could not have written this book
without assistance and support from others. I am especially grateful to Ann
Cook and Imelda Mulholland. Ann read every word—sometimes several
times—and provided me with a clear and honest appraisal of the book's con-
tents and its readability. Imelda served as my information specialist, tracking
down obscure references, gathering books and articles, photocopying, deliver-
ing and mailing, saving me uncounted hours and untold headaches. Others
were invaluable as sources of support and encouragement, both for the book
and the life that surrounded it; my sincere thanks especially to Marjorie Leidig
and Glenda Russell. The course was developed and the book written while I
was on leave from Metropolitan State College of Denver, and I am indebted to
the college both for the time and for the support the leaves represent.

I am also grateful to Philip Rappaport, who was the psychology editor when
I decided to list the book with Routledge. He was inspiring and helpful, and
convinced me that the book was important when I was still unsure. In his
absence, Jonathan Korzen has been both supportive and encouraging, and I
appreciate his commitment to the book. Margaret Buttenheim provided a very
affirming and very constructive review of the book in its last stages, reaffirm-
ing its value and suggesting some useful directions for change.

Finally, the students in the Psychology of Sexual Orientation course have
my profound gratitude. I have learned a great deal from them and their enthu-
siasm for this material brought it to life for me.

GLOSSARY

NOTE: THE ACRONYM **LGB** is shorthand for lesbian/gay/bisexual. It is used throughout this list for the sake of brevity.

Words printed in **bold** are terms that appear elsewhere in this list.

AFFECTIONAL ORIENTATION. A recent term used to refer to variations in object of emotional and sexual attraction. The term is preferred by some over **sexual orientation** because it indicates that the feelings and commitments involved are not solely (or even primarily, for some people) sexual.

AIDS. The acronym for Acquired Immune Deficiency Syndrome. AIDS affects the immune system and makes one susceptible to a wide range of opportunistic infections. The disease is caused by HIV, the human immunodeficiency virus.

AMBISEXUAL. This term is sometimes used to refer to a sexual orientation that is not exclusively homo- or heterosexual; it is roughly equivalent to **bisexual,** which is the more familiar term. Kinsey and others prefer this term, as it expresses the fluidity of some individuals' ability to eroticize both sexes under certain circumstances, whereas the term **bisexual** implies a more static, equal orientation toward same and other sex individuals.

BIOLOGICAL SEX. The dichotomous distinction between female and male based on physiological characteristics, especially chromosomes and external genitalia.

BISEXUAL. A person whose **affectional** and **sexual orientations** are to members of both sexes, either serially or simultaneously. Sometimes referred to as **ambisexual.**

BUTCH and FEMME. Terms referring to gender stereotyped roles of "masculine" and "feminine," respectively. The primary use of the term is in describing roles assumed by some **lesbian** couples. "Butch" describes a woman who assumes stereotypically "masculine" behavior, mannerisms, and dress. "Femme" describes a woman who behaves in a stereotypically "feminine" way. More broadly, the terms are sometimes used to refer to others, including **straights** and **gay men.**

CLOSET, IN THE CLOSET, CLOSETED. This term is used to describe a **lesbian, gay male,** or **bisexual** individual who hides her/his sexual orientation.

COHORT, COHORT EFFECT. A cohort is a group of people who share similar experiences, typically based on age and the historical contexts of their lives. These shared experiences often translate into common world views and attitudes. The cohort effect refers to the fact that different cohorts may understand and respond to similar phenomena in very different ways.

COMING OUT (of the **Closet**). The sequence of events through which individuals come to recognize their **sexual orientation** and disclose it to others. Since heterosexuality is taken for granted and there is generally no conscious process of discovery or disclosure for straight people, the term is applied almost exclusively to **lesbians, gay males,** and **bisexuals.**

COMMUNITY/LGB COMMUNITY. The social, emotional, and political network within which **LGB** people create and maintain contacts with others, affording opportunities for the sort of interaction and mutual support that are provided for straight people by mainstream institutions.

DRAG. Being "in drag" involves overt violation of **gender** role prescriptions. Most obviously, it means dressing in clothing usually prescribed for the other sex; beyond this, one also mimics the make-up, hair styles, and mannerisms of the other sex. Drag queens are men who appear in public in drag, often performing in drag shows. They may or may not be **gay.**

DYKE. Slang term for a **lesbian,** usually having the connotation of traditionally "masculine" appearance, speech, and manner. In this meaning, it is a stronger form of **butch** and is often intended to convey contempt.

Increasingly, the term "dyke" and its variations are used among lesbians themselves to reclaim the word and deprive it of its negative power. Employed in this way, the word becomes a statement expressing pride in lesbians' freedom from traditional **gender** stereotypes.

ESSENTIALISM. In reference to **sexual orientation,** this approach argues that one's sexual orientation is a core part of her/his being and identity (whether its origins are biological, social, or both). The approach argues that homosexuality (and heterosexuality and bisexuality) have always existed, across history and across cultures, and thus reflect an essential aspect of human experience. This view is contrasted with **social constructionism.**

FAGGOT, FAG. Slang term for a **gay** man. The term "faggot" also means a bundle of sticks. Its use to refer to gay men may derive from the time when men who were accused of homosexual acts were burned along with witches. This origin is also suggested by the term "flaming faggot," a reference to extreme or exaggerated "feminine" behavior.

Like **dyke**, the term has historically had a negative connotation, but is now often used among gay men themselves as an affirmation of gay pride.

FEMME. See **butch/femme**.

GAY. The term applied to a person (especially a man; see below) who is emotionally and sexually attracted to members of the same sex. The most specific definition reserves this term for those who are attracted to men, identify themselves as gay, and see themselves as members of the gay community.

Traditionally, "gay" has been a generic term used to refer to both women and men. However, it has also been used to refer to men only (as the word "man" has been used to refer to all humans and specifically to males). Because this generic use makes women invisible, the current preference in much of the LGB community is for the term "gay" (or gay male) to refer to gay men and "**lesbian**" to refer to women. This usage is advocated by the American Psychological Association.

GENDER, GENDER ROLE. "Masculine" and "feminine." The attitudes and behaviors one is expected (and socialized) to exhibit based on one's **biological sex**. Gender is the socialized consequence of our belief that men and women are and should be different in a wide range of behaviors and experiences. The complex of those expectations constitutes the gender role: the "feminine" role details how women should be, and the "masculine" role defines appropriate behavior for men.

GENDER BENDING (sometimes "gender blending"). Any form of behavior that challenges traditional, stereotypical expectations for "gender appropriate" behavior. **LGB** individuals engage in gender bending/blending by virtue of their involvement with members of the same sex, because this violates "appropriate" (i.e., heterosexual) pairings. Other forms of gender bending (e.g., cross-dressing, exaggerated cross-sex mannerisms, and so forth) may be particularly offensive to some people, but are often seen by the LGB community as intentional affirmations of the freedom to bend gender rules.

HETEROPHILIA. From the Greek *hetero* (other) and *philia* (love). This term is an alternative to heterosexual, preferred by some because it stresses the love between women and men rather than the sexual nature of the relationship.

HETEROSEXISM. The belief that **heterosexual** identity and behavior are normal and legitimate, whereas any other **sexual orientation** is deviant, perverse, abnormal. Institutionalized heterosexism occurs where social institutions assume the legitimacy of heterosexuality and support it with public policies, rituals, and resources while ignoring, demeaning, or even punishing other sexual orientations.

HETEROSEXUAL. From the Greek *hetero*, meaning other. The term refers to an **affectional** and **sexual orientation** toward members of the other sex.

HETEROSEXUAL ASSUMPTION. The belief that everyone is or should be **heterosexual**. This assumption is manifested in cultural norms and institutions that portray heterosexuality as the only possibility, in daily interactions where others assume that one is heterosexual, and in the life scripts we hold for ourselves and each other while growing up.

HOMOPHILIA. Taken from the Greek *homo* (same) and *philia* (love), this term is an alternative to homosexual. Some prefer this term because it stresses the love between people rather than the sexual component of same-sex relationships.

HOMOPHOBIA. Technically, irrational fear of **homosexuality** (from the Greek, *homo*, same + *phobes*, fear). The term has come to refer to an aversion to and prejudice and discrimination against **lesbian, gay**, and **bisexual** people, the traits that characterize them, their sexual practices, lifestyles, and beliefs.

HOMOSEXUAL. From the Greek *homo*, meaning same. This is a clinical or diagnostic term for a person whose **affectional** and **sexual orientation** is toward members of the same sex.

The term is disliked among many LGB people and their supporters for two reasons: (1) it is a clinical term, long used to label LGB identity as a medical or psychological disorder; and (2) it emphasizes the sexual aspect of LGB experience, thereby disregarding the multi-faceted nature of LGB identity.

INTERNALIZED HOMOPHOBIA. The psychological consequence of living in a **homophobic** (or **heterosexist**) society, this term refers to a hatred or denigration of homosexuality that has been internalized by **LGB** people themselves. Internalized homophobia may be expressed through self-denigration, substance abuse, depression, or suicide; as verbal or physical aggression toward other LGB people; as hatred of qualities stereotypically attributed to LGB; or in other forms.

LGB (or LBG or GLB). A shorthand term for **lesbian/gay/bisexual**. **Lesbigay** is often used in a similar manner. Occasionally LGBT or GLBT is used to include **transgender** people. **Queer** (see below) is a rough synonym, acceptable among many in the LGBT community.

LESBIAN. A woman who is emotionally and sexually attracted to other women. The term comes from the isle of Lesbos, where the poet, Sappho, established a community of women in the seventh century BC. Much of Sappho's poetry spoke of love for women.

Currently, the term "lesbian" is popular in many segments of the LGB community and is the term deemed appropriate by the APA to designate **homophilic** women. It is preferred over the generic "gay" as a term that makes women clearly visible, acknowledging that lesbian issues are not entirely the same as **gay** men's issues. However, some members of the LGB community are not comfortable with this term. Some believe it is too political and may be divisive; others feel that it sounds too clinical or pathological.

LESBIGAY. Shorthand for **lesbian/bisexual/gay**.

LIFE PARTNER. The person with whom one shares a committed relationship. In many senses the term is comparable to "spouse" or "lover" in **heterosexual** relationships. Because there are no clear models or "rules," there are no definitive patterns for these relationships, and creativity is the norm.

LOVER. Traditionally the term has been used among **LGB** people to refer to a primary partner, with or without commitment to a long-term partnership. The term is rejected by some LGB people because it implies that the relationship is purely sexual, thus neglecting the many other facets of the relationship and reinforcing stereotypes.

OUT, OUT OF THE CLOSET. The state of being aware of and open about one's **sexual orientation**. Coming out is a continual process rather than a single event, and people can be out in varying degrees; some are out only to themselves, some are out to their family, some are out to coworkers, some may be out to some friends and not to others, and so forth. The term is almost exclusively applied to **LGB** people, because **straight** people are automatically out as a result of **the heterosexual** assumption.

OUTING, TO "OUT" SOMEONE. To "out" someone is to reveal her/his **sexual orientation** without consent. Some activists have argued that it is crucial that powerful and important **LGB** people be visible, and that when such people choose to remain **closeted**, the entire LGB cause suffers. Using this rationale, they publicly expose the sexual orientation of people who themselves have chosen to remain closeted. Less blatant forms of outing also occur, as when a person mentions the name of someone she/he knows to be LGB, thus inadvertently revealing that person's sexual orientation to people who might otherwise not be aware of it and whom the individual might not have chosen to tell.

While outing in the intentional, politically motivated sense is highly controversial in the LGB community, inadvertent outing occurs frequently, as people share stories about their lives, seek out community, try to make new contacts, and so forth. **Straight** people, of course, are outed regularly and without controversy ("I know her husband," "She dated my brother"). The sharing of information about sexual orientation is only a risk for LGB, for whom even inadvertent and apparently innocent outing can be damaging.

PARTNER. See **life partner.**

QUEEN. A **gay** man, especially one who is particularly "feminine" in manner and dress. The term is usually used by others derogatorily, but may be used by gays themselves as an affirmation of their comfort with violating norms for "masculine" behavior.

QUEER. A slang term traditionally used to refer to **lesbians** and **gay** men; increasingly it refers to all alternative **sexual orientations** and identities (lesbian, gay, and bisexual; often it also includes **transgender**). Historically a derogatory term, this word has recently been claimed by LGB (and transgender) people as a term of pride used among themselves, reflecting their shared freedom to engage in **gender bending.** It provides a convenient umbrella term and also expresses many LGBs' conscious desire to challenge the norm, to be different, odd, queer. However, many LGBs are very uncomfortable with the word, because it has been used so negatively in the past and precisely because it means odd, different, queer.

SEXUAL ORIENTATION. One's sexual orientation is defined by the sex (same or other) of the people to whom one is emotionally and sexually attracted. While the term emphasizes the sexual component of interpersonal relationships, in reality any sexual orientation involves a wide range of feelings, behaviors, experiences, and commitments.

SOCIAL CONSTRUCTIONISM. In reference to **sexual orientation,** this approach argues that **"homosexuality," "heterosexuality,"** and **"bisexuality"** as we understand them are products of particular historical and cultural understandings rather than being universal and immutable categories of human experience. Although same-sex attachments and sexual activity may have occurred throughout history and across cultures, this approach argues, such behavior is not necessarily viewed as we view it. One's self-identity as homosexual (or heterosexual or bisexual) is seen as a product of similar forces. If the culture did not define identity by the sex of one's partner, neither would we define ourselves in that manner. Thus, sexual orientation is not *inherently* a core, immutable part of identity, but comes to be experienced in that way because the culture defines it thus. This view is contrasted with **essentialism** (see above).

SODOMY. This term is taken from the biblical town of Sodom, which was destroyed by God as punishment for its sins. In its broadest sense, the term sodomy refers to any "unnatural" sex act, that is, any sex act that is not directed toward reproduction. The term has taken on a narrower meaning, usually referring to anal sex. In many situations, sodomy is synonymous with

homosexual sex (where "homosexual" means **gay** male sex)—hence the references to gay men as "sodomites." Laws against sodomy are commonly prosecuted as laws against (usually male) homosexuality.

STIGMA, STIGMA MANAGEMENT. The term "stigma" literally means a physical mark that labels an individual (e.g., a scarlet "A" to denote an adulteress; a yellow star to denote a Jew). More broadly, it refers to a trait or attribute that causes others to label someone as deviant, even if that quality is invisible—such as being LGB.

Individuals characterized by stigma must develop strategies for coping with the negative consequences of this label. These stigma management techniques may consume inordinate energy, commensurate with the degree to which the stigma is seen as a pervasive and seriously deviant aspect of the individual's identity.

STRAIGHT. A slang term historically referring to people who are generally conventional in their behavior, conforming to cultural norms. Its most frequent current use is in the context of **sexual orientation**, where it refers to **heterosexual** identity.

TRANSSEXUAL, TRANSGENDER(ED). In most sources, these terms are nearly interchangeable, with both terms referring to individuals who have chosen to live as a member of the sex other than their own **biological or birth sex**. "Transgender" is a more recent term, reflecting a movement to the use of "gender" rather than "sex" in most discourses about male/female, feminine/masculine distinctions. Transgender individuals express a feeling of being "in the wrong body" and choose to correct the error. They may choose to change their sex/gender identity completely, undergoing hormone treatments and surgery to give them the correct body, as well as changing their behavior, hair style, dress, mannerisms, and so forth.

In some discussions, the distinction between transsexual and transgendered rests in the meaning given to these feelings of being in the wrong body. The term transsexual focuses on the physical and sexual aspects of one's identity. Transgendered, on the other hand, focuses on the broader psychological and social meanings of being a man or a woman. Some transgendered people do not undergo physical changes, choosing instead to live as the other sex while retaining the physical body of their birth sex.

In other sources, transsexual is reserved for those who undergo a complete sex change, whereas transgender refers to anyone who blurs traditional gender lines: transsexuals, transvestites, cross-dressers, drag queens, **butch lesbians, gender blenders/benders** (who assume some parts of both roles), androgynes (who are comfortable in either role and are not committed to one or the other), etc.

Transsexual/transgendered people represent a dimension different from **sexual orientation**. For example, a male-to-female transsexual may, subsequent to the undergoing a sex change, form relationships with men. Such relationships are **heterosexual** according to the social roles (**gender**) and the external genitalia of the partners, although both are genetically male. If the same person formed relationships with women, those would be **lesbian** relationships according to the external genitalia and social roles of the people involved, even though they are genetically of different sexes.

TRANSVESTITE. A person who dresses in clothing generally deemed appropriate for the other sex and who derives sexual gratification from this practice. Some sources refer to any cross-dressing as transvestitism, but most reserve the term for people who are conventional in other areas of their lives and who engage in cross-dressing in well-defined and circumscribed circumstances. Most commonly, transvestites in this latter sense are **heterosexual**, often married with children.

The Symbols of LGB Identity

LAVENDER. The color that represents LGB identity. Probably this comes from a merging of pink (feminine) and blue (masculine), signifying the freedom from gender stereotypes made possible by living outside the heterosexual norm. Some authors point to lavender as a transitional color—between pink and blue, but also between dark and dawn, day and night. Thus, the color signifies an intermediary state, a transitional position in human experience.

INVERTED PINK TRIANGLE, BLACK TRIANGLE. During the reign of Hitler, gay men and lesbians were taken to concentration camps, as were other minorities, to be used for forced labor and medical experiments and often to be exterminated. Just as the Jews were required to wear a yellow star of David (two yellow triangles), other prisoners were identified by particular triangles. Gay men wore pink triangles. In some camps, lesbians wore black triangles (which generally designated social misfits), while in others they, too, wore pink triangles. The pink triangle has become a symbol of LGB pride.

RAINBOW. The rainbow denotes the wide diversity in the community, an emphasis on the fact that there is no "typical" lesbian, gay, or bisexual, that **LGB** individuals come in all colors, races, religions, ages, occupations, social classes, family patterns, etc. The "official" LGB flag, recognized by the International Congress of Flag Makers, consists of six horizontal stripes: red, orange, yellow, green, blue, and lavender.

λ (The Greek letter LAMBDA.) According to legend, this symbol adorned the shields of warriors in the Sacred Band of Thebes, a particularly brave and fierce band of warriors in ancient Greece, comprised of 150 gay couples. In ancient Greece, the lambda symbolized justice and a reconciliation of opposites.

COMING TO TERMS

SEXUAL ORIENTATION, sexual preference, sexual identity, gay rights, Queer Nation, dykes on bikes, fairy circles . . . who are these people and what is their proper name? Why are they so vocal and what do they want? Why do they elect to live a detested identity and how can such egregious deviation from the norm be considered anything other than pathological? Does the word "gay" disguise an existence that is sad and lonely? Is bisexuality an evasion or an expanded level of existence? How do people come to call themselves homosexual, bisexual, lesbian, gay, queer? What are the joys and risks, the costs and benefits, of nonheterosexual identity? What does any of this have to do with being "womanly" or "manly?" Who knows the answers to these questions? And why should anyone care?

In recent years, numerous events have drawn attention to the place of gay, lesbian, and bisexual people in this society. Consider the litany: electoral initiatives to restrict so-called gay rights; contentious discussions about accepting gays in the military; incidents of appalling violence against lesbian, bisexual, and gay individuals and the addition of this class of violence to the list of designated "hate crimes"; numerous court cases where the parental rights of lesbians and gay men have been contested; the implementation of regulations ensuring protection for bisexual, lesbian, and gay pupils in public schools; the heightened visibility of (especially) gay males incident upon the HIV/AIDS epidemic; the steady barrage of condemnation from the religious right.

This magnifying attention has occurred against a background of opinion little informed by scholarship. As portrayed in the public discourses that frame these debates, the conflicting positions are forged from profound and irreconcilable differences in values. The tacit message is that these positions have no scholarly mooring, and are therefore not amenable to serious intellectual analysis. In reality, there is a great deal of significant scholarship pertinent to gay, bisexual, and lesbian experience—as well as to heterosexual experience; much of this work is in the field of psychology.

Simultaneous with increasing public focus on these issues, psychology has labored to become more responsive to the breadth of human diversity. Students taking psychology courses and persons entering into the psychological professions are increasingly called upon to consider the impact of cultural variations on individual and group psychological functioning. The intersection of these two developments—the burgeoning awareness of lesbian, bisexual, and gay issues and psychology's recent commitment to pluralism—has led psychology to direct attention to the distinctive experience of lesbians, gay males, and bisexual individuals. We now find in the psychological literature frequent admonitions that a familiarity with this experience is essential if one is to work effectively with bisexual, lesbian, and gay people living in a heterosexist world.

From this awareness and the initiatives it has spawned have emerged a need for resources that provide access to the burgeoning psychological scholarship addressing the experience of LGB persons. The purpose of this book is to introduce the reader to this literature with an eye toward providing a sound basis for living and working in a society where some percentage of individuals identify as bisexual, lesbian, or gay, and where that identity is stigmatized.

The Question of Terms

It is difficult to find terms that are adequate to identify the many people we want to discuss here. This book primarily addresses the experience of individuals whose primary attachments are not (or not solely) to members of the other sex. But the term "homosexual" is problematic, both because it focuses on sexuality to the disregard of the complexities of identity, and because it is the term long used as a medical and psychological diagnosis and therefore carries pathological undertones. "Homophilia" is better, in that it refers to love between same-sex individuals, thus avoiding the sexual implications and pejorative tone of homosexual, although bisexuality is still not explicitly included in the term. But this term is not widely known, and its usage is often awkward. Although both words fail explicitly to address bisexuality, they do include the nonnormative dimension of bisexual identity, namely same-sex attachments.

The generic "gay" is sometimes used to refer to both men and women who identify as homosexual or bisexual, but this term shares the same problem as the generic use of "man" to name everyone—women are invisible, and their distinctive needs and experiences are therefore easily missed. In fact, considerable scholarship points to profound differences between the experiences of lesbians and gay men, as well as of male and female bisexual individuals. Alternatively, the word "queer" can be used as an umbrella term to include lesbian, gay, bisexual, and perhaps other nonstraight identities. However, this word has carried extremely negative connotations, so that many people find it offensive.

There simply is no universally acceptable collective term. The American Psychological Association recommends using "lesbian" to refer to homophilic women, "gay males/men" to refer to homophilic men, and "bisexual" to refer to both men and women who so identify. However, in discussing the collective, this convention creates quite a lengthy string of terms, which quickly becomes tedious. Accordingly, I will usually use the abbreviation "LGB" to refer to lesbians, gay men, and bisexual persons; sometimes I will use the generic "homophilia." Where the context demands it, I will use the terms "lesbian," "gay," and/or "bisexual" individually. And on rare occasions, I will use "homosexual," especially where referring to others' work that has employed that term.

The Terminology of Sex and Gender

To provide consistency to this discussion of LGB experience, a brief tour through basic terminology is in order. The word *sex* refers to one's biological status as female or male. Most commonly, one's sex is defined by external genitalia or by chromosomal make-up. However, even in this most rudimentary of distinctions, confusion can arise. It is possible, for instance, to have external genitalia not in keeping with internal organs or with chromosomal sex, and it is possible to have chromosomal make-up that does not match either of the two simple categories we designate as male (XY) or female (XX).[1] To complicate further the matter of defining sex, we usually do not know the chromosomal sex of others, nor do we usually inspect their external genitalia. Rather, we draw conclusions about people's sex based on other, readily visible criteria, usually having to do with gender.

The term *gender* refers to the behaviors, attitudes, and other attributes that are deemed appropriate for an individual based on her or his biological sex. Gender is usually denoted by the terms "feminine" and "masculine." We are socialized into particular *gender roles*—that is, we are taught these roles, both blatantly and subtly—throughout life. To the degree that this socialization is successful, our gender role will correspond to our sex: women will be feminine and men, masculine. These gender expectations include attributes ranging from dress, hair styles, and mannerisms to interests, abilities, values, and beliefs, and they vary from culture to culture and across history. We typically determine another's sex from visible indicators of gender as we understand it, concluding that her/his sex corresponds to these signals or "gender display" (West & Zimmerman, 1987).

---

1. These complexities are beyond the scope of this book. For discussion see Fausto-Sterling (1992), Money (1987, 1988), or a human sexuality text.

4   Some writers use the term, "sex role" or "social sex role" to refer to these socialized attitudes and behaviors (e.g., Gonsiorek & Weinrich, 1991; Shively & DeCecco, 1977). However, major work in the area of gender abandoned the term "sex role" some time ago, both because it disregards the distinction between biological (sex) and sociological (role) constructs, and because it distracts from the socialized nature of these qualities by implying a fixed correspondence between the role and one's biological sex (see, e.g., Unger, 1979). Consequently, a distinction has been drawn between sex-as-biological and gender-as-socially-created.[2] Accordingly, the term "gender role," now common in the psychology of gender literature, will be employed here rather than sex role.

Sexual identity is the phrase used to refer to one's sense of the sex category to which she or he belongs. Thus, to identify oneself as a woman or a man, as male or female is to express sexual identity. Some writers use the term "sexual identity" rather than or interchangeably with sexual orientation. Again, while this usage has some merit, it is not the terminology commonly found in psychological writings, and so will not be used in this manner here. Additional confusion, though, is introduced by a discrepancy between terminology currently accepted in psychology of gender and that commonly suggested in work on sexual orientation. Some sources in the latter group (e.g., Gonsiorek & Weinrich, 1991; Shively & DeCecco, 1977) have used "gender identity" to refer to this sense of one's identity as male or female. However, as is true with the terminology regarding gender/sex roles, the use of "gender" here conflicts with the use now common in gender theory and research, where (socialized) gender is distinguished from (biological) sex. Accordingly, "sexual identity" will be used here to refer to a sense of being female or male, since those terms represent biologically based (sex) rather than socialized (gender) identity.

Finally, *sexual orientation,* which has largely replaced "sexual preference" in the psychological literature, is defined by the *sex* (not the gender) of the people to whom one is erotically and emotionally attracted. In keeping with arguments perhaps most cogently articulated by Money (1987), this usage is intended to convey that LGB identity is not (simply) a preference but is as much a given as is handedness; it is not a choice, nor is it synonymous with same-sex acts. At the most basic level, same-sex orientation, or homosexuality, is contrasted with other-sex or heterosexual orientation and with bisexuality (or ambisexuality). Money argues that the definitive criterion is falling in love; if one falls in love with one's own sex, she or he is lesbian or gay; if one falls in

2.   Recent work recognizes that even the concept of sex entails socially constructed meanings and cannot be understood as a simple biological given (e.g., S. Bem, 1993a, 1995; J. Butler, 1990; Kessler & McKenna, 1978; Ortner & Whitehead, 1981; Tiefer, 1987, 1991; West & Zimmerman, 1987). For our purposes, however, the basic distinction between sex and gender seems crucial to the discussion of terminology here.

love with both men and women, he or she is bisexual; if one falls in love only with the other sex, he or she is heterosexual. As will soon become clear, defining sexual orientation is not this simple.

The terms sex, gender, and sexual orientation are often confused in common language (and even in the professional literature, as we will see). However, conceptually they are independent dimensions. Masculine men may or may not be gay; heterosexual women may or may not be feminine; feminine individuals may or may not be men; masculine women may or may not be attracted to men; individuals whose sexual identity is not compatible with their biological sex may or may not be heterosexual; bisexual individuals may or may not behave in a manner typically defined as gender-role appropriate, and so forth.

The Complicated Meaning of "Coming to Terms"

This book is about the *psychology* of sexual orientation; it is not intended to resolve the sociopolitical issues that currently command our attention. It is not the conclusive answer regarding the morality of LGB behavior, nor the military preparedness of LGB persons, nor their place in religious beliefs and institutions. The aim is not to answer the convoluted social, political, and ethical questions that are stirred by considerations of LGB experience. Although the work we will consider here certainly has the potential to shape our answers to questions such as these, resolution of these controversies is not our goal.

The approach taken in the book is not, for all of that, free of controversy. Two distinctive meanings are implied by the title, and this intentional ambiguity reflects a duality of understanding that will serve as a touchstone for discussion throughout the text: the distinction between essentialist and constructionist renderings of sexual orientation. In order to frame the meaning of the title and the aim of this book, let us consider these two very different perspectives on sexual orientation and their relevance here.

Essentialism and Sexual Orientation

The dual meaning expressed by "coming to terms" perfectly sets the agenda for this book. On the one hand, the phrase refers to the struggle to accept, to come to terms with one's identity as a member of one or another category of sexual orientation. Coming to terms in this sense points to the process of recognizing, accepting, and integrating sexual orientation into one's overall sense of identity. Seen this way, one comes to terms with her or his sexual orientation as an essential, core aspect of personal identity, as a quality that defines who one is as well as how one behaves and feels. This meaning represents an *essentialist* interpretation of sexual orientation, wherein sexual orientation is seen as a trait or attribute intrinsic to individuals.

6   From an essentialist perspective, sexual orientation exists as a freestanding quality of individuals, present whether or not it is acknowledged by the individual, observed by others, or given meaning by the culture. It is a fundamental and definitive axis of each individual's core self, regardless of how that self may be manifested (or hidden) in varying situations. In addition, essentialism posits historical and cross-cultural dimensions to the meaning of sexual orientation, as well. Sexual orientation as an element of individual identity has existed across history and across cultures; in every time and locale, there have been individuals who were fundamentally gay, heterosexual, lesbian, and bisexual. Whether there were words to designate these identities, whether there was an identifiable LGB community, whether these people made a point of revealing their identities, there have always and everywhere been people who define themselves in terms of the sex of those they love.

From an essentialist stance, then, sexual orientation is an extant trait of the individual, a core aspect of one's character; such an identity is grounded in the sense that sexuality itself—and, more specifically, the sex of one's partner—is definitive of one's being. Although attitudes toward variations in sexual orientation may differ across time and culture, these identities themselves have existed always and everywhere, and thus represent a fundamental, essential form or manifestation of human experience.

The task of science, from this perspective, is to discover the phenomena that define these identities and to answer meaningful questions about them; this is the posture that psychology has taken toward sexual orientation. The psychology of sexual orientation is a study of the process of *coming to terms* with life as a heterosexual, bisexual, lesbian, or gay person. In part, this book will appeal to this meaning of the phrase "coming to terms," and will explore in depth the fundamental salience to LGB experience of the process of coming to terms with a stigmatized identity and a stigmatizing world.

Constructionism and Sexual Orientation

On the other hand, the phrase "coming to terms" might describe the manner by which we collectively come to terms, come to shared understandings about how to identify and describe particular events or individuals. This meaning of the phrase appeals to social constructionism, a fairly recent approach to the question of how we know or what we take for "knowledge." Social constructionism argues that we do not know reality directly. Rather, what we take as truth—that is, what we take to be an accurate description of reality—is in fact a hypothesis, a best guess based on the limited information available to us. Thus, we do not firmly "know" in the usual sense of having access to an accurate rendition of reality. Rather, we come to particular understandings based on the means of knowing that are available to us. Such understandings are indelibly marked by the beliefs and prior interpretations imbedded in our own culture, by the concepts available to us to organize our understandings, and (especially) by the language we employ and the categories we create to define and describe reality.

Once achieved, this so-called knowledge does not seem to us to be a hypothesis but seems self-evidently true. We believe we have "discovered" and are describing reality, when in fact we are describing a limited perspective available to us through the particular lens of our own context. Rather than describing a freestanding reality, the particular discourse—the language, beliefs, statements, terms, and categories—we employ to express our so-called knowledge does not simply represent reality, but endows experience with meaning, actually forges the meanings that we take as reality. Our experience is thus formed by discourse rather than by reality itself (e.g., Berger & Luckmann, 1967; Gergen, 1985; Hare-Mustin & Marecek, 1988, 1990; Sampson, 1993).

Applied to sexual orientation, the constructionist approach suggests that sexual orientation is not a trait or quality of individuals. Rather, it is a socially constructed notion that imbues certain acts and experiences with a particular meaning: they are taken as expressions of an identity grounded in (what we term) sexual orientation. By defining individuals in terms of their erotic and affectional attachments and by enumerating categories to describe such attachments, we actually create precisely the situation we believe we are describing. Individuals do, in fact, understand their identity to be grounded in the nature of their affections—more precisely, in the sex of their partners.

However, these experiences we take as indications of sexual orientation are not intrinsically or necessarily manifestations of identity, nor need identity be organized around the nature of one's erotic and affective attachments. Viewed from a different historical or cultural position, these same phenomena would carry a very different meaning. Same- or other-sex attachments would not necessarily be seen as constituting identity; indeed, there might be no construct of sexual orientation at all, no sense that the sex of one's partner is significant to one's sense of self. In Padgug's words, "The members of each society create all of the sexual categories and roles within which they act and define themselves. The categories and significance of the activity will vary as widely as do the societies within whose general social relations they occur" (1989, p. 60).

The terms we employ and, most importantly, the meanings they convey are socially constructed; as such, they bear the imprint of the context from which they emerge. Once we have come to such terms, we collectively accept them as descriptions of a reality that we take to be separate from the terms themselves. By *coming to the terms*, we construct the very phenomena that the terms designate. Thus, experiences come to define individual identity; the adjective "homosexual" used to define a particular quality of some experiences becomes a noun (the homosexual) that identifies and defines an individual. The concept of sexual orientation transforms something one experiences into something one *is*.

From a social constructionist view, sexual orientation is a term to which we have come (as is bisexual, lesbian, gay, or heterosexual) and that we use in naming experience and thereby defining or constructing the meaning of that experience. We will frequently return to this interpretation of the phrase, "coming to terms," exploring the terms employed in discussions of sexual orientation and attempting to unravel the implicit meanings they convey and the personal and social consequences they render.

Constructionism and "Truth"

Importantly, the constructionist argument asserts that no matter how self-evident our own particular construals appear, they are no more certain, no more directly representative of "truth" than are other, very different understandings. If we cannot know reality directly but only through the limited vision of our own position, then there is no way to assert that our rendition correctly taps some core truth about human experience.

Faced with the question of why one or another idea/construction holds sway, constructionists argue that the preference for one construal over another occurs for good reason, and that it is possible to dismantle (or deconstruct) a given pattern of so-called knowledge to determine why this particular piece of certainty has evolved. Thus, we can ask the questions "Why this understanding, in this culture and at this time? And what would be the consequences of our adopting a different understanding?" (see especially S. Bem, 1993a, 1995; Kitzinger, 1987, 1995). Questions such as these will arise throughout the book, and we will return to these notions in the conclusion.

Constructionism, Essentialism, and the Psychology of Sexual Orientation

Considerable recent scholarship has explored a constructionist perspective on sexual orientation, detailing its rationale and implications.[3] In combination, these works suggest that constructionism promises an enriching analysis of how individuals' lives are framed by their culture's understanding of sexual

---

3. For further discussion of the social construction of sexual orientation, see S. Bem, 1993b, 1995; Butler, 1990, 1993; D'Emilio, 1983, 1992; Foucault, 1979; Greenberg, 1988; Haumann, 1995; Kitzinger, 1987, 1995; McIntosh, 1968; Plummer, 1981b; Richardson, 1987; Rust, 1993; Stein, 1992; Tiefer, 1987; Weeks, 1981, 1989.

orientation and by their own self-identification as lesbian, gay, bisexual, or heterosexual.

However, this social constructionist approach to sexual orientation is not widely known outside of academia, nor has it guided the psychological literature on the subject to any marked extent. Psychological research and theory, which is the primary focus of this book, derives almost entirely from an essentialist approach; this is true in two senses. First, the psychology of sexual orientation is grounded in the presumption that, by conducting proper research, one can discover and describe the "true" nature of LGB experience. This position stands in contrast to the constructionist perspective asserting that there is no independent reality to be discovered, investigated, described, or explored; the very object of our curiosity is a social construct shaped by our means of knowing rather than an autonomous phenomenon that can be known directly.

Second, most work in the psychology of sexual orientation begins from the essentialist assumption that sexual orientation is a primary, nuclear quality of self with which each individual must come to terms. In this assumption, the field of psychology reflects the understanding of the culture in which the discipline has evolved; this notion of sexual orientation as an essential attribute of individuals and as constitutive of the self is precisely the understanding widely held in society at large. Psychology has contributed to as well as been shaped by this cultural understanding of sexual orientation as an essential trait of individuals.

Although the absence of a constructionist perspective in psychology may separate the discipline from a perspective now prevalent in many disciplines, a thoughtful juxtaposition of essentialism and constructionism suggests that psychology has a distinctive contribution to make to our understanding in this area. Psychological approaches to sexual orientation may point to an intersection between the essentialist and constructionist views where the two are not so discrepant as they might first appear, and it is this: The individual's coming to terms with her/his identity involves creating narratives or descriptions about who she or he is. The conceptual categories and the language available for those narratives necessarily consist of the terms to which we have come in our collective constructions of the notion of sexual orientation. At present, those terms are essentialist; the culture we live in constructs sexual orientation as a core, nuclear, essential defining attribute of identity, which can be defined by membership in one of two (or at best, three) discrete categories. Hence, individuals living in this culture assume this understanding and therefore experience their own and others' sexual orientation in these terms.

Sexual orientation may well be a socially constructed meaning imposed on experiences that could equally well accommodate myriad other meanings.

10   However, *this particular meaning* is the one that individuals in this culture are likely to embrace and with which they must come to terms (cf. Cass, 1984, 1990; Schippers, 1987). These understandings will inevitably be reflected in their psychological functioning.

Weise provided an anecdotal illustration of this phenomenon:

> I know a woman who was a lesbian for seven years. Then one day she admitted she desired men, so she stopped being a lesbian and became a heterosexual. Whereas seven years earlier she had undergone a process of redefining her past . . . she now did the same in reverse. . . . For each transformation, she rearranged her interior landscape of desire. . . . She felt as if there were only two possibilities, so she had to fit her feelings and desires into the narrow confines given her, like Cinderella's stepsisters cutting off their toes and heels to get the glass slipper to fit. (1992, p. xi)

Psychological models that are premised on an essentialist rendition of sexual orientation—insofar as they reflect the internalized, socially constructed understandings of those they strive to depict—accurately represent the subjective experiences of individuals coming to terms with their sexual orientation. That they come to these particular terms—sexual orientation, homosexual, bisexual, gay, lesbian, heterosexual, queer, dyke, fag, straight—may be a social construct, but these are indeed the terms to which they come.

Given that our cultural understandings take this form, essentialist questions such as those raised by psychological research and theory are indeed meaningful, for they address the subjectivity of individuals and the collective understanding of this society. Here, then, is a merger of essentialist and constructionist views that sets the unique role to be played by psychology: to develop an understanding of how individuals and society come to terms with those phenomena we understand as manifestations of sexual orientation in a culture that construes sexual orientation as an intrinsic aspect of individual identity.

PART I

Conceptual Frameworks

CHAPTER ONE

THE (UNCERTAIN) MEANING
OF SEXUAL ORIENTATION

As SUGGESTED IN THE INTRODUCTION, the concept of sexual orientation is not as straightforward as everyday conversations, media accounts, and political slogans would imply. Rather, the topic is fraught with vagaries, the terminology is ambiguous and ill-defined, and the apparently exclusive and stable categories commonly employed actually disguise complex dimensionality and fluidity. The aim of this chapter is to explore in some depth the uncertain meaning of sexual orientation, and in the process to destabilize the simplistic understandings we tend to carry regarding this topic.

Cultural and Historical Contexts

As preface to this discussion, recall the social constructionist suggestion that what we take as truth is actually a situated understanding, whose content is shaped by the context in which it was developed. From our shared perspective, these mutually constructed understandings seem to be not constructions but self-evident descriptions of reality. It follows that our present understanding of sexual orientation is inextricably rooted in our own context, is a culturally and historically specific concept. We grant a particular meaning to this group of experiences that in other places and in other times have been understood quite differently because those understandings evolved in differing contexts. In Blumenstein and Schwartz's (1990) words, "desire is created by cultural context. Sexuality emerges from the circumstances and meanings available to individuals; it is the product of socialization, opportunity, and interpretation" (p. 310). A few examples will illustrate this point.

13

Cultural Variations

First, let us consider the cultural specificity of the notion of sexual orientation as we understand it. A great deal of anthropological research has explored behaviors and experiences that we regard as manifestations of sexual orientation and has convincingly demonstrated the diversity of meanings that can be attributed to these phenomena, and the variety of categories that can be created to accommodate them. The literature on this topic is now vast, and only a few illustrations will be offered to demonstrate the concept.

In many Melanesian cultures, for example, homosexual activity between male youths and adult men is an integral aspect of young males' growing into men. While there are variations among these societies in the specific elements of underlying beliefs, at the core is the assumption that a boy achieves manhood by ingesting the semen of older men. Thus, homosexual activity is essential to rather than a threat to masculinity. Once thus initiated, this younger man will, in turn, become a source of manhood for youth who come of age later. He will also move on to form heterosexual relationships. At no time is this behavior seen as defining a man's identity; no label "homosexual" is applied to the act or the individual. Behaviors that to us bespeak a homosexual or bisexual identity are simply manifestations of this people's cultural beliefs and practices that identify one's membership in the group and in no sense speak to the individual's core sexual identity (e.g., Adam, 1986; Herdt, 1984).

In Mexico, it is common for men to engage in what we would term bisexuality, that is, having both male and female sexual partners. However, having sex with another man is only viewed as an indication of nonheterosexuality for the partner who is the recipient of the sexual act (or "passive"); such receptivity is seen as "feminine" and therefore as an abdication of heterosexuality. For the active partner, there is no such approbation, because his behavior is seen as appropriately "masculine" (e.g., Carrier, 1976, 1989; Taylor, 1986). This perception of sexuality as defined in terms of activity-passivity rather than the sex of partner may have an impact on identity formation for Mexican/Latin American men (Almaguer, 1993). In some Brazilian cultures, a parallel distinction is made between passive ("feminine") and active ("masculine") roles in male-male sex. However, the term "homosexual" as referring to an individual who prefers relationships with members of his own sex fits neither of these roles, which are both internally complex and sometimes reciprocally interchangeable (e.g., Fry, 1986; Parker, 1986). In each case, in contrast to our own understandings, only in limited circumstances is identity defined by the sex of one's partner, and even then, the categories do not correspond to our own.

In a number of African cultures, same-sex relationships are common among women, particularly among cowives in polygynous societies; some of these relationships even include formalized commitment ceremonies. These women are not considered homosexual or lesbian, and their involvement in traditional heterosexual practices is not in question. These relationships are fully integrated into the cultural norms of their society, and may be more or less formal and more or less acknowledged, depending at least in part on the class structure of the society. But in no case are relationships with other women considered definitive of these women's sexuality or core identity (e.g., Blackwood, 1986a; Wieringa, 1987).

As late as the mid 1930s, some Chinese women joined together in the "marriage resistance movement," forming sisterhoods that served as extended families for these women who chose not to marry. Often, close relationships, including sexual intimacy, formed among pairs or small groups of these women (Blackwood, 1986a; Sankar, 1986; Wieringa, 1987). In Lesotho, close friendships between adolescent girls and young women, referred to as "mummy-baby" relationships, frequently include an element of sexual intimacy (Gay, 1986). In neither case does an identity as homosexual coalesce around these relationships.

In many Native American tribes, some men and women assumed cross-gender roles, participating in the dress, activities, and roles usually assigned to members of the other sex. This cross-gender role frequently involved taking a same-sex spouse; thus men would take husbands, and women, wives. However, neither the cross-gender individual nor the partner was seen as homosexual. Rather, the cross-gender individuals, often designated by the generic term, *berdache*,[1] were often viewed as blessed, as merging feminine and masculine energies, as "two-spirited." In none of the instances where this pattern has been identified have the *berdache* traditionally been considered homosexual, nor have they been viewed as deficient, demented, or disturbed (e.g., Allen, 1986; Blackwood, 1984, 1986b; Roscoe, 1987; Weinrich & Williams, 1991; Whitehead, 1981; Williams, 1986b).

With the encroachment of other cultures, these traditional values have often been displaced, so that in many cases current attitudes within these groups have come to match our own. Williams (1986a), for instance, wrote of the discrepancy between the high regard accorded the *Winkte* (the Lakota term for biologically male *berdache*) and the comparative disdain expressed toward contemporary "gay" Lakota members. This transformation in meaning illustrates the initial point: the significance given to particular behaviors and experiences

---

1. The term *berdache* comes from the French word for male prostitute. The use of this term is evidence of the European invaders' misunderstanding of this tradition. They observed men acting in women's roles and taking men as sexual partners. The European cultural tradition provided only one meaning for such behavior: male (homosexual) prostitution. The term has became standard, although it misrepresents the meaning of this tradition to Native Americans themselves.

is a product of context. In this case, the importation of European attitudes acted to alter the understandings of the Lakota, so that their perspective now reflects European beliefs rather than those of their Lakota ancestors.

Historical Variations

The cultural distinctiveness of our particular understanding of sexual orientation is matched by its historical specificity. Focusing on our own, western cultural tradition, we discover that the very notion of sexual orientation as "the distinguishing characteristic of a particular kind of person" (Weeks, 1981, p. 81) is a recent construct.[2] Let us trace major steps in the journey to our current conceptions.

In ancient Greece, it was accepted—indeed, expected—that men would have male youths as sexual partners. These same-sex relationships existed in addition to rather than instead of heterosexual marriage, and were so integrated an aspect of society that there were protocols for their proper conduct. This behavior was not taken as a manifestation of sexual orientation but as an expression of power and status—variables that also legitimized the rape of vanquished enemies and sex with women and with servants. Thus, having same-sex sex did not define one's identity but merely served as the expression of cultural norms.

During the emergence and then the dominance of Christianity in Europe and in the early United States, same-sex sexual activity came to be seen as a sin against God and, eventually, a crime against the state. However, until at least the 18th century, homosexual acts were seen simply as *acts*, and not as defining one's identity. They were condemned and punished as sins or as crimes, just as adultery or bestiality were sanctioned. But there was no attribution of a distinctive *identity* to the person performing these acts.

Even into the nineteenth century, intimate relationships or "romantic friendships" between women were common, often expressed in poetry and in correspondence that can only be described as love letters. As some women gained access to higher education and became able to support themselves without marriage, these relationships sometimes evolved into shared lives, or "Boston marriages." Yet no category of lesbian or homosexual was invoked to define these bonds, nor were they stigmatized by society. Indeed, romantic friendships often existed side by side with heterosexual marriage and family, and were seen as complementary to those relationships. In other cases, women "passed" as men, sometimes taking wives. Ultimately it was the gender viola-

---

2. For a more thorough discussion of the historical evolution of this construct see Adam, 1986; Altman, Vance, Vicinus, & Weeks, 1987; D'Emilio, 1983; D'Emilio & Freedman, 1988; Faderman, 1981, 1991; Foucault, 1979; Greenberg, 1988; Halperin, 1989; Plummer, 1981b; Smith-Rosenberg, 1975, 1985; Vicinus, 1988; Weeks, 1977, 1985; Weinberg, 1983.

tion inherent in this lifestyle rather than the implied or potential lesbianism,
per se, that was the focus of the rhetoric that condemned these women.

Beginning in the nineteenth century, however, acts were transmuted into identities. A growing interest in sex, heightened by Freud's focus on sexuality as central to human development and experience, spawned the new science of sexology, which granted a central role to sex in characterizing individual personality and identity. As sexologists began to describe and catalogue the range of human sexuality, they employed Freud's distinction between the object of sexual expression and the aim of that expression; a preference for a same-sex rather than other-sex object thus defined a major axis of sexual identity.

In the latter half of the nineteenth century, a group of sexologists undertook to investigate and explain what Karl Ulrichs termed "the riddle of love between men" (Kennedy, 1980); others prominent in this field included Magnus Hirschfeld, Richard Krafft-Ebing, and Havelock Ellis. The then-prevalent understanding of "homosexuality," a term first used in 1869, was most often expressed by the term "inversion." This condition was believed to represent cross-sex identity, a third sex, "a woman's soul in a man's body." The biological determinism of the time, a product of Darwin's pervasive influence, led these writers to postulate a biological origin for homosexuality. They were convinced that such an explanation would end the legal and religious discrimination against homosexuality that had long dominated western culture.

By the twentieth century, sexuality had come to be seen as core to personality, and categories of sexual practice and object were construed as central to and consubstantial with identity. The term homosexual now designated an entire individual ("the homosexual"), and that individual's own private experience was inevitably shaped by this new conception. Thus, in D'Emilio's words, the "transformation of homosexuality, both conceptually *and in its actual expression*, from a sexual act to a personal identity" was complete (1983, p. 5; italics mine). Heterosexuality, which was simply that form of sexuality left over after the "perversions" were catalogued, was taken as normative. The movement toward biological and, ultimately, medical explanations of all non-heterosexual identities led to homosexuality's being considered a medical "condition," a form of pathology amenable to "treatment."

Psychology's Role. Psychology's formal participation in the matter of homosexuality begins here, as early psychiatrists and psychologists accepted this disease model of homophilia and contributed their own variations on the theme. Freud's followers in the psychoanalytic tradition, particularly in America, took the professional lead in the movement to pathologize homosexuality (Abelove, 1993; Lewes, 1988; Morgan & Nerison, 1993). Psychoanalytic psychiatry's attitudes were transplanted to psychology largely intact.

Early research supported the view that homosexuality was related to mental illness. Since samples for this research came from among prisoners and patients in psychotherapy, it is not surprising that these individuals were found to be less well adjusted than the average person. In the name of curing this condition, individuals diagnosed as homosexuals (especially men) were subjected to all manner of treatment. Long-term psychotherapy was perhaps the least aversive of these, but even this approach undoubtedly caused tremendous pain, as it reinforced the client's perception of himself (or, more rarely, herself) as diseased. More damaging still were various biological treatments: chemically induced seizures (to "free energy" to its proper use), castration and clitoridectomy, implanting of "normal" testes, administration of estrogen (to decrease "abnormal" sex drive) or androgens (to increase "normal" sex drive), and even lobotomies. Numerous forms of behavior therapy were also invoked, such as aversion therapy (associating electric shocks or nausea-inducing substances with homosexual stimuli or fantasies), and orgasmic reconditioning (associating heterosexual stimuli or fantasies with masturbation) (Coleman, 1978; Haldeman, 1991; Martin, 1984; Silverstein, 1991).

Such treatments were justified by the consensus that homosexuality was a treatable disorder. The original 1952 issue of the American Psychiatric Association's *Diagnostic and Statistical Manual* (DSM), the approved listing of mental disorders, listed homosexuality as a sociopathic personality disorder. Beginning in the 1950s a series of research projects, especially the work of Evelyn Hooker, began to dismantle the contention that homosexuality was intrinsically pathological. Hooker (1957) compared heterosexual men with a sample of well-functioning (rather than imprisoned or disturbed) homosexuals and found that there was no difference in their adjustment. In her research, experts in the field of personality testing were unable to distinguish between the responses of homosexual men and their straight peers. However, the 1968 edition of DSM still listed homosexuality as a mental disorder, not as sociopathic but as a "sexual deviation." Subsequent research activities continued to yield results corroborating Hooker's work, and psychiatry and psychology were ultimately persuaded to rethink this position (e.g., Siegelman, 1972a, 1972b; Thompson, McCandless, & Strickland, 1971).

On the basis of empirical evidence, and having been stimulated to action by the emerging gay rights movement (discussed below; also see chapter 8), the American Psychiatric Association in 1973 removed homosexuality from the DSM. In 1975, the American Psychological Association (APA) issued a resolution of agreement with this stance, further urging that "homosexuality per se implies no impairment in judgement, reliability or general social and vocational capabilities . . . [and mental health professionals should] take the lead in removing the stigma of mental illness long associated with homosexual orientation" (Conger, 1975, 633; see also Bayer, 1981; Gonsiorek, 1991).

Still included in DSM, however, was the diagnosis "egodystonic homosexuality," a term referring to cases where individuals are distressed about their homosexual identity—that is, experience it as incompatible (or dystonic) with the ego (or sense of self). Thus, while homosexuality itself was not seen as intrinsically pathological, discomfort with and a desire to modify it was. This diagnosis allowed mental health professionals to continue treating dissatisfied homosexuals, using "reparative" therapies to attempt to alter homosexual orientation in order to resolve this dystonia or discomfort.

Gradually, as the understanding of homosexual experience was transformed, due in large part to scholarly work motivated by the burgeoning gay rights movement, an alternative view evolved, namely that the problem was not the individual's displeasure with her or his identity but the societal attitudes that condemned that identity and thereby made its adoption painful. Also, emerging models of LGB identity development (see chapter 4) indicated that a period of doubt and discomfort is a common developmental phenomenon as individuals come to terms with an identity stigmatized by society. Thus, a period of "ego dystonia" is an understandable part of the evolution of LGB identity, and should be seen as a normal aspect of the process of managing denigrating attitudes. It is those attitudes, not the identity, that need to be "repaired."

Psychologists were challenged to consider the ethics of "conversion" therapies, even where discomfort accompanied LGB identity. Egodystonic feelings, it was argued, are actually internalizations of society's condemnation of homophilia, and addressing them therapeutically only reinforces the perception that homophilia is a disorder whose correction is a legitimate aim of psychology. Furthermore, such therapy detracts from the needed focus on modifying the prejudicial attitudes that result in internalized homophobia (e.g., Begelman, 1977; Haldeman, 1994; Halleck, 1971; T. Murphy, 1992). By 1987, psychologists were urged by the APA not to use the diagnosis of egodystonic homosexuality, and in the 1987 revised edition of the DSM, the diagnosis was removed (Morin & Rothblum, 1991).

Also contributing to psychology's gradual rejection of reparative therapies was the mounting evidence that such treatment is ineffective. Reviews of research on the outcomes of such therapies have revealed only minimal levels of success, and even these "successes" are rendered questionable by a large body of scholarship documenting pervasive theoretical and methodological shortcomings of research projects purporting to support reparative therapies.[3] Two examples will illustrate these problems.

Masters and Johnson (1979) reported their therapeutic work with a group of

---

3. For critiques of reparative therapies, see Blair, 1982; Coleman, 1978; Davison, 1991; Haldeman, 1991; T. Murphy, 1992; Silverstein, 1991.

20 fifty-four "dissatisfied" gay men who had come to them for help in altering
their sexual orientation. Of these men, only nine described themselves as
almost exclusively or exclusively homosexual (5 or 6 on Kinsey's scale—see pp.
25–26 for a more detailed discussion of Kinsey's scale); the others (83 percent)
ranged from a rating of 2 on Kinsey's scale (predominantly heterosexual with
more than incidental homosexual responses) to a rating of 4 (predominantly
homosexual with more than incidental heterosexual responses). They were not
exclusively heterosexual, but neither would they be considered clearly gay,
opening to question the meaning of "conversion" to heterosexuality. Of the
initial 54 subjects, 30 percent were lost to follow-up, so there is no way to be
certain that any of those identifying as Kinsey 5-6 were included in the follow-
up sample. Final results reported 73 percent "non-failures," a classification
that is not clearly defined and that included nineteen subjects described as
"uncooperative."

Pattison and Pattison's (1980) study of "ex-gays" reported successful treatment "in a spiritual context" of eleven gay men. However, these eleven
individuals were from an initial pool of 300 "dissatisfied" gay men, of whom
thirty were studied in this research project. There is no explanation of why
the other 270 (of the initial 300) were excluded, nor why the other nineteen
from this sample of thirty were not followed. Although success was defined
by these authors as a complete shift in sexual orientation, of the eleven "successes," only three (of eleven, of thirty, of 300) reported no lingering same-
sex fantasies.

Increasing criticism of reparative therapy—accompanied by a growing conviction that the problem lies not in variations in sexual orientation but in intolerance toward such variations—has gradually led psychology to abandon the
position that nonheterosexuality is in need of cure. The discipline has moved
instead toward efforts at enhancing the psychological well-being of individuals
who identify as bisexual, gay, or lesbian and countering the prejudicial attitudes that condemn these orientations. This LGB-affirmative stance has
recently flourished in the literature as well as influenced programmatic efforts
within the formal structures of the discipline.

Currently, organized psychology plays an active role in attempting to
rectify not only the discipline's own treatment of LGB issues but society's
attitudes, as well. Special-interest groups within the field have flourished over
the past twenty years, and the APA has issued numerous policy statements
and *amicus curiae* (friend of the court) briefs in court cases affecting LGB
individuals and groups. APA task forces have published reports on bias in
psychotherapy, bias in language, and bias in research; bibliographies regarding major topical issues, such as gay and lesbian parenting; listings of gradu-
ate faculty interested in the psychological study of LGB experience; special
issues of major journals addressing LGB issues; and numerous other docu-

ments intended to support a movement toward LGB-affirmative psychology.[4]
In addition, psychologists are beginning to address the challenges presented
by new approaches to LGB issues, including social constructionism (e.g.,
Kitzinger, 1995; Richardson, 1987).

Not all psychologists and psychiatrists, however, have participated in this
shift. Some practitioners have remained extremely vocal in their insistence that
LGB identities are expressions of psychopathology (e.g., Bieber, et al., 1962;
Nicolosi, 1991; Socarides, 1975, 1978), and research indicates that heterosexist
bias persists in psychotherapy (e.g., Committee on Lesbian and Gay Concerns,
1991d; DeCrescenzo, 1985; Rudolph, 1988). Also, participation in research and
theory in this topic area remains professionally risky, suggesting that attitudes
within psychology toward the topic of sexual orientation remain ambivalent, at
best (Rothblum, 1993).

Despite evidence of lingering bias, the progression of attitudes reflected in
the contemporary summons to LGB-affirmative psychology culminates in a
remarkable metamorphosis in perspective over the past few decades. This
change in approach represents a profound shift within the discipline, as in
society as a whole, in our understanding of the phenomena we construe as sexual orientation.

The Emergence of Community. The emergence of the contemporary LGB community (hereafter, the "Community"[5]) has overlapped and interacted with
these shifting attitudes in psychology and in society at large. Although the
topic of the Community will be discussed in depth in chapter 8, a few major
elements of its evolution will be presented here, by way of demonstrating the
formative connections among history, politics, knowledge, and personal experience. It is clear that the Community evolved in response to and has, in turn,
exerted profound influence on the changing understandings of LGB experience, and that the experience of individual LGB persons has been powerfully
shaped by these events. A few historical mileposts will suffice to make this
point clear, until we return to the topic in chapter 8.[6]

Prior to World War II, being lesbian, bisexual, or gay usually meant living a

---

4. For discussions of LGB-affirmative psychology, see Bersoff & Ogden, 1991; Committee on
    Lesbian and Gay Concerns, 1991a, 1991b, 1991c, 1991d; Garnets, Hancock, Cochran,
    Goodchilds, & Pepleau, 1991; Herek, et al., 1991; Melton, 1989; Morin & Charles, 1983.

5. There is, of course, no single gay/lesbian/bisexual community, any more than there is a
    single heterosexual community. However, the very construct of a community that joins
    these individuals who share a core sense of identity and, therefore, of commonality—this
    construct is helpful in understanding how individual lesbians, gay men, and bisexuals
    structure their lives and experience.

6. For a more detailed discussion of these and related events, see Cruikshank, 1992; D'Augelli
    &Garnets, 1995; D'Emilio, 1983; Duberman, Vicinus, & Chauncey, 1989; Katz, 1992;
    Miller, 1995.

very closeted life. There was no highly visible label for what one felt; there were no models for how one might live as a homophilic individual; there was no Community to provide information, resources, contacts, or support. During World War II, homophilic people found their counterparts in the mass comings together that accompanied the war—most obviously in the armed forces, but also in cities where same-sex segregation in work environments was common. After war's end, these people gathered to sustain those relationships, especially in large cities and especially along the coasts, where many service people were discharged. The first homophile organizations emerged in California in the early 1950s, acting with the explicit intent of supporting lesbian and gay individuals in efforts to achieve acceptance within mainstream society.

However, such acceptance was not readily forthcoming. On the contrary, gays and lesbians became a major target of the anticommunist rhetoric of the early 1950s, in which homosexuals were portrayed as equally complicitous in the move to destroy the nation. In this climate, gay men and lesbians were at serious risk, as the mere accusation of homosexuality was cause for losing one's job, one's home, and very likely one's family and friends. Compounding the stigma, psychology and psychiatry still judged homosexuality to be a mental illness. People who came to terms with LGB identity during this era were likely to come to very negative terms, indeed.

The severe persecution that emerged during the McCarthy era persisted into the 1960s, forcing most lesbians and gay men to remain deeply closeted and leaving them constantly at risk of being exposed. Thus, it was an event startling for its daring when a group of gay men and lesbians, patrons at a bar in Greenwich Village when the bar was raided, refused to be herded into police vans. The infamous riots that followed inaugurated the contemporary gay rights movement; dubbed "Stonewall" after the bar where the riots began, this insurrection of June 1969 marked a turning point for the Community.

After Stonewall, there was a gradual but persistent growth in the movement toward lesbian and gay rights. Homophile organizations emerged and grew, community centers sprung up across the country, lesbian/gay publications flourished, and political activism became more visible and more vocal. However, "Gay Liberation" held different meanings for lesbians than for gay men, reflected in a growing antagonism between some lesbians and some gay men.

For the individual LGB person, this vigorous political activity marked a new epoch. Suddenly there was a highly visible and intensely energetic movement with which to identify; in fact, there were several, loosely connected movements. People coming to terms with their homophilic identity after Stonewall had new terms that carried far more positive connotations. Indeed, the use of the designation "gay" sets the movement apart from earlier homosexual identity, which had been grounded in an individual's sexual and affectional preference, to a new identity that emerged since Stonewall and that implies a self-selected, socially and politically aware, community-oriented identity.

In this new context, coming out was seen as a political act, and coming out now also meant "coming in" to a supportive Community. It was just four years after Stonewall that the diagnosis of homosexuality as a mental disorder was removed from the DSM, initiating the movement toward LGB-affirmative psychology. While the decision was based partly on empirical evidence that homosexuality was not related to mental illness, there is no doubt that the political milieu also played a role (Bayer, 1981).

At the same time that increased visibility and successful activism provided a positive venue for people coming to terms with a lesbian or gay identity, it also exacerbated the threat of LGB identity. With the conservative political trend that dominated American politics in the 1980s, this visibility made the Community a ready target. Psychology avoided this conservative movement, accelerating its efforts toward improving the life conditions of LGB people and toward addressing the discipline's own lingering heterosexist biases.

Beginning in the early 1980s, the Community faced yet another enemy: AIDS. Using human and political resources that had coalesced around gay rights, the Community undertook to serve its own. The epidemic has had profound effects on the Community as a whole and on the individuals within it. It has also served to reenergize the virulent homophobia that had characterized earlier periods, to aggravate the already burgeoning trend against gay rights, and thereby to erode some of the progress of the post-Stonewall gay rights movement. In this atmosphere, coming out has become more risky, even with the presence of a strong Community.

The collective response of the LGB Community to the AIDS crisis has demonstrated its resources and its strengths, has forged new bonds between gay men and lesbians, and has hastened the active incorporation of bisexual individuals into the Community. Professional psychology has responded with numerous publications focusing on AIDS and its psychological concomitants, with a continuing commitment to the 1973 resolution that our goal should be "reducing the stigma."

These elements of history are crucial to our understanding of the contemporary meaning of sexual orientation, for individuals as well as for society. For, as social attitudes have changed, as the Community has evolved, and as psychology's perspective has been transformed, individuals' experiences have unavoidably been affected. Coming to terms is markedly different where there is Community than where there is not, where one risks life and livelihood for being honest than where one is honored for it. No person experiences her or his identity in isolation from the surround; the meanings of our lives are written in the terms provided to us.

Summary: The Situated Nature of Sexual Orientation

As we have seen, the phenomenon we take as reflecting a primary axis of identity, i.e., sexual orientation, assumes entirely different meanings depending on context. In other cultures, the same phenomena are understood in ways unrecognizable to us, for our categories simply do not encompass them. Even within our own culture, they have taken on entirely different meanings across time: from sin to crime to medical condition to personality disorder to normal—although stigmatized and socially condemned. The locus of the problem has moved from an internal one of character defect to an external one of social attitudes. Our understanding of the appropriate target for corrective action has shifted from sinful acts to homosexual identity to homophobia and heterosexism—and perhaps, given the current political climate, back to sinful acts and discredited identity. Our approach, accordingly, has changed from prayer to punishment to "reparative" therapy to LGB-affirming approaches—and, in some circles, back again.

Shifts in psychology's perspective on the phenomenon we term sexual orientation represent a microcosm of the variability we discover when we explore the historical and cultural specificity of this concept. Our present conception of sexual orientation is historically and culturally located, as specific to its societal location as is any culture's understanding, and as amenable to change as were earlier understandings. The material covered in these pages has illustrated the wide variations in meaning that can be ascribed to overtly similar behavior and how those variations in meaning in turn serve to shape—and even to constitute—individuals' identities as well as cultural designations of normality and deviance.

Contemporary Conceptions: No Less Uncertain

But this is not to say that the understanding of sexual orientation held at this time, in this culture, is any more certain than past or foreign understandings. On the contrary, if we look simply to very recent work in the area and focus on our own contemporary conception of homophilia, we discover not clarity but confusion. To begin to understand the perplexity behind this superficially elementary construct, let us begin with the most uncomplicated (and the most commonplace) contemporary rendition, the notion that people can be grouped into two categories based on sexual orientation: homosexual and heterosexual. This conception of sexual orientation is the understanding that underpins most everyday conversations about the topic, as well as media presentations and political discussions about topics such as gay rights, a gay gene, and gays in the military.

Further, it is this model that underlies the question, asked so frequently, about what proportion of the population is heterosexual or homosexual. To ask this question presumes that it is possible to group people into these two categories and simply count them. I will reserve a discussion of this subject until we have explored the difficulties with defining what homosexual and heterosexual mean; it will become clear how thoroughly unanswerable this question is.

The popularity of this dichotomous portrayal—homosexual and heterosexual—is remarkable, given that its inadequacy was established over forty years ago, when Kinsey and his colleagues demonstrated that this binary depiction of sexual orientation is flawed (Kinsey, Pomeroy, & Martin, 1948; Kinsey, et al., 1953). Through extensive interviews with thousands of subjects, these investigators revealed a range of self-reported sexual orientation best described not by discrete categories but by a seven-point continuum, ranging from exclusive homosexuality (6 on Kinsey's scale), through varying degrees of bior ambisexuality (scores of 5 to 1), to exclusive heterosexuality (0 on the scale) (see Figure 1.1).

Kinsey's work not only discredited the notion that people can readily be categorized into two groups, but also suggested that sexual orientation is not entirely defined by sexuality, per se. His interviews included questions about psychological aspects of attraction as well as actual sexual activity; an individual's placement along the continuum reflected both overt and "psychic" reactions.

In addition, Kinsey's work suggested that people's self-defined position along this continuum may change over time, so that many subjects identified periods in their lives when their sexual orientation was quite different from how they would now identify themselves. This research also demonstrated that the inadequacy of the heterosexual-homosexual dichotomy is not resolved by simply adding a third category, bisexuality. The dimension described here is not composed of discrete categories, whatever the number, but of vague, permeable, and potentially shifting "locations" along the continuum. Adding yet another unclear classification—namely bisexuality—does nothing to resolve the complexities inherent in defining sexual orientation.

The research conducted by Kinsey and his colleagues is not the only work to challenge the conventional construal of sexual orientation. Subsequently, others elaborated further on the intricacies of sexual orientation, progressively expanding the complexity of models offered. For example, Shively and DeCecco (1977) and Storms (1980) joined Kinsey in rejecting a dichotomy in favor of a continuum, and further argued that not one but two continua are necessary: heterosexuality and homosexuality, they argued, are separate dimensions. A person might have strong heterosexual feelings *and* strong homosexual ones, a high level of attraction to one sex and none to the other, moderate attraction to both, none to either, or any other possible combination. For Shively and DeCecco, physical/sexual interest and affectional attraction were presented as independent phenomena, so that an individual could experience intense emotional attractions to members of her/his own sex, but sexual

Figure 1.1

Kinsey's Sexual Orientation Continuum

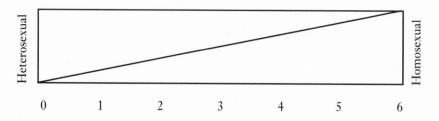

0   No physical contacts resulting in erotic arousal or orgasm and no psychic response to individuals of own sex. Sociosexual contacts and responses are exclusively with other sex.

1   Only incidental homosexual contacts which have involved physical or psychic response, or incidental psychic responses without physical contact. The great preponderance of sociosexual experience and reaction is with the opposite sex.

2   More than incidental same-sex experience and/or respond rather definitely to homosexual stimuli. Heterosexual experiences and/or reactions still surpass homosexual, although both might be frequent. Usually recognize quite specific arousal by homosexual stimuli, but heterosexual responses are still stronger.

3   About equally heterosexual and homosexual in overt experience and psychic reactions. Accept and equally enjoy both types of contacts, and have no strong preference for one or the other. Actual experience in one category or the other may predominate, but psychic reactions indicate that both forms of contact are equally desired.

4   More overt activity and/or psychic reactions to same-sex stimuli, while also experiencing a fair amount of heterosexual activity and/or psychic response. (The reverse of 2).

5   Almost entirely homosexual in overt activities and/or psychic reactions. Incidental physical experience with the opposite sex and sometimes react psychically to the other sex. (The reverse of 1).

6   Exclusively homosexual, both in regard to overt experience and in regard to psychic reactions. (The reverse of 0).

Adapted from Kinsey, Pomeroy, & Martin, 1948; Kinsey, et al., 1953.

attraction primarily to the other sex, both emotional and sexual attractions to only one sex or to both, and so forth.

In another variation on the theme of dimensionality, Klein and his colleagues (Klein, 1993; Klein, Sepekoff, & Wolf, 1986) offered a view of sexual orientation as a multivariate and dynamic process. In this view, sexual orientation is best defined as a constellation of seven components: (1) sexual behavior; (2) emotional preference; (3) sexual fantasies; (4) sexual attraction; (5) social preference; (6) life style, social world, and community; and (7) self-identification. Each of these can be rated along Kinsey's seven-point scale from 0 (exclusively heterosexual) to 6 (exclusively homosexual). There may be little or no similarity among ratings on different variables, or they may be highly congruent.

In addition, these ratings can be used to describe independently past, present, and ideal future positions along each dimension, allowing for variations in the ratings over time. Thus, a hypothetical individual might rate her/himself as a 6 on some variables, a 0 on some, and in between on others; the ratings that describe one's sexual orientation today might not at all mesh with ratings for a year ago or for a future ideal. Using this model, there are uncounted possible categories into which individuals would fit, based on the overall configuration of their ratings. The very notion of categories becomes meaningless here, and the need to recognize the unique qualities of each individual's identity becomes apparent.

These and other multivariate perspectives point up, as well, how futile it is to define sexual orientation by sexual activity alone. Indeed, sexuality per se may even be irrelevant in some circumstances. Some people identify as lesbian or gay without ever having had a same-sex experience, just as most heterosexuals identify as straight prior to having actual sexual experiences. Many people who identify as lesbian or gay have had heterosexual sexual experiences, and many people who identify as heterosexual have had same-sex sexual experiences. Some identify with a particular sexual orientation even though celibate. For men, sexual fantasies and acts are often the key indicator of their sexual orientation, whereas for women intense emotional ties are primary. Indeed, Blumenstein and Schwartz (1990) argue that:

> If Kinsey had used female sexuality as a model, his scale might have been conceptualized not in terms of accumulated acts and psychic preoccupations but rather in terms of intensity and frequency of love relationships, some of which might have only incidental overt erotic components. (p. 311)

Thus, it is clear that it is not sexual activity in itself that defines one's sexual orientation, but a far more complex assortment of variables.

In addition to establishing the profound complexity of sexual orientation, all of these models also acknowledge that people's understanding of their sexual orientation may shift over time. Research has repeatedly demonstrated that, for

28   many people, sexual orientation is not the same today as it would have been in the past or might be in the future. For other individuals, self-labeled sexual orientation may remain the same even though this identification no longer meshes with current sexual activity and emotional commitments. Such shifts in identity are readily explicable within a framework that understands identity as necessarily shaped by shifting social contexts. From this perspective, "changes in self-identification are to be expected of psychologically and socially mature individuals" (Rust, 1993, p. 68)

The gradual recognition that sexual orientation is neither dichotomous nor inflexible has also provided a more adequate basis for understanding bisexuality. The persistent belief that sexual orientation could be described as bipolar has supported the notion that bisexuality was somehow pathological—perhaps a defense against homophilic feelings or a denial of one's "true" homosexual identity. More complex models that recognize self-identification, affect, social relations, and community as well as sexual behavior, and that acknowledge the potential for internally divergent identity and flexibility across time, are far more adequate to portray bisexual identities.

As the work summarized here amply demonstrates, the concept of sexual orientation as a simple dichotomy (or even trichotomy) of identities defined by sexual behavior and consistent over time is simply untenable.[7] Given these critical challenges to the customary perception of sexual orientation, it is clear why the question of "how many" people belong to any particular category is impossible to resolve. In order to answer this question, we must define precisely what are the criteria for membership in each group. This would mean determining, first, what variables will be selected to define sexual orientation and what rating on each is required for membership in a group. Must one be a Kinsey "0" to qualify as heterosexual, or will a "1" do? Or, to invoke Klein, on how many of the seven relevant variables must one reach a "0"? Is sexual activity more crucial to this definition than is, say, social preference? Why? And then there is the question of time. Must one have always been a "0"? Or if one just came to this identity a few months ago, but now feels quite certain, is that enough? How about self-defined gay men or lesbians who have "occasional" heterosexual feelings or experiences (Kinsey's "4")—in which group do they belong? What about a person who identifies as bisexual but is currently in a committed heterosexual relationship? What if she or he is in a committed same-sex relationship? And then, of course, there is a methodological dimension to this definition: subjects must also be willing to identify their sexual orientation to the researcher.

---

7. For discussions of the complexity and potential flexibility of sexual orientation, see Bart, 1993; Bell & Weinberg, 1978; Blumenstein & Schwartz, 1977, 1990; Brown, 1995; Cass, 1990; Coleman, 1987, 1990; Fox, 1995; Golden, 1987, 1994; Gonsiorek, 1995; Kinsey, Pomeroy, & Martin, 1948; Kinsey, et al., 1953; Kitzinger & Wilkinson, 1995; Klein, 1993; Rothblum, 1994; Rust, 1993; Sophie, 1986; Suppe, 1984; Weinberg, Williams, & Pryor, 1994.

The number of individuals identified as heterosexual, lesbian, gay, or bisexual depends entirely on how group membership is defined and determined. As a case in point, a recent, much publicized study reported that the incidence of homosexuality among U.S. residents is far lower than the 10 percent commonly cited in the LGB literature. Laumann, et al. (1994) reported that 2.7 percent of men and 1.3 percent of women in their survey told interviewers that they had same-sex sexual experiences in the past year. This study is questionable on several grounds. First, about 20 percent of those contacted chose not to participate; it seems likely that LGB identity would be a reasonable motive for declining to participate in a study regarding sexual experience. Second, there is no way to know how many individuals who did participate were unwilling to answer this question honestly when it was posed by an unknown interviewer, regardless of guarantees of confidentiality.

Finally, the time span covered by the question regarding same-sex experience has effects that cannot be measured. Kinsey's classic research, for example, found that 10 percent of men reported having been primarily or exclusively homosexual (Kinsey ratings of 5 or 6) for three or more years during some period of their life. This is a far different criterion from having had same-sex sex in the past year. Thus, the answers one gets depend not only on the nature of the sample and on subjects' trust in the researcher, but also on precisely what questions are asked. No definitive answer to the question of the incidence of homosexuality (or heterosexuality or bisexuality) is possible given the intricacies of meaning that presently pervade this topic area.

Of greater importance than the numbers is the question of why they should matter. If, as psychologists, we strive to understand human experience, we cannot disregard that experience for a group of people simply because we believe their numbers to comprise 3 percent rather than 10 percent of the population. Just as it is important to appreciate the lives of other numerical minorities, so is it important to develop as deep as possible an understanding of the lives of LGB individuals, regardless of their numbers. The fact that the question is unanswerable only serves to spotlight this important issue.

Sexual Orientation and Psychological Research

The inexact meaning of sexual orientation has profound implications for psychology's attempts to understand the experience of those who identify (or whom psychology identifies, by whatever means) as lesbian, gay, or bisexual. The nature of psychological theory and research is such that it is well suited to sorting individuals into groups and attempting to draw generalizations about and explain differences between those groups. However, given the very nebulous meaning of sexual orientation, it is impossible to create legitimately defined categories or to assign individuals to them.

Further, the categories imply internal homogeneity but actually disguise important variations among their members. The category "homosexual," for instance, is assumed to include both gay men and lesbians, so that conclusions drawn about the group are presumed applicable to both groups—this despite evidence that being a lesbian is profoundly different from being a gay male. (The same can, of course, be said for heterosexual or bisexual men and women.)

These difficulties notwithstanding, when we turn to the psychology literature regarding sexual orientation, we discover work premised on the assumption that it is possible to create distinct categories. This presumption is crucial for theory that contrasts LGB with heterosexual experience, and it is fundamental to research designs that aim to describe the psychological functioning of any single group or that draw comparisons among these groups. Yet it is apparent that this premise is indefensible; on the contrary, the very meaning of sexual orientation is itself in question. In truth, the difficulties of accurate assessment leave any research or theoretical project in this area open to question, and comparability across projects is even more problematic (Brown, 1995; Patterson, 1995b).

In addition to the conceptual and pragmatic difficulties entailed in identifying discrete groups, of equal consequence is the issue of self-protection and its impact on subjects' self-identification. In a world where LGB identities are stigmatized, we can readily anticipate that many individuals will be unwilling to reveal such self-labels. Therefore, the group identified as heterosexual might be more accurately described as consisting of open heterosexuals and closeted LGB individuals. The LGB group actually includes only that sample of individuals who self-identify as lesbian, gay, or bisexual (which, incidentally, may not include all individuals that a psychologist with access to all possible information might label as belonging to this group)—*and* who are willing to disclose this identification to the researcher.

Amidst this morass of confusion, the one certainty is precisely the uncertainty of the meaning of sexual orientation and the impossibility of identifying individuals or groups that actually reflect the separate, internally homogeneous, and stable categories we use in everyday language. Our own clarity about questions relating to sexual orientation is limited by these vagaries, as are the issues that psychology can address in any definitive manner.

Again and ever more profoundly, the very notion of sexual orientation as a phenomenon that exists independent of the meanings created for it is called into question. Yet the presumption that sexual orientation is a freestanding phenomenon, to be discovered, validated, measured, and described underlies work in the psychology of sexual orientation. And, because it also underlies the understanding that we hold—both individually and collectively, as a society—a psychology that strives to understand this experience is, without doubt, an important undertaking.

CHAPTER TWO

HETEROSEXUALITY, GENDER, AND HETEROSEXISM/HOMOPHOBIA

THE GOAL WE ARE MOVING TOWARD is an understanding of the psychological experience of bisexual, gay, and lesbian people. In keeping with the contextual emphasis of the first chapter, it is paramount that we recognize that no aspect of that experience occurs in a vacuum. On the contrary, the nature of LGB experience is thoroughly shaped by the conditions that surround homophilic individuals and their communities. In particular, the psychological reality of each individual who identifies as lesbian, gay, or bisexual is unavoidably infused with attitudes that permeate society.

In order to understand LGB experience, we must understand the place of heterophilia and homophilia in this society. And we must recognize the compelling impact of coming to terms with a society that denigrates one's own identity, the impact of identifying as LGB and living in the constant company of homophobia and heterosexism.

Heterosexuality: Theorizing the Norm

Consider these questions: What do you think causes heterosexuality? Is it a reaction to bad experiences with members of one's own sex? Why are heterosexuals so flagrant about their lifestyle—wearing wedding rings, holding hands and even kissing in public places, flaunting their sexuality by appearing in public pregnant, acknowledging children admittedly conceived through heterosexual intercourse? Why do heterosexuals try so hard to recruit children to their way of life, by insisting on other-sex dating, romanticizing marriage, and purveying films and fiction that portray rampant heterosexual bonding? While these questions may seem ludicrous, their counterparts do not; substitute "homosexual" for heterosexual, and the questions are common fare. This exercise illustrates the degree to which we take heterosexuality as the norm and in need of no explanation, while deviations from it are seen as requiring explanation, even justification.

Locating our understanding of sexual orientation in a particular time and place, as we did in the previous chapter, allows us to ask important questions about notions that otherwise seem self-evident and beyond question. When we recognize that our concepts of sexual orientation are situated, are products of particular historical and cultural perspectives, we are able to see that our construction of normative heterosexuality is as open to appraisal as are other constructs. What happens if we attempt to reverse the tables, if we problematize heterosexuality, present it as a phenomenon open to critique and explication, as an object worthy of theoretical analysis?

The Meaning of Heterosexuality

Heterosexuality, like homosexuality, is a relatively new category for organizing human experience. The term heterosexuality first appeared in the early twentieth century; the 1901 *Illustrated Medical Dictionary* defined it as having an "abnormal and perverted sexual appetite toward the opposite sex" (Penelope, 1993, p. 262). In the later nineteenth century, as sexology progressed in its efforts to describe the range of human sexual experience, heterosexuality evolved as the term designating the space left after the perversions were delineated (Katz, 1992).

Classical Theory: Natural versus Unnatural Acts.
As the concepts of heterosexual and homosexual identity solidified, tacit beliefs in the normalcy of the former and the deviance of the latter were articulated more formally. The crux of the argument was that heterosexuality is natural, while other expressions of sexuality are unnatural. This position actually entails at least three distinct arguments: (1) homosexuality is unnatural because it does not occur in nature (that is, in other species); (2) what is natural is that which leads to reproduction; homosexuality does not, thus it is unnatural; and (3) the natural expression of sexuality is made clear by the sexual organs, which obviously are intended for heterosexual intercourse.

Before we discuss these arguments, note that all are addressed to sexual activity. As we have seen, sexual orientation, whether homophilic or heterophilic, is a far more complex phenomenon than can be neatly distilled into sexual behavior. None of these arguments addresses the question of how we are to determine under what circumstances it is natural for one human being to love another.

This limitation aside, each of these arguments is flawed. First, same-sex sexual behavior does occur in other species, from octopi to rats to primates

(Kirsch & Weinrich, 1991; Vasey, 1995). Second, if the criterion for a sexual act's being natural is the possibility of reproduction, then we must declare all nonreproductive sex unnatural—including masturbation, oral sex, foreplay, birth control, and celibacy, as well as intercourse after hysterectomy, vasectomy, or menopause.

Finally, the argument that sexual organs clearly dictate a particular form of sexuality is not persuasive. It is no more obvious that the genitals are exclusively designed for heterosexual intercourse than that the mouth is designed solely for eating rather than for language, or the hands for tool use rather than for clapping. Organs serve multiple functions. Even those that serve basic biological needs allow for wide variation; eating is not always purely life-sustaining, but is often directed by pleasure, social acceptability, and other contextual determinants. Why might not the same variability be equally natural in activities involving the genital organs?

One final topic within the general domain of "nature" is the argument from evolutionary biology. The assertion here is that only those systems will persist that confer some evolutionary advantage for a species. Quite evidently, heterosexuality affords such an advantage: reproduction and thereby survival of the species. By the same token, homosexuality must serve an evolutionary purpose, or it would not have persisted across the ages. Leaving aside the question of whether homophilic *identity* as we know it has always existed, it appears that homosexual *behavior* has been present among humans over at least several thousand years and is also found in other species. This raises the question of what evolutionary purpose it serves. Much has been written about this topic (see Kirsch & Weinrich, 1991, for a summary) without achieving a resolution. Of especial interest here, however, is that this line of reasoning makes homosexuality *as natural as* heterosexuality, a variation in human experience that serves some purpose—albeit an unidentified one—for the species.

Contemporary Theory: Gender and the Heterosexual Assumption.
Rather than striving to "naturalize" heterosexuality and thereby justify the deprecation of homophilia, contemporary theory has undertaken to theorize heterosexuality itself, to ask what are the assumptions that underlie it, what is the origin of the hostility toward LGB identity, and what is the impact on human experience of the privileging of heterosexuality.

This theorizing begins by illuminating the preeminence of the heterosexual assumption—the presumption that everyone is and should be heterosexual. A powerful elaboration of the potency of this assumption is found in the work of Adrienne Rich (1980). Rich spoke specifically of women, but much of her argument addressed the institution of heterosexuality and therefore has implications for men, as well. In her analysis of the institution of "compulsory heterosexuality," Rich exposed how thoroughly our lives are constrained by the expectation that heterosexuality will define the course of our existence. The possibility

34   for any life other than a heterosexually defined one is thoroughly impeded by our daily experiences; any other life is made invisible and devalued where it appears; and both social norms and formal institutions are structured so as to compel individuals to embrace the heterosexual manner of living.

For women, in particular, this compulsion is damaging, because heterosexuality as we understand it is grounded in male dominance and privilege. Thus, women are constrained not only in their options for how life might unfold, but also in the choices required of them that may be detrimental to their own well-being. Further, Rich argued, the very categories we have developed to label sexual orientation serve the function of reinforcing compulsory heterosexuality. When women bond with other women, they are a risk to male dominance. To the degree that society is able to render such bonding pathological (by labeling women-identified-women as "lesbians" and defiling that identity), we protect male-dominated heterosexuality (or patriarchy). As corrective, Rich proposed the "lesbian continuum," which defuses the pejorative quality of the label by seeing all women-bonding as lesbian, as woman-affirming, and as active opposition to patriarchy.

In a parallel argument, Lillian Faderman (1994) suggested that lesbianism is a socially constructed category, whose consequence is precisely to pathologize attachments among women. While such bonds have been common across time and across cultures, the creation of a category that is defined by sexuality and impugned in our society effectively precludes most women from pursuing such attachments. If the only choice a woman-loving woman has is to term herself a lesbian, and if that term as she understands it (that is, as the culture constructs it) does not coincide with her sense of self, such a relationship is not conceived as viable. There is no category available that affirms her commitment to women without pathologizing her identity.

Kitzinger (1987) pursued the notion that categories of sexual orientation are closely tied to the sociopolitical meanings of gender. The social construction of lesbianism as a category of sexual orientation, she argued, actually acts to reaffirm heterosexuality and thereby to support traditional gender roles. Specifically, insofar as lesbianism is seen as a distinctive form of identity whose origins can be sought and whose "nature" psychology strives to understand, the political meaning of lesbianism is subverted. Lesbianism becomes simply a "variation" in human sexuality, rather than a penetrating assault on gender politics.

Other theorists, too, have noted how pervasive is the role of gender in our construction of heterosexuality. Gregory Herek's (1986) analysis of "heterosexual masculinity" examined masculine identity, pointing out that masculinity as we construct it is grounded in heterosexuality (including being active heterosexually and vigorously affirming that sexuality), dominance (and the eroticization of dominance), and avoiding at all costs any appearance of femininity. Female heterosexuality, in turn, is grounded in submission to male dominance. Herek argued, as did Rich, that these strictures serve to lock individuals in delimited roles, defined by their sex and expressed in gender expectations, and to punish any deviation from these.

Numerous writers, including Sandra Bem (1993b), Alan Hunter (1993), and Suzanne Pharr (1988), have rounded out the argument by illuminating how these gender expectations interact with sexual orientation: any deviation from gender roles is taken as a violation of heterosexual masculinity/femininity (that is, of compulsory heterosexuality) and therefore leaves one open to accusations of homosexuality. The threat of such indictment acts to reinforce traditional norms of appropriate heterosexuality, thus controlling everyone's behavior—straight and homophilic alike.

These role expectations are especially rigid for men. While parents might be delighted with an assertive and achieving daughter (even a "tomboy"), they are unlikely to express pride in their son the sissy. Evidence indicates that both men and women hold more rigid attitudes about men's roles than about women's, and both are more likely to be disturbed by a man's stepping out of his role. The demand that men live according to gender norms or risk being identified as gay thus acts to reinforce heterosexual masculinity, including the submersion of any quality that might be deemed feminine. It also serves to legitimize male violence, for one element of male heterosexuality is dominance and its eroticization (Kokopeli & Lakey, 1992).

This tolerance for violence as an expression of masculinity together with the fear of appearing feminine come together in what Herek sees as normative homophobia embedded in heterosexual masculinity. Men must affirm their own masculinity, which by definition entails heterosexuality, by attacking those who transgress the rules that define masculinity—namely, LGB individuals; they must affirm who they are by vigorous assault on those who they are not (Herek, 1990).

For women, gender expectations limit opportunity by locating all behavior construed as nonfeminine beyond the boundaries of acceptability. On one level, such behavior risks one's opportunities for achieving the very heterosexuality that is deemed compulsory. Yet, achieving heterosexuality puts one in jeopardy, not only because it is limiting, but also because the institution as we know it legitimizes male dominance over and violence against women and prohibits deep ties with other women. On another level, gender-inappropriate behavior—including refusing heterosexual advances—opens one to charges of lesbianism.

Thus, the anchor of heterosexuality is gender-role compliance. It may be that the greatest risk posed by LGB identity is precisely the profound transgression of gender norms implied by such identities. Indeed, the very existence of same-sex relationships is an affront to gender roles. If men are supposed to be dominant over women, who is to dominate when there are two men? If women are to be submissive to men, who is to submit to whom in a lesbian relationship? Our inability to transcend this heterosexual norm may be at the root of the common stereotype that gay men are effeminate (because surely they must assume a submissive role) and lesbians are masculine (because surely someone must be in command). Also, the notion that in same-sex couples one partner plays the role of "wife" and the other, the role of "husband" clearly reflects our deep-seated incapacity to conceive of a relationship between equals. In short, same-sex intimate relationships threaten "to sever the comfortable connection of sex and power" that is fundamental to heterosexuality (Bleich, 1989, p. 24).

Gender and Homosexuality

The intermingling of gender and sexual orientation that appears in this analysis of heterosexuality also suffuses the literature on homosexuality. In particular, we find throughout the lay and professional literature the assumption that lesbian or gay identity necessarily entails cross-gender behavior, or behavior deemed appropriate to the other sex. Thus, common stereotypes portray gay men as sissies and lesbians as mannish, and parents worry that boys who play with dolls will be gay and girls who prefer football will be lesbian. As might be expected, when subjects in psychological research are asked to give characteristics that typify lesbians and gay men, their descriptions closely match traditional gender stereotypes for the other sex (Kite, 1994; Kite & Deaux, 1987).

The same assumptions carry over into professional thought (S. Bem, 1993b; DeCecco & Parker, 1995; Pillard, 1991; Ross, 1985b). Early medical and psychological theories of homosexuality presumed gay men to merge a woman's soul in a man's body, and both lesbians and gay men were defined as "inverts." The first psychological scale designed to measure masculinity and femininity (M-F) was grounded in the assumption that homosexuals would be found largely among those whose M-F score differed from their biological sex (Terman & Miles, 1936). Animal research seeking biological origins for homosexuality has interpreted cross-sex behavior in animals (including both sexual behavior and other sex-typical acts) as equivalent to homosexuality (Haumann, 1995; Parker & DeCecco, 1995). In recent human research, men's sexual attraction to men has been presumed to reflect female brain organization (LeVay, 1991). Extensive research has searched for a connection between cross-gender behavior in childhood and later gay or lesbian identity (Bailey & Zucker, 1995).

This conceptual merging of gender and sexual orientation has profound consequences both for the study of sexual orientation and for our daily lives. Research and theory based on essentialist understandings of sexual orientation, of gender, and of the conflation of the two may miss provocative and surely important questions. If we recognize that these two are separate (if often intersecting) constructs, then we can see more clearly the complexity of their interaction.

For example, gender expectations vary across cultures, as do understandings of sexual orientation. Ross (1985a) has demonstrated that the correlation between gender and sexual orientation depends on cultural definitions of those two constructs. Yet psychological research, particularly that seeking biological roots for sexual orientation, has been remarkably blind to cross-cultural and historical variations in the relationship between gender and sexual orientation. The failure to take such variation into account renders ambiguous the outcome of much psychological research.

As an illustration, consider research reporting a correlation between cross-sex behavior in children and later LGB sexual orientation. This finding is interpreted as demonstrating that cross-sex behavior is predictive of homo-sexual orientation, either because the former predisposes the latter or (more commonly) because both reflect some underlying, probably biological factor that causes both cross-sex behavior and homosexual orientation.

But what does such a finding actually tell us? If we consider that the definition of "cross-sex" behavior is culture specific (i.e., what is cross-sex here may be gender appropriate elsewhere), other interpretations are possible. It might be that what we have observed is a relationship between sexual orientation and these particular behaviors, regardless of their relation to culture-specific gender expectations. In this case, the correlation says nothing whatever about gender per se, since these behaviors may be unrelated to gender in some cultures. Or perhaps it is the fact of deviance or difference of any kind, here manifested in cross-sex behavior, that correlates with same-sex orientation. In this case, gender deviance would be only one difference among many that might correlate with sexual orientation. The point is not that one or another (or some entirely different) explanation is correct, but that we foreclose the possibility of such queries if we fail to address the arbitrariness of both constructs—gender and sexual orientation—and of our presumption that they are related.

In our daily lives, the equation of gender with sexual orientation is the cognitive error that allows the control of one by the other. We dare not violate gender roles precisely because any such infraction is presumed to be indicative of homophilia. As long as we live in a heterosexist society where homophilia is condemned, the behavior of all of us—lesbian, gay, bisexual, and hetero-sexual—is effectively controlled by epithets such as "fag," "lezzie," "homo," and "queer." Correlatively, compulsory heterosexuality is sustained and strengthened by insistence on rigid role adherence. The reification of compul-sory heterosexuality relies on a category of anomalous behaviors, "deviations," to define and reinforce the boundaries of what will be tolerated (cf. S. Bem, 1995; J. Butler, 1992; Sampson, 1993).

This is a fine illustration of the constructionist notion that ideas serve a function; one is chosen over another because it serves a purpose for the culture. Here, rigid gender roles serve to maintain normative heterosexuality and to punish other sexual orientations; the heterosexual assumption, in turn, serves to reinforce gender roles by prescribing those behaviors that will protect against charges of deviance. Thus, existing social structures are buttressed by our construal of gender and sexual orientation as coextensive.

Homophobia and Heterosexism

This discussion leads us to consider why insinuations of nonheterosexual identity, often wrapped in charges of gender deviance, carry such potency. The ideological expression of the heterosexual assumption is found in homophobia and heterosexism. Homophobia, a word coined by George Weinberg in 1972, has become the most commonly used term for negative attitudes toward and prejudice against LGB people. This word refers to an irrational fear (phobia) of homosexual people and the qualities attributed to them; by extension, it describes a fear of being associated or in close company with these individuals.

Many have argued that homophobia is not the best term to describe negative attitudes toward LGB people, or homonegativity. First, these attitudes are not necessarily a reflection of fear nor are they necessarily irrational. As we will discuss shortly, homonegative attitudes may reflect a complex range of motives and values that may or may not include fear. Further, in psychological jargon the word phobia refers to a trait of an individual, an internal, irrational fear of some object or event. Using this term to describe homonegativity implies that the problem is simply a character defect of individuals, and that if we could cure a few mentally ill or phobic individuals, homonegativity would vanish. In reality, negative attitudes toward LGB people thoroughly permeate our society and are formalized in and justified by our institutions, norms, and language. As Shields and Harriman (1985) pointed out, homophobia is the only "phobia" where the phobic person attributes her or his problem to the feared target; spider phobics accept responsibility for their difficulty and are not encouraged to regard it as emotional illness on the part of the spider. The difference lies in societal evaluations of homophilia and of spiders.

The term "heterosexism" is preferred by many to highlight the systemic character of homonegativity. A parallel can be drawn to racism, sexism, classism, and other forms of institutionalized prejudice. Racism is grounded in the belief that one race is best and that others are inferior and are therefore justifiably demeaned. Similarly, heterosexism implies that heterosexuality is the one acceptable sexual orientation and that all others are deviant, disturbed, and

inferior, and are therefore legitimately the target of both individual and institutionalized prejudice. Also, by imbedding the term, "sexism," heterosexism
points to the defining role of gender in homonegativity.

Homophobia or heterosexism exists in many forms and on many levels of
experience. *Personal homophobia* (Blumenfeld & Raymond, 1993) is reflected in
an individual's personal prejudice against LGB individuals (and traits stereotypically associated with these). *Interpersonal homophobia* is evidenced when
one's personal attitudes are expressed in relationships with others. It is here
that personal bias leads to actual discriminatory acts, such as homophobic jokes
and verbal or physical violence, but also including avoidance, rejection, and
withholding of support. Herek (1995) has suggested the term *psychological
heterosexism* to refer to these two levels of heterosexist attitudes; this term has
the advantage of avoiding the misrepresentations contained in the word homophobia while retaining the emphasis on individual attitudes and beliefs.

Institutionalized homophobia (Blumenfeld & Raymond, 1993) or *cultural
heterosexism* (Herek, 1995) entails the promotion by society in general of
heterosexuality as the sole, legitimate expression of sexuality and affection.
This includes not only the embedment of this ideology in the explicit teaching
of heterosexual normativity, but also the tacit communication of this ideal via
society's norms, institutions, laws, cultural forms, and even scientific practices.
Cultural or institutional homophobia/heterosexism is so pervasive, so taken for
granted, as to escape notice. The tacit acceptance of this world view is revealed
by a glimpse at the range of privileges accorded to heterosexuality; some
elements of this *heterosexual privilege* are summarized in Figure 2.1.

The target of such prejudice, on both the individual and the institutional
level, is nonheterosexual identity. Thus, it is not only homosexuality that
elicits heterosexism attitudes but also bisexuality. The tendency to demean
bisexual identity is manifested both by heterosexual and by homosexual people
and is reflected in *biphobia*—that is, the discomfort that people experience
regarding bisexuality.

For heterosexually identified people (and from the cultural stance that
privileges heterosexuality), any deviation from normative heterosexuality is
suspect. Thus, the same-sex aspect of bisexual identity is as open to condemnation as is exclusive homosexuality. In addition, the failure of bisexuals to
disclaim openly a particular category of relationships—in this case, same-sex
relationships—challenges common understandings of dichotomous categories
of sexual orientation. Further, bisexuality may be seen as a risk to heterosexual
relationships, as it is often assumed that bisexual individuals' real allegiance
is to same-sex relationships—otherwise, surely they would simply identify
as heterosexual.

Despite having experience with the pain of discrimination, many gay
and lesbian individuals hold negative attitudes toward bisexually identified

Figure 2.1

What Is Heterosexual Privilege?

- Taking for granted everything on this list. Living without ever having to think twice, face, confront, engage, or cope with any of these things, seeing them as given rather than as privileges.

  – Heterosexual people may reflect on these privileges, but they are not forced to by their personal identity and experience.

- Coupling and marrying ... which include the following privileges:

  – Public recognition and support for your intimate relationships (e.g., receiving calls or cards of congratulations celebrating your commitment, supporting activities and social expectations for longevity and stability in your committed relationships)
  – Joint child custody
  – Paid leave when grieving the death of a spouse
  – Leave to care for an ill partner or for a funeral or other crisis in your partner's immediate family
  – Immediate access to your loved one in case of emergency; the right to make medical and financial decisions when your partner is unable to do so
  – Support for and pride in your relationship from your family of origin

- Self Acceptance: Knowing your sexual orientation is acceptable

  – Having role models from childhood who show your affectional and sexual orientation as normal
  – Learning about romance and relationships you can identify with from fiction, movies, and television
  – Having positive public role models with whom you can identify

- Validation from the culture in which you live

  – Dating the people you are attracted to in your teen years
  – Talking about your relationship, including whatever projects, plans, vacations, activities you and your partner undertake
  – Expressing pain when a relationship ends from death or separation, and finding acknowledgment and support from others
  – Receiving social acceptance from neighbors, colleagues, friends
  – Not having to hide or lie about single-sex social activities
  – Living your life without always being identified by your sexual orientation (e.g., you get to be a farmer, a teacher, etc., without being labeled the heterosexual teacher)

- Institutional acceptance:
  - Employment opportunity: socializing with colleagues increases opportunities for getting a job, receiving on-the-job training, and promotions; no risk of losing your job because of your sexual/affectional orientation
  - Property laws, filing joint tax returns, automatically inheriting from your partner under probate laws
  - Sharing health, auto, and homeowners' policies at reduced rates; having both partners and all children covered by one partner's health insurance
  - Receiving validation from your religious community; being able to celebrate your relationship within that community; being a member of the clergy
  - Being able to work as a teacher in preschool through high school without fear of being fired if you are discovered; no one assumes that you molest or recruit children to your way of living
  - Adopting children, serving as a foster parent
  - Raising children without the threat of their being taken from you and without having to worry about whether their friends might reject them because of their parents' sexual and affectional orientation
  - Being able to serve in the military without having to cover up who you are

- Integrity about who you are, safety in your identity

persons. At times, hostility is expressed by actively excluding bisexual individuals from social circles and activities, at other times by denying the legitimacy of bisexual identification. Lesbian and gay people's discomfort often derives from a belief that the claim of bisexuality is merely a matter of clinging to heterosexual privilege or a protection against the painful realities that come with the acknowledgment of lesbian or gay identity. Also, many gay men and lesbians see bisexuals as untrustworthy. The absence of a singular commitment to one's own sex is taken as implicit loyalty to heterosexuality, so that the individual is presumed likely to reject same-sex relationships in favor of heterosexual ones if given the opportunity. An additional impetus for gay and lesbian biphobia may derive from the fact that many lesbians and gay men define their identities not only by whom they love but also by the explicit abdication of heterosexual relationships. Bisexual individuals expressly repudiate this position by their willingness to form heterosexual relationships, thus defining a fundamental difference between their own identity and that of exclusively gay or lesbian people.

Finally, for heterophilic and homophilic people alike, stereotypes of bisexual infidelity, indiscriminate sexuality, claims to heterosexual privilege, and transparent denial also interfere with the acceptance of those identifying as bisexual. We will discuss scholarship addressing these stereotypes of bisexuality in chapter 4.

Personal and cultural heterosexism share elements with other forms of stereotyping and prejudice. A consideration of the dynamics of prejudice will provide the groundwork for a more thorough analysis of homonegativity.

Stereotypes and Prejudice

Stereotypes are exaggerated beliefs about and portrayals of groups of people, derived from meager and often distorted information; typically, these are pejorative beliefs and depictions. Stereotypes, in turn, provide a bulwark for prejudice, a word that derives from the Latin for prejudge. Prejudice involves negative attitudes toward a group based on preconceptions and stereotypes, which lead one to judge individuals within the group not by their personal qualities but by their membership in the stigmatized group. The behavioral expression of prejudice is discrimination, where members of a devalued group are treated in harmful ways. Such maltreatment, in turn, is justified by invoking stereotypes that "prove" the inferiority of and/or the risk presented by the denigrated group.

Once formed, prejudices typically do not change with new information. Whereas people who are not prejudiced tend to make judgments based on individual cases, prejudiced individuals retain stereotypes and behave accordingly (Kite, 1994). Clearly, there are dynamics underlying prejudicial attitudes that make them so resilient, even in the face of discrepant information

Contextual Sources of Prejudice

The *sine qua non* of prejudice is unequal status and unequal power. When a particular group inhabits a devalued position within the society and lacks the power to assert its own perspective, the group and its members easily become the targets of prejudice. The stereotypes that evolve to characterize demeaned groups serve to justify their vilification and to legitimize prejudice and discrimination against them. Such stereotypes usually present the group as inferior in some way (less intelligent, lazy, emotional, weak) and/or as a threat to the social order (promiscuous, a risk to children, dishonest, unhealthy).

Prejudice is grounded in particular social and historical contexts. Which groups are to be designated as social outcasts, what stereotypes will evolve to support their condemnation, what social norms and institutions will be invoked to maintain the distribution of power and privilege—all these are dependent on situated cultural understandings. The specification of what is "good"—and therefore characteristic of the dominant group—varies across cultures and across time, as does the specification of what is bad.

Social norms and institutions evolve within societies to maintain both these designations of relative status and the privilege afforded the dominant group. The criteria for exclusion from privilege may be sex, race, ethnicity, sexual orientation, or other differences from the dominant group. In any case, the ultimate foundation of prejudice is the benefit that accrues to those with privilege from maintaining other groups in inferior and disparaged positions (Henley & Pincus, 1978).

As Allport (1954) argued in his classic treatise, prejudice develops not from contact with members of devalued groups but from contact with prejudicial attitudes toward them. These attitudes and the stereotypes that support them have evolved as elements in a complex social system, whose stability relies on maintaining order; the maintenance of order, in turn, requires that the distribution of power within the society be justified. The devaluation of certain groups lends credibility to their exclusion from power and simultaneously elevates the status of the dominant group and thus legitimizes its power. Thus, in the service of social systems, individual prejudices are continually reinforced.

Psychological Correlates of Stereotyping and Prejudice

Even in the face of such systemic support for prejudicial attitudes, some individuals are more accepting than others. Substantial research has attempted to identify psychological characteristics that predispose individuals toward prejudiced attitudes—or, correlatively, greater acceptance. Among the variables that have been investigated are cognitive and personality characteristics.

Cognitive Sources of Prejudice

Human beings are cognitive creatures; we respond to our reality according to how we conceptualize and understand it. The cognitive strategies that we employ to comprehend our world provide part of the groundwork for prejudice.

Categorization. One way to manage the tremendous complexity of our world is to group similar events so that we can respond to them all in a like manner, rather than having to deal with each one separately. Stereotypes provide convenient schemas for such groupings. Once we create categories, we tend to exaggerate similarities within each group and to magnify differences between groups. This makes the categories more efficient and more stable; if everything in class A is good and everything in class B is bad, we know precisely how to respond to any A or any B in any situation.

We also tend to understand groups in terms of their relationship to ourselves. Our own group, the *in-group*, is highly regarded, while the other group, the *out-group*, is devalued. This out-group effect (or in-group bias) occurs even where groups are created artificially and for trivial reasons, such as by the flip of a coin or eye color.

This phenomenon is further complicated by the *out-group homogeneity effect*, the tendency to see all members of the out-group as alike while recognizing diversity within our own group. Thus, we speak easily of the shared "national character" of individuals from other countries, although we recognize the wide diversity among our own country's people; political slogans refer to "the homosexual agenda" as if there were only one homogeneous amalgam of gay people who all share a common perspective, although we recognize a variety of perspectives among heterosexuals (no one speaks of "the heterosexual agenda"). This out-group homogeneity effect allows us to condemn all members of a group, disregarding the reality that there are individual differences within every group.

Vivid cases. We especially notice, recall, and pass judgment about events or individuals that are unusually intense or distinctive. Some of the very qualities that differentiate out-groups from the dominant group may be qualities that in some ways violate the expectations of that dominant group. Thus, what may seem ordinary from the perspective of a particular out-group is seen as outrageous from a mainstream perspective. Consider, by way of comparison, customs and rituals of other societies that seem bizarre to us.

Because such vivid cases may be disquieting, they have the particular power to shape attitudes. When an out-group is already disparaged, it is relatively easy for prejudice against them to be exacerbated by the presentation of vivid cases of behavior that is discomforting to the dominant group. For example, materials designed to appeal to racist prejudices may depict dangerous crimi-

nals who are African American. Similarly, anti–LGB materials often portray, as
if they were representative, attire and behaviors that are likely to offend mainstream audiences.

Selective perception, selective recall. It is not possible for us to perceive all the
events that happen around us; rather, we attend to those that seem most salient
and disregard others. Similarly, we cannot remember every event, but select
only those that have particular importance. Overall, our recall is but a small
sample of the events we have actually experienced. The simplest way to store
and retrieve (or to perceive and recall) events is to classify them using existing
concepts, labels, and categories.

The upshot of this process is that we are most likely to notice, to remember,
and to recall events that fit what we already "knew." Events that violate our
expectations are likely to be disregarded, distorted, or written off as exceptions
that do not challenge our initial understanding. As it affects prejudice, clearly,
this means that we are most likely to notice and remember events that confirm
existing stereotypes. We take note of and recall the poor people of color we
encounter and dismiss the wealthy as exceptions to a general rule. We notice
and recall the gender-bending drag queen and disregard the gay athlete.

Illusory correlation. This is closely intertwined with selective perception and
recall. We often perceive connections that do not in fact exist but that fit our
expectations—relationships or correlations that are, in reality, illusions. We
may be convinced that women dominate conversations, when in fact women
are less likely to speak, especially in mixed-sex groups. This is an illusory
correlation: a nonexistent (but perceived) relationship between sex and
verbosity. Research has demonstrated that both psychologists and lay people
perceive a correlation between homosexuality and characteristic responses to
personality tests, even though no actual differences in response are present
(Chapman & Chapman, 1969). These people are reporting an illusory correlation—a nonexistent (but perceived) relationship between sexual orientation
and test outcomes.

The fundamental attribution error. The tendency to see other people's behavior
as resulting from their own internal qualities, rather than its being a product of
the situation, leads us to believe that other people are responsible for what
happens to them. Companion to this is the *just world phenomenon,* our collective wish to believe that the world is a just place and that bad things don't
happen to good people. Together, these lead us to blame victims of oppression
for their own plight—they are responsible for what happens to them (the
fundamental attribution error), and if something bad happens, it was because
they deserved it (the just world phenomenon). Thus, the poor are shiftless and

deserve their poverty; a lesbian who gets beat up coming out of a bar is flaunting her perversity and deserves to be punished for it.

Cognitive dissonance reduction. Cognitive dissonance, or internal conflict, further shapes our responses to others and occurs where our beliefs are incompatible with our actions. If one believes that prejudice is wrong but continues to engage in prejudicial actions, that person is faced with cognitive dissonance. We can resolve such dissonance either by changing our beliefs or by changing our behavior. If one believes in equal rights but also believes that LGB teachers should not be allowed to work with children, one can reduce this dissonance by deciding that such restrictions are a realistic response to a group of people who are justly excluded from certain roles. Participation in activities opposing LGB teachers would then not be dissonant with the belief that prejudice is wrong.

In combination, these cognitive mechanisms provide a framework for the beliefs we hold, whether they are prejudicial or not. Their use to create and sustain prejudicial beliefs is potentiated by other characteristics that lead some individuals to employ these strategies in support of poorly informed and denigrating attitudes toward others. Among these factors are personality and demographic correlates of prejudice (Adorno, et al., 1950; Allport, 1954; Altmeyer, 1988; Herek, 1995). While much of this work has focused on racism and anti-Semitism, the principles can be fruitfully applied to other prejudices as well. Indeed, research has demonstrated that prejudice against quite distinct outgroups reflects a "generalized attitude" (Bierly, 1985), a finding that leads us to expect similar underpinnings for various forms of prejudice.

Personality and Motivational Correlates of Prejudice
There is some criticism of scholarship that approaches prejudice in terms of psychological characteristics rather than focusing on the social context that shapes and supports prejudicial attitudes—a critique in keeping with this book's emphasis on context (e.g., Henley & Pincus, 1978). However, much of the psychological work addressing heterosexism has invoked these concepts, so that their inclusion here seems worthwhile. Certain personality and motivational characteristics have been found to be correlated with prejudice.

Low self-esteem and a need for status appear to underlie many prejudicial attitudes (Blumenfeld & Raymond, 1993; Kite, 1994). Individuals who are unsure of their own power or their own intrinsic worth may elevate their sense of self by diminishing the value of others. Rejection of an out-group serves to define one as a member of the dominant group, thereby granting one the status of that group. This tactic also allows the individual to project unacceptable feelings onto members of the out-group (they are evil; I am not), thereby reasserting her or his own superiority over the out-group and escaping responsibility for personal qualities deemed undesirable.

On a societal level, prejudicial attitudes tend to increase where there is a perception that power or status is being lost by those who have traditionally held it. Thus, we might expect an increase in prejudice during more difficult economic times or when social change has led to greater opportunity or recognition for members of traditional out-groups.

The authoritarian personality is a constellation of traits initially reported in a classic work by Adorno, Frenkel-Brunswik, Levinson, and Sanford (1950); their aim was to understand the psychological basis of the extreme anti-Semitism of Nazi Germany. These researchers found that individuals who held prejudicial attitudes shared a pattern of authoritarian tendencies. Among these was a tendency to see relationships as structured by power, authority, and obedience. Each person has a proper place in such relationships, which are highly structured with firm rules. If one is a subordinate, then obedience to authority is essential; if one is the superior, then dominance, power, and unquestioned authority are to be expected. Accompanying this world view is a high degree of conformity to social norms and an intolerance for ambiguity that makes for rigid distinctions between right and wrong (see also Altmeyer, 1988; Herek, 1995).

As a substratum of prejudice, the authoritarian personality provides members of the in-group with the firm conviction that they are in power, that they are right/good, and that it is the proper role of out-groups to accede to their privilege. Such power is justified by existing social stratification, so that the whole system is self-perpetuating. Those in power know themselves to be right because they are the ones in power; out-groups are expected to comply with mainstream values because they are bad/wrong, as is evidenced by their out-group status. Because authoritarian tendencies increase in times of economic hardship and social upheaval, we can expect that prejudice would increase during such times, as well.

The *frustration-aggression hypothesis,* initially proposed and extensively investigated by a group of psychologists several decades ago (Dollard, Doob, Miller, Mowrer, & Sears, 1939), provides yet another element to the matrix of prejudice. When the needs or goals of an individual or group are blocked, the result is often hostility. When the cause of the frustration is difficult to identify and/or is not a safe target for one's feelings of anger, aggression may be expressed toward an alternative safer object—a scapegoat.

Prime targets for such scapegoating are individuals and groups who are already demeaned. The people who are the targets of such hostility may have nothing whatever to do with the frustration of its perpetrators; rather, they are simply a safe target because they have little power with which to protect themselves or to retaliate, and are seen by society at large as legitimate targets of anger. The more denigrated the group, the more suitable a scapegoat it becomes.

Homophobia, Heterosexism, and Values

Thus far we have been discussing prejudice and stereotyping in general, and it is apparent that these dynamics help us to understand the working of heterosexism, as well. In addition, considerable research has investigated stereotypes of LGBs and homophobia or psychological heterosexism, specifically. It is to this work that we now turn.

Stereotypes of LGBs

As discussed previously, stereotypes serve as a foundation for prejudicial attitudes, justifying discrimination and reinforcing existing beliefs. This is certainly true of homonegative attitudes. Research exploring stereotypes toward LGB individuals has consistently revealed two constellations of images. The first harkens back to our earlier discussion of the mingling of gender and sexual orientation, centering on gender-role deviation as a common characteristic. Gay men are characterized as stereotypically feminine and lesbians as stereotypically masculine. The second set of stereotypes focuses on abnormality, portraying LGBs as perverted, mentally ill, maladjusted, and sexually deviant (e.g., Kite, 1994; Kite & Deaux, 1986, 1987).

The role of stereotypes is also evident in the impact of HIV/AIDS on homonegativity. The HIV/AIDS epidemic provides an excellent illustration of the fact that historical events are often assimilated to stereotypes, reinforcing preexisting assumptions about particular groups. Prior to the epidemic, gay men were already stereotyped as unhealthy and sexually promiscuous. Thus, when the disease disproportionately affected gay and bisexual men, it was easy for many people to perceive it as a "gay" disease, because this analysis was compatible with existing stereotypes.[1] Coming as it did in the early 1980s—an era of growing political conservativism—HIV/AIDS built on existing stereotypes and served as a lightning rod for homophobia, whose overt expression had been more subdued in the relatively progressive '70s (Eliason, 1995).

Correlates of Psychological Heterosexism

The research on homophobia/heterosexism has largely consisted of correlational studies that identify the demographic and psychological characteristics of those with high scores on measures of homophobia or psychological hetero-

---

1. Cognitive mechanisms are also apparent in arguments for increasing discrimination against LGBs in the wake of HIV/AIDS: gay men's own actions have brought this on (fundamental attribution error); those who are not evil will be protected (just world phenomenon).

sexism. Correlational studies do not demonstrate causation, but are helpful in identifying characteristics shared by people with similar attitudes.

One drawback to this research is that it focuses on negative rather than positive attitudes toward LGBs and thereby misses important information about individual differences in attitudes (e.g., Kite, 1994). Also, by construing heterosexism as an internal trait of individuals, this work may distract attention from the institutionalized heterosexism that is arguably the deeper root of homonegativity. Nevertheless, this research does provide a glimpse at certain characteristics of people who express homonegative attitudes, at least as defined by these scales.

Herek (1984, 1988, 1995) and Eliason (1995) have summarized this extensive body of work, distilling from it the following key correlates of homonegativity. Individuals who score high on scales of homophobia or psychological heterosexism:

1. have had little contact with known LGBs

2. are less likely to have engaged in same-sex sexual acts or to identify as LGB

3. are likely to believe that their peers hold similar negative attitudes, especially among males

4. tend to live in geographic areas where homonegativity is likely to be the norm—the midwest, the south, and rural as opposed to urban areas

5. tend to be older and less well educated on average than those with more positive attitudes

6. are more likely to identify themselves as very religious, and are especially likely to identify with conservative or fundamentalist religions

7. express conservative political views

8. hold traditional attitudes toward gender roles (this is especially true for men)

9. have conservative attitudes toward sex in general

10. display a pattern of traits comprising the authoritarian personality, including dualistic thinking and low tolerance for ambiguity

11. evidence greater prejudice toward other out-groups as well as toward LGBs

12. are more likely to be men than women—on average, men express more homophobic attitudes overall, especially toward gay men (this sex difference may not hold among African Americans)

An additional consideration is in order. Prejudices are social constructions, and individual prejudices are personal elaborations of these constructs. Thus, the nature of an individual's homonegative attitudes depends in part on what stereotypes he or she holds about LGBs. Antigay attitudes will take one form for the person who sees gay men as predatory and another for the individual who sees them as passive and effeminate. People may fear lesbians if they perceive them as rapacious, but pity them if they believe them to be unhappy and failed women. Thus, it is more accurate to speak of "homophobias" or "homonegativities" to highlight that homonegative attitudes can represent very different feelings and beliefs.

The Function of Attitudes

Social psychologists have argued that attitudes, including prejudicial attitudes, are best understood in terms of the function they serve for those holding them. When looked at in this way, prejudicial attitudes cannot be readily dismissed as simply bigoted and ignorant, but rather must be understood as representing strategies for coping with one's own life. Understanding the function that attitudes serve allows us to consider attitude-change strategies that take the psychological basis of these values into account.

Herek (e.g., 1984, 1986, 1995) has explored at length the roles served by homonegative attitudes, and has offered an analysis that includes several possible values functions. The first is an *experiential function*, where the individual develops attitudes to make sense of her or his own experience. People whose judgment of homophilia is based on personal contact with LGBs would fall into this category. This belief-function is compatible with the correlation between psychological heterosexism and the absence of contact with openly LGB individuals; those with more contact form attitudes based on actual experiences with LGB individuals, rather than on pejorative stereotypes.

Some circularity is evident in the correlation between contact with known LGBs and decreased homonegativity. It appears that homophilic people are more apt to disclose their sexual orientation to people who are likely to be acceptant (such as younger, well-educated, politically liberal individuals). Thus, the people who know self-identified LGBs (and thereby rate high in contact) are the people likely to have more positive attitudes in any case. By the same token, this may help to explain gender difference in acceptance. Perhaps people are more likely to disclose LGB identity to women, because they sense greater acceptance; hence fewer men than women have contact with self-declared LGBs, and so their attitudes have less opportunity to change toward the positive (Herek & Glunt, 1993).

However, even contact may not alter convictions. Selective perception, selective recall, and other cognitive strategies may work to prevent one from changing stereotypes and negative attitudes even when faced with information refuting those beliefs. In addition, an individual's beliefs and ideologies may be so firm and themselves serve such crucial psychological functions that even positive contact is dismissed as irrelevant.

The second broad class of attitudes discussed by Herek is those that serve a *social-identity* function. In this case, one's attitudes reflect deeply held beliefs connected to one's own identity and to membership in social reference groups. Two closely related functions are included here. Attitudes serving a *value-expressive* function express core beliefs or values that are central to one's identity and self-esteem. Religious beliefs and strongly held political ideologies are examples of values. This function might explain the correlation between psychological heterosexism and conservative political beliefs, as well as the relation to religiosity, especially a commitment to conservative religious institutions whose teachings about homophilia are extremely negative. Indeed, the religious argument for homonegativity is arguably the most powerful force in contemporary social movements to limit gay rights. Also, the frequent finding that homonegativity is correlated with other forms of prejudice may be explicable from this perspective. The cohesiveness of these attitudes suggests that they serve an important function for the individual.

A second group of attitudes within the social-identity category is that serving a *social-expressive* function. These attitudes derive from the individual's need to belong to social reference groups and to find support for her or his attitudes from the group. This function is likely reflected in the relationship between attitudes toward LGBs and such variables as geographic location, where one holds the attitudes supported by the surrounding community; age, where the individual's attitudes parallel those of his or her cohorts; and the belief that friends agree with one's own attitudes, a finding suggesting both that we select friends in part for their similar attitudes and also that we seek support from friendship groups for our ideas. Some attitudes—for instance, religious and political affiliation—may serve both value-expressive (through the ideology) and social-expressive (through the camaraderie) functions, thus offering dual support for homonegative beliefs that are commensurate with political or religious doctrines.

The third major function that values might serve is an *ego-defensive* function. In this case, one espouses attitudes that serve to protect oneself by projecting unacceptable feelings onto others. To understand how this function operates in the particular case of homophobia, recall the earlier discussion of the conceptual conflation of gender and sexual orientation. We understand the two to be inseparable, with deviations from prescribed gender roles as an indication of homosexuality. For men, especially, heterosexual masculinity requires complete adherence to requirements that one express no qualities that might be regarded as feminine, and that one assert his masculinity through heterosexual sexuality and a condemnation of homosexuality.

Under these circumstances, any doubts about one's thorough identification

52   with gender roles or any sense that one might have same-sex feelings would be extremely threatening. One way to handle such a threat is to deny those doubts and/or feelings in oneself and project them onto others. Maligning those others, then, serves two purposes: it reinforces and demonstrates one's own belief that those qualities are despicable, and it proves that one is "normal" in gender-role and sexual orientation.

A common piece of lay wisdom is that people who are extremely homophobic are actually denying their own homosexual impulses. While this may be true for some people, Herek's work demonstrates that the issue is not so simple. First, defensive attitudes might also protect against fears of gender deviance as well as fears of nonheterosexual orientation. Given the rigidity of (especially male) gender roles, we might expect this to be a common concern for men, and their need to demonstrate their masculinity (as gender role identity) a common motive for much of their behavior. In this case, psychological heterosexism would reflect gender anxiety rather than anxiety about one's sexual orientation. Also, it is important to recognize that only a small percentage of Herek's subjects could be described as defensive in their homophobic attitudes. Thus, such ego-defensiveness appears not to be the most prevalent underpinning of psychological heterosexism.

This defensive value function would be compatible with a number of correlates of homophobia. Traditional attitudes toward gender might support hostility toward or envy of the gender flexibility available to LGB people; this gender rigidity might also make one anxious about any real or imagined gender deviation in oneself, raising the issue of the merger of gender and sexual orientation. Conservative sexual attitudes might bespeak anxiety about sexuality that would be elicited by LGB identities, especially in light of stereotypes of LGBs as sexually promiscuous. The cognitive/motivational correlates of homophobia—rigidity, authoritarian personality, and especially intolerance for ambiguity—all suggest a defensive posture. And, finally, people tend to express greater hostility toward homophilic individuals of their own sex, suggesting that these same-sex individuals are a greater threat to the exposure of their own unacceptable feelings. This is especially true for men, pointing once again to the normative homophobia that characterizes heterosexual masculinity (Herek, 1986).

Heterosexism and Violence

The most blatant manifestation of heterosexism is violence directed against LGB individuals (or those who are perceived as such) with no provocation other than their (perceived) sexual orientation. Such violence serves many purposes: it reaffirms the assailant's position as anti-LGB (and therefore, presumably, as straight); it reminds the lesbian, gay, or bisexual victim that he or she is at constant risk of such attack; and it reasserts the societal condemnation of the LGB identity.

For a number of reasons, it is impossible to determine the incidence of anti-LGB violence (Berk, Boyd, & Hamner, 1992). For one thing, few law enforcement agencies keep separate statistics on these acts. It is only recently that anti-LGB violence has been considered a hate crime, and the meaning of this term, where it is applied, is ill-defined, at best. Furthermore, an unknown proportion of attacks are never reported to police, because reporting such events amounts to coming out, and many people are not willing to make such a disclosure on public record. Also, many victims have little confidence in law enforcement procedures, and feel that reporting will put them at great risk with little hope for gain. In fact, the police are often themselves perpetrators.

Statistics kept by LGB-sponsored programs typically show a far higher rate of such occurrences, indicating that official records are, indeed, inaccurate (e.g., Berrill, 1992; Collins, 1992; Comstock, 1991; Herek, 1992). Every attempt to compile figures measuring rates of violence has demonstrated that a significant proportion of LGB individuals have experienced violence or victimization of some form. Furthermore, those who have been victims overwhelmingly report more than one incident (Berrill, 1992; von Schulthess, 1992).

Not all anti-LGB attacks take the form of "rolling queers" or "gay bashing"—the too-familiar physical assaults that commonly take place around gay male bars and other known gathering places. Violence ranges from verbal harassment to homicide; its victims range in age from school children to the elderly; it may target women as well as men, although gay and bisexual males are more likely to be targets of physical assault as well as verbal harassment and threats from police and at school. Lesbians and bisexual women are more likely to be victims of verbal assault by family members, to express greater fear of violence, and to encounter more discrimination—perhaps because they face greater risk of attack and of discrimination as women as well as for their sexual orientation. Gay and bisexual men are more likely to be assaulted in public places known to be frequented by gay men; lesbians and bisexual women are more likely to be victimized at home or in public settings that are not LGB-identified. Lesbian, gay, and bisexual people of color are at greater risk for assault than are white LGBs, reflecting the pervasive impact of racism as well as heterosexism. Children are most commonly victimized by their peers, although violence also occurs when adolescents come out to their families (Berrill, 1992; Comstock, 1991; Icard, 1986).

One thing is clear: reports of anti-LGB violence have increased dramatically in recent years. A National Gay and Lesbian Task Force report culled from the records of police departments in five major U.S. cities found an increase in anti-LGB episodes of 161 percent between 1988 and 1991 (Berrill, 1992). This increase may have to do in part with heightened consciousness on the part of the LGB community and a growing willingness to resist rather than quietly succumb to heterosexism. It may also reflect increased awareness on the part of law enforcement officials, and a greater willingness to respond to such claims seriously.

But the increase in reported violence may reflect actual increases in attacks against gay, lesbian, and bisexual people, occasioned by recent historical trends: LGBs' heightened visibility since the political awakening of Stonewall, public reaction to the HIV/AIDS epidemic, and recent political trends toward reasserting the primacy of heterosexuality. The fact that increasing anti-LGB violence has coincided with growing violence against other out-groups, including ethnic, racial, and religious minorities as well as women, suggests that a general mood of hostility toward out-groups is involved (Herek & Berrill, 1992). As discussed above, certain correlates of prejudice appear to increase during periods of social upheaval, particularly if the dominant group perceives its power as being threatened. Perhaps the current trend of increasing animosity toward diverse out-groups reflects this dynamic.

The Perpetrators

It appears that the vast majority of anti-LGB crimes are committed by late adolescent and young adult males, usually acting in groups (Berrill, 1992; Collins, 1992; Comstock, 1991; Harry, 1992; Herek, 1992). Herek's (1992) discussion of how violence against LGBs might serve various functions is useful here.

In particular, the preponderance of young males among those engaging in anti-LGB violence suggests that, for many of perpetrators, this behavior serves social identity and/or ego-defensive functions. Attacks on gay men, especially, would serve to demonstrate young (presumably heterosexual) men's antagonism toward gay identity, both as sexual orientation and as gender violation. This antagonism, in turn, affirms their own heterosexual orientation and their own masculine gender identity. Such behavior also serves as an acceptable outlet for the violence that is a part of our understanding of masculinity, one that carries little risk of loss to the attacker (Ehrlich, 1992). In addition, the collective affirmation of masculinity—both as gender display and as assertion of heterosexual orientation—provides an opportunity for group cohesiveness that fulfills social identity needs (Ehrlich, 1992; Herek, 1992).[2]

Other functions might also be served by anti-LGB violence, although the connection of these to the predominance of young male perpetrators is less clear. An individual who has had a particularly bad experience with an LGB

---

2. Weissman's (1978) conversation with "kids who attack gays" is invaluable in bringing these dynamics to life.

person might engage in violence as a reaction to or in retaliation for that event; this violence would serve an experiential function. A value expressive function might condone anti-LGB violence where deeply held beliefs deem homophilia an abhorrent identity that should legitimately be punished and even eliminated.

Notice that in both cases, social as well as individual values are served by anti-LGB violence. Unpleasant experiences with others do not typically lead to violence; however, in this case, violence is potentiated by social systems that legitimize anti-LGB aggression. Similarly, where such violence expresses beliefs endorsed by institutions or organizations, institutional values as well as individual values are served.[3]

The Consequences

The psychological impact of anti-LGB violence is tremendous, even for those who are not directly victimized. This includes heterosexuals, who, ironically, are at risk because the mere suspicion of homosexuality may be sufficient to justify violence. Within LGB communities, people are quite aware of the threat of violence even if they have not personally been victimized. A major national survey completed by National Gay and Lesbian Task Force in 1984 found that 83 percent of LGB individuals surveyed believed that they might be the victim of violence in the future; 62 percent reported that they felt their safety was at risk; 45 percent arranged their lives so as to reduce the possibility of attack (Berrill, 1992). Many of these people learned to fear future violence from direct experiences with verbal harassment, which serves as an effective reminder that one is constantly a potential target (Garnets, Herek, & Levy, 1992).

The individual who is the direct victim must deal not only with the immediate trauma, be that psychological or physical hurt, but also with the aftermath. Victims of any violent crime report ongoing psychological difficulties in response to victimization; for LGB individuals, these are exacerbated by cultural heterosexism. When an individual is attacked specifically because of her or his sexual orientation, then internalized homophobia, or one's own lingering feelings that LGB identity is wrong in some way, may be intensified, leading to self-blame and self-denigration. Further, the sense of vulnerability that results from any victimization becomes, for an LGB individual, directly associated with being gay, lesbian, or bisexual. As a result, one's sexual orientation is experienced as a source of anxiety and punishment rather than as a positive aspect of self (Garnets, Herek, & Levy, 1992).

Others, too, are victimized. The family, partner, and/or friends of the primary target must not only support that person in recovering from the assault

---

3. Comstock (1991) presented a detailed discussion of religious underpinnings of anti-LGB violence that is informative here.

but also address the issues it raises for them. Their own internalized homophobia may emerge, causing LGB individuals to question their own worth, renewing doubts among family members, and perhaps evoking enough discomfort to cause people to withdraw from the victim. On the other hand, the support of significant others may help to mediate the consequences of victimization (Garnets, Herek, & Levy, 1992; Hershberger & D'Augelli, 1995).

The community as a whole must somehow integrate the reality that many of its members are victims, that all of its members are potentially at risk, and that many of society's institutions appear indifferent to this risk. The belief in a just world is under constant attack in this situation, and people may respond by condemning the victim in order to make themselves feel more protected: "He is too open about being gay; I'll be safe." Such blaming of the victim serves only to reinforce the perception that the source of the problem is LGB identity rather than the cultural and psychological heterosexism that led to the violence. In addition, this reaction encourages others to remain closeted for fear of similar victimization, with negative consequences for their own mental health as well as for the gradual improvement of the position of LGBs in this society. On the positive side, the community provides crucial support and resources for coping with victimization, especially for those who are well integrated into community networks (Garnets, Herek, & Levy, 1992).

Politics and Psychological Trauma

Prejudice against LGBs takes many forms, and serious psychological consequences may result from events that would not ordinarily be construed as violent. For example, Russell (1995) reported on the psychological impact of Colorado's Amendment 2, a ballot initiative that repealed existing gay rights ordinances in the state and prohibited the passage of new ones. During the campaign preceding the vote, LGBs were subjected to pervasive, relentless, and virulent homophobia; public pronouncements, publications, and media presentations were rife with gross distortions of homophilic feelings, behavior, and identity. Having heard their lives misrepresented and vilified for months, Colorado's LGBs were further traumatized when the amendment, which polls indicated would be defeated, in fact passed. Many felt shocked; many felt betrayed by friends, family, and coworkers who had voted for the amendment. Many were traumatized by the process and its outcome.

Russell's research revealed that the state's LGBs paid a psychological price. Among her sample of over 650, she found significant increases in self-reported depression and anxiety after the vote, as well as in symptoms of posttraumatic stress disorder. Also identifiable in her data were indications of profound internalized homophobia, often reinforced by the vote, and many individuals reported increased fears for their safety. Some retreated more deeply into the closet. On the other hand, some respondents reported a sense of empowerment and used the amendment's outcome as a stimulus to personal growth and increased political involvement.

This research illustrates two important points. First, although physical and verbal attacks on LGBs are abhorrent, they are but one form of the attacks on personal integrity and psychological well-being with which LGB individuals must daily contend. Feeling hated hurts, even when one is not the victim of direct personal attacks. Second, it is often possible to use a traumatic experience as a catalyst for growth. If the damage is not too great (and this is an important "if"), recovering from such experiences may grant new and empowering psychological resources. As we will discuss later, some argue that LGBs are in a unique position to develop remarkable psychological strength by virtue of the constant need to cope with the impact of homonegativity.

Altering Homonegative Attitudes

There are significant practical advantages to viewing prejudicial attitudes in terms of the function they serve for the individual who holds them. In particular, when we recognize what purpose is served by a particular value, we can tailor attitude-change strategies to address that function (Herek, 1984, 1992). For example, knowing that experiential attitudes are shaped by actual experience, we would expect that positive interactions with LGB people would facilitate reductions in heterosexism. Since approximately 70 percent of Americans report knowing no (openly) LGB people, the functional approach to attitude change indicates that here lies a huge potential for decreasing psychological heterosexism, with potential benefits for reductions in cultural heterosexism, as well.

Indeed, research has demonstrated that ongoing contact with people who are openly lesbian, gay, or bisexual is the best predictor of positive attitudes. Even within a particular demographic group, those with the most contact tend to have the most positive attitudes (Herek & Glunt, 1993). Given our understanding of how attitudes are formed, we would expect that such contact would change cognitions by providing information that refutes common misconceptions. Without such contact, the only basis for attitudes is socially constructed "knowledge," which often consists of stereotypes, further supported by dynamics such as selective perception and misattribution. Also, contact would be expected to affect feelings toward LGB individuals by providing a positive emotional experience.

For such contact to reap maximum benefit, it needs to be continuous, to occur in an atmosphere that encourages cooperative efforts toward shared goals, and to involve common interests, beliefs, and standards. This litany perfectly describes interactions with family members, close friends, and

58   coworkers. It is this profile of attitude change that undergirds the assertion that LGBs' disclosing their sexual orientation to important people in their lives will foster positive attitudes toward homophilia in general (Herek, 1984, 1992). These guidelines for effective contacts also provide direction for how cultural change could occur, through the creation of such opportunities and their sanctioning by significant institutions.

Value-expressive attitudes, on the other hand, may not change even with positive contact. Here, attitudes have little to do with LGB persons, but rather are reflective of one's own identity. Homonegative attitudes of this sort may change if the individual recognizes a conflict between this value and another she or he firmly endorses (e.g., individual freedom), or if this value threatens another need that is of substantial personal importance (e.g., a close friendship). In either case, dissonance reduction might be invoked, resulting in a movement toward more positive attitudes. Alternatively, attitudes might change if a revered authority, such as a member of the clergy or a biblical scholar, were to present a more positive view of LGB experience, still grounded in religious teachings.

Attitudes serving a value-expressive function for individuals also serve a purpose for institutions. Where homonegativity is a fundamental aspect of the belief system of an institution, it reinforces the legitimacy of that institution's beliefs and the superiority of its (heterosexual) members. Altering institutional or cultural heterosexism grounded in this value-expressive function will necessitate changes in institutional support for it, which will require, in turn, that other beliefs emerge that are acceptant rather than prejudicial.

Values serving a social-expressive function may be amenable to change under a variety of circumstances. These values may alter if one's reference group changes; for instance, college attendance is typically associated with more liberal attitudes. Alternatively, significant others may gain access to information and/or to personal contacts with LGB people, and modifications in their attitudes may influence one's own beliefs.

Cultural heterosexism can also be understood in terms of social-expressive functions, suggesting additional means by which such values may be altered. As broad social norms shift, individuals' reference groups can be expected gradually to alter their attitudes in synchrony. Individual attitudes may adapt in response, providing support for institutional change. There is little doubt that we have seen in recent years a growing attention to and acceptance of human diversity; some argue that we are currently confronting a backlash that bodes comparably significant adjustments in the other direction.

Perhaps the most difficult attitudes to change are those that serve an ego-defensive function, because they are so closely connected to profound fears about one's own identity. Close contact is unlikely to be effective, for it may simply arouse anxiety. Information that might diminish homonegativity, similarly, is threatening and likely to be avoided or distorted through selective perception. While it might be possible to short-circuit the defensive motive behind homonegativity by identifying it to the individual, this tactic is also likely to lead to denial and heightened defensiveness.

Many scholars who work in this area point to gender roles as the key, and suggest that reducing the heterosexism that thrives in the service of this defensive function will require broad cultural change. Only by dissolving the rigid boundaries we impose around gender propriety, only by severing the link between gender and sexual orientation, only by allowing people (especially men) to recognize a wide range of human experiences as normal will we prevent their demeaning others out of their own fear that they may be deviant (Herek, 1986; Kitzinger, 1987, 1995; Pharr, 1988; Rich, 1980).

Prejudice against many out-groups has met with growing social condemnation over recent decades. Overt racism is no longer socially acceptable, at least in most groups, and is legally prohibited; overt sexism, while still popular in some quarters, is also generally regarded as inappropriate and is similarly punishable by law. Anti-LGB prejudice, in contrast, faces little societal condemnation and is still entirely legal in most contexts. Being homophobic is not widely seen as besmirching one's character. In fact, individuals who are highly prejudiced against LGB express "global discomfort but not compunction" for the discrepancy between how they believe they should behave and how they actually would behave toward LGBs (Kite, 1994, 36).

While individuals' cognitive and motivational functioning may contribute to heterosexist beliefs and actions, those individual dynamics are nourished by a social and political atmosphere that permits and even encourages homonegativity. Diminishing anti-LGB prejudice and discrimination will require institutional as well as individual change.

PART II

Lesbian/Gay/Bisexual Identity

THE QUESTION OF CAUSATION

Origins of Sexual Orientation

When addressing issues of sexual orientation, perhaps our greatest curiosity is reserved for the question of causation: what is the origin of sexual orientation? In practice, the question is usually more specific: what causes an individual to be nonheterosexual? However, it is as important to explore the etiology of heterosexuality as of any other sexual orientation. Indeed, the existence of culturally sanctioned bisexuality in societies throughout history and across cultures speaks to the bisexual potential of human beings, and indicates that monosexual orientation of any sort is as arbitrary as any other identity (Adam, 1986; Money, 1987).

One might well ask why it matters what causes one or another sexual orientation. During the period when homophilia was viewed as a disease, the answer to this question was couched in terms of the need to prevent and to cure this "disorder." Today, the search for an answer persists in part because of remnants of this view.

But other motives, as well, might underlie our interest in this question. Perhaps it is simply curiosity, the desire to understand the variety of human experience. Yet the questions asked reveal not broad curiosity but a focused interest in LGB identity. As Pattatucci (1992) points out, differences among people are important only when they are accompanied by differences in power and status; significantly, these are the very ingredients that make for prejudice (see chapter 2). Why don't we ask whether lesbians find women more loving than men? Or how gay men resist the pressure to conform to heterosexual masculinity? Why not ask whether heterosexuality reflects a symbolic self-denigration, expressed by loving only people different from oneself? If we were simply curious, answers to these questions would be sought as eagerly as are the causes of homosexuality.

But it is the anomalous we seek to understand, and as a culture we still view homophilia as a deviation from the norm and therefore in need of explanation—and even justification. This cognitive bent shapes the questions that are asked and how they are framed. Thus, research seeks hormone imbalances in homosexuals, whereas hormone levels in heterosexuals are regarded as normal; investigators search for distortions in early family experiences of LGB people, while the families of heterosexuals are assumed to have been normal. Questions such as these presuppose their conclusion: homosexuality is presumed to be abnormal, so whatever qualities characterize homosexual persons are deemed abnormal.

Accordingly, the most compelling question raised in discussions of sexual orientation is what causes homosexuality. Considerable research and theory have been aimed at answering this question. Before we review scholarship addressed to this topic, however, let us recall the concerns raised earlier about difficulties in defining sexual orientation, and consider the problems they must raise for investigations of causation. We have discussed the inadequacies of essentialist understandings of sexual orientation, and asking questions about causation demands an essentialist approach. The questions presume that there exists a phenomenon, termed sexual orientation, that can be defined and measured and whose origins can be discovered.

As we have seen, this assumption is problematic, at best. If we cannot clearly define the phenomenon of interest, if we cannot identify who belongs to one or another group, if individuals alter their self-identified sexual orientation over time, and if people behave in ways that are not compatible with their self-identification, how can we presume to ask or answer questions about origins? Of precisely what are we seeking the origin? How do we decide who epitomizes whatever it is we are trying to investigate? And if we cannot constitute discrete and coherent groupings, how can we presume to identify etiological events that differentiate these (indefinable) groups from one another?

Despite such fundamental uncertainties, the bulk of research and theory in this area presumes that it is possible to sort individuals into two (or at best, three) discrete categories, and that sexual orientation is an enduring characteristic, usually established early in development—all despite evidence to the contrary. Research also often relies on a unidimensional definition of sexual orientation—i.e., sexual activity—despite evidence for a distinction between sexual acts and LGB or heterosexual identity. And both theory and research frequently equate gender compliance with sexual orientation, taking cross-sex behavior as indicative of homosexuality and vice versa. This bias is so pervasive that it may constitute the core ideology of etiological theorizing, particularly in the biological sciences (DeCecco & Parker, 1995; Haumann, 1995). In addition to these widespread problems, specific methodological issues are intrinsic to particular studies or models; we will address these as they arise.

It is imperative that we keep in mind that one's assumptions shape the questions asked, the methods employed to address those questions, the interpretation of outcomes, and the application of those interpretations. In Brown's words, "the tendency to see [sexual orientation] in one or another manner leads to models which are descriptive and predictive of those outcomes" (1995, p. 7). Furthermore, "which answer a scholar chooses reflects a willingness to align primarily with certain explanatory models" (p. 9).

With these cautions in mind, let us begin a review of major approaches to the puzzle of causation. Three classes of explanations can be identified: biological, environmental, and cognitive/volitional.

Biological Explanations

Recent years have seen a pronounced movement toward biological explanations for many phenomena long thought to be psychological and/or environmental in origin. The reasons for this turn to biology are many and complex. Increasingly sophisticated techniques have contributed to the growth of knowledge in this area, and major research projects such as the human genome project regularly provide new perspectives on the role of biology in human life. In addition, research seeking environmental explanations for sexual orientation has failed to identify experiential precursors to homophilia, leaving open the possibility that LGB identity is biologically based.

Sociopolitical forces amy also contribute to this biological turn. The idea that biology is an objective, value-free science may blind us to the fact that this, like all human endeavors, is influenced by cultural beliefs and unacknowledged preconceptions. A number of scholars have asserted that a movement toward biological explanations commonly characterizes relatively conservative political periods, perhaps because biological explanations serve well to support the status quo.[1] If it can be argued that people are as they are because it is their nature to be so, then pressure for change appears futile and even counterproductive.

Whatever the underlying bases, research striving to identify biological underpinnings for homosexuality, while not novel, has flourished in the past decade. Several interacting categories of explanations can be identified. Some

---

1. In addition to the topic of sexual orientation, the trend toward biological explanations of human experience is reflected in recent work on mental illness (especially schizophrenia and mood disorders) and on gender. The latter, in particular, illustrates the social utility of biological arguments in maintaining the status quo. For examples of this critique see Doell, 1995; Fausto-Sterling, 1992; Gooren, 1995; Haumann, 1995; Pattatucci, 1992; Shields, 1975.

appeal to genetic mechanisms, some to hormonal, and some focus on brain structures that presumably reflect genetic and/or hormonal influences.

Genetic Explanations

Chromosomal Sex. Early attempts to resolve the riddle of homophilia relied on longstanding assumptions that a homosexual man (and presumably woman) was a cross between a man and a woman, having the genetic make-up of the other sex (Richardson, 1981). This simplistic model was quickly disproved once it was possible to test for chromosomal make-up. Its importance here lies in the reiteration of the assumption that homophilia is identical to cross-sex identity, a theme that reverberates through this research even today.

Statistical Approaches. Recent, more sophisticated attempts to discover genetic bases for sexual orientation have relied on statistical analysis. Such analyses search for *concordance,* or the degree to which there is agreement between two individuals on a particular trait. Identical twins, who have identical genetic make-ups, would approach 100 percent concordance for any trait that is completely genetically determined; fraternal twins and nontwin siblings, who share half of their genes, will show a concordance rate of approximately 50 percent for a genetically determined trait. Lower concordance in either case indicates an environmental component in the determination of that trait.

A study by Bailey and Pillard (1991) investigated the sexual orientation of the siblings of 110 gay men. These researchers found a concordance rate of 52 percent for identical (monozygotic, or MZ) twins, 22 percent for fraternal (dizygotic, or DZ) twins, 9 percent for nontwin brothers, and 11 percent for adopted brothers. In a similar study with lesbians and bisexual women, Bailey, Pillard, Neale, & Agyei, (1993) reported a concordance rate of 48 percent for MZ twins, 16 percent for DZ twins, 14 percent for nontwin sisters, and 6 percent for adoptive sisters. These findings suggest that there may be a genetic component to homosexual orientation (although they do not speak directly to heterosexuality). The concordance rate increases as the degree of genetic similarity increases, as would be expected from a genetic hypothesis.

However, if sexual orientation were entirely genetic, we would expect concordance nearing 100 percent for MZ twins. And, the higher concordance for DZ twins than for nontwin siblings (whose genetic similarity is the same) indicates that the greater similarity of environment increases the concordance rate for DZ twins over nontwins. Also, the figure for adoptive siblings should be lower than that for nontwin, biological siblings, but this is not the case for the sample of gay men. Thus, while the data provide some support for a genetic explanation of sexual orientation, they indicate that other factors are involved, as well.

These studies suffer additionally from methodological flaws. The samples were obtained through newspaper advertisements, a technique that might bias the results in unknown ways. In addition, unless twins are reared apart, it is impossible to separate the role of genetics from the role of the environment (Byne, 1994; Byne & Parsons, 1993).

Another recent and well-publicized research project investigated the family history of a group of gay men, and then attempted to identify the actual genetic element that underlay their homosexuality (Hamer, et al., 1993). These researchers interviewed seventy-six gay men to determine whether there were other LGB persons in their families. Outside their nuclear families, subjects reported more homophilic relatives on the mother's side of the family. To the researchers, this finding indicated that the critical genetic information predisposing homosexuality must be on the X chromosome, since that is the chromosome that men receive from their mother.

DNA samples were then taken from forty pairs of gay brothers. Thirty-three pairs were found to share a particular segment of the X chromosome, called Xq28. The researchers concluded that the gene or genes that predispose homosexuality almost certainly lie in this region.

What appears to be a fairly incontrovertible bit of research, though, is open to criticism (Byne, 1994; Byne & Parsons, 1993; DeCecco & Parker, 1995). First, there are the usual problems of how one identifies the sample: Who counts as gay among subjects and among their relatives? Second, the fact that these men knew of more homophilic relatives in their mother's family may simply reflect the fact that mothers tend to be closer to their families than do fathers, so that offspring are more likely to know the mother's extended family. Finally, and perhaps most importantly, it would have been appropriate to use heterosexual siblings as a control group; without such a control, there is no way to know whether Xq28 might be shared by all siblings, rather than only by gay brothers.

Even if we disregard these problems of methodology, the conclusion that a gay gene has been located is not warranted. The research does show that some gay men share a particular genetic element, but Xq28 could represent some other shared characteristic that is unrelated to sexual orientation. And remember that only thirty-three of the forty pairs shared Xq28; if homosexuality is genetic, how do we explain the other seven pairs? Also, even for those pairs who share Xq28, the genetic sequence located there is not the same throughout the thirty-three pairs; that is, there is no specific genetic coding that is shared by even these subjects.

Recent research by Hamer and his colleagues has addressed some of these criticisms and has also raised new questions (Hu, et al., 1995). In a study investigating further the role of Xq28 in the etiology of sexual orientation, these researchers used heterosexual siblings as controls and included lesbians in their sample. Results confirmed a high degree of concordance between gay male brothers, along with significantly lower concordance between gay and heterosexual siblings. Although it is still possible that this concordance reflects some shared trait other than homosexuality, these results add weight to the original conclusion that there is a link between Xq28 and sexual orientation in men. Results for women, however, found no difference in concordance between lesbian sisters and lesbian-heterosexual sibling pairs. Thus, the researchers concluded that Xq28 is not related to sexual orientation in women.

While this project lends further support to the original conclusion, problems of methodology and interpretation remain. First, gay male pairs were only included if there was no indication of "paternal transmission" (i.e., a father, son, or paternal half-brother who was also gay). Thus, the findings tell us nothing about the etiology of sexual orientation among those individuals. Similarly, the study explicitly excluded bisexuals and others whose sexual orientation was uncertain; again, an unspecified segment of the LGB population was ignored. Combined with the finding that Xq28 is not implicated in lesbian identity, we are left with an explanation that accounts for only one (perhaps narrow) segment of the nonheterosexual population.

Finally, in the researchers' own words, the identical twin of a gay or lesbian individual "still has a 50 percent or more chance of identifying as heterosexual" (Hu, et al., 1995, p. 252). Although this research may indicate one element of the complex determination of sexual orientation in some individuals, it does not point to "the gay gene" in any meaningful sense of that term.

Finally, data reported by Pattatucci and Hamer (1995) indicated significant "familial clustering" of nonheterosexuality among women. That is, nonheterosexual women were more likely than heterosexual women to have nonheterosexual sisters, daughters, nieces, and women cousins through a paternal uncle. However, this research was unable to differentiate between genetic and environmental sources for this clustering.

In summary, results of research exploring the possible genetic origins of sexual orientation is tantalizing but not decisive, and conceptual and methodological deficiencies make it impossible to derive definitive conclusions (Diamond, 1993; McGuire, 1995). Thus, we are left with an unsatisfying conclusion: for some people there may be a genetic component to the development of same-sex orientation.

Hormonal Explanations

Adult Hormonal Imbalance

Women and men both have "male" and "female" hormones; what is different between men and women are the relative levels of these hormones. Early researchers seeking a hormonal explanation for homosexuality reported a lower than normal ratio of androgen (male hormone) to estrogen (female hormone) in gay men, suggesting that gay men were hormonally "feminized." Other research followed, characterized by serious methodological flaws, failures to replicate, and findings suggesting that adjusting hormone levels did not alter sexual orientation (although it might alter sexual drive). A summary of this research concluded that the bulk of evidence demonstrates no relationship between adult hormone levels and sexual orientation (Meyer-Bahlburg, 1984, 1995).[2]

Early Hormonal Determination of Brain Organization

Arguably the most popular current explanation for a biological underpinning to sexual orientation focuses on the role of hormones in prenatal development. The basic position is that prenatal hormones influence not only the differentiation of the genitalia but also the sexually differentiated organization of the brain. This hormonally regulated brain organization is seen as underlying sex differences in behavior. By extension, similar underpinnings are sought for sexual orientation. Specifically, it is proposed that homosexuality is a manifestation of cross-sex identity—as revealed by attraction to the same sex—and is therefore likely to derive from cross-sex brain organization. This proposal rests on several assumptions: (1) that prenatal exposure and sensitivity to sex hormones influence sexually differentiated brain organization; (2) that this brain organization is expressed in sex-typical behaviors; and (3) that lesbian and gay identities are examples of cross-sex behavior and therefore reflect cross-sex brain organization: gay men have brains organized like heterosexual women, and lesbians have ones like heterosexual men.

This position represents an extension of the theory that sex differences (as distinguished from sexual orientation) are mediated by hormonally determined brain differentiation. Accordingly, we will first consider research supporting the notion of sex differences in brain organization.

Sex differences in brain organization. Early theories that attributed homosexuality to the presence of a woman's soul in a man's body are not far distant from current biological theories for the origin of sexual orientation. The basic argument is that early in embryonic development, female and male hormones act to organize the differentiation of the external genitalia and reproductive organs. Organisms are initially fundamentally female, in that the emergence of male-typical development requires the presence of male hormones; in their absence, female development will occur.

---

2. This lack of evidence did not, however, prevent the development of treatment techniques to "cure" male homosexuality, including both castration and the administration of male hormones.

In addition to the differentiation of reproductive tissues, the sex hormones also influence prenatal brain organization, resulting in sexually dimorphic structures in the brain—that is, structures that are different in females than in males. These structures are activated by sex hormones produced after puberty. Hormonal impact on brain development is reflected in the behaviors of organisms, so that male typical behaviors indicate the presence of male hormones during brain organization and activation, and female-typical behaviors reflect a relative absence of or insensitivity to male hormones (DeCecco & Parker, 1995; Meyer-Bahlburg, et al., 1995; Money, 1987, 1988).

Considerable research has been performed using animals to explore the effects of sex hormones on the brain and on behavior. Although criticized as overly simplistic even as it applies to animals (Fausto-Sterling, 1995), this research has provided the theoretical foundation for human research, and thus a brief review is in order.

Among the indicators of the sexual dimorphism of the brain are two mating-related behaviors, mounting and lordosis. Male animals mount females from the rear during intercourse; females assume a position termed lordosis, with back arched and tail held to the side. In practice, both sexes engage in both behaviors to some degree. Research indicates that in the presence of androgens (male hormones), the brain is "masculinized" and the individual, male or female, is predisposed to male-typical behavior such as mounting. The absence of or insensitivity to androgens predisposes the individual, female or male, to female-typical behaviors such as lordosis (DeCecco & Parker, 1995; Money, 1987, 1988).

In support of the notion that these differences do in fact indicate sexual differentiation in brain organization, several studies have identified a specific location in animal brains that appears to be sexually dimorphic. The sexually dimorphic nucleus, or SDN, is located in the hypothalamus, a brain structure known to be involved in mating behavior (DeCecco & Parker, 1995; Money, 1987).

Similar research with humans is difficult, as the manipulation of hormones and the surgical removal of gonads are not possible with human subjects. However, some information is provided by "experiments of nature," where the typical process of differentiation is altered by physiological anomaly. In some cases, there appears to be a relationship between such distortions and gender atypical behavior, so that androgenized females or androgen-insensitive males, for instance, show more cross-sex behavior than do hormonally typical subjects (Money, 1987).

In response to the question of whether such differences in behavior reflect hormone-induced brain organization, recent research has suggested the existence of several sexually dimorphic structures in the human brain, although the precise functions of these structures are not clear (Byne, 1995). Currently, a number of major research projects are exploring possible sex differences in brain function and their implications for gender as we understand it. This work is one illustration of the trend toward biological explanations of phenomena traditionally considered psychological and social in nature.

Brain organization and sexual orientation. For our purposes, the central question is whether hormone-induced "sexualization" (i.e., masculinization or its absence) of the brain is related not only to sex-typical behaviors but also to sexual orientation. In other words, does the masculinization of the brains of females or its absence in males predispose homosexual behavior in animals and also homosexual behavior and/or LGB identity in humans?

The animal research appears to demonstrate a relationship between hormones and sexual orientation. When hormones are altered, male rats become receptive and females assume the dominant role; it appears that we have created homosexual rats by inducing cross-sex brain organization. But the message of this research is not so simple. When a male assumes a receptive position, what are we to say of the male who mounts him? Which one is "homosexual"—the demasculinized one, as this theory would have it, or the one who mounts, whose brain is normally "masculine," but who is the initiator of same-sex sexual activity? If a neo-"lesbian" rat mounts another female, is the mounted female, who evidences lordosis in response to another female, heterosexual because she still behaves in a female-typical manner, or homosexual because she is receptive to another female?

Beyond such confusions of interpretation, note that the definition of sexual orientation here is completely grounded in sexual behaviors, in contrast to the convoluted meaning of sexual orientation discussed previously. Consider the huge pragmatic, theoretical, and philosophical leap from simple behaviors of mounting and lordosis to the complexities of lesbian, gay, or bisexual identity. Reflexive mating postures of rats are surely not comparable to the cortically mediated sexual activity, partner choices, and emotional attachments of human beings (Byne, 1994; Byne & Parsons, 1993; Doell, 1995).

When we turn to research with humans, we find two bodies of evidence regarding the role of hormones in the organization of human brain. The first sees a relationship between early cross-gender behavior in children (especially boys) and later LGB identity as evidence for cross-sex brain organization, which is manifested as gender deviance in childhood and as LGB identity after puberty (Bailey, 1995; Bailey & Zucker, 1995). Much of this research has been criticized, however, for its reliance on retrospective reports. That is, these findings may simply reflect gay men's tendency to reconstruct their memories of the past to fit their current self-understandings, selectively recalling gender-atypical behavior.

However, recent longitudinal research indicates that extreme cross-gender behavior in boys is indeed somewhat predictive of later gay identity (Bailey & Zucker, 1995). Because the boys included in this research were taken from a clinical population of boys who evidence extreme gender-atypical behavior, it is impossible to say what these findings might mean for LGB individuals in general (Baumrind, 1995). Other qualifications stem from the lack of comparable work with girls, which would be necessary for the hypothesis to be fully explored, and from the imperfect relationship between gender atypicality and sexual orientation; some stereotypically "masculine" boys grow into men who identify as gay, and some boys who engage in much cross-gender behavior later identify as heterosexual. Still, the relationship is intriguing. The question is what does it mean.

It may be that early cross-sex behavior does indeed reflect underlying brain organization, and that this organization is also causally implicated in LGB identity. However, an alternate explanation is possible. The term "cross-gender" is relative; behaviors that are seen as cross-gender in this culture are not in others (Risman & Schwartz, 1988). It may be that biologically based behaviors predict same-sex orientation only where they are seen as gender-inappropriate.

In this culture, for example, an aversion to aggressive play, which may be biologically based, would be seen as gender inappropriate for boys. In such circumstances, perhaps the boys discussed above experienced an awareness that they were "different," based on peer and adult responses to their cross-gender behavior. At adolescence, when the development of a sense of identity is focused so intently on sexuality, this diffuse sense of difference might coalesce around one's sense of sexuality. This is particularly likely, since the culture provides all the labels for the transformation of gender into sexuality: "sissy" equates with "fag," and "masculinity" means both dominance and heterosexual sexuality. An adolescent boy who embodies—in his own mind and in the judgment of his culture—the first (sissy) and fails at the third (macho) might well conclude that he is gay. Thus, the relationship between early cross-gender behavior and later gay identity may afford a glimpse into how socially constructed meanings move from cultural beliefs to individual identities.

The second body of research addressing the role of hormonally directed brain organization in humans looks at the influence of varying hormone levels on behavior. Although Money (1987) reported a relationship between hormonal abnormalities and nonheterosexual orientation in some cases, other research has found conflicting results, including that the majority of individuals exposed to abnormal hormone levels identify as heterosexual (Byne, 1995; Meyer-Bahlburg, 1995). Furthermore, alternative explanations for any relationship cannot be ruled out; it might be that in those cases where hormone-related cross-gender behavior precedes LGB identity, the relationship reveals how the individual and the culture evaluate gender deviance rather than demonstrating an underlying cross-sex brain organization (Bleier, 1984; Byne & Parsons, 1993). And, as Money himself points out, such atypical cases tell us nothing about the development of sexual orientation in average LGB individuals. Indeed, no differences have been found between heterosexual and nonheterosexual individuals in the somatic symptoms that indicate such hormonal abnormalities (Meyer-Bahlburg, 1995).

Despite these ambiguous findings, the assumption that there must be a relationship between prenatal hormones, the sexual organization of the brain, and sexual orientation is deeply entrenched. Consider Money's description of "masculinized" girls who are described as "tomboyish" but who later identify, contrary to predictions, as heterosexual. Money proposed that "possibly the prenatal hormonal effect was too weak or did not persist long enough to have an enduring effect on the brain" (1987, p. 391). There is another possibility: perhaps such hormonal effects do not determine sexual orientation (cf. DeCecco & Parker, 1995).

Brain Structures and Sexual Orientation

In keeping with the notion that homosexual individuals have the brain organization of the other sex, sexually dimorphic structures have been an object of study for those seeking brain bases of sexual orientation. Some researchers have reported differences in the brains of heterosexual and homosexual individuals in areas unrelated to reproduction, and have asserted that these findings point to early prenatal hormonal influences that broadly affect the brain (Bailey, 1995; Swaab, Gooren, & Hofman, 1995). However, other researchers have failed to replicate these findings, and some have come up with contradictory results (Byne, 1995; Byne & Parsons, 1993; DeCecco & Parker, 1995; Gooren, 1995).

Perhaps the most important research in this area, both for its content and its public visibility, was LeVay's (1991). LeVay began from the assumption that the brains of gay men would be similar to those of women, because both evidence female-typical behavior as defined by their sexual attraction to men. He chose to investigate one part of the brain previously reported to be dimorphic by sex in humans: the interstitial nuclei of the anterior hypothalamus (INAH). He expected to find that these structures in gay men would be similar to the same structures in women, that is, would be smaller than in heterosexual men.

LeVay studied the brains of forty-one deceased individuals: nineteen self-identified gay men who had died from complications of AIDS; sixteen men presumed to be heterosexual, of whom six had died from AIDS and ten from other causes; and six presumably heterosexual women, one of whom had died of AIDS. He found that INAH-3, one of the nuclei within INAH, was on average twice as large among the heterosexual men in his sample as in his female subjects, and two to three times as large in his sample of heterosexual men as in his gay subjects.

Although these findings have never been replicated, they are still widely cited as definitive. LeVay appears to have identified a specific structure that differentiates subjects by sexual orientation. However, the study is replete with weaknesses that make any such conclusion impossible (Byne, 1994, 1995; Byne & Parsons, 1993; Doell, 1995).

In addition to the theoretically problematic assumption that homosexual orientation equates with cross-sex brain organization, the study reflects troubling methodological problems. The sample was extremely small. It was comprised of individuals many of whose sexual orientation is uncertain; the nongay identified men and the women were only presumed to be heterosexual, and no allowance was made for the difficulties in defining what constitutes gay or heterosexual identity. The absence of lesbians as subjects means that half of the original hypothesis was not considered. Finally, there was considerable overlap between groups; for most individuals, it would not be possible to categorize a subject as gay, heterosexual male, or female from the size of INAH-3.

There are also substantive problems of interpretation. The use of straight men who had died of AIDS was intended to assure that any differences between groups would not be attributable to AIDS but to sexual orientation. However, heterosexual men with AIDS have usually contracted HIV through intravenous drug use, which is related to lower socioeconomic status, poor overall health, and earlier death from the disease. Individuals who live longer with the disease would be expected to show its effects more profoundly. For instance, cognitive deficits are common in the late stages of AIDS and reflect brain damage that might well extend to INAH-3. Also, AIDS alters testosterone levels, a change that might influence brain structures—including INAH-3.

Finally, correlation does not imply causation. Even if these methodological and theoretical problems were addressed and the outcome remained unchanged, this would not demonstrate that INAH-3 is causally implicated in sexual orientation. There is ample evidence that experience alters neurological structures and also influences the production of hormones, which, in turn, affect neurological structures. There is no reason to prefer a causal explanation that privileges brain over other biological systems or over experience. Finally, it is possible that any relationship between sexual orientation and INAH-3, if indeed such a relationship exists, reflects the action of some third factor, an event intrinsically unrelated to sexual orientation but that has the effect of altering the size of INAH-3 *and* is implicated in the etiology of sexual orientation. In this case, sexual orientation and the size of INAH-3 might be related without having any causal connection whatever.

Gooren (1995) reviewed research on brain organization and sexual orientation and also reported on attempts to replicate previous research. He concluded that no credible evidence exists at this time supporting the notion of cross-sex brain organization in LGB individuals. Nor is there clear evidence regarding differences between the brains of homosexual and heterosexual individuals. Byne's (1995) review of this research concluded that even if currently uncorroborated reports prove replicable, our knowledge of brain function is insufficient to explain their meaning. Nor are we capable of constructing an argument for the leap from quantitative differences in brain tissue to "qualitative variation in psychological phenomena as complex and multifaceted as sexual orientation" (Byne, 1995, p. 6). Thus, as with the other areas of biological research, no unequivocable conclusion is possible regarding the role of brain differentiation and sexual orientation.

Biological Explanations: A Summary

At this point, the most popular hypothesis regarding the role of biology in the etiology of sexual orientation appears to be a neuroendocrinological one. This theory argues for hormone-induced brain organization as the basis for sex differences, and further postulates that homosexuality is a manifestation of differential, cross-sex organization (Bailey, 1995; Money, 1987).

Popular though this model may be, research exploring the question of whether sexual orientation can be attributed to particular biological mechanisms is open to serious theoretical and methodological critique and cannot be taken as definitive. We are left with two schools of thought. One review of evidence to date concluded by arguing that "research into possible biological bases of sexual preference has failed to produce any conclusive evidence" (Parker & DeCecco, 1995, p. 427). In contrast, Gladue (1993) observed:

> One can only conclude that, while imperfect, and while still in search of a perfect set of data that will yield uncontestable findings, the evidence to date grows in support of the notion that the development of sexual orientation ... is early and critically based upon a myriad of biological factors. (p. 450)

This is not to say that biological models are either right or wrong; it is only to say that we cannot know.

Environmental Explanations

Often the debate about the origins of sexual orientation is phrased in terms of the perennial nature-nurture controversy: is behavior caused by biology or by environment? Those approaches that urge an environmental origin can be roughly divided into two categories. Psychodynamic approaches propose that homophilia reflects personality dynamics caused by particular formative experiences, usually in early childhood. Behavioral approaches propose that sexual orientation is the product of specific experiences of association, imitation, reinforcement, and/or punishment.

Psychodynamic Approaches

Traditional Psychoanalytic Theory.
The staunchest advocates of a psychodynamic explanation of sexual orientation come from the psychoanalytic school descended from Sigmund Freud. Contrary to popular belief, Freud himself did not see homosexuality as pathological, nor did he believe that it should be socially condemned or legally punished. Rather, he theorized that all human beings are intrinsically bisexual and that the emergence of heterosexuality required explanation as much as did homosexuality (Jones, 1965).

Although Freud's contention that homosexuality is a developmental distortion is hardly an affirming position, it does not approach the pathologization of LGB identity that would follow. Freud's successors, especially among American psychoanalysts, believed homophilia to be a form of mental illness, one amenable to psychotherapeutic cure (Abelove, 1993). This interpretation supported a movement from the construal of homosexuality as a sin and a crime to its redefinition as a sickness. It also effectively forestalled any proposition that homosexuality was a normal variation of human biology, as many early sexologists had proposed. Based on the presumption that homophilia was a mental illness, the search for its psychological roots and for treatment modalities began. The cause was sought in early childhood experiences, especially in the child's relationships with her or his parents.

A vast array of possible etiologies accumulated: Homophilia is a form of autoeroticism or narcissism wherein loving one's own sex amounts to self-love. Homosexuality bespeaks an aversion to and fear of the genitals of the other sex. Gay male identity reflects a man's unresolved castration anxiety, so that a woman partner, who has no penis, evokes one's own fears of castration. Homophilia reflects a developmental arrest, where one fails to move beyond the normal same-sex attachments of latency. Gay men hunger for masculinity and search for it in relationships with other men. A girl's anger at her father for rejecting her as his partner causes her to hate men. A girl's strong attachment to her father leads her to lesbianism as a means of avoiding incest fears. Lesbianism is an expression of "masculine protest," a woman's desire to assume the preferred male role. For both lesbians and gay men, the root problem is a mother fixation. These illustrations suggest the variety of etiologies prosed within a psychoanalytic framework. The most prevalent theme was that the mothers of male homosexuals were close-binding and seductive, and that their fathers were absent or distant.

In each case, homophilia is interpreted as a disturbance in the normal course of development. Not simply a variation, it is symptomatic of a pathological condition that requires treatment. The prescription was for long-term psychoanalysis (or other form of intensive psychotherapy), whose intent was to restructure the personality so as to eliminate psychopathology and thereby cure homosexuality.

One major research project purported to support the most widely accepted of these hypotheses, namely that male homosexuality is the product of an overprotective mother and a distant father. Bieber, et al. (1962) conducted an extensive study, wherein they asked a large group of psychotherapists to describe the childhood backgrounds of their gay male patients. A consistent pattern emerged of an overly intimate and controlling mother and a distant father.

However, this study was severely flawed. First, the sample consisted entirely of gay men already in therapy. Second, the reports of patients' backgrounds were secondhand, having been solicited from the therapists rather than from the patients themselves. The problem with this approach is that a therapist's expectations influence what a client says as well as how the therapist interprets those comments. A therapist trained to expect this sort of family constellation in the background of his gay male clients is likely to hear just that and report just that. To complicate this point further, recent research demonstrates that if there is a connection between gay identity and fathers' distance, it may be that fathers' aloofness follows rather than precedes their sons' homophilic tendencies (Bell, Weinberg, & Hammersmith, 1981).

In sum, there is no reliable evidence to support psychoanalytic interpretations of homophilia. On the contrary, extensive research has found no familial variables that are consistently related to sexual orientation (Bell, Weinberg, & Hammersmith, 1981). Both the fact that research has demonstrated that homophilia does not reflect a mental disorder and the persistent failure of psychotherapy to alter sexual orientation militate against models that present homosexuality as a form of psychopathology susceptible to psychotherapeutic change (Gonsiorek, 1991; Haldeman, 1991, 1994; Silverstein, 1991).

Contemporary Feminist Psychoanalytic Theory
A recent variation on traditional psychoanalytic theory, based on the work of Chodorow (1978), has intriguing implications for sexual orientation—particularly for lesbianism. Chodorow suggested that girls and women form their identity through a close relationship to their mother, with the result that their sense of self is deeply grounded in close relationships. Boys and men, in contrast, develop identity by distancing themselves from their mothers, creating identity that is defined by separation and independence.[3]

---

3. Chodorow acknowledges that this formulation reflects an affluent, western, white perspective, although others have been less conscientious in acknowledging the model's culture-bound roots.

Self-in-relation theory (e.g., Jordan, Kaplan, Miller, Stiver, & Surrey, 1982) elaborates on the implications of this model for women's identity. The core argument is that, because of its importance to women's sense of self, the first intimate relationship—that with the mother—becomes a prototype for subsequent interpersonal connections. Since men's identity is not comparably imbedded in a close relationship—is, indeed, defined by separation—women's need for intimacy cannot be met by men. Hence, women turn to other women to meet their relational needs.

In terms of sexual orientation, the question this model raises is why more women are not lesbians (Brown, 1995). Since a woman's first intimate relationship is with another woman (the mother), and since her relationally defined self finds connection most readily with other women whose sense of self is similarly grounded in connection, the question becomes what generates heterosexual attachment. This is a provocative transformation of the usual query about sexual orientation. However, without resolving this quandary, self-in-relation theorists present heterosexuality as the normative outcome of personality development, although women are regarded as the continuing primary emotional support for each other.

Self-in-relation theory has been criticized for its ethnocentrism, for its essentialist rendering of gender (Bohan, 1993; Brown, 1995), and for its lack of evidence that women are intrinsically more relational than men, or that the early relationship with the mother is exclusively or even predominantly determinant of later personality. Still, women's relationality and men's independence are persistent themes in both lay and professional discourse. Given these pervasive cultural constructions of feminine and masculine identity, one might well ask why women don't more readily turn to other women for their primary relationships.

One particular strength of this model is its focus on the nature of relationships rather than on sexuality per se. Evidence suggests that women tend to define their sexual orientation in terms of relationship variables—intimacy, falling in love, special friendships, and so forth—whereas men define theirs in terms of sexual experience and fantasies (Garnets & Kimmel, 1993). This finding appears to support the self-in-relation model, and suggests that this approach might offer some meaningful insights into sexual orientation for women.

Social Learning Theory Explanations

Social learning theory is a form of behaviorism asserting that it is possible to understand even complex behaviors by analyzing the environmental forces that shape those actions. This approach relies on a few key principles: Associations are formed between events that occur together, so that experiences gain meaning from the contexts in which they occur. We increase the performance of behaviors that have positive consequences or are reinforced; we decrease behaviors that have negative consequences or are punished. And we learn both behaviors and their potential consequences by observing others. The term *social* learning focuses on the assumption that, for humans, the vast majority of our learning experiences take place in social settings, involve social stimuli, and are shaped by social consequences.

From a social learning perspective, sexual orientation of any sort is learned, and it is (at least theoretically) possible to determine exactly what learning experiences shape one or another sexual orientation. The task is to identify those events that might be associated with same-sex or other-sex experiences, and to determine what learning experiences might lead one to imitate (and therefore be more prone to), might reinforce (and thereby increase the probability of), or might punish (and thereby diminish) a particular sexual orientation. These same questions could, theoretically, be asked about heterosexual as well as LGB behavior, though they rarely are. A number of experiences have been theorized as leading to LGB identity.

Heterophobia

One hypothesis is that homophilia reflects "heterophobia," a fear of the other sex, often based on performance anxiety or a fear of rejection. Thus, heterosexual behavior is punished by rejection or embarrassment, making it less likely. However, it is unclear why one would be more afraid of poor performance with or rejection by the other sex than one's own. Also, this would not explain why people who have reason to fear the other sex because of past experiences still identify as heterosexual, nor why gay men and lesbians who have positive heterosexual experiences do not question their sexual orientation. In fact, far from fearing heterosexual experience, many lesbian and gay individuals experience heterosexual arousal, and many have heterosexual masturbatory fantasies.

Perhaps most importantly in terms of understanding LGB experience, this hypothesis presumes that LGB identity is a second choice, a fall-back position rather than an affirmative identity. Loving someone of one's own sex need have nothing to do with negative feelings toward the other sex, any more than heterosexual love entails negative feelings toward members of one's own sex.

Seduction or Recruitment

A second hypothesis is that LGB individuals were seduced or recruited— usually as children—by other LGBs. Where this refers to sexual molestation of a child by an adult, evidence indicates that the vast majority of sexual abuse of children is committed by heterosexual males; most commonly, the victim is female (Finkelhor, 1986; Jenny, Roesler, & Poyer, 1994; Patterson, 1995b). Women, including lesbians, are extremely unlikely to molest children, and gay men are no more likely to do so than are heterosexual men. There is no evidence that unwilling participation in same-sex sexuality is related to later LGB identity.

If "recruitment" is taken to mean that participation in same-sex relationships initiates one's LGB career, an important point arises. Because of the heterosexual assumption, heterosexual individuals needn't question their sexual orientation, and therefore the moment when they come to that identity is not defined by a particular experience. In contrast, the achievement of a lesbian, gay, or bisexual identity may indeed require experience with same-sex attraction, attachments, and/or relationships to ground an identity that contradicts that assumption. However, lesbians and gay men do not typically participate in same-sex sexual activity until well after they become aware of same-sex feelings (Bell, Weinberg, & Hammersmith, 1981). Thus, it is not that LGB individuals are recruited, but that, unlike heterosexual people, their sexual orientation is not automatically assumed and can only emerge in the context of connections to others of their own sex.

First Sexual Experience
A third hypothesis holds that if a child's first sexual experience is with same-sex peers, sexual arousal becomes associated to members of one's own sex, and homophilia results. This proposal does not explain, however, why the majority of people identify as heterosexual, since most children engage in their first, exploratory sexual behavior with same-sex peers. A similar hypothesis is that sexual orientation reflects masturbatory fantasies; whatever fantasies are associated with sexual satisfaction become the object of sexual desire and therefore determine sexual orientation. However, this hypothesis also falls short because many LGB individuals report predominantly heterosexual fantasies and many heterosexual individuals engage in homosexual fantasies. Notice again how both these explanations define LGB orientation entirely in terms of sexual activity.

Negative Heterosexual Experiences
Yet another proposal is that LGB identity derives from a damaging sexual experience with a member of the other sex. This theory, too, fails to find supportive evidence. First, to reiterate an earlier point, many LGBs have had good sexual experiences with the other sex. Further, many heterosexuals have had painful sexual experiences, such as rape or incest, but do not question their sexual orientation; and many LGB individuals have had no such experiences. The presumption that such a relationship exists once again reflects the belief

that LGB identity indicates something gone wrong, is a negative response against the other sex rather than an affirmative love for one's own.

Exposure and Imitation

One theory holds that LGB identity is a result of exposure to LGB models. This "contagion" hypothesis, together with the recruiting or seduction hypothesis, lies at the heart of proposals that children be kept away from LGB individuals. Like the recruitment theory, this one has no empirical support. Recent research—for example, on children raised by lesbian and gay parents— demonstrates that children who are exposed to LGB adults are no more likely to identify as LGB than are children of heterosexual parents (Patterson, 1992, 1995a). Indeed, if this modeling or imitation hypothesis were an adequate explanation of sexual orientation, we would be hard pressed to explain the existence of homophilia, since the vast majority of LGB individuals were raised by heterosexual parents and as children had little or no contact with (openly) LGB adults.

Gender Deviance

One supposition connects learning principles with concepts discussed previously. This theory asserts that, at least for boys, homosexuality is a result of gender deviance that was not punished; as it flourished, so did a gay identity. On a theoretical level, this position is problematic because, once again, it merges gender and sexual orientation, implying that if cross-gender behavior were eliminated, gay identity would be, as well.

This hypothesis finds some support in research discussed previously, which demonstrates a relationship between cross-gender behavior in children and later LGB identity (Bailey, 1995; Bailey & Zucker, 1995). It may be, as suggested by this hypothesis, that a failure to punish cross-gender behavior results in LGB identity, in a simple behavioral model. Or it may be that the process is far more complex than that, and that it relies not solely on biology and/or behavioral learning but also on complex cultural understandings and the individual's transformation of those understandings into personal identity. As discussed above, this linkage between gender atypicality and later LGB identity may reflect the process by which individuals come to terms with their own atypical identity by internalizing the terms of identity provided by their culture. They may be aware of themselves as different and incorporate society's label for that difference: homosexuality.

Here the conflation of sexual orientation and gender roles is highlighted by the question that is not asked. Given that the core of LGB identity is precisely relationships with the same sex, why do we look to cross-gender behavior rather than same-sex attachments for its predictors (Berenbaum & Snyder,

1995)? Posing the issue in terms of gender deviance rather than same-sex attachments denies the central meaning of LGB identity and embraces instead the socially constructed belief that sexual orientation and gender-role performance are interchangeable.

Social Learning Theory: A Summary

In sum, research has failed to yield support for hypotheses that specify environmental origins for LGB identity. The one social learning hypothesis that seems beyond question addresses heterosexuality rather than nonheterosexuality; it is simply that heterosexuality is consistently and pervasively modeled and reinforced, so we would expect it to be far more common than other forms of sexual orientation. LGB identity, on the other hand, is relatively invisible and is punished, so we would expect it to be relatively uncommon, as indeed it is. The dilemma here, of course, is how one explains the persistence of LGB identity despite this situation.

Interactionist Explanations

Most contemporary scholars insist that it is pointless to ask whether sexual orientation—or any other human characteristic—is caused by nature *or* nurture, biology *or* environment. Rather, any phenomenon as complex as this reflects an interaction between biological substrata and environmental influences. Interactionist models of sexual orientation propose that there is a biologically based predisposition to one or another sexual orientation, and that particular environmental events act to actualize or minimize this predisposition.

Money (1988), for example, suggested that sexual orientation results from a biological predisposition acted upon by particular environmental events during a critical developmental period. The result is the formation of a "lovemap," a blueprint for the ideal relationship that, once developed, is fixed. This theory, unfortunately, does not identify either the critical period or the crucial environmental triggers that establish the lovemap, and, as we have seen, the notion of a biological underpinning remains open to question. Also, the assertion that sexual orientation is fixed once developed ignores evidence for fluidity and choice in sexual orientation. However, the approach is valuable for its attention to the probable complexity of the development of sexual orientation.

Some models recommend a more indirect etiology. For instance, Byne and Parsons (1993) proposed that the process begins with a biological predisposition not to a particular sexual orientation but to some set of traits that in turn shape an individual's experience; these experiences, in turn, influence the development of sexual orientation. For example, a boy may be biologically predisposed to be withdrawn and low in energy. If as a result the child does not participate in active group sports, he may be ostracized by his peers and eventually incorporate the label they offer—seeing himself as a sissy and therefore as gay. One advantage to a model such as this is that it allows for many paths to the same identity and acknowledges the differential impacts of biology and environment in individual cases. However, it does not explain same-sex orientation where the individual does not engage in gender-atypical behavior, nor does it address those cases where sexual orientation is an active choice.

Finally, Daryl Bem (in press) has proposed that sexual orientation derives from a complex process by which "exotic becomes erotic." Bem suggests that biological variables predispose not sexual orientation, per se, but childhood temperaments, which in turn predispose sex-typical or sex-atypical patterns of behavior—aggression or activity level, for instance. The child who is prone to sex-atypical behavior feels different from her or his same-sex peers, who, in turn, are experienced as unfamiliar and exotic. This gender-nonconforming child is likely to be ostracized by age-mates, leading to anxiety and discomfort, which, in turn, trigger nonspecific physiological arousal. This arousal thus becomes associated with (different or "exotic") same-sex peers and is subsequently eroticized, leading the child to develop romantic and sexual feelings toward members of her or his own sex. This pattern persists through childhood and adolescence, and the result is a gay or lesbian adult.

Children whose biologically based temperament predisposes gender-conforming behavior, in contrast, perceive the other sex as different from themselves, as unfamiliar and therefore exotic. These feelings of unfamiliarity also elicit anxiety, which becomes associated with other-sex peers; over time, this leads to heterosexuality. Variations in this process lead to bisexuality in its many forms, as well as accounting for the fluidity of sexual orientation for many people, and for situations where various elements of sexual orientation (feelings, actions, self-identification, and so forth) are incongruent. Finally, Bem's analysis incorporates the impact of systems of socially constructed beliefs, highlighting especially the centrality of gender polarization to the very notion of sexual orientation.

Bem's model is remarkable for its grounding in a wide range of research and its attention to the complexity of forces that must underlie a phenomenon as convoluted as sexual orientation. It is also intriguing for its notion of same-sex peers as different. This is in contrast to most approaches to understanding LGB experience, which point to the role of similarity between partners as central to same-sex relationships—particularly in terms of the empathy possible between two people whose shared gender makes for very similar life experiences.

What is not clear in Bem's model is why the nonspecific physiological arousal generated by feelings of difference necessarily becomes eroticized. Why, for instance, doesn't the anxiety that becomes associated with the "exotic" lead children to fear and avoid, even loathe members of their own sex? Further, Bem acknowledges that this model cannot explain those women who choose a nonheterosexual identity; other choices are also precluded here, such as elective heterosexuality. The theory is also unable to accommodate those LGB individuals who did not sense themselves to be different during childhood, nor the heterosexuals who did.

Interactionist Models: A Summary

Interactionist models are extremely important for their incorporation of a wide variety of factors in the etiology of sexual orientation and their openness to the possibility of very different individual paths within their general frameworks. However, they leave some questions still unanswered, particularly the quandary of how one comes to a self-identification as gay, lesbian, bisexual— or heterosexual. Without this element, even these complex models miss an important element of LGB experience. In Daryl Bem's own words, "issues of sexual orientation *identity* are beyond the formal scope of [such] theory" (in press, p. 12) [italics in original].

Volitional and Cognitive Explanations

Theories postulating that sexual orientation is caused by biology, by environmental forces, or by an interaction between these disregard the role of cognition and thereby mask a third possibility: that sexual orientation is a matter of cognitive processing and conscious choice. Although science, operating from a deterministic paradigm, has avoided the question of volition, the debate about whether or not sexual orientation is a choice currently dominates public discourse on the topic. A number of researchers have addressed this question.

This work focuses almost entirely on women, and some writers have proposed that choice plays a greater role in lesbian than in gay male identity (e.g., Cass, 1990; Haldeman, 1994; Jeffreys, 1993; Kitzinger & Wilkinson, 1995; Rothblum, 1994). Indeed, scholars in the area contend that the deterministic bent of sexual orientation theory and research reflects a male bias: it is based on men's experience, has often not included women, and has failed to take into account the impact of feminism on women's identities. Even some writers who generally argue for biological underpinnings of sexual orientation suggest that the path to same-sex orientation may be very different for women than for men, with biology perhaps playing a more demonstrable role in male than in female sexual orientation (e.g., Gladue & Bailey, 1995; Hu, et al., 1995).

Perhaps the first indication that choice is a relevant variable in the understanding of sexual orientation comes from feminist thought. Especially in the 1970s, a politically radical branch of feminism supported the adoption of lesbian identity as a positive alternative to patriarchal heterosexuality. Choosing lesbianism became a political act, and some women who had previously identified as heterosexual chose to invest their political, social, emotional, and sexual energies with other women (e.g., Faderman, 1991; Golden, 1994).

Fluidity and Choice

Research that emerged after this movement was well underway identified two very different "identities in the lesbian world." Reporting on her research exploring lesbian experience, Ponse (1978) distinguished between primary lesbians, who felt they had always been lesbians, and elective lesbians, who saw their lesbian identity and lifestyle as a conscious choice. This choice often derived from a feminist stance, which supported the lesbian choice as the affirmative selection of a life that transcended heterosexuality. Golden (1987, 1994) explored this distinction further, interviewing heterosexual, lesbian, and bisexual women. Her results demonstrated that choice is a major component of sexual orientation for many lesbian, bisexual, and—significantly—heterosexual women.

Among her college subjects, Golden identified primary lesbians who believed they always had been and always would be lesbians. Their understanding of their sexual orientation was essentialist; they saw themselves as "true" lesbians, in contrast to some others who were seen as less authentically so. In contrast, elective lesbians reported having made a conscious decision to consider lesbianism. Some of these women also had an essentialist view of their lesbian identity, interpreting their past to fit this identity and not believing they could ever be other than lesbian in the future. Other elective lesbians saw this identity as less essential and as potentially flexible or changeable in the future.

Most heterosexually identified college women could be considered primary heterosexuals; they were perplexed by a question asking when they first knew they were heterosexual, and could not imagine being otherwise. However, there were also elective heterosexual college women, who saw sexual orientation as potentially fluid. These women had been or could imagine being attracted to women, but chose not to explore this possibility, often citing the difficulties of living a nonheterosexual life.

Golden's sample of older women came from feminist groups and included women from their late-20s to early 50s. Among this sample, primary lesbians, like their college-age counterparts, believed their lesbianism was a fundamental and unchanging aspect of their identity. Elective lesbians, on the other hand, saw their lesbianism as reflecting one option of many available to them. Some elective lesbians had come to this perspective from a more essentialist view. Earlier in their lives they had thought their sexual orientation was fixed and fundamental to their identity; later they came to see it as more fluid and flexible, with lesbianism now a conscious choice. Others saw their identity as increasingly fixed, anchored in a firm commitment to women and to the lesbian community.

Among these women, Golden also identified elective heterosexuals. These women had been or could imagine being attracted to women as well as men, and almost always preferred women as emotional partners. Although they currently identified as heterosexual, many were open to involvement with women, and believed that if the circumstances presented themselves, they would prefer to have a relationship with a woman.

Tenacity Despite Change

In a variation on the theme of fluidity and choice, Bart (1993) explored "the tenaciousness of lesbian identity" in the face of apparent heterosexuality. Bart interviewed a number of women who formed intimate relationships with men after having identified as lesbian. Despite their involvement with men, these women refused the label "heterosexual," and indicated that their next partner might be a woman. Thus, although the current behavioral manifestation of their sexual orientation pointed to heterosexuality, their self-identification remained lesbian. It appears that several choices were involved here: the selection of partner, the selection of identity, and the choice to maintain one even when it was incommensurate with the other.

The Creation of Narratives

Other models focus on the role of cognition in supporting and making sense of transitions such as those reported by Golden and Bart. Drawing attention to the role of cognition in mediating changes in sexual orientation, Kitzinger and Wilkinson (1995) interviewed a large group of women who currently identified unequivocally as lesbian, and who had previously held an equally firm heterosexual identity.

The women who had made a shift in identity cited a variety of barriers to their assumption of lesbian identity, including both external constraints, such as compulsory heterosexuality, and personal barriers, such as their own internalized homophobia. However, once having overcome these impediments, these women's transitions to lesbian identity was clearly a cognitively mediated undertaking, moving from a sense of profound awakening through a continuing process of defining what it means to be lesbian and to transact life from that position. Each phase of this transition was marked by the utilization of cognitive strategies that made sense of the process and gave meaning to life choices.

Detypification

Jennes (1992) offered yet another cognitive model, based on the notion of detypification. Exploring how women come to self-identify as lesbian, Jennes sketched a process that begins with an awareness of the category, "lesbian." The movement to lesbian identity entails reassessing the social category implied by that term and detypifying it, or stripping it of its stereotypic and negative connotations. As the category takes on increasingly personal and positive meaning, identity shifts to meet the new category. In keeping with this model, Cass (1990) argued that our behavior is actually shaped by our identity. To the degree that we assume one or another sexual orientation identity, our behaviors follow. Thus, detypifying the category of lesbian, for instance, by making it positive and personal, will influence subsequent behaviors, leading them to conform to this new identity.

Because the meanings of social categories are constantly shifting, identity can be expected to be fluid: "As our understandings of the meanings associated with the kinds of people it is possible to be in society undergo substantive changes, we continually reassess the personal applicability of any given category" (Jennes, 1992, p. 69). This perspective opens the provocative possibility that, as meanings continue to change, so, too, will our identities.

Volitional and Cognitive Models: A Summary

The volitional and cognitive models discussed here all deal with women, and, as noted above, some work urges that women's adoption of one or another sexual orientation is, overall, more fluid than is men's. Yet, it seems probable that many men make comparable choices. Surely many men choose to identify as heterosexual because of the stigma attached to gay or bisexual identity, and there is evidence that many men make a transition from a heterosexual to a gay identity, a transition that entails cognitive reframing of past and present experience.

What makes this research with women particularly significant is that it points to the role of social, historical, and political contexts in understanding sexual orientation. Over the past few decades, women have forged a political and philosophical lens that grants new perspectives on their place in society. Feminism offers not only a critique of existing systems but also a prospect for change; among the opportunities it promises are relationships that transcend the gendered power dynamics of traditional heterosexuality. Thus, feminism provides a philosophical base for consciously rejecting heterosexuality and choosing lesbianism as an affirmation of one's own and other women's worth. There is no comparable philosophy to support men in a parallel decision. On the contrary, to reject heterosexuality is, for men, precisely to renounce the unquestioned superiority of heterosexual masculinity.

Another benefit of volitional models is the perspective they provide on biological and environmental determinisms. When we view deterministic explanations from a volitional perspective, some interesting questions emerge: Do elective lesbians' brains change as they assume this new identity? What happens to Xq28 with shifts in sexual orientation? If elective heterosexuals really have lesbian brains, how are they able to resist that prenatally entrenched predisposition? What parenting styles "cause" elective lesbianism? Did elective heterosexual women have bad experiences with women as children? Or was it with men? Posing such questions makes clear how thoroughly grounded psychological theory and research are in essentialist views of sexual orientation. When confronted with the role of cognition and volition, determinist questions and answers are puzzling.

Perhaps the greatest benefit of considering volitional models is the role they play in destabilizing the categories we adopt so easily. They illuminate the fact that, at least for some people, sexual orientation is not constitutive of self but is a potentially temporary claim. Such fluidity of identity demands that we consider the social and political meanings—indeed, the arbitrary nature of the very construct of sexual orientation.

A Panoply of Answers

Consider the enormous array of elements that comprise the complicated phenomenon that we know as sexual orientation, the vast assortment of variables discussed in chapter 1. Given such complexity, the potential diversity of individual identities is staggering, and attempting to encompass such variety under the rubric of a single explanatory construct seems futile. It is reasonable to expect that the origin and the development of sexual orientation vary widely among people, with various components contributing differentially and at different times to the course of each person's evolution. For some, biology may play a major role; for others, choice predominates; for each, environmental forces likely contribute; for all, the meanings given by society shape how experiences will be understood and identities will be defined.

The Role of Cultural Meanings

Whatever the source of same-sex attachments and sexual activity, the development of an identity grounded in the sex of one's partners is a result of internalized social meanings. One only identifies as bisexual, lesbian, heterosexual, or gay because those are identities provided by the pattern of meanings this society gives to affectional and sexual attachments. Even fluidity in sexual orientation rests on cultural meanings; changes in sexual orientation are an expectable product of "individuals [responding] to changes in the available social constructs, the sociopolitical landscape, and their own positions on that landscape" (Rust, 1993, p. 74).

Thus, there is an inescapable social-cognitive component to identity grounded in sexual orientation; we experience it as the culture presents it to us, in the terms the culture gives us. Those meanings are internalized and become the terms by which we define ourselves—whatever the etiology of the experiences they label.

So What? The Implications of the Answers

It was suggested previously that particular understandings assume prominence not because they are intrinsically superior but because they have a place, make sense, serve a purpose within society. If this is the case, we might ask what would be the implications of these various explanations? What consequences would follow from each? Who would benefit and how? What would one or another mean to the society as a whole? Let us consider each class of explanations from this perspective.

The Implications of Biological Explanations

On the positive side, many contend that a biological answer to the question of causation will support an end to discrimination against LGBs. If sexual orientation is a biological given, much like race, then LGB individuals cannot rightfully be persecuted. The acceptance of such a tenet would eliminate concerns about "contagion" and recruitment, because one can't "catch" or be persuaded to adopt a genetic trait.

However, past attempts to guarantee protection based on biological arguments have not succeeded; indeed, biological explanations have historically been employed to support efforts to eliminate homosexuals and homosexuality through the administration of hormones, castration, and even brain surgery DeCecco & Parker, 1995). Consider the parallel to racism, which has not ceased because race is believed to be biologically determined. In addition, fears of recruitment and contagion would not necessarily be assuaged. Throughout recent history, theorists have differentiated between true or congenital homosexuals and those who are their victims, the recruited innocents.

Nor is the argument for nondiscrimination based on biological causation necessarily persuasive. It would still be possible to insist that homophilia is a sin or a sickness and to demand that individuals not act on that identity. By analogy, it is generally believed that alcoholism has a biological underpinning, but we still expect alcoholics to stop drinking.

Finally, we might ask why any group must claim a biologically based identity in order to achieve equal rights. Religion is not biologically determined but is legally protected from discrimination nevertheless.

Perhaps of greater importance are the ethical and personal implications of biological explanations. The attitude of helpless victim—"I know it's wrong, but I can't help it; it's in my genes"—is hardly an affirming position for LGB individuals to assume, and in fact reinforces pejorative judgments of homophilia. This assertion disregards the experience of many individuals for whom homophilia is explicitly a conscious choice. Ignoring this group may serve to distract from their powerful case against patriarchy and heterosexism, but it does not alter the reality that sexual orientation is a choice for some.

Finally, biological explanations imply simple, concrete solutions to complex, multifaceted phenomena. Such reductionist approaches disregard the psychological and social realities of human experience. Indeed, given their theoretical and methodological inadequacies, we might wonder at their current popularity. As mentioned previously, constructionism asks precisely such questions, and Byne offers a provocative answer: "Support for these theories derives as much from their appeal to prevailing cultural ideology as from their scientific merit. This appeal may explain why seriously flawed studies . . . remain viable even when replications repeatedly fail" (1995, p. 304). In other words, research that appears to support dominant beliefs may not be held to the rigorous standards we usually expect of science. As constructionism would suggest, it appears that we believe most easily that which supports current world views.

The Implications of Environmental Explanations

Determinist environmental explanations might carry some of the same implications as biological explanations. If sexual orientation is a product of specific, early experiences, then it is not a choice and should not be persecuted as willful sin or deviance.

Depending on which environmental factors are invoked, however, such explanations could reinforce claims of contagion and recruitment—and the discrimination they support. For instance, the belief that people become LGB because of exposure to other LGB individuals, would support discriminatory treatment. In addition, the identification of environmental "causes" for homophilia might well lead to programs designed to prevent LGB identity through careful environmental control.

Environmental determinism also recreates the victim status produced by biological determinism, with only a slight variation: "I know it's wrong, but I can't help it; it stems from my childhood." Finally, environmental (like biological) determinism overlooks the experience of those who consciously choose one or another sexual orientation and at the same time silences their reasons for making that choice.

The Implications of Volitional Explanations

An important ramification of volitional models may be that they affirm the legitimacy of *any* sexual orientation and they acknowledge the reality that, for many, sexual orientation is not fixed but fluid. No external excuse is invoked; individuals choose the form of relationship that is most fulfilling to them. Equally important, these approaches point to social ills that should command our attention—such as the rigid gender roles that undergird heterosexuality (and its political manifestation, patriarchy) and are damaging to us all.

Cognitive models point to the role of higher mental processes in an aspect of human experience that is otherwise at risk for being reduced to behaviors and biology. To the extent that human beings are cognitive creatures, we will be unable to explain sexual orientation without appeal to the role of cognition.

Still, volitional and cognitive models can also be invoked to support homonegative attitudes among those who see homophilia as a sin or a perversion. From this position, for people actively to engage in homosexual behavior is anathema, to choose an LGB life is morally repugnant, and no cognitive reframing of an identity's meaning diminishes its depravity.

The Implications of Complex Interactionist Explanations

Complex models that incorporate a role for each of these elements—biology, environment, choice, and cognition—arguably have the greatest potential for encompassing the vast range of experience that we understand as sexual orientation. However, their very complexity mitigates against their acceptance in society as a whole. As we discussed while considering prejudice, human beings tend to categorize and homogenize, not to differentiate and individualize.

The current sociopolitical atmosphere begs for a simple explanation for this phenomenon, because it carries such profound implications for beliefs about human experience that are currently under negotiation. Our understanding of sexual orientation is deeply embedded in our beliefs about gender, about relationships, about right and wrong. The very fact that it touches so many firmly held convictions makes us, as a society, yearn for an uncomplicated resolution to the questions it raises. A single gene or an identifiable experience might be the cleanest answer and perhaps the most utilitarian in terms of putting the question to rest. But we must ask what are the costs of such a simple "solution."

CHAPTER FOUR

LESBIAN, GAY, AND BISEXUAL IDENTITY

Stigma Management, Identity Formation, and Coming Out

PSYCHOLOGY IS PRIMARILY concerned with individual experience, and our understanding of the individual is centered on identity—the individual's unique sense of who she or he is. Clearly, we must understand the individual within her or his social context; identity is chiefly forged by social experience, and each person's sense of self is framed by the meanings provided by the culture. Still, psychology is most interested in the product of that process, in identity itself. Thus, the heart of the psychology of sexual orientation is found in attempts to understand the impact on individual identity of one or another position in the matrix of sexual orientations.

Before we explore theory and research in this area, it is important to revisit briefly certain concepts we have covered previously. A discussion of LGB identity development presumes that we know what we mean by the categories of lesbian, gay, and bisexual. It also presumes that identity development for individuals in these categories is more or less homogeneous, reflecting under-lying processes common to LGB persons. As we have seen, the first of these presumptions cannot be supported; on the contrary, the meaning of these terms and the categories they delineate are nebulous, at best. The second is equally untenable. Lesbians' experiences are not the same as those of gay men, and bisexual individuals of either sex clearly face developmental quandaries different from those of gay men or lesbians.[1] In addition, of course, each indi-

---

1. It has been argued that the impact of gender socialization is more powerful in defining

vidual has unique experiences that render any generic model of identity development inadequate.

The salience of these issues becomes clear if, following Brown (1995), we consider whose experience we are trying to describe with models of LGB identity development. Is it the gay man who has "always known" he was gay, or is it the elective lesbian who consciously chose this identity at midlife? Is it the woman whom others may refer to as bisexual but who self-identifies as lesbian despite her involvement in a heterosexual relationship, or is it the man who was happily heterosexually married and raised children before falling in love with another man? Is it the man who has frequent sexual encounters with other men but steadfastly insists that he is not gay, or is it the two women who regard themselves as a lesbian couple but whose relationship is not sexual?

Innumerable such questions could be asked; if we do not include all of these individuals (and others), we have not described LGB identity development. The diversity of identities represented here hints at the impossibility of a single model of development incorporating all variations on LGB identity formation.

Stigma and Stigma Management

Whatever path leads one to identify as lesbian, gay, or bisexual—or to be so labeled by others—those coming to terms with such identities must deal with the omnipresent stigma attached to homophilia. In its literal meaning, the term stigma refers to a physical mark identifying an individual or group as deviant or outcast, such as the scarlet "A" that branded Hawthorne's character an adulteress or the yellow star worn by European Jews during the Nazi regime. In a broader sense, the word also encompasses invisible traits, and includes any attribute that causes others to label an individual as deviant. Thus, LGB identity carries a stigma, albeit usually an invisible one; this identity is likely to elicit condemnation if it is detected.

Typically, members of stigmatized groups are not seen as complete persons. Rather, the stigmatizing quality assumes primacy, anchoring a "master status" or "transsituational identity" so that the stigmatized identity is deemed salient even where it is irrelevant. Thus, one is first LGB and only incidentally any other descriptor: the gay cop or lesbian teacher or bisexual parent. By contrast, nonstigmatized identities do not assume such master status; imagine a newspaper's referring to a "straight teacher" or a "heterosexual actor."

---

individual experience than is sexual orientation (see Brown, 1995; Cass, 1990; Garnets & Kimmell, 1993; Gonsiorek, 1995). In other words, the experience of lesbians and bisexual women is more like that of heterosexual women than of gay and bisexual men, and vice versa. To the degree that this is the case, generic models of LGB identity are destined to fail.

The stigma attached to homophilic identity serves as a backdrop for all LGB experience. Anyone whose life is framed by a label of or self-identification as gay, bisexual, or lesbian in a heterosexist society must cope with the stigma this designation bears. Hence, the development and expression of homophilic identity necessarily centers on managing this stigma.

Internalized Homophobia

A primary consequence of the stigma attached to homophilia is internalized homophobia or internalized homonegativity—the incorporation by LGB individuals themselves of the culture's vilification of gay, lesbian, and bisexual identities. Internalized homophobia/homonegativity is the unavoidable result of having grown up in a heterosexist society.

Although heterosexism shares much in common with other prejudices, it is distinctive in that this form of prejudice is socially condoned, whereas others generally are not. Furthermore, most minority individuals find within the family a sense of shared identity, a safe haven from prejudice, and a place to learn skills for dealing with prejudice. Most homophilic individuals, in contrast, grow up with heterophilic parents, knowing their family's disdain for LGB identity, and unable to learn from them strategies for managing heterosexism. For the individual coming to an LGB identity, this early, profoundly personal lesson in homonegativity becomes directed at oneself: it is no longer some anonymous "they," but *I* who am the target of heterosexism—including that of my own family. Internalized homophobia is the result of these early lessons in homonegative attitudes learned within both within and outside of the family.

The concept of a "qualifying difference" illustrates how minority-group members internalize cultural prejudices against them. The question posed here is how much deviation from the norm is acceptable before it qualifies for intolerance. In concrete terms, how "white" must an African American person look and act, or how straight must an LGB individual appear in order to avoid discrimination?[2] The role of the qualifying difference is reflected in prejudicial attitudes within minority communities, where lighter-skinned blacks and straighter-acting LGBs are favored by many, while those most obviously exhibiting traits that identify them with the stigmatized group are denigrated by some members of their own community. The discomfort of many LGBs with blatant gender bending, for instance, can be seen as reflecting internalized homophobia: these qualities evoke in LGBs as well as in straight society the anxiety associated with stigmatized and denigrated, nonnormative behavior.

---

2. The current "don't ask, don't tell" military policy relies on this dynamic. The position is that LGB identity will not be challenged, so long as the individual does not act on it—in other words, so long as the individual does not qualify for discrimination by doing anything offensive to mainstream sensitivities.

Internalized homonegativity takes many forms. At its most blatant, it is reflected in self-hatred specifically attached to one's LGB identity. The desire to renounce homophilia and somehow become acceptably heterosexual also reflects a condemnation of this identity. Internalized homophobia may also be expressed more indirectly—through low self-esteem, isolation, self-destructive behaviors, substance abuse, even suicide. Behavioral patterns that reaffirm one's inferiority may also be indicative—self-defeating behaviors, tolerance for prejudicial treatment, the sense that one deserves ill fortune. Remaining closeted may demonstrate internalized homonegativity in that it reveals feelings of shame at one's true identity.[3]

Just as the cultural condemnation of homophilia is internalized by gay and lesbian individuals, we might expect that bisexually identified people would internalize the hostility or "biphobia" expressed toward that identity by both heterosexual and homophilic communities. Two parallel dynamics seem important. First, bisexual individuals are likely to experience internalized homophobia as regards the same-sex component of their identity; hence, we might expect manifestations of this dynamic similar to those seen in gay men and lesbians— rejection of apparently homosexual qualities in oneself and others, self-denigration, self-destructive behaviors, and attempts to hide this aspect of identity. Second, in their interactions with lesbian and gay people and communities, we might expect internalized heterophobia—nondisclosure of the heterosexual aspect of their bisexual tendencies, denigration of qualities and individuals perceived as heterosexual, and devaluation of their own heterosexual feelings.

Stigma Management

Given the profound and pervasive impact of internalized homophobia and biphobia, mental health requires that LGB individuals overcome this self-devaluation and reevaluate the meaning of LGB identity in order to achieve a positive sense of self. To accomplish this, the individual must develop means for managing both the stigma attached to the emerging identity and the self-devaluation this stigma generates.[4]

de Monteflores on the Management of Difference

de Monteflores (1986) has delineated a number of stigma management techniques employed by those deemed "different" by their society. Her catalogue

---

3. For a more detailed discussion of the impact of internalized homophobia, see Bickelhaupt, 1995; Brown, 1986; Gonsiorek, 1995; Kominars, 1995; Malyon, 1982; Margolies, Becker, & Jackson-Brewer, 1987; Shidlo, 1994; Sophie, 1987.

4. Allport's (1954) "traits due to victimization" bear a striking resemblance to certain manifestations of internalized homophobia and to strategies for stigma management.

provides an outline of the range of strategies available to individuals identifying as LGB.

Assimilation

One strategy for self-protection is to present oneself in a manner that duplicates as closely as possible that of the dominant group. In the case of LGB
individuals, this entails appearing as straight as possible—in physical appearance, behaviors, relationships, and so forth. The most common form of
assimilation is "passing," where one strives to go unrecognized as LGB, to
be considered heterosexual. By providing a strategy that minimizes one's
association with the denigrated group and maximizes connection with the
valued group, passing protects against both the self-effacing impact of stigma
and the hostility of society at large. Because of the power of the heterosexual
assumption, carefully orchestrated passing can be a very successful strategy
for avoiding stigma; unless rather clear information to the contrary is offered,
people will generally accept the ruse and believe one to be straight.

Assimilation has its costs, however. First, attempts to pass suggest an underlying internalized homophobia that may impede movement toward a positive
LGB identity. This tactic reveals that the individual herself or himself accepts
the societal condemnation of LGB identity, agreeing that it is somehow wrong
and in need of suppression.

Another consequence of assimilation is that it creates a fragmented and
marginal status. The individual has one foot in each culture, trapped between
living a homophilic identity and assimilating to the heterophilic world. Such
marginality may generate a crisis of allegiance. The individual is likely at some
point to ask herself or himself probing questions: Just who am I and to which
community am I committed? What does it say about my lesbian/gay/bisexual
identity that I deny it in order to make myself and others comfortable in
heterosexist society? How much energy am I spending protecting myself that
might be more fruitfully used elsewhere? How will mainstream attitudes
change if the average person never knows an LGB individual because we all
hide? Questions such as these often lead the person to seek other stigma
management strategies.

Ghettoization

For de Monteflores, one way of avoiding stigmatization without the moment-
to-moment conflicts that may be caused by assimilation is to segregate one's
LGB identity from the life where passing seems essential. Some people practice geographical isolation, even to the point of actually working and living—
passing as straight—in one city, and participating in an LGB community in
another. More common is social isolation, where one's LGB connections are

carefully kept from one's straight acquaintances. This sort of distancing allows the LGB person to find support and validation for his or her identity, while yet minimizing the risks associated with that identity's being known in mainstream society.

However, Davies (1992), who referred to such practices as *compartmentalization,* has pointed out the lingering risk of information diffusion inherent in attempts to keep elements of one's life separate. The safest tactic for insuring that this compartmentalization of information is maintained would be to assure that no one who knows one's sexual orientation knows anyone who doesn't. Leading such a double life, however, depends on maintaining impermeable boundaries between identities, a task that is difficult, precarious, and emotionally draining. As an alternative means of managing information, Davies points to the tactic of *collusion,* which entails telling only selected others who agree to keep one's identity a secret. Again, the possibility of information diffusion persists.

There are only two guaranteed strategies for avoiding information's reaching the wrong people: either no one knows or everyone knows. Any other position leaves one vulnerable to being outed—that is, to one's LGB identity being revealed (intentionally or inadvertently) by others, without one's permission.

Confrontation

A very different strategy for dealing with stigma involves an open acknowledgement of one's difference from the norm, an active self-affirmation that presents this difference in a positive light, transforming the apparent defect into an asset. For LGBs, this means coming out, disclosing one's LGB identity and living openly in the face of stigma.

The availability of a supportive community is of paramount importance in the decision and ability to confront rather than avoid stigma. An awareness of a community of others like oneself diminishes the sense of isolation that comes with exclusion from mainstream society and provides a forum to address feelings of anger and sadness that arise from marginalization and stigmatization as well as from one's own internalized homophobia. Often, confrontation includes reframing one's own past as well as claiming the history and culture of the new-found community, as the individual gradually constructs a new identity grounded in a self-affirming society. Public acknowledgement of LGB identity and burgeoning group allegiance round out the transition from hiding to affirming one's LGB identity.

Troiden on Stigma Management

Troiden (1989) distinguished among techniques for coping with stigma in terms of when various strategies are likely to be invoked during the process of identity formation. This discussion provides a finer analysis of de Monteflores' principles.

Early Strategies

When the individual first begins to experience feelings or to engage in acts that might indicate an LGB identity, strategies used to manage these experiences often reveal the extreme discomfort that such awareness may evoke. *Denial* occurs where the person simply refuses to believe that he or she is having such feelings. If these experiences become too compelling to deny, one might resort to *repairing*, apologizing, repenting, and promising that they won't occur again. Another way of dismissing these events is to acknowledge their occurrence but to *redefine* them as not indicating a homophilic identity. As one might expect, given our patterns of gender socialization, men are more likely to deny affect as a means of excusing the act (I was drunk; we were just experimenting), whereas women are more likely to justify the experience precisely in terms of their feelings (this is a very special friendship; I love a person who happens to be a woman). Notice that all these approaches reflect internalized homophobia—here expressed as the belief that LGB identity must somehow be avoided or escaped.

The individual who moves beyond these strategies to an acknowledgement or *acceptance* of her or his LGB identity is likely to begin seeking out information and gradually to become more comfortable with this identity. Still, this greater comfort does not necessarily mean a willingness to be entirely open about one's new-found identity.

Midlevel Strategies

The most common technique for dealing with a self-acknowledged but still largely private LGB identity is *passing*, discussed above. The aim of passing is to make one's LGB status invisible (note the internalized homophobia this suggests), and the control of information this requires can be a very demanding undertaking. Techniques for maintaining invisibility may include changing pronouns to disguise the sex of friends and lovers—changing "she" to "he" or always speaking about one's activities in the singular. Fictitious relationships may be invented to discourage curiosity; this is especially common to ward off parents' insistence that one date and marry—heterosexually, of course. The physical environment must be controlled, as well: the second bedroom that is never used, the picture of one's pet rather than of one's partner on the office desk, separate home telephone numbers to avoid the "wrong" person's answering a call, clearing the shelves of LGB-related books before guests arrive.

Even the homophilic relationship itself must be managed: there can be no show of affection in public; pet names and endearments must be avoided whenever others are around; partners must introduce each others as "roommates"; work-related activities that include heterosexual partners must be attended alone or with a stand-in; joint financial ventures are made difficult or impossible by the need to disguise the nature of the relationship; other claims on one's time take precedence over the relationship, to avoid its being seen as central to one's life.[5] Thus, although often an effective strategy for concealing LGB identity, passing is extremely costly psychologically to both the individual and the relationship.

Another drawback to living as if one were heterosexual is how it militates against one's finding a supportive community of other LGB individuals. Not only is such isolation costly in terms of social contacts, but it also precludes the individual's finding the validation of identity and affirmation of personal worth that are essential to a positive sense of self. Access to a community is of tremendous value to the well-being of LGB individuals, as we will discuss in chapter 8.

Another strategy described by Troiden, *capitulation,* entails accepting society's condemnation and avoiding participation in homophilic activities or relationships. This move clearly reflects internalized homophobia and risks ongoing self-devaluation for the individual, as well as creates a struggle to contain the feelings that are being suppressed.[6] A very different tactic is *minstrelization,* where the individual openly exhibits the new identity, typically in a highly stereotypic manner, satirizing cultural images as a defiant assertion of LGB status. As a stigma management strategy, this tactic risks alienating not only straight society but other LGBs as well, depending on how blatantly the behavior violates the qualifying standard.

In Troiden's formulation, a final strategy for coping with a newly achieved LGB identity is *group alignment.* Here, the sense that one belongs to one community is matched by the awareness that one is explicitly excluded from another—the mainstream, heterosexual community. With this recognition, the salience of the LGB community escalates, and the individual may become thoroughly immersed in the institutions and activities of that community, sometimes actively avoiding interaction with heterosexual people. Often, the homophile community is lionized in this process, with all LGBs seen in a favorable light and heterosexuals collectively maligned.

Late-Stage Strategies

As the individual becomes increasingly dedicated to LGB identity, new techniques emerge that reflect this growing commitment. An individual in this

---

5. Kirk's (1987) humorous and poignant "Hetiquette" depicts the extremes of caution dictated by careful passing.

6. "Don't ask, don't tell," again. See footnote 2 this chapter.

position might employ *covering,* where she or he does not deny LGB identity—sometimes because it is already known—but does strive to diminish its impact. Typically, this entails a lifestyle that is the epitome of respectability and that essentially duplicates the heterosexual norm, despite one's often apparent homophilic identity. Similarly, people who use *blending* as a strategy focus their efforts on behaving in gender-appropriate ways, disguising their LGB status by the apparently normative quality of their lives. If pressed about their sexual orientation, these individuals simply argue that one's sexual orientation is irrelevant. Covering and blending differ only slightly from passing; the distinction lies in the diminished need for active deceit that stems from a willingness to admit to one's sexual orientation, though avoiding its becoming an issue.

Finally, some people *convert,* that is, acquire an ideology that supports their active confrontation (in de Monteflores' terms) with rather than avoidance of stigma. For these people, the problem at hand is not LGB identity but society's heterosexist prejudices. Therefore, rather than concealing their identity and striving to avoid the consequences it brings, these individuals face the stigma and work to change homonegative attitudes.

As is clear from this discussion, LGB identity formation is profoundly affected by the reality that such an identity is maligned by society. How each individual handles this stigma reflects an interaction between his or her characteristic modes of coping and the particular demands of LGB identity. Some individuals pay a huge psychological price for this struggle, particularly those whose mental health was compromised prior to grappling with LGB identity (Gonsiorek, 1995; Ratner, 1988; Saunders & Valente, 1987). However, what is most remarkable is that the vast majority of LGB individuals successfully negotiate the passage to homophilic identity, emerging with exemplary mental health and personal well-being (D'Augelli, 1994).

Most depictions of LGB identity formation stress the very difficult struggle toward self-acceptance and the perpetual battle against heterosexism. Even the LGB community is often portrayed as a position of retreat, the last bastion of safety beset by a hostile world. In contrast to this picture of perpetual victimization, D'Augelli (1994) proposes an "affirmation assumption," asserting that most LGB individuals come through this process, perilous though it may be, with a generally positive sense of self and able to function happily and productively in society. It is true that divergence from the heterosexual norm imposes an enormous strain on the individual's coping abilities, but it also encourages the development of adaptive strengths. From this perspective, the struggle to achieve a positive sense of one's lesbian, gay, or bisexual identity in the face of stigma and prejudice is not a source of inevitable pathology but a crucible for potentially exceptionally healthy development.

Identity Formation

The pervasive impact of stigma on LGB experience is clearly illuminated by theoretical models of LGB identity formation. A few general comments about identity development are in order here to preface our consideration of work in this area. First, during the course of psychological development, LGB individuals face the same tasks that characterize development for all individuals. The particular issues raised by bisexual, lesbian, or gay identity therefore must be addressed *in addition to* and not instead of the usual developmental tasks. Second, because nonheterosexual orientation is generally viewed as a trans-situational identity, issues related to LGB status permeate every developmental task and, conversely, each step in lesbian, gay, or bisexual identity formation is colored by developmental tasks common to us all. Third, any understanding of LGB identity development must take into account the profound cohort effects that have framed LGB experience over the past century. Coming to terms with such identity is emphatically not the same today as it was a decade or a generation ago.

Finally, the formation of lesbian, gay, or bisexual identity involves embracing a particular label as descriptive of who one is. That label may carry a variety of meanings for different people, so that naming oneself "lesbian," for example, may have very different implications for different women; the same is true for gay men and bisexual individuals. And the act of assuming the label will not only influence the nature of one's intimate relationships but will also affect one's other social relationships and will have as yet little-explored implications for one's actions, cognitions, and feelings—in short, for one's future self. In a circular manner, how we label ourselves shapes how we experience life; this, in turn, has consequences for identity and for behavior (Blumenstein & Schwartz, 1990; Cass, 1990; Jennes, 1992; Rust, 1993). Thus, "there is no such thing as a single homosexual identity. Rather, its nature may vary from person to person, from situation to situation, and from period to period" (Cass, 1984, p. 111).

Models of Homophilic Identity Development

As we look across a number of theories of LGB identity development, certain commonalities become apparent. These models present identity formation as a prolonged quest involving a number of transitional periods. The process moves at varying paces for different individuals, and the stages delineated do not necessarily proceed as described for everyone. In general, however, the journey toward identity is portrayed as moving in an identifiable pattern from a sense of confusion through an emerging clarity about one's sexual orientation to a growing desire to express one's identity in more and more settings and to make public the formerly concealed sense of self. Intertwined with this, both cause and result of the wish to disclose, is burgeoning involvement with and a sense of belonging to the LGB community.

With these general principles as outline, we move to a brief summary of models of gay and lesbian identity formation. Following this, we will consider perspectives on bisexual identity development.

Gay and Lesbian Identity

Cass's Identity Development Model

Perhaps the best known description of gay and lesbian identity formation is found in the work of Cass (1979, 1990), which identifies characteristic stages of identity formation and further proposes that identity foreclosure may occur at any stage, effectively stalling development at that level.

Everyone first sees himself or herself as heterosexual by default; when homophilic experiences or feelings challenge that certainty, the incongruity between the heterosexual assumption and one's own experience leads to the first stage of gay and lesbian identity development: *Identity Confusion*. At this stage, the person begins considering the possibility that he or she might be gay or lesbian. The individual may simply disavow this possibility, denying or reframing the experience to make it compatible with a heterosexual sense of self. Alternatively, the person might believe that she or he is lesbian or gay but find the identity unacceptable. Such rejection of same-sex feelings can lead to identity foreclosure: the individual is unable to move beyond this self-denigration and therefore avoids homophilic experiences and strives to suppress gay or lesbian identity.

Optimally, the individual feels generally comfortable with the emerging homophilic feelings and seeks out further information. This leads to the second stage, *Identity Comparison*, where the person examines the implications of this possibility. The previous life plan based on the heterosexual assumption is seen as no longer relevant, and the individual realizes that there are no guidelines to replace those cultural expectations. Faced with this sense of alienation from the dominant society, the individual may retreat into identity foreclosure, rejecting gay or lesbian identity and working to eradicate her or his own same-sex feelings.

More positively, the vacuum left by the irrelevance of heterosexual norms may be filled by a growing sense of belonging to the gay and lesbian community, which affords opportunities to rewrite one's life script in a positive way. At this stage the individual commonly avoids direct personal confronta-

tion with heterosexism by cultivating a heterosexual image, carefully controlling personal information, and avoiding visible associations with LGB issues.

During stage three, *Identity Tolerance,* the person becomes more certain that
she or he actually is lesbian or gay. This conclusion both heightens the sense of
separation from the heterosexual community and diminishes the turmoil and
confusion of earlier stages. However, homophilic identity is tolerated rather
than celebrated, and its self-acceptant quality is tenuous. If early experiences
with the LGB community are negative, they may arouse internalized homophobia and self-devaluation. If this leads to a withdrawal from LGB contacts,
identity foreclosure may follow. On the other hand, good experiences with
other LGBs and incorporation into the LGB community will serve to support
the movement toward an affirmative sense of oneself as gay, bisexual, or lesbian.

The fourth stage, *Identity Acceptance,* reflects a growing commitment to a
lesbian or gay identity, a thriving sense of the normalcy of this identity, and a
sense of belonging and validation within the community. If one's reference
group only partially legitimizes gay or lesbian identity—that is, communicates
a belief that it should be kept private—the individual is likely to continue to
use passing as a strategy for avoiding confronting the hostility of heterosexuals,
who are presumed to be, as a group, homophobic. If this strategy is successful,
identity foreclosure at this stage is likely.

Alternatively, if one's reference group fully legitimizes gay and lesbian identity and encourages disclosure as a self-affirmative step, the incongruity
between passing and valuing one's own identity motivates the abandonment of
a closeted position and the adoption of disclosure as a coping style. In this fifth
stage, *Identity Pride,* the individual experiences and expresses strong group
commitment, becoming immersed in LGB community and culture. Gay men
and lesbians in this stage often see LGB identity as preferable to heterosexual
identity, and believe that LGB's as a group are better in many ways than are
heterosexuals as a group. The increased disclosure that accompanies this sense
of pride not only brings one's private and public identities in line, but also
opens possibilities for increased confrontations with overt homonegativism.

If the response to such a disclosure is negative, one may retreat to the closet,
succumbing to identity foreclosure. On the other hand, if the response to
coming out is affirming, the individual may move on to the sixth stage, *Identity
Synthesis.* Here, lesbian or gay identity becomes just one—albeit an admittedly
very salient—aspect of identity, rather than the sole preoccupation. Both the
heterosexual and the LGB communities are seen as diverse, with some heterosexually identified individuals recognized as truly acceptant of gay and lesbian
identity. There is also a synthesis between public and private identities; one no
longer needs to maintain boundaries between homophilic identity and daily
life, which allows for greater integrity in one's sense of self.

A more recent model developed by Troiden (1989) provides a slightly different perspective that synthesizes the work of Cass and others. The first stage in Troiden's depiction of gay and lesbian identity, *Sensitization,* points to early experience with the cultural devaluation of homophilia. Crucial here is the point that lesbians and gay men learn to despise homophilic identity and behavior before they apply these categories to themselves. This sets the task for healthy gay and lesbian identity formation: to reevaluate this label as it applies to oneself and forge an identity that incorporates the label but with a transformed meaning.

Troiden suggests that the second stage, *Identity Confusion,* commonly occurs in adolescence.[7] Here, the individual begins to recognize his or her feelings as potentially homophilic, an awareness that generates confusion and uncertainty. The sense that one might be or even most likely is lesbian or gay follows this initial confusion, leading to the third stage, *Identity Assumption,* which, according to Troiden, commonly occurs during late adolescence or early adulthood. Gender differences are important here. The assumption of lesbian identity typically emerges in the context of one or a series of intense emotional attachments; identity assumption for gay men is usually a result of sexual contacts with other men. Initially this identity is merely tolerated; it comes to be accepted as the individual becomes more involved with other LGB individuals and with the community.

Finally, in the fourth stage, *Commitment,* the individual adopts gay or lesbian identity as a way of life, as a comfortable and natural self-definition. This comfort, in turn, underpins an eagerness to express one's identity and a growing involvement with the community. The culmination of this process is the formation of intimate one-to-one relationships, which, for Troiden, marks the highest level of gay and lesbian identity.[8]

Bisexual Identity

The literature on bisexual identity development remains small relative to that dealing with gay men and lesbians. Indeed, the very existence of authentic bisexual identity has been questioned by scholars as well as lay people, and the topic of bisexuality is laden with stereotypes and misconceptions (Fox, 1995). Many have assumed that those claiming bisexual identity are simply in denial, refusing to acknowledge their "true" homosexual identity. However, over four

---

7. Other work indicates that the ages suggested by Troiden for this and other stages do not accurately depict the experience of many LGBs. We will return to this issue.

8. This sequence may apply more accurately to gay (and bisexual) men then to lesbians (and bisexual women). This point will be considered later.

decades ago, research first demonstrated that a large percentage of individuals
experience emotional and erotic attraction to both women and men, and recent
work indicates that more people may display bisexual than exclusively same-
sex attraction and sexual behavior (Kinsey, Pomeroy, & Martin, 1948; Kinsey,
et al., 1953; Zinik, 1985).

The belated recognition of the validity of bisexual identity is reflected in a
growing literature that portrays bisexuality as a healthy and arguably a
uniquely flexible mode of being, and it has helped to dismantle longstanding
misconceptions.[9] For example, the common belief that there is no "true"
bisexuality—that those who identify as bisexual are merely confused, in denial
about their true sexual orientation, or partaking of heterosexual privilege while
pursuing same-sex relationships—is supported neither by first-person
accounts nor by research. For instance, Klein and his colleagues (Klein, 1993;
Klein, Sepekoff, & Wolf, 1986) have elaborated on the complexity of bisexual
identity in the context of their multivariate model of sexual orientation. As you
will recall, this approach portrays sexual orientation as a constellation of
numerous experiences, each of which varies independently along a continuum
from homosexual to heterosexual orientation (see chapter 1). Given the complexity of this model, it is apparent that many individuals have at least some
experiences that deviate from exclusively same-sex or other-sex orientation.
Thus, bisexuality broadly defined can be seen as normative and "monosexuality" as the more atypical phenomenon.

Additionally, the notion that bisexual persons are sexually indiscriminate
and willing to have sex with anyone is unwarranted. People who identify as
bisexual, like those who identify as monosexual, are selective in whom they
find attractive, with whom they have sex, to whom they devote their emotional
energy. The difference is that the other's sex is not a salient criterion in that
selection; rather, the choice is based on personality characteristics, appearance,
one's mood at the time, and so forth (Ross & Paul, 1992; Weinberg, Williams,
& Pryor, 1994). The range of possibilities may be greater, but the choices are
no less discriminating.

Nor are bisexual individuals unavoidably promiscuous. The fact that they
can choose either a female or a male partner does not mean that they *must* have
both male and female partners, either simultaneously or sequentially. Some
bisexual individuals do indeed pursue both same-sex and heterosexual relations
simultaneously; others do not (Weinberg, Williams, & Pryor, 1994). A bisexual
person can be as faithful (or as unfaithful) to a given relationship, and relationships can be as open or as exclusive, as among monosexual individuals.

---

9.   For examples of affirmative perspectives on bisexuality, see DeCecco, 1985; Fox, 1995;
     Geller, 1990; George, 1993; Hutchins & Kaahumanu, 1991; Klein, 1993; Klein & Wolf,
     1985; Rust, 1992, 1993; Weinberg, Williams, & Pryor, 1994; Weise, 1992; Zinik, 1985.

As is true with lesbian, gay, and heterosexual identity, there is no typical bisexual person, although several writers have offered schemes for cataloguing the varieties of bisexuality (e.g., Klein, 1993; Ross, 1991; Weinberg, Williams, & Pryor, 1994). It is clear that people who identify as bisexual differ from each other in many ways—whether they define themselves as bisexual on all dimensions that might be construed as sexual orientation or only on some; whether they prefer relationships with one sex over the other; whether they actually have partners of both sexes or are aware of but do not act on bisexual feelings; whether they consider their bisexual identity transitional or fixed—in these and countless other ways, bisexual individuals do not form a homogeneous group (Fox, 1995).

Despite progress in dissolving longstanding stereotypes, perspectives on identity development specific to bisexually identified individuals have been sparse. Some authors have attempted to extrapolate from gay (and perhaps lesbian) to bisexual identity, arguing that the salient issues raised by bisexuality derive from the same-sex (rather than the heterosexual) components of that identity. However, it can be argued that such transposition of gay and lesbian experience does violence to the distinctive struggles of coming to a bisexual identity. For instance, it is difficult for a bisexual individual to see herself or himself holistically. No single relationship (unless it involves more than two people) is bisexual, so that the temptation to regard oneself as sometimes homosexual and sometimes heterosexual is great. Thus, bisexual persons may see their identity as merely additive—as homosexual plus heterosexual—rather than as a distinctive manner of being that is itself a viable framework for understanding oneself and one's relationships (Rust, 1993). Such fragmentation of experience further feeds the perception of bisexuality as incomplete homosexuality or inadequate heterosexuality.

Perspectives on Bisexual Identity
Zinik (1985) presented two opposing models of bisexuality, the conflict model and the flexibility model. The former corresponds to common presumptions that portray bisexuality as stemming from identity confusion and as a transitional stage en route to lesbian or gay identity. The flexibility model is more in keeping with currently evolving understandings of bisexual identity as unique in its adaptability and its promise. For example, Klein (1993) offers an analysis of the potential of bisexuality—and, simultaneously, of the restrictiveness of monosexuality. In Klein's view, the homophobia imbedded in heterosexuality and the heterophobia lodged in homosexuality derive from a fear of intimacy with those excluded by our dualistic categories. Specifically, the fear is that emotional intimacy with the forbidden sex (the same sex for heterosexuals, the other sex for lesbians and gay men) will lead to sexual intimacy. Since sexual intimacy with the "other" is precluded by both categories of exclusive monosexual orientation, emotional intimacy is thwarted. Bisexual identity, in

contrast, is first and foremost an ability to engage emotionally with members of   *107*
both sexes, a capability that creates as well the possibility for flexibility in the
expression of physical intimacy. Such intimacy is made possible and is
sustained by the capacity to transcend traditional understandings of gender
and forge with members of either sex relationships grounded in equality as well
as complementarity.

Bisexuality not only allows for flexibility in partner choice but may foster
adaptability in interpersonal style, as well. Because women and men have
been socialized to interact in different ways, an intimate relationship with a
woman is necessarily different from one with a man. The bisexual individual
must develop a wide range of interactive skills and versatility in behavior to
accommodate the very different requirements of same-sex and heterosexual
relationships.

Models of Bisexual Identity Development
Early work by Blumenstein and Schwartz (1977) explored the processes by
which bisexually identified men and women came to (and sometimes dis-
carded) that identity. These researchers gathered longitudinal data, following
many of their subjects over several years' time. Their findings regarding bisexuality have been echoed in other work since, and make clear that there is no
"typical" pattern of identity development for bisexually-identified individuals
(see also Fox, 1995; Rust, 1992, 1993).

More recently, Weinberg, Williams and Pryor (1994) proposed a sequential
model of bisexual identity development, based on longitudinal data from a large
sample of bisexual-identified women and men. Although their sample reflected
the usual problems in terms of generalizability, results provide one look at the
process of bisexual identity formation. The sequence described in this work
begins with *initial confusion,* as individuals wrestle to understand feelings of
attraction that are incompatible with their previous sexual orientation.

This confusion may last for years, until some event leads the individual to
find and apply a label to these attractions. For some, this involves simply
encountering the term "bisexual," along with its meaning; for others, it may
result from a first heterosexual or a first same-sex experience; for yet others, it
may be a response to others' encouraging the person to identify her or his feelings as bisexual. *Settling into the identity* follows this labeling and self-identification. Gradually, the individual completes a transition to the new identity, a
process marked by growing self-acceptance. Even in this stage, many bisexual-
identified people believe that this identity—or at least its behavioral manifestations—might change in the future, particularly if they enter into an intense
monogamous relationship. In this sample, men were more likely to anticipate a
movement to heterosexuality; women were more likely to believe they might
move toward lesbianism.

The hallmark of bisexual identity formation appears to be *continued uncer-*

tainty, which persists even after the settling-in stage. Intermittent doubt appears to result in part from the absence of social validation for bisexual identity, as well as from pressure in gay and lesbian communities to adopt a gay or lesbian identity (see also Rust, 1993).

Characteristics of Bisexual Identity

Some general observations can be extracted from scholarship dealing with bisexual identity. First, bisexual individuals typically (but not always) come to this identity later than lesbian and gay people come to theirs. This is not surprising, given the culture's dichotomous view of sexual orientation. Most realize their bisexuality after already having established a heterosexual identification, although some individuals come to a bisexual identity from a homophilic identity. Conversely, many individuals who identify as bisexual change this identification over time, taking on a heterosexual or homosexual identity with equal comfort and assurance. That such movement may occur in any of the many possible directions is testimony to the potential fluidity of sexual orientation of which we have spoken previously (Blumenstein & Schwartz, 1977; Rust, 1993; Weinberg, Williams & Pryor, 1994).

Some individuals engage in relationships with members of both sexes but do not necessarily identify as bisexual; conversely, others do so identify, although they have not had sexual relationships with both sexes—especially with members of their own sex. Fox (1995) suggests that the variability and open-ended nature of bisexual identity development reflects the complexity inherent in considering patterns of both same-sex and other-sex attachments.

Important gender differences appeared in Blumenstein and Schwartz's research, as well. Women appeared to have less difficulty than did men incorporating same-sex feelings or actions into their identity. They were prone to see such experiences as extensions of typical female expressions of affection (i.e., as gender appropriate) and were less likely to identify as lesbian on the basis of such events. For men, in contrast, a single same-sex experience was likely to lead them to question both their masculinity (i.e., their gender appropriateness) and their sexual orientation. In response, they were more prone to take such experience as clear evidence of their "true" gay identity, accepting the cultural dichotomy between exclusive heterosexuality and homosexuality. Men, in turn, had greater difficulty accepting a homophilic label than did women, revealing the greater stigma attached to a gay male than to a lesbian identity. Weinberg, Williams, and Pryor (1994) also found gender differences, with women's identity grounded more in romantic feelings and men's in sexual feelings and behaviors.

Clearly, bisexual identity is a subjective phenomenon, involving the application of idiosyncratic meanings to experiences that could yield to many interpretations. Weinberg and his colleagues and Blumenstein and Schwartz suggest several variables that might be significant in interpreting life events as indicative of a bisexual identity. One important factor is *labeling*. When one is identified by others as being bisexual (or straight, lesbian, or gay), this shapes one's own self-definition and thereby one's feelings and actions, as well. Bisexual identity is also facilitated by *conflicting events,* such as new sexual feelings toward one's own sex, that point up the inadequacy of one's former identity. Often such events lead people to reframe previous experience in order to incorporate it into the new identity. For instance, a movement from a heterosexual to a gay identity, which might be seen as sequential bisexuality, is frequently reinterpreted as the discovery of the "real" (gay) self.

Finally, *reference group* contact influences how individuals identify themselves. People who are well integrated into a lesbian and/or gay community, for example, are likely to be labeled and treated by others as lesbian or gay and to see themselves as such. Bisexual feelings are easily reinterpreted within such a community as defensive or merely transitional, while bisexual identity is discounted. Each of these variables—labeling, reframing previous experience to fit existing categories, and reference group influences—reveals one manner in which social meanings are translated into individual identity.

The Impact of AIDS on Identity Formation

The added stigma and fear associated with HIV/AIDS have further complicated identity development for LGB individuals. The struggle to accept homophilic feelings and attractions is made more difficult by the realization that homophilic identity is so closely connected to HIV/AIDS, so that identifying as LGB now carries added approbation, and the expression of homophilic feelings may put one at lethal risk. Thus, the process of coming to terms may be forestalled and the emergence of a positive LGB identity and involvement in supportive communities thereby postponed.

The direct impact of AIDS on identity is seen in longitudinal research with bisexual-identified men and women, which was begun before the epidemic was recognized. Many of these individuals changed their identification as a direct result of AIDS. Many bisexual women adopted a lesbian identity, ending their relationships with men. Some bisexual men relinquished gay relationships and came to identify as heterosexual; others, perhaps in response to rejection by women who feared relationships with bisexual men, embraced a gay identity (Weinberg, Williams, & Pryor, 1994).

Critiques of Identity Development Models

These portrayals of identity formation serve the invaluable function of making sense of a process that might otherwise appear disjointed and even disturbed.

110   To realize that self-denigration and confusion about one's identity and deep involvement with a community of marginalized peers are predictable and understandable components to the formation of a sense of self is crucial to any affirmative understanding of LGB experience.

However, these depictions also have serious shortcomings that need to be considered lest they be inappropriately applied. The theories of gay and lesbian identity formation, in particular, describe a stage-wise process that cannot be universally applied. Not all gay men and lesbians pass through these stages at the times suggested, in this order—or, indeed, at all. Furthermore, although discussions of bisexuality highlight the fluid nature of sexual orientation, models of gay and lesbian development ignore the plasticity of sexual orientation that is clearly evident in the literature. In doing so, they fail to address those situations where the evolution of sexual orientation identity is not a one-time discovery but a continuous process.

Recent research suggests that self-awareness and disclosure among youth may now occur far earlier than in the cohorts represented in these models (e.g., D'Augelli & Herschberger, 1993; Fox, 1995; Herdt, 1992). However, many individuals come to their LGB identity only later in life. This is no trivial matter, for, although all may experience confusion, surely the impact of these first glimmerings of homophilic feelings are far different on, for instance, an adult who has long lived a heterosexual life than on a teenager; the impact is far different on a fourteen-year old with many years left at home than on an eighteen-year old near emancipation.

As we try to apply these models to individual development, it is particularly important that we consider carefully the portrayal of coming out—ideally, in a very public, even political way—as the epitome of healthy identity development. Research indicates that coming out is indeed correlated with mental health in some populations (Garnets & Kimmel, 1993; Gonsiorek, 1995). However, the renditions of identity formation considered here have been derived almost entirely from work with selective samples comprised largely of young, educated individuals, open enough about their identity to be visible to theoreticians or to participate in research projects. In addition, the work undergirding these models comes largely from highly educated, professionally secure, LGB or LGB-affirmative scholars. We must consider the possibility that, while such a depiction may say much about the identity formation of well-educated and visibly "out" LGBs, it may say less about individuals who are comparatively less educated about LGB issues, less occupationally secure, and/or less integrated into a community that values disclosure and political activism.

A model of identity development describing the experience of this latter group might well reveal less attention to coming out as the height of self-acceptance, less focus on community involvement as crucial, and more concern with the forging of resilient boundaries to protect one's identity and privacy.

Indeed, some research indicates that the major motivation for many individuals' nondisclosure is not self-devaluation but concern about others' responses (Franke & Leary, 1991). At least for some populations, there is no correlation between the level of disclosure and psychological well-being (Eldridge & Gilbert, 1990). As D'Augelli (1994) points out, LGB individuals evidence a wide assortment of healthy life patterns that do not entail disclosure and community involvement. It is likely that no single mode of dealing with stigma is intrinsically more advanced; rather, each reflects a mode of coping that meets the needs of particular individuals.

A related critique argues that these models disregard cohort effects. For instance, the experience of coming out today is strikingly different than it was before World War II; surely the likelihood of being out and the psychological correlates of self-disclosure are different for LGBs who are now sixty than for those who are now twenty. Similarly, feminism provides an ideology whose availability clearly distinguishes the experience of contemporary women from that of women who came of age before the contemporary feminist movement. Correlatively, the HIV/AIDS epidemic has profoundly altered the process by which men come to identify as gay and bisexual and to act on and disclose that identity. None of these historical changes is easily accommodated by the approaches discussed above, rendering their broad applicability questionable.

This work has been criticized also for its male bias (e.g., Brown, 1995; Cass, 1990; Sophie, 1986). Whereas these models present a linear, step-wise progression from self-discovery toward self-disclosure, women's experiences in coming to terms with one or another sexual orientation are often not unidirectional, are perhaps more fluid, and are thus not well represented by this portrayal. Furthermore, these models place considerable significance on sexual experience as the catalyst for assuming an LGB identity and as being definitive of such identity. However, emotional attachment and political beliefs appear to play a greater role than sexuality per se in the formation and expression of women's identities. Also, the sequence of experiences portrayed may more accurately represent the experience of (most) men than of (most) women. For example, Troiden's model describes identity formation as culminating in the formation of one-to-one relationships. However, the literature indicates that most lesbians and bisexual women first come to their nonheterosexual identity in the context of precisely such relationships. Similarly, involvement in the community is portrayed as an early step in LGB identity formation, whereas for women, close relationships appear to be more common early, with involvement in the broader community a relatively late event.

Finally, these models are clearly essentialist in their assumptions. They presume that sexual orientation is a given, an attribute or quality of the individual that develops early, is stable across time, and requires only to be discovered and (perhaps) disclosed by the individual. As we have discussed, these assumptions are open to serious question. As Rust (1993) points out, whereas essentialist models have difficulty explaining the demonstrable variability and flexibility of sexual orientation, a constructionist view of identity normalizes plasticity precisely because it reflects individual accommodation to changing social contexts. Recent work has begun to explore how we might address questions of identity development from a more flexible, even a constructionist perspective (e. g., Cass, 1990; Jennes, 1992; Kitzinger, 1987, 1995; Richardson, 1987; Rust, 1993; Schippers, 1987). We will explore these ideas in the Conclusion.

Coming Out

Despite the limitations of these theoretical models, both research and personal accounts agree that a central element of lesbian, gay, and bisexual identity development is the process of coming out—embracing for oneself and disclosing to others one's sexual orientation. Although the term may imply a single event, in reality coming out is a prolonged, perhaps even an unending process, and it demands considerable psychological agility. Not only does coming out challenge cultural norms in the abstract; it also means risky and potentially painful revelations to significant others in one's life. Crucially, it violates what the individual herself or himself has learned. Because we have all absorbed heterosexist attitudes, coming out requires overcoming a lifetime of learning and choosing to act in direct contradiction to those early lessons.

If one chooses to take even tentative steps toward disclosing LGB identity to others, decisions regarding coming out must be made constantly, in nearly every situation one encounters. Each decision is laden with conflict. Hiding one's LGB identity risks detection; revealing it risks discrimination and psychological and physical abuse. Remaining in the closet implies lack of self-acceptance; coming out may diminish one's worth in the eyes of others. In addressing these very real conflicts, some suggest a strategy of "rational outness," where one strives to be "as out as possible . . . , as closed as necessary" (Bradford & Ryan, 1987, p. 77).

The nature and difficulty of the coming-out process differ among individuals. Cohort effects here are profound (Herdt, 1992; Troiden, 1989). Older cohorts who came of age before World War II usually discovered their same-sex attraction in isolation, and often never came out to anyone other than their immediate partner(s). Those who came of age during the McCarthy era had the benefit of the emerging postwar community but an intense fear of persecution engendered by the repressive atmosphere of the time. Many never came out except to a circle of known LGB friends and acquaintances; the few who came out publicly commonly strove to assimilate, to be as acceptable to mainstream society as possible.

After Stonewall, the emergence of an active LGB community supported more individuals in coming out; indeed, coming out became a political statement, a tool employed by the gay rights movement to raise consciousness and to lobby for civil rights. More recently, the HIV/AIDS epidemic has heightened the stigma of LGB identity, and has combined with a revitalized conservative political movement to increase the risks associated with coming out. On the other hand, coming out now means "coming in"—into a visible and welcoming community with extensive resources to support the individual in coming to terms with an emerging LGB identity. (The community's role in LGB experience is the topic of chapter 8.)

Bisexually identified individuals face dual risks in coming out. In the context of heterosexism, coming out as bisexual exposes one to all the penalties heaped upon nonheterosexuality. In addition, coming out as bisexual within the LGB community risks losing the support of that community, which serves as a buffer against the heterosexism of the broader society. Thus, the wider opportunities for relationships provided by bisexual identity bring with them greater possibilities of encountering lack of acceptance, as well.

Steps in Coming Out

In the face of these complex cost-benefit scenarios, most LGB individuals do disclose their sexual orientation to at least some people. For those who decide to come out in varying degrees, disclosure typically takes place in gradual steps and over a period of time (Coleman, 1982b). The first step, necessarily, is acknowledging to oneself same-sex feelings and what those mean for identity.[10] This immensely difficult step—sometimes referred to as awareness, signification, or identification—requires that one overcome the whole weight of cultural conditioning embedded in the heterosexual assumption and manifested in internalized homophobia (or internalized biphobia). At whatever point in the life course it occurs, this step is the precursor to the struggles we have discussed with stigma management and subsequent decisions about coming out.

After coming to a self-identification as bisexual, gay, or lesbian, further steps involve disclosing this identification to others. Many scholars and therapists see the initial disclosures as important indicators of self-acceptance, expressed by seeking validation of one's worth from significant others. The response to initial disclosures is crucial. If it is negative, the internalized homophobia (or biphobia) which is still very near the surface is likely to be aroused, and the LGB indi-

---

10. Terminology appropriate to coming out as bisexual is complex because of the many avenues to that identity. Coming out as bisexual means acknowledging same-sex feelings if one's previous identification was heterosexual or other-sex feelings if one previously identified as gay or lesbian. Adjustments in wording can be made throughout this discussion.

vidual's tentative sense of self-esteem is at risk. It the response is positive, self-esteem is reinforced and subsequent disclosures become less risky.

A typical, but by no means universal, pattern of disclosure to others might proceed as follows. The first revelation is often to a romantic partner and involves simply acknowledging to oneself and each other that this is a gay or lesbian relationship (or a relationship defining one as bisexual). Next usually come disclosures to other LGB individuals, who provide the surest source of affirming feedback for this revelation. Even at this juncture, however, some people remain closeted with many LGBs.

Disclosures to heterosexual significant others are more difficult, for one can reasonably expect that they will not understand. Virtually nothing in our society provides even the most open and caring individuals with the where-withal to understand LGB experience. On the contrary, throughout our lives, homophilia has been portrayed as perverted, sick, sinful, and unnatural, and most people have nowhere seen, heard, or read realistic depictions of the actual experience of living as a nonheterosexual person in a heterosexist society. Despite this risk, the motivations discussed above lead many LGBs to reveal their sexual orientation to important heterosexual people in their lives.[11]

Typically, the first revelations are to close friends. Research with gay men and lesbians indicates that just over half have told their close heterosexual friends. Siblings are the next most common confidant; for both gay men and lesbians, sisters tend to be told more often and sooner than are brothers. This trend is compatible with the finding that women tend to be more acceptant than are men. Parents tend to be next in line, with mothers being told earlier and more often than fathers; nearly half have told their mothers and about a third, their fathers. Coming out to one's family of origin is a very significant event for both the LGB individual and the family; we will consider this topic in greater depth at the conclusion of this chapter.

Self-disclosure at work is relatively rare. Most LGBs reveal their identity to no one at work or to only a few select coworkers, and the vast majority feel sure that their bosses do not know. This reticence is understandable, as most believe that it would create a problem at work if their identity were known, and many report direct negative consequences when they have been open.

As LGBs disclose to individual people, they also typically explore the LGB culture and community. Initial involvement with the LGB community is usually in relatively protected activities, such as friendship circles; LGB estab-

11. For representative figures on the proportion of people who disclose to others, see Eldridge & Gilbert, 1990; Kitzinger, 1991; Troiden, 1989. Most research in this area is relatively old, and the numbers may have changed significantly. In any case, the individuals surveyed cannot be taken as representative—people who are deeply closeted are unlikely to tell researchers their sexual orientation. The crucial point is that even among those who are open enough to participate in research, a relatively small proportion disclose their sexual orientation to important people in their lives.

lishments, such as bars, coffee houses, or community centers; and exclusively
LGB events. This may be followed by participation in increasingly public
events, such as political rallies, fund raisers, or LGB-related cultural events.
The final step in thoroughly coming out entails public declarations of one's
LGB identity, including such actions as openness and advocacy at work,
involvement in local or national political work, and speaking engagements or
publications where one expressly discloses LGB identity.

Reasons for Disclosure

A wide range of motivations may underlie the decision to come out in particular circumstances (Cain, 1991). In some cases, coming out takes the form of
therapeutic disclosure; revealing one's LGB identity serves as a means of
enhancing self-esteem and seeking support for the task of dealing with stigma.
Relationship-building disclosure reflects a desire to improve a relationship with a
significant other, motivated by a realization that, so long as this aspect of who
one is remains a secret, a truly honest and close relationship is impossible.
Situational problems created by secrecy about one's sexual orientation may be
resolved by *problem-solving disclosure*. For instance, parents' persistent questions about one's (heterosexual) romantic life or peer pressure toward (heterosexual) sexual activity can be curtailed by coming out.

Preventative disclosure is designed to prevent potential problems from
emerging. An LGB individual might reveal her or his identity to a potential
employer or landlord rather than risk dismissal or eviction if it is discovered in
the future. Sometimes coming out takes the form of *spontaneous disclosure*,
where unplanned revelations occur through slips of the tongue, because an
opportune moment arises, or in response to feelings of unusual comfort and
safety with another individual.

Finally, *political disclosure* is intended to make LGB individuals and issues
more visible, to change attitudes, to provide mentors and role models, or to
offer visible support to the LGB community. The decision to be out in a
visible and vocal manner requires that one work diligently at overcoming
the resilience of the heterosexual assumption. If successful, this undertaking
may generate charges of "flaunting," of making an issue of LGB identity
even where it is irrelevant. If it is unsuccessful, the individual's goal of visibility is forfeited.

Reasons for Nondisclosure

There are also many reasons why individuals choose not to disclose their LGB
identity. In some cases, the individual might feel that coming out is *inappropriate*. One might perceive sexual orientation as irrelevant in this situation, or

might not care whether this particular person knows one well or not. A *lack of pay-off* is another reason for avoiding disclosure. If there is little to be gained, a person might feel that it is not worth the risk of possible rejection and lack of understanding that she or he might face. In other situations, one might avoid disclosure out of *deference* to others' beliefs and feelings. One might feel that others would be hurt or could not possibly understand, or that others would be offended because of their religious beliefs.

Some individuals might avoid disclosure for *political* reasons, believing that coming out might actually hamper acceptance by calling attention to LGB identity and the LGB community. Alternatively, one might refuse to acknowledge one's LGB identity as an expression of the refusal to accept the heterosexual assumption: straight people don't need to come out, one might argue, so why should I? Finally, some people explain not coming out by simple *avowal of responsibility*. The individual identifies covertness as a problem and credits his or her own fear and insecurity for the choice not to come out.

It is apparent that coming out is not a process that can be described in simple terms applicable to each person. Inevitably, decisions about disclosure reflect the unique psychological realities of each individual as well as her or his particular life circumstances. For some individuals, the movement toward near-complete disclosure may be supported by substantial psychological and interpersonal resources, whereas for others the psychological costs are too great. For some, life may be secure enough to allow the sort of openness about one's sexual orientation that enhances self-esteem and encourages attitude change in others. For others, the potential dangers prohibit broad disclosure, and one's personal and social welfare are best served by relative secrecy. As is true with other developmental issues, individual diversity is the rule, and no single course of action can be recommended for everyone.

Coming Out to Family of Origin

Many lesbians, gay men, and bisexual individuals never come out to their biological families, because the potential cost seems too great. For others, however, coming out to family is the most important in a series of revelations. Indeed, the self-help literature stresses the importance of this step, as well as its potential pitfalls. One may come out to family in adolescence or in adulthood; in either case, it is a landmark event. If the response is positive, one's self-esteem is enhanced and subsequent disclosures occur against a background of self-acceptance. If the response is negative, the individual risks loss of self-esteem as well as the loss of important relationships (Savin-Williams, 1989).

Because of the potential for rejection, LGB persons must "strike a devil's bargain in which a stilted or distant relationship is weighed against the possibility of no relationship at all" (Brown, 1988, p. 67). On the other hand, that stilted relationship may be abdicated in hopes of a more honest and intimate relationship than is possible so long as one remains closeted. The decision to come out to family is fraught with anxiety and hope, and the struggle is usually prolonged.

Sometimes the choice is foreclosed by the family's discovery of a member's LGB identity through other means. One of the painful tragedies of the HIV/AIDS epidemic is seen in the lives of those individuals whose illness has outed them, so that they have to deal simultaneously with the stigma of the disease and the complicated and often rejecting responses of their families to their homophilic identity. In other cases, particularly with adolescents living at home, families might find love letters or discover their child engaging in intimate interactions, and thereby force a confrontation that is difficult under the best of circumstances.

Family Responses to Coming Out

Whatever brings it about, the response of family members is an important element in the LGB individual's process of coming to a positive sense of self. The precise reaction to a family member's coming out is unpredictable, but is almost invariably initially negative (Borhek, 1988; Savin-Williams, 1989). This negative reaction appears to have two central components. First, the family is likely to respond out of their own homonegative attitudes, perceiving LGB identity as sick and/or sinful. Negative stereotypes disrupt their previous positive feelings toward their loved one, and she or he may seem like a complete stranger. Second, there are no clear family roles for the LGB person, and the family is thrown into confusion about where this person fits if not in the neat heterosexual identity previously allocated (Strommen, 1989).

Several authors have proposed models that depict typical stages in the family's response to a child's coming out. As with all stage models, these cannot be taken as descriptive of all families' reactions to this disclosure. Some families skip stages, many remain stuck for short or very long periods in one or another stage, others react in a manner not adequately depicted by these models. A synthesis of the work of DeVine (1985) and Wirth (1983) suggests a multistep process as families adapt to a child's disclosure; different families will manifest different reactions, and not necessarily in the sequence described.

Prior to the actual disclosure, the family often experiences *subliminal awareness,* where family members have a sense that a child might be LGB. Considerable energy may be spent in covert denial, avoiding situations that might reveal this possibility and stressing those that imply heterosexuality. This tactic is brought to an end when the LGB individual comes out. The disclosure itself may be gradual or abrupt, but in either case moves the family to the *impact* stage. Often they are shocked, paralyzed, even hysterical;

commonly, they resort to *denial.* The family may refuse to acknowledge this identity, declaring it a phase or denying the existence of a lover. Efforts may be made to "fix the problem," such as religious intervention, sending the individual to a therapist, or arranging heterosexual dates. It is also common for the family to search for external "causes" on which they can place blame for the condition. They may *blame* the current lover or other acquaintances for seducing or recruiting the individual, or anonymous social forces for having damaged their loved one; parents may blame each other for what is perceived as poor parenting that resulted in their child's becoming LGB. The family may also react more strongly, refusing to address the issue, even expelling the LGB family member.

After the initial shock, family members may experience *confusion and guilt.* As it becomes clear that the family member's LGB identity is real and cannot be wished away, families face a sense of confusion, shame, and loss. They often go through a period of mourning the loss of the person they thought they knew and of the (heterosexual) dreams they had for this person (Borhek, 1988). Still mired in the belief that LGB identity is wrong, many parents experience intense guilt, presuming that they have contributed to this identity and therefore done harm to a loved one.

As families come to terms with the reality of LGB identity, considerable *anger* may be expressed toward the LGB member. Some may resort to financial or emotional blackmail, banning the LGB person from family gatherings, disowning or disinheriting the person, insisting that coming out was a "hostile gesture" because it hurts others—rather than a loving one, because it allows for honesty and intimacy. Some family members attempt to disrupt any relationships the LGB individual forms (Brown, 1988).

In the *bargaining* phase, families may engage in a variety of techniques designed to manage the stigma of having an LGB family member. Some families attempt to maintain family integrity and the family's social image by keeping a member's LGB identity secret. Here, acceptance depends on the LGB individual's keeping silent, not "flaunting" her or his identity. Often family relations are carried on as before, but there is an agreement that the topic will never be discussed, and that the LGB person will act as if she/he were straight in order not to disrupt family harmony.

For movement beyond these emotionally costly adjustments to occur, family members must address their feelings. The LGB member must deal with the fear of rejection and alienation from the family that characterized life before the disclosure, as well as anger at the lack of acceptance and compassion that followed it. Other family members must deal with their sense of loss and mourning, as well as the guilt and shame that derive from longstanding heterosexist attitudes. If the family is able to do this, they can move toward *acceptance and resolution.* This movement allows the family to adjust to the reality of a member's LGB identity, modifying family relations to accommodate the individual and her or his relationships. Often this move is accomplished with the support of groups such as PFLAG (Parents, Families, and Friends of Lesbians and Gays), a nationwide organization that provides information and resources, as well as the personal support of others who have dealt with the same issue.

At its very best, this process leads to *integration,* where the family includes the LGB member in an affirmative and joyous way. They come to cherish and celebrate the difference that this person embodies, and take pleasure in her or his happiness. Often this step means that family members become actively involved in the political and social issues raised by LGB identity.

As Brown (1988) pointed out, the family itself can be regarded as passing through its own "coming out" process. Because they are so closely associated with a stigmatized identity, they also bear an element of that stigma. They must decide whether, when, and to whom to reveal this information and thereby expose themselves to a degree of the hostility and hatred that are regularly expressed toward LGBs. The stigma management strategies we have discussed for individuals may also be employed by families. For instance, they may "pass," even to the extent of manufacturing a fiance(e) for their LGB relative; they may "cover," avoiding the topic but not denying it if it arises. And they may "convert," becoming active allies in support of LGB issues.

A national survey conducted by Robinson, Walters, and Skeen (1989) looked at how parents deal with their children's coming out. Because their subjects were recruited from PFLAG and similar organizations, this sample represented a limited segment of parents—namely, those far enough along in the process toward acceptance that they were willing to declare their association publically and were actively seeking information and support. Still, the results are informative.

The majority of these parents reported that they had passed through a five-stage progression: shock, denial, guilt, anger, and acceptance. Some were relieved to have long-dormant suspicions confirmed. Many reported that their learning this information was comparable to a child's death, and was followed by intense grief and mourning. However, despite initial largely negative reactions, 97 percent reported that they had worked through their early feelings and arrived at a stage of acceptance. These hopeful results suggest that, while the process may be long and difficult, many families are able to move beyond initial negative reactions and come to an acceptance of LGB members.

Coming Out to Spouse

For many reasons, some people who identify as gay and lesbian have married, and many of them have children. Some, particularly men, are aware of their same-sex feelings prior to marriage; others, especially women, realize these feelings only after they are married. Among those who are aware of or act on homosexual attractions prior to marriage, some people discuss these feelings with their future spouse in advance of marriage, and the two decide that this will not pose a threat to the relationship. In other cases, homosexual feelings or activities are not discussed, often because the individual believes or hopes that marriage will eliminate them.

While the hope of ending same-sex feelings is one motivation for marrying for some individuals, most reasons for marrying are similar to the things that lead anyone to marry: social pressure, belief that marriage is necessary for happiness, a desire for children, and genuine love for the spouse (Bell & Weinberg, 1978; Bozett, 1980; Coleman, 1982a; French, 1992; Strommen, 1989). Even so, some people who experience same-sex feelings later determine that they cannot deny those attractions, and decide to disclose their feelings to their spouse and/or children.

A prominent motive for such disclosure is feelings of role conflict. Bozett (1980, 1981) found that men who do not disclose are likely to feel that their role as husband and father is incompatible with their gay identity and tend to be unhappy in their marriages, although they may remain married because of their attachment to their children. These feelings of conflict are often exacerbated by guilt and anxiety deriving from secretive sexual encounters, leading many men to reveal their identity. For some, this decision results from a crisis, as the gay man becomes aware of previously unrecognized homosexual feelings. For others, especially those who have been aware of their feelings for some time, there is a gradual distancing from their wives, which eventually compels disclosure (Bozett, 1982; Strommen, 1989).

A husband or wife's responses to a gay or lesbian spouse's revelations may be similar to parents' reactions. These might include a preliminary period of latent but unacknowledged awareness, followed by shock, denial, a sense of estrangement, and confusion and guilt. Recently, HIV/AIDS has added a new dimension for the wife of a gay or bisexual man, namely the fear that her husband has been exposed and might, in turn, have exposed her to the virus. Thus, an added layer of anger and betrayal might intensify her negative response to her husband's coming out. The sense of isolation, stigma, and loss are made more difficult by an absence of support from significant others and the broader community (Gochros, 1985).

When a man discloses a gay identity to his wife, the most common eventual outcome is divorce. Some couples arrive at other solutions, such as an asexual "companionate" marriage or an open relationship that allows the husband to pursue same-sex relations as well as to continue a sexual relationship within the marriage. Such open relationships are made more complicated by HIV/AIDS, which creates a continuing source of anxiety and potential conflict. The possibility of the relationship's surviving is far greater for bisexually identified men than for gay-identified men, and is greater where the husband's same-sex feelings and activities are openly acknowledged (Brownfain, 1985; Buxton, 1991; Coleman, 1982a, 1985a, 1985b; French, 1992; Gochros, 1985, 1989; Matteson, 1985; Strommen, 1989).

Relatively little research is available on the process and consequences of lesbians coming out to husbands, but it appears that these marriages are even more likely to end in divorce (Coleman, 1985a, 1985b). Many women may leave a marriage without revealing their sexual orientation, often to protect against the possibility of losing custody of their children. Additionally, some research suggests that when husbands are told, they tend to react in an angry and hostile manner, perceiving their wife's lesbianism as a personal affront to them. The predominant reasons for women's leaving once they become aware of same-sex feelings include a lack of sexual interest in the husband, their own intolerance for nonmonogamy or secretive relationships, and husbands' unwillingness to accept their wives' bisexuality (Buxton, 1991; Coleman, 1985a, 1985b; Garnets & Kimmel, 1993; Strommen, 1989).

In another vein, research has not systematically explored the experience of women who come to a lesbian identity as a political choice, and how this very different experience might affect the process and outcome of disclosure to husbands. French (1992) presented case studies that suggest very different processes for elective lesbians leaving marriage. In particular, this work points to the contrast between egalitarian lesbian and inequitable heterosexual relationships as opposed to the discovery of an irrepressible, essential identity. Details of such dynamics remain to be explored.

Coming out to one's spouse is further complicated by the presence of children. It is the loss of a close connection with their children that most concerns many gay or bisexual men, and the potential loss of custody may motivate women to avoid disclosure. In either case, the parent must deal with the issue of coming out to children. Because this topic can be seen as one aspect of lesbian and gay parenting, we will return to consider it in chapter 7.

The Bottom Line: Identity is Individual

The intertwined tasks of identity development, stigma management, and coming out lie at the very heart of LGB experience; this complex process creates who one is and negotiates a place for that identity in a painfully hostile world. Despite its social roots, identity is a uniquely singular construction, and its creation is distinctive for each individual, as the demands of this identity interact with the unique psychological realities of each person. To understand a given individual's experience as she or he comes to an LGB identity, one must first understand that individual; LGB identity formation is an addition to and not a substitute for the developmental process we all pursue.

CHAPTER FIVE

DIVERSITY AND LESBIAN/GAY/BISEXUAL IDENTITY

Intersecting Identities, Multiple Oppression

THUS FAR WE HAVE SPOKEN of the stigma attached to homophilic identity and the need to come to terms with that denigration in the struggle to find acceptance and self-worth. Although it is doubtless true that managing homonegativity (both external and internalized) is core to LGB experience, this is not the only form of stigma faced by many LGBs. Lesbians, gay men, and bisexual persons who are also members of other minority groups—as defined by ethnicity, race, religion, physical characteristics, or other criteria—must deal with the convoluted meanings and overlapping oppression of a dual or multiple minority status.

Minority LGBs have (at least) three social reference groups: the larger society, their own minority community, and the LGB community. Each group is an important source of information, resources, and coping techniques for the individual. At the same time, each denies and/or denigrates significant parts of one's deepest sense of self. Misogyny further complicates this situation for women, whose position in many LGB and minority communities mirrors the sexism of the broader society, leaving them with little power and little affirmation for their own needs.

In this chapter, we will consider the impact on LGB-identified individuals of membership in another stigmatized minority—or, phrased differently, the impact of LGB identity on members of stigmatized minority groups. Each such intersecting identity bears unique qualities; being an African American lesbian is not the same as being a Hispanic/Latino gay man. However, it is possible to identify certain common principles. We will discuss these first, and then explore in greater depth the unique characteristics of several such identities.

Minority Identity Development

Just as models have been developed to describe the process of lesbian and gay (and, to a lesser extent, bisexual) identity development, so has minority identity development been conceptualized as a stage-wise process. Atkinson, Morten, and Sue (1979) proposed the Minority Identity Development Model, which describes a series of steps toward full integration of minority identity. The first stage, *conformity,* is characterized by acceptance of dominant cultural beliefs regarding one's minority culture, along with a devaluation of the minority culture and commensurate preference for the dominant culture. The second stage, *dissonance,* reflects growing confusion and conflict as the individual begins to question these values. During stage three, *resistance and immersion,* the individual rejects the beliefs of the dominant society and devalues that society while lionizing and becoming deeply involved in her or his own minority culture.

This is followed by the stage of *introspection,* when the person begins to question the narrow perspective of the previous stage, and experiences a conflict between loyalty to her or his own culture and a desire to be free of the constraints on personal autonomy imposed by the earlier intense loyalty to its norms. Finally, the individual may move to the stage of *synergetic articulation and awareness,* which reflects comfort with one's minority identity, together with an ability to evaluate cultural expectations individually and accept or reject them as befits the circumstance. A desire to eliminate oppression in all forms typically accompanies this stage, as well.

The similarities between this model and the descriptions of lesbian and gay identity development are remarkable. In both cases, the individual starts in a stage where dominant prejudices—racism, homophobia, and so forth—are incorporated without question and where the individual accepts the views of mainstream society. From this emerges a period of confusion and conflict, as the person recognizes the self-denigration implied in these values and strives to reevaluate earlier beliefs. Immersion in the culture and institutions of one's minority/LGB community follows, and the individual begins to move toward a positive minority/LGB identity. Finally, one is able to transcend the dichotomous view of earlier development, to evaluate beliefs on an individual basis, and to work toward the elimination of prejudices of all sorts.

These parallels suggest the complexity of the task of identity development for minority LGBs. They must simultaneously negotiate a passage through two different but interrelated processes of identity formation, juggling the costs and benefits of each identity in light of its reciprocal impacts upon the other. In this process, progress toward a firm and positive identity in each area is bound to be affected by one's position in the other.

For most people, minority identity is salient far earlier in development than is LGB status. Because it is also often undeniable, an individual must begin to deal with the minority identity's impact early in life. Since this identity is likely to be shared with many or most significant others in one's life—especially the family and the minority community—the emergence of homophilic identity may create a sense of betrayal of one's already established minority identity and of the minority community (Sears, 1989).

For some, however, minority status may be less salient and therefore receive less attention—perhaps because it is not visible and does not demand attention, because one's reference group has avoided addressing issues of minority status, or for other reasons. In this case, LGB identity formation may occur against a background of unaddressed issues related to minority identity, and would not be experienced as a specific challenge to one's minority identity. These and other interactions between minority and LGB identity formation may lead to quite diverse patterns of coping with dual stigmas. The complexity of this interaction illustrates how futile it is to attempt to describe the experience of a "typical" individual, even an individual more specifically defined as minority and lesbian, gay, or bisexual.

Intersecting Identities, Multiple Oppression

The key issue in understanding the experience of minority LGBs is the notion of multiple oppression. For minority LGBs, multiple oppression means not only facing discrimination from the dominant society both because one is minority *and also* because one is homophilic. It also means facing prejudice from other members of one's minority group for one's LGB identity, and from the LGB community for being a minority person. Doucette (1989) describes the experience from her perspective as a disabled lesbian:

> We are seen, and see ourselves, as outsiders—outside the mainstream, rejected by the disabled community, excluded by the lesbian world. We have no community of our own. (p. 17)

To understand the dilemma that this situation creates for minority LGBs, we can refer to Goffman's (1963) distinction between *discredited* and *discreditable* identity. The former refers to identity that is not only devalued but also visibly marked so that it is obvious and immediately elicits prejudice. In general, membership in a racial minority is a discredited identity—as are sex (female or male), some physical disabilities, age, and sometimes ethnic or religious identification, especially if these are distinguished by special physical markings. A discreditable identity, although devalued, is not visible and therefore elicits prejudice only if something brings it to attention. In general, LGB identity is discreditable, although some expressions of LGB identity may be visible.

The effects of stigma are different in these two cases. A discredited identity, because it cannot be hidden, requires the development of techniques to cope with inescapable prejudice and discrimination. A discreditable identity can be hidden, and therefore demands continuous decisions regarding whether to conceal the identity. The choice to remain invisible or "closeted," in turn, requires techniques not for managing prejudice and discrimination, but for controlling information about one's identity, and for coping with acceptance that one knows to be contingent on deception.

In light of this distinction, consider the situation of an individual whose minority status is discredited (as is her sex, in the case of lesbians) and whose LGB status is discreditable. If one chooses not to disclose LGB identity, a judicious use of information management protects one's position in and support from the minority culture. At the same time, the decision to remain closeted leaves the individual with no sense of affirmation for his or her LGB identity.

Alternatively, the minority individual may choose to reveal the discreditable identity by coming out as LGB. However, this revelation may result in the loss of acceptance by the minority community and one's own family. An African American lesbian explains:

> The family is very contradictory for us. There are emotional involvements, there are ties, the roots that it represents for us all as individuals in a fundamentally sexist/racist society. That's why Black people may decide not to come out as lesbians or gay for fear of being rejected by a group of people whom you not only love but who represent a real source of security, of foundation. (Garnets & Kimmel, 1993, p. 333)

This decision is further complicated in the case of individuals whose life course involves migration or other separations from cultural roots, which may make remaining ties to community even more crucial (Espin, 1994).

The minority LGB is inevitably caught in the margin, between identities. If minority identity and LGB identity are seen as antithetical, a minority individual's identifying as LGB is taken as disloyalty, as a rejection of her or his own culture (Sears, 1989; Morales, 1990). On the surface this means that if one is true to her or his cultural heritage, she or he will have no part of LGB identity. Beneath the surface, this creates a fundamentally untenable position for the individual who is, in fact, both LGB-identified and a member of a minority group.

Not surprisingly, many minority LGBs report living with an almost constant sense of such crisis. Audre Lorde's words capture this dilemma:

> As a forty-nine-year-old Black lesbian feminist socialist mother of two, including one boy, and a member of an interracial couple, I usually find myself part of some group defined as other, deviant, inferior, or just plain wrong... I find I am constantly encouraged to pluck out some aspect of

myself and present it as the meaningful whole, eclipsing or denying the other parts of self. But this is a destructive and fragmenting way to live. (1984, p. 114)

A position at the intersection between or among stigmatized identities leaves the minority LGB individual without escape from prejudice; rather, each potential haven from one sort of prejudice is a bastion of another. These inter-secting oppressions magnify the consequences of LGB identity formation. Anyone who contemplates being open about LGB identity may be silenced by the potential costs of such disclosure. But for minority LGBs, the tendency toward secrecy is exacerbated by the potential loss of vital community and family support. Anyone who identifies as LGB deals with the marginalization that results from living in a society where one is simultaneously a participant and an outcast. But for minority LGBs, there is the additional marginalization that results from the erasure of one's minority identity in the LGB community and of one's LGB identity in the minority community.

Racism in LGB Communities

The LGB community is in many ways a microcosm of the larger society and therefore reflects its values—including its prejudices. Accordingly, minority LGBs are likely to encounter the same racism, classism, anti-Semitism, and other prejudices in homophilic communities as they face in society as a whole (Garnets & Kimmel, 1993; Greene, 1994a, 1994b; Icard, 1986; Morales, 1990; Tremble, Schneider, & Appathurai, 1989). Sometimes such prejudice takes overt forms, such as exclusion from or differential treatment in LGB estab-lishments, organizations, or events; relegation to subservient or stereotyped roles in LGB settings; and assorted forms of isolation and marginalization that make minority individuals feel out of place, discounted, and unwelcome.

Prejudice may also be manifested more subtly. A common occurrence is for minority LGBs to feel that their own values and perspectives are entirely disregarded and that they are expected, without the issues ever being addressed, to think and behave in keeping with the mainstream LGB culture. Yet another form of prejudice is seen with sexual stereotypes—sometimes referred to as "sexual racism"—where ethnic/racial stereotypes are expressed in interpersonal relationships among LGBs (Garnets & Kimmel, 1993).

Such prejudice and discrimination interfere with LGB communities' being the comfortable and affirming places so integral to the process of coming to terms with one's lesbian, gay, or bisexual identity. In response to this dilemma, some minority LGBs have joined together to form supportive communities of their own. Thus, in many large cities one can discover organizations and support groups for African American, Hispanic/Latina(o), Asian American, or other minority LGBs. Additionally, a growing literature of first-person accounts speaks to the unique experiences of these intersecting identities, and increasingly these individuals find themselves and their issues represented in the professional literature.

Still, specialized organizations are the luxury of those living in cities large enough and with LGB populations visible and active enough to create and sustain such efforts, and a very large proportion of minority LGBs does not have ready access to such affirmative resources. Many minority groups are so small that the development of communities responsive to their distinctive needs is virtually impossible. Thus, many minority LGBs continue to experience a sense of invisibility and marginality.

Homonegativity in Minority Communities

Some have argued that homonegativity is greater in minority communities than in the culture as a whole. Little systematic empirical research has addressed this question, and results do not support simple generalizations about homophobia in minority communities (e.g., Bonilla & Porter, 1990; Ernst, Francis, Nevels, & Lemeh, 1991; Loiacano, 1989). However, there are dynamics that might contribute to homophobia in minority communities, and a discussion of these factors tells us something about the lived experience of minority LGB individuals.[1]

First, there is the issue of pride in one's minority identity and a commensurate rejection of traits seen as characteristic of the dominant society. Here, homonegativity may reflect internalized racism (a concept parallel to internalized homophobia), where one's efforts to be a "credit to one's race" are expressed by rejection of qualities seen as negative. An acknowledgment of homophilia within one's own minority group amounts to an admission of negative qualities among that group; denial that it occurs affirms that one's group is without such flaws. Thus, homophilia may be seen as a "white people's problem," and assuming an LGB identity as a sign of assimilation, of capitulation to white values.

A second dynamic derives from the fact that, in many minority cultures, the (heterosexual) family holds particular salience as the fundamental means of survival for the culture, as well as the foundation for individual psychological well-being. Intertwined with the issue of family is the powerful role played by gender expectations in many minority cultures. LGB identity violates traditional gender roles, as we have seen, and as such threatens a set of values that

---

1. For further discussion of these dynamics see Dworkin & Gutierrez, 1992; Garnets & Kimmel, 1993; Greene, 1994a, 1994b; Hidalgo, 1995; Morales, 1990; Savin-Williams & Rodriguez, 1993; Tremble, Schneider, & Appathurai, 1989.

is viewed as core both to the structure of the family and to the well-being of the culture as a whole.

On an institutional level, the importance of religious beliefs and institutions in many minority communities must be considered. In cultures where religion plays a major role in community life, extremely negative attitudes of the church toward LGB identity reinforce homonegative judgments among members of the community. In addition, many minority communities have had concrete experiences with conflict between their own and the LGB community that have led them to perceive LGBs as genuinely threatening. For instance, in some locales, minority communities have been systematically displaced as LGB property owners have led the way in the "gentrification" of older neighborhoods.

Finally, because minority individuals are excluded from the many realms of privilege enjoyed by those in power, heterosexual privilege may be the only privilege accessible to them. This may be particularly true for minority women, who enjoy literally no other form of privilege. That people might respond to their own oppression by expressing prejudice toward the one group over whom they can exercise privilege is completely understandable, as is clear from our earlier discussion of prejudice (see chapter 2).

This tendency to devalue others may extend to discounting others' oppression. That is, some members of minority groups express a belief that LGBs' claims to oppression are specious, and that LGB identity is not comparable to ethnic, racial, religious, or other minority status. From this perspective, their own group is the true victim of oppression; LGBs are pretenders and therefore the more to be dismissed.[2]

These factors point to important aspects of the experience of minority LGB individuals. To the extent that their cultures embrace these rationales, identifying as gay, lesbian, or bisexual is tantamount to challenging values that define the very essence of one's culture and therefore of oneself.

Affirmative Possibilities

We might expect that minority LGBs would suffer severely from this inescapable web of oppression, their sense of self and their means of coping almost inevitably damaged by the barrage. This risk might be exacerbated by the fact that minority LGBs appear to be less likely to seek psychological help than are mainstream LGBs. Such reticence may leave them at greater risk for negative psychological consequences of stigmatized identities.

---

2. Many authors have protested against this tendency, urging that "there is no hierarchy of oppression" (Lorde, 1983, p. 9), and arguing that homonegativity in minority communities and prejudice in LGB communities serve to distract from the common goal of resisting oppression in all its forms (e.g., Clarke, 1983; Gomez & Smith, 1990; hooks, 1989; Lorde, 1984; Smith, 1993).

On the other hand, recall D'Augelli's (1994) "affirmation assumption," *129*
which suggests that living with the stresses induced by stigmatized identity
may facilitate the development of unusual coping skills. If this is true of LGBs
in general, perhaps it is even more true of minority LGBs, who must cope with
the dual stigmas of LGB identity and minority status, as well as with the
multiplicative effects of the intersection of the two (Greene, 1994a). By this
model, minority lesbians might be expected to demonstrate exemplary coping
abilities because of the added stress of dealing with sexism. Whether this is
true remains to be answered, but this perspective provides an affirmative position from which to consider the experience of minority LGBs.

Illustrations of Specific Cultures

Although the general principles discussed above may illuminate the struggle of
minority LGBs as a whole, each culture has its own distinctive perspective on
homophilia. Differences among minority cultures, indeed, are complex and
multidimensional. For instance, Bonilla and Porter (1990) found that African
Americans tend to hold more conservative attitudes toward the morality of
homophilia than do Latin Americans, but more liberal attitudes regarding the
civil liberties of LGBs. Such differences highlight both the complicated nature
of attitudes toward homophilia and the complexity of various cultural perspectives. This diversity renders the experience of coming to terms with LGB
identity distinctive for members of each community. We will consider here
several variations on the broader theme of intersecting minority and LGB
identities. This is by no means an exhaustive discussion, but will provide some
insights into the unique dilemmas, struggles, and strengths of LGB individuals
who are also members of various minority groups.

African Americans

The experience of African American lesbians, gay men, and bisexual persons
epitomizes many of the dynamics described above. Some of the most virulent
racism of American society has historically been expressed toward African
Americans, and the salience of community is correspondingly heightened for
individual African Americans. Thus, the conflict between the search for validation for one's LGB identity and the necessity of acceptance within the
minority community is central to psychological health.[3]

The category, African American, includes a broad range of cultural backgrounds. Most contemporary African Americans trace their ancestry to the

---

3. More detailed discussions of issues related to African American LGB identity, along with
   more extensive references, can be found in Folayan, 1992; Greene, 1994a, 1994b; Gutierrez
   & Dworkin, 1992; Icard, 1986; Loiacan, 1989; Mays & Cochran, 1988; Mays, Cochran, &
   Rhue, in press; Peterson, 1995.

forced immigration of peoples from Western Africa through the slave trade. Some are immigrants or descendants of immigrants from Caribbean countries, whose background reflects the impact of Europeans who colonized parts of the Caribbean (Silvera, 1991). In addition, many African Americans claim Indian and European roots.

Even across these differences, the experiences of African Americans share certain qualities, many of which help to illuminate the realities of African American LGBs, who often perceive their community as being more homophobic than society at large. For there are certain aspects of the African American communities that might predispose its members to homonegative attitudes.

First, the African American experience is deeply imbedded in a sense of community and an involvement in the extended family, both of which provide support and nurturance to and expect reciprocal commitment from the individual. Historically, the family has been the bulwark of individual safety and simultaneously the guarantor of continuity for the community. The very real threat of genocide and the intentional dismemberment of the family that characterized the historical experience of African Americans have combined to make the heterosexual family and the collective rearing of children essential strategies for survival. Additionally, there is genuine concern within African American communities about the shortage of marriageable men—a result of high rates of incarceration and elevated rates of homicide, substance abuse, and AIDS.[4] Given these considerations, LGB identity is easily seen as a threat to the community and its values. The individual gay or lesbian individual is perceived as rejecting core cultural values related to reproduction and family, and as putting the community at risk of extinction.

An additional issue is the fact that African Americans have historically been stereotyped as sexually promiscuous. Insofar as homophilic individuals are also perceived as sexually profligate, the presence of LGBs within the African American community threatens to reinforce that stereotype. Thus, hostility toward homophilia may be in part an expression of internalized racism—the desire to distance the community from any negative qualities that have been associated with African Americans.

Religion also plays a central role in the lives of many African American communities, and the Christian church's condemnation of homosexuality serves to reinforce existing homonegativism. The role of traditional views among African Americans may contribute to homophobia in other ways. A recent movement toward "Afrocentrism" strives to reframe African American experience in terms of its cultural roots in African societies. From this perspec-

---

4. This concern, coupled with the complete absence of any privilege other than heterosexual privilege among African American women, may explain research indicating that heightened homonegativity in the African American community may primarily reflect more negative attitudes on the part of African American women (Ernst, Francis, Nevels, & Lemeh, 1991).

tive, homosexuality is a product of western societies and directly incompatible with Afrocentric values. Although some research indicates that homophilia is found in African societies, LGB identity is seen as a form of corruption and a denial of one's African roots.

The strength of family and community ties often means that the African American lesbian, gay, or bisexual individual will not be entirely banished from that network of support. As Tremble, Schneider, and Appathurai (1989) pointed out, placing the blame for homophilia on sources external to the family and the community—a "white people's disease"—allows the group to condemn LGB identity without explicitly rejecting its LGB members. However, tolerance depends on silence about one's homophilic identity, so complete acceptance and validation of one's full sense of self are not forthcoming.

The failure to find active validation within the family may lead the individual to the LGB community—but full acceptance is not assured here, either. African American LGBs commonly report direct experiences of racist treatment, such as exclusion from and discriminatory treatment within LGB establishments and organizations. More subtle forms of racism occur, as well, such as the expectation that racial stereotypes will be played out in relationships— the African American partner viewed as a "stud" or a servant, for instance (Garnets & Kimmel, 1993).

The meager research that has addressed the impact of this dual prejudice suggests that both forms of hostility—racism among LGBs and homonegativity in the African American community—have an impact. The perception of intense hostility toward homophilia within the African American community encourages its LGB members to remain closeted, thus creating a degree of deceit in their relationships with other members of that community. On top of this, African American LGBs report finding less support from LGB communities than do white LGBs, and are more likely to feel isolated and tense. African American LGBs also appear to maintain close contacts with non-LGB members of the African American community, to maintain a strong allegiance to that community, and to see their African American identity as paramount (Greene, 1994a, 1994b; Icard, 1986; Loiacano, 1989).

As an illustration of how intersecting identities may have concrete impact on minority LGBs, we can look to research on HIV/AIDS and African American gay and bisexual men. The fact that little research has addressed this issue points not only to societal racism but also to the invisibility of gay and bisexual African Americans—a result of refusal by the African American community to acknowledge the existence of LGBs among their numbers, as well as LGBs' fear of rejection by the African American community. What little research is available indicates that a higher proportion of African American men identify as bisexual than do whites or Hispanics. One possible explanation for this phenomenon is that gay identity is so vilified in the

African American community that men reject that identity for themselves and identify as bisexual instead. Because of this identity, they are more likely to have sex with women as well, thus exacerbating the risk of HIV transmission within the African American community. And, because of the racism inherent in the LGB community, AIDS education and support programs are not geared to the specific experiences of minority LGBs, leaving them without the resources easily accessible to white LGBs (Peterson, 1995).

Asian Americans

The Asian American population includes a vast array of nationalities and subcultures whose diversity is belied by the collective term, "Asian." We tend to think of Asian Americans as Chinese and Japanese, but the category includes also Korean, Laotian, Vietnamese, Thai, and many others—each of which, in turn, encompasses great cultural diversity. In addition, groups of Asian ancestry are often grouped with Pacific Islanders, the resulting "Asian/Pacific Islander" (API) category forming an amalgam of radically different cultures including Hawaiian, Filipino/a and others. While some academic literature and a growing number of anthologies of personal commentary have begun to address this diversity, most psychological research on Asian American LGBs deals with those of Chinese and Japanese heritage; accordingly, these two groups will be the focus of this discussion.

Many of the principles discussed above as common to the experience of minority LGBs can be identified among Asian Americans; some factors are distinctive to Asian American or API cultures.[5] Particularly salient is the role of the family in Asian cultures. This includes the expectation that complete respect and obedience be granted to one's parents, as well as the conviction that an individual's actions reflect directly on the family. Rigid gender roles prescribe that men should carry on the family name through marriage and child rearing, and that women should find satisfaction through dutiful devotion first to the family of origin and later to husband and children. Traditionally, marriage has been viewed as an inevitable linkage not between individuals but between families, intended for the betterment of both families rather than for individual fulfillment.

Given this foundation, it is easy to see how LGB identity would be seen as a flagrant transgression of fundamental cultural norms among Asian Americans. Lesbian or gay identity directly defies expectations for marriage and child rearing, and also appears to place one's personal wishes above family

---

5. For further references and more detailed discussions of issues for Asian, Asian-Pacific, and Asian American LGBs, see Chan, 1987, 1989, 1992; Choi, Salazar, Lew, & Coates, 1995; Garnets & Kimmel, 1993; Gock, 1992; Greene, 1994a, 1994b; Tremble, Schneider, & Appathurai, 1989; Wooden, Kawasaki, & Mayeda, 1983.

and the community. The importance of carrying on the family name and bringing honor to the family and the community is violated by what is perceived as a conscious choice to defy the family and the values of the culture. A child who is lesbian or gay may be regarded as a source of tremendous shame, especially for the mother, whose role is to raise children who bring honor to the family.

Also involved in the rejection of homophilia in Asian American communities is the clear division of gender roles. Man's role is to father children and to expect obedience from women; woman's role is to bear children and to be dutiful, submissive, and self-effacing. Same-sex relationships preclude such role divisions based on sex, so that their very existence threatens cultural norms.

Attitudes toward sexuality are also important. For women, sexuality is presumed to be unimportant, so that relationships between women may be seen as inconsequential unless the label "lesbian" is attached to them. Asian American men, similarly, may have sexual relations with other men without those relationships being seen as gay. In both cases, it is the designation of homosexuality, the label "gay" or "lesbian," that renders one's identity shameful. Accordingly, Asian Americans who do identify as gay or lesbian risk ostracism from the family and the community. Indeed, most experience deep concern about revealing their sexual orientation to other members of the Asian American community for fear of meeting with hostility and rejection.

To complicate the matter further, many Asian American LGBs argue that the Asian American community is largely oblivious to LGBs among their numbers. Rather, homophilia is perceived as a "white problem." This situation makes it more uncomfortable for Asian American LGBs to come out within their community or to their families, because they feel that "there is no frame of reference to understand homosexuality in Asian American culture" (Chan, 1989, p. 19).

As is true for African American LGBs, this denial of the existence of LGBs in the Asian American community contributes to complications surrounding HIV/AIDS and its impact on Asian American gay and bisexual men. Data indicate a relatively lower rate of HIV/AIDS among Asian American or API populations; it appears that this reflects both a later entry of the virus into this community and significant underreporting. Illness is a taboo topic in the community in any case, and both AIDS and LGB identity are severely stigmatized and would therefore bring shame to the family; hence, many cases probably go unreported. The same stigma precludes gay and bisexual API men from turning to their community for support, but—with a few recent exceptions—few programs in the LGB community have addressed the specific cultural, linguistic, and social needs of Asian American LGBs. The meager research available that specifically addresses HIV/AIDS among API individuals suggests that gay men engage in high levels of unsafe sex, perhaps because existing programs have not been successful in reaching them (Choi, Salazar, Lew, & Coates, 1995).

Gender differences are also apparent in the experience of Asian American LGBs. Chan (1989) found that Asian gay men experience discrimination more because of their sexual orientation than because of their Asian identity; this differs from other minority groups, who generally report greater discrimination based on ethnicity than on sexual orientation. In contrast to their male peers, Asian American lesbians report greater discrimination because they are Asian than because they are lesbian. These findings highlight the role of gender as it interacts with ethnicity and sexual orientation, and point out again the futility of making generalizations about such complex phenomena.

Asian American LGBs also experience racism within the LGB community, sometimes in the form of stereotypic expectations for behavior, at other times in the form of explicit discriminatory treatment. Asian American LGBs often feel that they are required to choose between allegiances. In Chan's (1989) research, when forced to choose one identity as primary, most described themselves primarily as lesbian or gay and secondarily as Asian. However, this was not universal, and many identified primarily as Asian. Which position an individual takes is surely affected by the interaction between levels of ethnic identity and LGB identity formation.

Moving beyond the more widely studied experience of Japanese and Chinese Americans, some literature has recently addressed the experience of South Asian LGBs—a category that includes those who identify as Indian, Pakistani, Nepalese, Sri Lankan, and some other nationalities. A brief discussion will highlight some key concepts.[6]

These cultures are characterized by rigid gender roles and by expectations of complete obedience to parents and compliance with social norms. Marriages are often arranged, and the pressure to marry is intense. LGB identity is condemned as a western phenomenon and is extremely stigmatized, a homonegative stance that in part reflects the long domination of colonial Britain. In fact, in India, relatively acceptant attitudes toward homophilia were supplanted by legal sanctions imported and imposed by the British. Because of the illegality of homosexuality, nondisclosure is often crucial for South Asian LGBs. In addition to legal threats, coming out also risks the loss of family support; in extreme cases, the LGB individual may be actively shunned by the family.

Those of South Asian ancestry who migrate to the United States find little acceptance here and little sense of community among mainstream LGBs. In addition to the generally exclusionary quality of many LGB communities, differing attitudes about relationships may distance those with South Asian

---

6. For more information about South Asian LGBs, see Greene, 1994a, 1994b; Jayakar, 1994; Ratti, 1993.

ancestry from mainstream LGBs. South Asians tend to believe in long-term relationships and to feel uncomfortable with public displays of affection, both of which may make them feel out of place in many LGB communities in this country. Thus, a cultural legacy of silence and invisibility combine with the racism and conflicting values of American culture to keep South Asian LGBs largely closeted in their own communities and without ready connection to the mainstream LGB community. Because their numbers are so small, the formation of self-contained South Asian LGB communities is extremely difficult.

Hispanic or Latin Americans

The category of Hispanic, Latin American, or Chicano/a is another that includes a wide variety of cultures, languages, and countries of origin or ancestry. In different parts of the United States, individuals or subcultural groups prefer varied generic designations (Chicano/Chicana, Hispanic, Latina/Latino), and some claim specific national identifications (e.g., Mexican American, Cuban American, Puerto Rican). The terminology bespeaks the diversity to be found among these groups. Still, research suggests some commonalities in values across Hispanic or Latin American cultures.[7]

In a theme that is now familiar, the Hispanic/Latin American family is of central importance, with strong ties of interdependence among family members. Clear gender roles differentiate the acceptable behaviors of men and women. Men are expected to display *machismo*, to defend and provide for the family and to eschew any traits that might be deemed feminine. Women are to exhibit *marianismo*, to be submissive, altruistic and virtuous, to defer to men, and to remain with the family of origin until marriage. These values are reinforced by the Catholic Church, which holds a position of significant influence in many Hispanic/Latin American communities.

Once again, the threat to these beliefs implied by LGB identity is profound. Those who identify as LGB do not fulfill cultural prescriptions for commitment to (heterosexual) families, nor do they abide by their community's gender role expectations. Here, as with other groups, the fact that lesbian, gay, and bisexual people *can* bear and raise children and *do* have families (if of a nontraditional sort) is deemed irrelevant. Such arrangements still violate traditional norms and patterns of family, and cannot assume the position of respect granted to the heterosexual family. Abdicating one's traditional role in favor of an individualistic identity as lesbian, gay, or bisexual may be taken as a selfish

---

7. More thorough discussions and references regarding Hispanic/Latin American LGBs can be found in Carballo-Dieguez, 1995; Carballo-Dieguez & Dolezal, 1994; Carrier, 1985, 1989, 1992; Espin, 1984, 1987, 1994; Greene, 1994a, 1994b; Gutierrez, 1992; Hidalgo, 1984; Morales, 1992.

136 denial of one's responsibility to the extended family and the community. Lesbian identity is an explicit violation of a woman's traditional child-bearing role that simultaneously threatens the presumed dominance of men.

Interestingly, in a phenomenon reminiscent of some Asian American communities, same-sex sexual behavior is not itself necessarily condemned in many Hispanic/Latin American communities. The physical expression of affection among women is accepted and is not presumed to indicate lesbianism, in part because women are expected to be ignorant about sexuality. More striking, it is not uncommon for men to participate in explicit same-sex sexual behavior without its being taken as indicative of homosexuality. In the latter case, the strong tie between gender and assumed sexual orientation makes it acceptable for a man to be the active, insertive partner in anal intercourse (i.e., to assume the "masculine" role), without his behavior or identity being stigmatized. The passive or recipient partner, however, is deemed "feminine" and regarded as homosexual, an identity that carries severe cultural condemnation. Among some groups, this phenomenon is class related, with men of a lower socioeconomic status more likely to adhere to these roles than men of a comparatively higher socioeconomic position. Thus, acts that might be seen as indicative of homosexual identity by the dominant culture are not necessarily interpreted as such. Only if the individual explicitly assumes a gay or lesbian identity will he or she necessarily confront the approbation of the family and community.

The phenomenon of men having sex with men but not identifying as gay—or even as bisexual—has important implications in this age of HIV/AIDS. Several factors are relevant here. First, at least among men of Mexican descent, it appears that anal intercourse is strongly preferred over other forms of sexual activity, making it more difficult to change sexual behavior toward safer sex practices. Second, some men who frequently have sex with other men still identify as heterosexual; indeed, sex with a "passive" man may be regarded simply as a release of sexual tension with someone who is "like" a woman. If these men equate HIV/AIDS risk with gay or bisexual identity rather than with specific unsafe practices, they may fail to see the danger of their own, unprotected sexual activity. Whatever their identification, men who have sex with men and with women risk transmitting the virus to women as well, to whom they usually do not disclose their bisexual activities (Carballo-Dieguez, 1995; Carballo-Dieguez & Dolezal, 1994).

Many Latin/Hispanic American LGBs indicate that their families and communities are tolerant, so long as their homophilic identity remains unspoken. This tacit acceptance earned through silence may derive from the culture's reticence to deal with sexuality of any sort, especially for women. And/or, direct disclosure may violate a cultural proscription against being direct or confrontative, particularly where directness might lead to a loss of face. In either case, in the name of receiving such tolerance and avoiding painful overt rejection, Hispanic/Latin American LGBs may not come out within the community or to their families, although they may feel sure that these people "must know."

Many writers suggest that, despite this quiet and tenuous tolerance of individuals believed to be LGB, homonegativism is stronger in Hispanic/Latin American communities than in the dominant culture, causing LGBs to remain closeted rather than face the hostility of their people. The importance of the community is demonstrated by the deep loyalty to it expressed by Latin/ Hispanic American LGBs, who often see their ethnic group membership as primary to their sense of identity.

As with other groups, Hispanic/Latin LGBs must cope with the racism of homophile communities. Hispanic/Latin American LGBs express dismay at this situation, realizing that in neither community are they able to find full acceptance. For example, Espin (1987) found that Cuban lesbians prefer to be in the company of white lesbians rather than heterosexual Cubans, but they regret the need to make the choice. In major cities with a large Hispanic/Latin American population, one can often find communities of Latin/Hispanic American LGBs; such groups serve a crucial role in offering their members both affirmation for their homophilic identity and support from others members of their own ethnic group. However, for those living in rural or smaller urban areas and for those who do not have access to such groups for other reasons, experiences that affirm both their ethnic and LGB identities may be unavailable.

Native Americans

Native Americans (or, as some prefer, American Indians) include many distinct nations, tribal groups, cultures, and languages; it is extremely difficult to draw any generalizations about the status of Native American LGBs. A few general comments will serve to raise some crucial points.[8]

Most cultural groups included under this rubric place considerable emphasis on spirituality, cultural identity, the importance of the family, and the need to preserve and continue the tribe. However, while these qualities sound similar to descriptions of other ethnic minority groups, Native American attitudes toward homophilia have historically been very different from those of other cultures.

In the traditional beliefs of many Native American tribes, gender was not inextricably linked to biological sex, nor was sexuality conceived of as a dichotomous variable—that is, as heterosexual or homosexual. Rather, the

---

8. Native American identity and its relationship to LGB issues is addressed in greater depth in Allen, 1984, 1986, 1989; Blackwood, 1986b; Grahn, 1986; Greene, 1994a, 1994b; Roscoe, 1987; Tafoya, 1992; Tafoya & Rowell, 1988; Weinrich & Williams, 1991; Whitehead, 1981; Williams, 1986a, 1986b; further references can also be found in these readings.

culture held a place for individuals who manifested all varieties of sex-gender combinations and all forms of sexual partnering. Thus, women might perform roles typically identified as male, and vice versa, and either men or women might have same-sex partners. None of these variants in identity was seen as pathological. Rather, individuals were presumed to come to their particular identity through spiritual guidance, and the same respect was accorded to those who devised a typical or an atypical identity. Indeed, in some tribal groups, so-called two-spirited people—those who manifested both "masculine" and "feminine" qualities—were especially revered for their ability to bridge differences.

These traditional, very acceptant, even reverential attitudes toward gender variation among Native Americans were effectively erased by white colonization, when traditional native beliefs were supplanted by European beliefs. The attitudes of Native Americans educated by white-run programs on the reservations came to reflect the homonegativity of the colonizers. Furthermore, the risk of genocide made the bearing and rearing of children a crucial survival strategy for Native Americans. As a result of these forces, contemporary Native Americans, particularly those living on reservations, tend to hold extremely negative attitudes toward homophilia.

The situation is not without its complexities, however. At least for lesbians, there is some possibility for and acceptance of their fulfilling their primary role in the culture—namely, the bearing and rearing of children, who are seen as the future of the tribe. In fact, Native American women who identify as lesbian are more likely than their counterparts from other minority groups to have heterosexual relationships and to bear children. Despite the allegiance to critical cultural values expressed by their bearing children and thereby contributing to the continuance of the tribe, however, lesbians' sexual orientation continues to be stigmatized.

For the majority of today's Native American LGBs, the reality of contemporary homonegativism is likely to be a stronger determinant of their experience than the earlier, far more positive attitudes. Because of the profound importance of group identity and the urgency of maintaining the culture, the process of coming to terms with a homophilic identity is particularly fraught for Native American LGBs. For those living on reservations, escape to large urban areas often seems the only way to cope.

In mainstream LGB circles, Native Americans are likely to encounter both subtle and overt racism. The former may be manifested as stereotyping of Native Americans—as exotic and noble, for instance. The latter emerges in the usual forms of exclusionary and discriminatory treatment by members of the LGB community. Because the population of Native Americans as a whole is so small, explicitly Native American LGB groups are exceedingly rare. Individuals may find a degree of support and affirmation in groups designed to address the

collective needs of those from a variety of minority backgrounds, but the Native   *139*
American experience (like every other) is distinctive, and those from other
minority communities may be unable to provide the unique forms of support
that might come from a community of other Native American LGBs.

Stresses and Strengths: Keeping Perspective

In this discussion, we have emphasized the very difficult position that minority
LGBs occupy—their self-esteem triply threatened, their places of haven also
sources of prejudice, the complexities of coming to terms with multiple stigmatized identities. However, the other, very affirmative side of this situation
lies in the opportunities it offers for personal growth and social awareness. The
demands placed on one's coping abilities by such circumstances and the potential for developing uncommon sensitivity and stress management skills are
truly exceptional. The individual who successfully navigates the maze of
minority LGB identity is likely to emerge with commendable social and
psychological strengths.

In discussing the experiences of LGBs from various minority groups, it is
paramount that we keep in mind the many layers of diversity—not only differences between these groups and majority cultures, not only differences among
these groups, but also variations within each group. Indeed, in some senses it
does a disservice to these groups to characterize them by using terms that
appear to homogenize and oversimplify cultures that are richly varied and
complex. Acknowledging the impact of minority group membership is a beginning. But the task of understanding individual experience demands a far finer
analysis than this—an undertaking psychology has only begun to address.

CHAPTER SIX

LIFESPAN DEVELOPMENT AND LESBIAN/GAY/BISEXUAL IDENTITY

THE AIM OF THIS CHAPTER is to explore specific developmental issues in the lives of people who identify as gay, bisexual, or lesbian—keeping in mind that these individuals face the same developmental tasks as do those who are heterosexually identified (who are, indeed, the unacknowledged subjects of traditional models of human development). In addition, LGB persons confront extraordinary issues raised by homophilic identity. The challenges of living a stigmatized identity and the accompanying constant demand to deal with heterosexism, internalized homophobia, and strategies of stigma management unavoidably complicate the process of development for LGB individuals.

Before reviewing this literature, it is important to reiterate problems mentioned earlier in our discussions. Research with LGB individuals is hampered by numerous methodological difficulties, chief among them the challenge of gathering a sample of LGB individuals who reasonably represent the broad homophile community. First, research subjects include only those individuals who are open enough about their sexual orientation to find their way into research. Then, subjects are overwhelmingly well educated, white, middle or upper class, urban dwelling, and young. The descriptions of LGB experience gleaned from such samples may tell us a great deal about the experience of this subset of LGBs, but we cannot know how well it describes the lives of less educated, nonwhite, working class, rural, older, or less open LGBs. As discussed in chapter 5, some of the literature documents the distinctiveness of nonmainstream LGBs; however, most work aimed at describing the LGB experience in general terms still relies on limited samples. We must be extremely careful not to generalize from this depiction about the lives of all LGBs.

Alert to the risk of such overgeneralization, we will consider how the particular characteristics of LGB experience, age-typical developmental tasks, and sociohistorical context interact to generate the unique experience of growing up and growing older as a lesbian, gay, or bisexual person. As a framework for this discussion, we will consider three developmental periods: adolescence, midlife, and aging. Each can be described in terms of distinctive developmental characteristics, and each presents unique challenges, risks, and opportunities to those identifying as LGB.

Adolescent Development and LGB Experience

The primary developmental task of adolescence is the achievement of identity, a sense of who one is, along with all this entails—values, beliefs, feelings, goals, skills, deficits, and sexuality, to name but a few elements of this sense of self. A secondary, derivative task is to learn to manage the social roles that accompany identity—to master, in short, the demands of one's particular place in society. For adolescents who identify as gay, lesbian, or bisexual, this undertaking is made more difficult by the need to cope with the discrepancy between one's sense of self and the culture's condemnation of that identity and of the roles the identity implies.

As discussed previously, many individuals first come to a sense of lesbian, bisexual, or gay male identity during adolescence. However, as Savin-Williams (1990, 1995) has pointed out, the formation of LGB identity is not as straightforward as it might seem from simplistic cultural portrayals of sexual orientation. We have seen that sexual orientation is difficult to specify among adults; the same is true of teens. One indication of its amorphous quality is the frequent asynchrony between self-identification and behavior. Many teens identify as LGB but have never had a same-sex sexual experience; this is especially true for lesbians, for whom identification as lesbian is likely to be grounded more in affect than in sexuality per se. Some adolescents who identify as LGB are not sexually active in any way; others are heterosexually active. Correlatively, many teens who identify as heterosexual have had no heterosexual sexual experience, and some engage in same-sex sexual acts. Such variability is not unique to adolescents, but is likely to be more common in this age group as teens engage in the complicated process of identity formation. Regardless of the sexual orientation with which teens eventually identify, many will explore a variety of relationships, both physical and emotional, because the task of adolescence is precisely to define one's sense of self through exploration.

This is not to say that adolescents who identify as LGB are simply "in a phase" that they will soon outgrow. It is a common belief that adolescents are too young to know that they are bisexual, lesbian, or gay—although the notion that they could know they are heterosexual is not questioned in the same way. Homophilic feelings or experiences are often interpreted as a phase that most will outgrow, with "true" LGB identity forming only in adulthood. In contrast to this view, it now seems clear that a significant segment of the adult LGB population can trace their certainty about their sexual orientation to adolescence—or even earlier, in some cases; research with LGB adolescents also indicates that many teens have come to a firm sense of LGB identity (see, e.g., D'Augelli & Hershberger, 1993; Gibson, 1989; Hershberger & D'Augelli, 1995; Remafedi, 1987a; Rofes, 1989).

Yet we needn't assume, either, that those who identify as LGB or as heterosexual are permanently fixed in that identity, as ample literature points to the flexibility of sexual orientation for some individuals (see chapter 1). Whether it is ultimately a lifelong identity, the assumption of LGB status during adolescence has profound effects on the experience of growing up.

Self-Identification: When Do They Know?

Research suggests that the age of first awareness of same-sex feelings has gotten younger in recent years. Early research typically reported self-awareness as occurring in the late teens or early 20s, with boys becoming aware earlier than girls. More recent research suggests that, at least in some samples, the age of first attraction to another member of one's sex may be as early as age ten for both boys and girls, first same-sex sexual activity at about thirteen for boys and fifteen for girls, and first disclosure to others at about age sixteen for both girls and boys (Savin-Williams, 1995).[1] While research with college students discloses that most of them did not come out to others until college, their recollections of self-identification as lesbian, gay, or bisexual generally occurred before the end of high school (D'Augelli, 1991).

There are, of course, tremendous individual variations in the timing of these events, as well as in their sequence. However, retrospective research with adults indicates that a positive LGB identity is related to the individual's engaging in exploratory same-sex sexual behavior prior to adopting an LGB identity. Perhaps this period of experimentation allows the person time to develop more adequate affective and social skills for coping with homonegativity (Adelman, 1991).

A consistent finding across studies is that awareness of same-sex feelings precedes self-identification as LGB, which in turn precedes disclosure to

---

1. These findings may in part reflect methodological differences among studies. The latest research (which shows the youngest age of self-definition) describes the experience of subjects who are participants in LGB youth groups; these individuals may not be representative of all who will eventually identify as LGB. The older research, in contrast, relies largely on adults' recollections of when they first identified as LGB; such reconstructions are subject to error.

others, typically by several years. Perhaps the most common experience
reported by LGBs, especially by men, is the very early sense of being
"different." This sense of difference usually does not have specifically sexual
connotations prior to adolescence.[2] Often, these early feelings have to do with
cross-gender interests and activities; many people recall having been taunted
for their difference long before they identified as LGB. The attribution of
sexual orientation to these feelings typically emerges after puberty.

The earlier reported age of self-awareness suggests a cohort effect. The very
notion of adolescent LGB identity may be a historically recent phenomenon, a
product of the growing visibility of the LGB community and LGB issues,
accompanied by now-familiar terminology to name the experience (Gibson,
1989; Herdt, 1989b). These factors may well have provided both the labels and
the support for youth to come to a homophilic identification earlier than was
possible in prior cohorts.

Early self-identification has tremendous psychological impact for youth.
First, it means a longer period during which one must deal with the stigma of
LGB identity *while still an adolescent.* The period shortly after one comes to an
LGB identity appears to be the most difficult time; about one-third of first
suicide attempts among LGB adolescents occur during the first year after self-
identification (Remafedi, Farrow, & Deisher, 1991). Thus, young adolescents
are far less well prepared to face the most treacherous period in the process of
coming to terms than are people who are older and have more psychological
and social resources (Adelman, 1991).

Some research does suggest, however, that early awareness of same-sex
attractions is correlated with higher self-esteem in adulthood—at least for
lesbians. It may be that higher self-esteem precedes this awareness, serving as
the grounding that allows these teens to acknowledge atypical feelings.
Alternatively, perhaps a longer period of coming to terms with these feelings
allows for the emergence of greater self-acceptance (Savin-Williams &
Rodriguez, 1993). A third possibility is that, for lesbians, this early awareness
helps them to resist the cultural devaluation of women that is grounded in
heterosexist beliefs about women's proper place.

A second important consequence of early self-identification is that the
earlier a teen comes to an LGB identity, the longer she or he must deal with
the implications for family relationships. If the individual reveals her or his
identity, negative reactions from the family may make the home environment
extremely aversive.

Although the LGB community would be the logical place for teens to find
aid in the process of coming to terms with their identity, these communities
have traditionally eschewed involvement with teens for fear of becoming

---

2.   However, many people—especially gay males—report specifically sexual feelings in early
     childhood. For a powerful first person account of such feelings, see Fricke (1981).

victim to old stereotypes—that LGBs molest and/or recruit children (Gibson, 1989; Gonsiorek, 1988; Rofes, 1989; Savin-Williams, 1990). To complicate things further, because most adult LGBs remain closeted, teens have few if any models or mentors to whom they can turn. Nowhere in their experience do they see models of how LGB life is or could be, other than the pejorative stereotypes learned in their childhood and reinforced in their daily lives. An eighteen-year-old lesbian notes:

> I see a lot of young lesbians out there. What happens when you get old?
> What happens to old lesbians? I don't know. I mean, do they live together
> or move out to the suburbs or something? (Schneider, 1989, p. 121)

With the LGB community inaccessible and its members largely invisible to adolescents, teens lack access to the information and the people who could ease this transition. Although it is not possible to draw causal conclusions, the added stress generated by this circumstance may help explain why both early self-identification and the length of time a teen has been out are correlated with low self-esteem,[3] a higher incidence of substance abuse, and perhaps a greater risk of suicide (Gibson, 1989).

Thus, today's adolescent LGBs live in a paradox: the greater visibility of the LGB community and its issues has proven a catalyst for the process of their own identity formation. However, even as that visibility contributes to their earlier LGB identification, they are left to deal with its consequences without the same level of support that the community provides for older LGBs.

Coming Out

Once they have self-identified, LGB teens begin the struggle over whether to reveal their identity and, if so, to whom. Some teens practice secrecy through-out their adolescent years; others choose to come out to at least some people in their lives. These decisions have profound consequences for LGB youth.

As we have seen, the process of coming out—to oneself and then to others—is fraught with confusion, conflict, and anxiety, regardless of when it occurs. For teens, an awareness of same-sex attractions is especially difficult. Adolescents lack many of the experiences and resources that adults enjoy: experience in managing stress and utilizing available support systems; psychological resources such as cognitive capacities, a clear sense of identity, solid

---

3. This appears to contradict the finding noted above indicating a relationship between early awareness and high self-esteem. However, that finding derived from research with adults, for whom current self-esteem was correlated with recollections of early awareness. Here we are dealing with teens whose current self-esteem reflects their struggle with coming to terms with a maligned identity.

self-esteem, and interpersonal skills; material resources such as access to relevant literature and community facilities; and social resources, such as models and mentors to provide guidance in how one lives this identity. In addition, most teens are still dependent on their families in many respects, and must cope in daily, concrete ways with their families' real and potential reactions to their LGB identity. At great risk of psychological difficulty and with few means of coping, adolescents approach the possibility of LGB identity from an extremely vulnerable position.

Despite the obvious pain of coming to terms with feelings that teens know to be unacceptable, many LGB adolescents do reach a point of coming out—initially by identifying their feelings to themselves, later by revealing them to others. It appears that this process is different for girls than for boys (Garnets & Kimmel, 1993; Gonsiorek, 1988; Malyon, 1981; Remafedi, 1987b; Schneider, 1989). Girls are more likely to experience intense same-sex connections as expressions of close friendship, and tend to respond to these feelings in a reflective, thoughtful manner. The process may be experienced as fluid and ambiguous. In contrast, boys are likely to experience homophilic attractions as more specifically sexual and to respond by engaging in same-sex sexual activity. Boys may also respond more dramatically to the crises of coming out, evidencing more psychological symptoms.

Accepting a gay identity is additionally complicated for boys by HIV/AIDS, particularly since so little information about HIV/AIDS is available to teens— a reflection of societal homophobia.[4] The fear of AIDS—of its stigma and of the disease itself—may delay adolescents from confronting the possibility of their own gay identity. Such delays may, in turn, prevent them from addressing crucial psychological and practical issues and may support unreflective acting out that puts them at risk ("I'm not gay or anything! How can a little experimentation hurt?"). Plus, it may prevent them from seeking out the resources and support that could help them cope in a more healthy manner with the difficult process of identity formation (Feldman, 1989). Additionally, the risk of depression and suicide is heightened by the sense that the identity to which one has come is both hated and potentially life-threatening.[5]

---

4. Because the public equates AIDS with homosexuality in general, lesbians must also cope with the increase in homonegativity that has occurred with the epidemic. However, lesbians in fact have the lowest risk for sexual transmission of HIV of any group, and thus do not have to deal with the intense fear that the expression of their erotic feelings will be life-threatening.

5. Of course homosexuality per se is not intrinsically dangerous. Unsafe sex—on the part of anyone—is potentially lethal. But public belief holds both that homosexuality is the cause of AIDS and that AIDS is the punishment for the evils of homosexuality. Many adults are unable to move beyond this distortion, so it is easy to understand why teens would not be able to transcend the fear and misunderstanding it represents.

Adolescence, Identity, and LGB Teens

Once the adolescent identifies as lesbian, gay, or bisexual, the process of coming to terms with that identity is superimposed on the already complex developmental task of adolescent identity achievement. The achievement of a firm sense of identity rests on two basic requirements: the opportunity for exploration and role testing, and the availability of social relations that support and assist the adolescent in coming to a sense of who she or he is. Both of these are problematic for LGB adolescents.

Opportunities for role testing allow the adolescent to explore a variety of qualities that might comprise an identity, gradually bringing together a distinctive constellation of traits that identify her or him as a unique individual. In addition, a great deal of role testing takes place vicariously, as the adolescent explores the meaning and consequences of roles she or he observes. The images and models available in popular culture serve important functions in providing adolescents with a vision of the options available to them.

Much of this exploration—both actual and vicarious—takes place in the peer group, where adolescents find support for their search and gather feedback about their own performance, and observe among their peers the variety of roles that are possible and the social implications of each. The peer group is crucial also as the locus for mastering the social skills that are the basis for interpersonal relationships. Acceptance by one's peer group is thus important in many respects: as fundamental to self-esteem, as a vehicle for role exploration, and as the primary means for developing social skills. The adolescent who fails to find such acceptance may be excluded from interactions that are crucial to identity achievement.

Adolescents are helped along in their identity seeking by cultural scripts describing how life is best lived and what expectations society holds. Children are socialized to match their own personal life scripts to these societal ones, a process sometimes referred to as *anticipatory socialization* (Herdt, 1989b). At adolescence, peers play an important role in this socialization, as well, mirroring in their interactions the judgments that they have incorporated through their own previous socialization.

As adolescents begin to define who they are, they compare their sense of self to these images and judge their place in society accordingly. Such scripts may vary considerably from one group to another; however, within a particular sociocultural framework there is considerable overlap, so that very different groups may share strikingly similar expectations in some areas. For example, as we have seen, heterosexism is pervasive in this society, so that across cultural and social groupings, heterosexuality is revered and homophilia is devalued.

Coming to Terms, Adolescent Style

Adolescents who are struggling with homophilic feelings face the same issues in LGB identity formation we discussed at length in chapter 4: denial, confusion, stigma management, and so on. But for teens, this process is greatly complicated by their developmental and social positions.

For adolescents whose sense of self includes an awareness of same-sex feelings, identity seeking is enormously complicated. It means coming to terms with an identity that they know to be condemned by their society—and also by themselves, since we have all learned homonegative attitudes. In addition, they are faced with a profound deficit in their preparation for the role they face, a deficit in anticipatory socialization. Every aspect of their socialization and all of the cultural supports for their transition to adulthood have presented the heterosexual script as the only life pattern available. Those of their peers who are also dealing with the same feelings are likely to remain hidden, so that each individual feels not only different from the cultural ideal and from his or her peers, but also totally alone.

LGB teens find few opportunities to explore the meaning of their feelings. Despite a few instances of same-sex dating that have captured media attention (see, e.g., Fricke, 1981), opportunities for open involvement in romantic relationships are simply not available for the vast majority of LGB teens. Although most LGB youth hope for a long-term relationship, they do not have the same opportunities to explore the possibilities of relationships as do heterosexual teens, who are free to engage openly in dating and other forms of peer socialization. The absence of opportunities for exploring intimate same-sex relationships is matched by an absence of models for how to conduct such relationships. The combination may leave adolescent LGBs at a loss for how one forms relationships or what those relationships might be like.

The task for LGB teens is thus quite complex. Not only must they negotiate a "role exit" from the heterosexual life to which they have been socialized (D'Augelli, 1993); they must also create a positive sense of themselves that incorporates a re-defined identification as LGB (Herdt, 1989b), and must do so essentially without templates for that identity. In short, the tools for optimal identity development are not readily available to LGB teens; they are left to construct an identity largely from scratch and often with a profound sense of isolation.

These feelings of isolation may take many forms (Martin & Hetrick, 1988). The sense that no one knows or understands one's feelings may result in *social isolation.* The need to hide one's identity and the constant fear of discovery may lead to social withdrawal, which is aggravated by persistent insecurity about acceptance by others. When LGB youth withdraw from social interaction and thereby from the peer group, their sense of difference—even of inferiority—is further reinforced, and they lose important opportunities to develop social skills and to benefit from peer support and feedback in the process of identity exploration. The failure to master social skills may lead to further withdrawal, and so on in a circle that may leave LGB adolescents at a clear disadvantage in the process of forming a healthy sense of identity (D'Augelli, 1993; Gonsiorek, 1988; Martin, 1982).

Emotional isolation may result from the adolescent's certainty that no one feels as she or he does, that no one can understand. This can lead, in turn, to avoidance of the intimate friendships that are crucial to adolescent development. Close relationships risk the possibility of misunderstanding and rejection if one is honest; if one is not, it is impossible to form a truly close relationship. Martin and Hetrick share the words of a young gay man:

> Why can't we say where we are really hurting? ... I was desperate—I wanted to tell you how much I need your help but I couldn't.... I was convinced that the only way I could be accepted was to remain hidden. I was sure that no one would love me if they knew. (1988, p. 172)

Social and emotional isolation are compounded by *cognitive isolation,* which results from adolescents' lack of access to information that would help them to move toward a more affirming sense of LGB identity.

It must be emphasized that the psychological difficulties depicted here— the sense of difference and inferiority, the social withdrawal, the difficulties in forming relationships—do not point to psychopathology on the part of LGB teens and, indeed, are not uncommon among adolescents in general. The problem is not homophilic identity in adolescence; the problem is homonegative attitudes in society. Coming to an LGB identity is not intrinsically different from coming to an identity as, say, an athlete or a scholar. The difference is entirely in the response of the culture to the identity in question. Were this not a heterosexist and homonegative society, LGB teens would face all of the same but no other struggles as adolescents who come to an identity as heterosexual.

Faced with circumstances that leave them potentially outcast and with profound feelings of self-denigration, adolescents may respond in a variety of ways. Many strategies employed by LGB teens parallel stigma management techniques discussed previously (see chapter 4). Some, however, bear particular relevance for adolescents because of their long-term implications. Emerging as they do during the process of identity achievement, these strategies may predispose the individual to patterns of functioning that subsequently shape life experiences in marked ways.

Denial is one understandable defense, a response to the invisibility of positive models and the devaluation of LGB identity expressed by common stereotypes. If these stereotypic images don't mesh with their own sense of themselves, LGB adolescents may be at a loss to understand their feelings. They may reject the possibility of LGB identity because it is so clear that the stereotypes do not describe them. This denial, in turn, may foreclose movement toward an affirmative homophilic identity.

Alternatively, in the absence of accurate information, some teens may conclude that they must live up to stereotypic images (Herdt, 1989b; Hetrick & Martin, 1987). This reaction can lead to the exaggeration of stereotypic—usually cross-gender—behaviors, a tactic that Troiden (1989) referred to as minstrelization. Such behavior is likely to earn disdain from peers, interfering with the peer group acceptance so necessary to optimal adolescent development. In either case, attempts to form an identity grounded in cultural images of homophilia interferes with adolescents' managing the dual task of adolescent identity achievement and coming to terms with homophilic feelings.

Passing, the most common strategy for adolescents (as for adults) may also have long-term implications for adolescent LGBs. Martin (1982) discusses adolescents' "learning to hide" and how the tendency toward secrecy and evasion may distort the process of identity formation. The constant possibility of exposure and the continual need to monitor their actions to disguise homophilic feelings force LGB teens to develop skills at managing social interactions through a veil of fear and deceit. This approach to interpersonal relationships leaves youth insecure in their relationships with others, ever fearful that if others truly knew them, rejection would follow. This pattern may become unconscious and pervasive, so that it may become impossible to conduct relationships that are honest and disclosive (Hetrick & Martin, 1987).

Similarly, the continual denial of homophilic feelings may lead some teens to deny feelings in general. This pattern, too, is reinforced by the fear that others will discover too much if they are allowed to know the person well. Adolescents who pursues this course toward self-protection may learn to discount their own inner life, closing themselves off from all emotions.

Yet another defense against unacceptable homophilic feelings takes the form of reaction formation. Teens who feel thoroughly unacceptable because of homophilic feelings might strive to overcome both their own and also others' judgments by becoming "the best little boy/girl in the world."[6] By over-achieving, being unusually competent, making admirable contributions to the community, being the kindest and most thoughtful possible son or daughter,

---

6. This phrase appears in the title of Reid's (1976) autobiographical, *The Best Little Boy in the World*, which depicts this dynamic, right down to the disclaimer in the front.

the best friend, and so forth, teens try to prove that this kernel of "evil" pales before their goodness. The hope is that being good enough will somehow erase homophilic feelings, or that exceptional goodness will outweigh the wrongness of those feelings. In both cases, such behavior reflects an attempt to eradicate the pain of being personally condemned for feelings deemed wrong by society.

Risks of Teen LGB Identity

Navigating the demands of adolescent identity formation while simultaneously striving to come to terms with homophilic identity in a heterosexist culture, LGB teens face genuine risks to their well-being.

External Risks

One of the greatest risks lies in teens' own families. Adolescents who success-fully hide their identity from their families live with the constant fear of discovery and its potential consequences. For teens whose families know, either because the adolescent comes out or because their identity is discovered, the risks range from anger and rejection to physical assault. In some cases, the reac-tion is extreme: about half of adolescent LGBs who are targeted for violence because of their sexual orientation experience that violence at the hands of their own families. Many youths are evicted from their homes—this is especially common for boys; girls are more likely to be verbally and physically abused. Both boys and girls may run away to escape abuse (Hetrick & Martin, 1987; Martin & Hetrick, 1988; Remafedi, 1987a; Savin-Williams, 1994).

Many LGB teens also worry about verbal harassment and the loss of friend-ships, should their identity be known. These fears are well-founded. Research indicates that over half of LGB teens have been victims of verbal abuse by their peers, nearly half have lost a friend due to their sexual orientation, and nearly all feel separated and emotionally isolated from their peer group. It appears that friendships are especially at risk for teens who are gender deviant, a finding very much in keeping with research on adult attitudes toward homophilia. Not surprisingly, the loss of friends is correlated with increased suicide risk, pointing to the crucial role of friendships and peer acceptance in adolescence (D'Augelli & Hershberger, 1993; Gibson, 1989; Remafedi, 1987b; Savin-Williams, 1995).

LGB adolescents also express concerns about the impact of their identity on job prospects. They are afraid to apply for a job for fear that their identity will somehow be exposed. If they succeed in getting a job, they fear that they will lose it if their identity is discovered. Again, these are realistic fears. Nearly a third of LGB teens report having experienced discrimination in education or employment (D'Augelli & Hershberger, 1993; Remafedi, 1987b).

Adolescents who identify as LGB fear that they will meet with violence as a result of their sexual orientation. Once more, their fears are justified. In one sample, about a third of LGB adolescents reported having experienced violence specifically because of their sexual orientation (Remafedi, 1987b). Of minority youth seeking services at a community program for LGB youth, half had been ridiculed and over half had experienced violent physical attacks (Savin-Williams, 1994). Retrospective studies with LGB adults reveal even higher rates of victimization during adolescence (Hershberger & D'Augelli, 1995). Among LGB college youth, over half report physical or verbal abuse from peers (D'Augelli, 1993). Assaults on adult LGBs (see chapter 2) serve to reinforce these fears and increase teen LGBs' sense of vulnerability.

LGB youth also face health risks related to their sexual orientation. Teens in general are often irresponsible about sexual decision making, in part because of the sense of invulnerability that accompanies adolescent psychological development. Thus, adolescents may engage in unprotected sex without any realistic consideration of its possible consequences. Lesbian teens may participate in heterosexual intercourse either to prove to others their heterosexuality or in hopes that sexual acting out will put an end to their lesbian feelings. As a result, lesbian teens may comprise a disproportionate percentage of pregnant girls (Hetrick & Martin, 1987; Schneider, 1989).

Gay male teens are at special risk for HIV/AIDS. Their sense of invulnerability may lead them to engage in unsafe sexual activity, to assume that they are not at risk. And since stereotypes that portray gay males as effeminate may persuade gay teens to "prove" their masculinity by acting out sexually, more sex may be equated with greater masculinity. Further, many run-away (or throw-away) teens—a group that includes a large proportion of gay, lesbian, of bisexual kids—survive through prostitution, and many are heavily involved in drug use; both behaviors put them at increased risk for HIV/AIDS. Because the latency between infection with HIV and the appearance of actual symptoms is typically two to ten years, it is unlikely that anyone in the teen's peer group is ill with AIDS; hence, the threat of contracting the virus seems remote or nonexistent. All of these concerns are exacerbated by the need to keep one's identity secret, which may preclude gay teens from receiving adequate health care or seeking out important information (Durby, 1994; Feldman, 1989; Pederson, 1994; Savin-Williams, 1994).

Psychological Risks

Adolescence is a stressful period for many teens; for LGB adolescents, the stress is multiplied by the necessity for dealing with an identity that violates fundamental social norms and for which there is no prior preparation and no current support. Coping in near isolation with this difficult undertaking exacts huge costs from some LGB teens. Because of methodological problems discussed previously, it is impossible to come to precise figures about the psychological impact of this situation, but there are several studies that provide glimpses of the prevalence of psychological problems among LGB youth.

Mental Health and Behavior Problems

Research suggests that teen LGBs have high rates of mental health problems, conflicts with the law, substance abuse, and poor school performance (Gibson, 1989; Hershberger & D'Augelli, 1995; Remafedi, 1987b; Savin-Williams, 1994). Many school-related problems—including truancy, dropping out, and low grades—may often be directly related to verbal and physical abuse from peers, which make school an unpleasant and even dangerous place. Unfortunately, most schools have done little to meet the special needs of LGB youth, or to offer them affirmative models.

LGB teens who come into conflict with the law often engage in illegal activities for the same reasons straight teens do. But other motives may be specific to the conflicts faced by LGB teens: substance abuse or sexual acting out may be a defense against homophilic feelings; running away and destructive behavior may express hostility toward society and toward the family for the rejection these teens encounter. Mental health problems are often directly related to the stresses of LGB identity: isolation, anxiety, depression, and internalized homophobia. To approach the issue from another direction, the single best predictor of mental health among LGB teens is self-acceptance (Hershberger & D'Augelli, 1995); correlatively, poor mental health is related to low self-acceptance, a direct response to societal condemnation of LGB identity:

> There was a total rejection of the idea of being a lesbian. Just a total and utter rejection of it. There was absolutely no way that I wanted to feel different and I felt very different from everyone and I didn't want that. So I didn't feel normal unless I had alcohol and drugs in me. (Schneider, 1989, p. 122)

Depression and Suicide

Research on depression and suicide indicates that LGB teens may be at particularly high risk; however, this work must be viewed with caution (Durby, 1994). The adolescents studied are not a random sample of LGB teens, but are teens who are involved in programs designed for LGB adolescents. These adolescents may be very different from those who do not seek out such support, and who may be adapting well—though invisibly—to the stresses of LGB identity. Since an individual's sexual orientation is usually not known, it is impossible to identify with any certainty the sexual orientation of most adolescents who attempt suicide.

This research is telling, however, in its demonstration of the distress of at least a subset of LGB teens. Among these selective samples, rates of depression and suicidal thoughts among LGB teens are high, with over half expressing severe anxiety or depression and over a third entertaining suicidal thoughts (D'Augelli & Hershberger, 1995). Suicide attempts are common, as well; various studies have reported rates of suicide attempts by LGB teens ranging from 20 percent to 40 percent (D'Augelli & Hershberger, 1993; Durby, 1994; Hetrick & Martin, 1987; National Gay and Lesbian Health Foundation, 1987; Savin-Williams, 1994). Remafedi and his colleagues found that almost half of the adolescents in their sample who had attempted suicide had done so more than once (Remafedi, Farrow, & Deisher, 1991). A report commissioned by the Department of Health and Human Services indicated that LGB teens are two to three times as likely to attempt suicide as are heterosexually-identified adolescents (Gibson, 1989).

These numbers are especially troubling given research indicating a very high rate of lethality in LGB suicide attempts—that is, these attempts tend to have a high probability of success and a low probability of lifesaving intervention (Kourany, 1987; Remafedi, Farrow, & Deisher, 1991). Indeed, based on a very limited sample, Gibson (1989) estimated that perhaps 30 percent of completed suicides among adolescents are LGB teens. If this estimate is correct, suicide may be the number one cause of death among LGB teens.

Not all LGB teens are at risk for depression and suicide; homophilia itself is not a cause of either (Rofes, 1982). The stresses of LGB identity formation may exacerbate the difficulties of adolescence, but other factors clearly play a role, as well. The risk of suicide is related to a number of variables that place any adolescent at greater psychological risk: low self-esteem, family problems, conflict with peers, other emotional problems, and so forth.

Among those LGB teens who do attempt suicide, such attempts are often related to those events that make LGB identity painful. Early coming out, gender-atypical behavior (especially for boys), and family problems are all correlated with higher rates of attempted suicide. Over 40 percent attribute their suicide attempt to family problems, one-third to turmoil over their self-identification as LGB (Remafedi, Farrow, & Deisher, 1991). Other precipitators often cited include depression, conflicts with peers, problems in romantic relationships, substance abuse, and anti-LGB violence. In this litany we can see many developmental issues common to all adolescents, but for LGB teens, the source of these problems is often specific to their homophilic identity and the support systems that might usher them through the difficulty are unavailable because of their sexual orientation.

It appears that all of these risks are greater for minority LGB teens. The combined effects of racism and homonegativity are involved here, as ethnic minority teens are more likely to be targets of harassment from peers and

154   adults. In addition, the complexity of dealing with both minority and LGB identity undoubtedly places greater stress on these individuals, a phenomenon reflected in higher rates of suicidal thoughts and suicide attempts among some minority groups (Gibson, 1989; Savin-Williams, 1994).

As noted above, we cannot be certain what the actual rates of suicide are among LGB youth. However, these data are indicative of a serious problem, and attempts to decrease the stressors that LGB adolescents must face certainly seems a worthwhile goal. More important than the question of how many LGB teens attempt suicide is the issue of heterosexism and its painful impact on teens whose striving to come to a positive sense of self can only be made more difficult by homonegative beliefs.

Relationship Formation
Finally, the ability to form meaningful relationships may be compromised by the nature of LGB teens' social opportunities. In the absence of sanctioned occasions for dating and socialization with other LGB teens, romantic attachments are usually pursued furtively and with the constant fear of exposure. Most high-school-age LGBs do have at least one romantic relationship, but these tend to be short-lived and stormy—no doubt at least in part because of their clandestine and forbidden nature. College-age LGBs appear to form more lasting relationships, although typically still covert and often turbulent (Savin-Williams, 1995).

Without occasions for safe and open exploration of relationships, and lacking models of healthy same-sex relationships, adolescent teens—especially boys—may have difficulty merging their need for emotional intimacy with their same-sex sexual desires. With no template to guide them, teens may believe that same-sex sex is independent of emotional attachment. This perception, in turn, allows for the pursuit of casual and emotionally shallow sexual liaisons that keep the adolescent from developing more substantive relationship skills (Remafedi, 1987b; Savin-Williams, 1995).

The emotional and social cost of this deficit of opportunity is difficult to assess. However, the sense of isolation and the missed opportunities for practicing social skills might well take a toll on the adolescent's self-esteem and thereby contribute to the elevated rates of mental health problems among LGB teens.

To Come Out or Not To Come Out

Teens who remain closeted must deal constantly with the risk of exposure, relationships that are based on deception, and a sense of isolation and difference. Those who are out, on the other hand, risk harassment, rejection, even violence. Given the potential negative consequences of disclosure, some have urged that teens should not come out. Indeed, it might be safer for adolescents

to suppress any movement toward LGB identity during adolescence (Malyon,
1981). Others, however, argue that coming out is the healthiest step lesbian,
gay, or bisexual teens can take. Savin-Williams and Rodriguez (1993), for
instance, point to research demonstrating a positive correlation between
disclosure and psychological adjustment, suggesting that nondisclosure may
actually be detrimental to adolescents' identity formation (cf. D'Augelli &
Hershberger, 1993; Garnets & Kimmel, 1993; Hershberger & D'Augelli,
1995). Recognizing the very real risks of visibility, these authors also suggest
that selective disclosure (rational outness) is the wisest strategy. From this
position, teens are able to acknowledge their homophilic identity to themselves
and thereby combat internalized homophobia and move toward integrating
that identity into their adult sense of self. Simultaneously, they can receive a
degree of validation and support from genuinely acceptant others, thereby
creating opportunities for the social interaction and external validation necessary for optimal identity seeking.

Promise and Potential

Recall once again D'Augelli's (1994) affirmation assumption. Given the
multiple, extreme stresses faced by LGB teens, the wonder is that most
traverse adolescence and move into adulthood essentially well-adjusted. Savin-
Williams (1990, 1995) makes a similar point. He argues that the negative view
of LGB youth so prevalent in the literature is a result of overrepresentation of
troubled youth in research samples. Extolling the "promise" and the
"resiliency" of LGB adolescents, Savin-Williams refers to the growing body of
research indicating that most LGB teens have high self-esteem and are coping
well with the challenges of their lives. He argues that the absence of high rates
of psychopathology among adult LGBs demonstrates that developmental tasks,
including those of adolescence, have been handled well. This is not to say that
the tasks of adolescence are not made more difficult by the need to cope with
homonegativity. It is simply to say that most LGB adolescents are resilient,
meet the test, and emerge intact and perhaps all the stronger for having
managed the challenges (cf. Boxer & Cohler, 1989; D'Augelli & Hershberger,
1993; Jackson & Sullivan, 1994).

In addition to these psychological strengths, future LGB adolescents will be
helped toward adulthood by support systems now emerging in LGB and
professional communities.[7] Coming out is increasingly "coming in" for LGB
teens, and this must surely make the transition to adult LGB identity smoother.

---

7. For representative discussions of the need for services for LGB youth, see D'Augelli, 1993;
    D'Augelli & Garnets, 1995; DeCrescenzo, 1994; Durby, 1994; Gibson, 1989; Hetrick &
    Martin, 1987; Herdt, 1989a; Jackson & Sullivan, 1994; Martin, 1982; Martin & Hetrick,
    1988; Unks, 1995.

Midlife and the LGB Experience

The substantial literature on LGB adolescence stands in stark contrast to the comparative dearth of scholarship regarding midlife lesbians, gay men, and bisexual people. Although several studies have explored in some depth the experience of midlife lesbians, no comparable research has portrayed that of gay men. In this already limited research, samples are selective and small in size, and no longitudinal data are available to answer the crucial questions of how midlife progresses (Kimmel & Sang, 1995). Accordingly, our view of midlife LGB experience is an aggregate of limited data, anecdotal evidence, and reasonable but unsubstantiated inferences drawn from examinations of LGBs' place in the culture.

Beneath any tentative conclusions we might draw, one thing is abundantly clear: Nowhere is the cohort effect more apparent or more important than in the range of experience of now-midlife LGBs. Those who came of age in the 1950s and early '60s have clearly had very different experiences than those who came of age in the '70s or early '80s. Thus, anything we say about midlife LGBs today will undoubtedly prove inadequate to our understanding of the next generation, which will have lived through a strikingly different era of LGB experience (Kimmel & Sang, 1995). All of these cohorts face midlife developmental tasks that affect everyone, regardless of our position in history. We will consider both of these forces—historical and developmental—and how they shape the experience of currently midlife LGBs.

Cohort Effects

Midlife LGBs who are presently in their fifties or early sixties came of age thirty or more years ago. This means that they are likely to have had their first lessons in the meaning of being homosexual at a time when homophilia was considered sinful, criminal, and perverted—in an era of intense repression and in the total absence of community. Many of these people have never come out to anyone except a limited circle of close friends, and are likely to lead relatively closeted lives and to be quite fearful of the consequences of being open about their identity. Such reticence is a product of historical context, of the incredible risks posed by LGB identity in their era.

Those currently in their forties came of age in the late 1960s and early '70s. Their early lessons about homophilia were largely negative—recall that Stonewall happened in 1969 and that psychology considered homosexuality a mental illness until 1973. However, the homophile movement had begun after World War II, and the social movement toward "gay pride" and "gay rights" began as this cohort entered adulthood. Thus, while homonegative attitudes certainly lingered, these individuals had access to far greater support for a positive LGB identity than had their predecessors. Accordingly, LGB individuals in this group are likely to have come out to a broader group of friends, to have formed friendship networks among themselves, to participate in LGB community events and perhaps in political activism. While they are still likely to be less open as a group than younger cohorts, neither are they as isolated as their predecessors.

Those who are now in their thirties (now young adults but soon to become the next cohort to enter midlife) came of age in the 1970s and early '80s, and came out into a rapidly developing and visible community. Lingering cultural heterosexism insured that they learned negative attitudes toward homophilia, but, among LGBs, being out was taken as an expression both of self-acceptance and of LGB pride. Extensive support systems, institutions, organizations, and public activism undergirded a vocal and enthusiastic movement toward gay rights.

Other events have had profound effects on these people's experience, as well. In the 1970s, the burgeoning feminist movement began to reshape the culture's understandings of gender and of relationships, and lesbian feminism emerged as a potent political and philosophical challenge to traditional understandings of both gender and sexual orientation. Beginning in the early 1980s, the HIV/AIDS epidemic and an increasingly powerful conservative political trend threatened to return LGB issues to an earlier, far more repressive era. The expectation that one be as out as possible, the presence of community, and the ideological support of feminism were countered by increased danger and growing homonegativism. This combination of forces means that the cohort of LGBs in their thirties is more likely to be out and to be involved in the community, while at the same time facing increasing risks because of political trends and decreased freedom of expression (particularly for gay men) because of HIV/AIDS.

This last cohort tends to be more out, more vocal, more active than their predecessors. They point to this openness as the key to progress in LGB rights, urging that only when the world knows LGBs as complete human beings and recognizes their right to satisfying lives will we transcend the homonegativism of previous generations. Their predecessors, on the other hand, point to current anti-LGB social trends as validating their own positions of relative secrecy. Such openness, they argue, is extremely risky for those who are out, who may find themselves in serious danger if conservative movements are successful in reestablishing the repressive policies of fifty years ago. They argue that this openness is dangerous to others, as well. The attention called to LGB identity, the "flagrant" behavior of certain activists, the demand for equal rights rather than simply for tolerance—all threaten the hard-earned gains of recent decades.

This is an important contrast. Each group's position is shaped by its distinctive history; each confronts current events from a perspective forged by earlier experiences. This is an excellent illustration of the meaning of the cohort effect.

But there is more. Each group is in a *developmentally* different position, as well; it is these developmental changes that define the period known as midlife. Let us consider some of the characteristics of midlife that have particular salience for LGBs.

Developmental Issues

Most research on midlife development has neglected the experiences of LGBs; in general, it addresses the lives of heterosexuals, primarily men, with a focus on the (heterosexual) nuclear family and its place in midlife transitions. However, a small body of scholarship is emerging that depicts the distinctive characteristics of LGB midlife.

To invoke what has now become a common theme, it is important to point out that there is no "typical" midlife lesbian, gay man, or bisexual woman or man. Rather, each individual's experience is deeply colored by her or his own personal experiences, by the sociocultural milieu, and by the historical context of his or her life. Indeed, Kimmel and Sang (1995) suggest that studies of LGB midlife reveal more flexible patterns of development than is true among heterosexuals. Because the cultural scripts for midlife development do not apply to their experience, LGB individuals are more free to follow developmental paths that are distinctive and fluid.

For some people, the first encounter with LGB experience or identity comes at midlife. This is particularly true for women, for whom, as we have discussed, sexual orientation appears to be more flexible. However, some men also come to a gay identity at midlife, having identified as heterosexual previously. Such a shift may be facilitated by the completion of one's former role and the freedom that allows. For women, especially, the end of child rearing may afford the opportunity finally to focus on the fulfillment of one's personal needs. For others, such a shift may be facilitated by developmental changes common to midlife, such as the lessened need to prove oneself in traditional ways, and a more central desire to define one's own goals and lifestyle. The choice to explore new forms of relationships might express a long-held interest, formerly suppressed because it would threaten one's position or one's goals.

For some individuals, this newfound identity is experienced as a discovery, a "coming home" after a lifetime of heterosexual identity (Kimmel & Sang, 1995; Kitzinger & Wilkinson, 1995; Sang, 1993). For others, movement to a homophilic identity may be experienced as a conscious decision. This is the case, for instance, for women who actively choose a lesbian identity as an expression of their feminist politics (Golden, 1987, 199 Ponse, 1978).

Most who identify as LGB at midlife have so self-identified for some time—
many since adolescence. These people, however, do not represent a homogeneous group, either. Many have been married and have children; others have children without having married; most do not have children. Some are in long-term relationships; some have been but are now single; others have been largely single most of their lives; still others are in relatively new relationships. Endless variations are possible. The point is that each such variable influences the experience of midlife for LGBs—as it does for heterosexually identified people. With this in mind, let us address a few key experiences in the lives of some midlife LGBs.

Gender and Balance
Some elements of LGB experience appear to confer a benefit on LGBs at midlife. As we have discussed, heterosexuality is grounded in gender roles that are seen as different and complementary; women and men are expected (and socialized) to assume roles that explicitly exclude qualities granted to the other sex. Many of the developmental tasks usually attributed to midlife have to do with bridging this dichotomy. Thus, men move toward greater investment in family, relinquishing some of the earlier, intense focus on achievement; women are freed from some family demands and move toward greater autonomy and pursuit of personal interests. Involvement in both roles is not new for LGB individuals; as a result they may be in a better position to nurture qualities of both genders and may reach midlife having already achieved a balance that stands as a developmental task for heterosexual people (Kimmel & Sang, 1995; Reid, 1995; Sang, 1993).

In other ways, too, the absence of traditional gender roles allowed by LGB identity may make midlife a more fulfilling period for LGBs and at the same time moderate some of the usual stresses of the period. Because LGBs enjoy the opportunity to engage in a wider range of behaviors without fearing condemnation, many LGBs come to midlife with a rich assortment of skills and interests that can enrich both midlife and aging (Friend, 1991; Kimmel, 1978). Consider the pleasure that might derive from feeling free to enjoy both vigorous sports and needlepoint, both cooking and carpentry.

Finally, lesbians are less likely than are heterosexual women to be preoccupied with advancing age and its implications for physical appearance. Research suggests that men tend to judge potential partners by physical appearance; women, however, do not, so that attractiveness is less an issue for lesbians than for straight women (but more an issue for gay men than for straight men) (Friend, 1987). In the words of one lesbian:

> One, if not *the* greatest blessing about being middle-aged dykes is that while heterosexual women are frantically chasing the rainbow of "lost youth" and

are frightened by their loss of "beauty" and "sex appeal"—we old dykes are daily growing more comfortable and *accepting* of our aging faces and bodies and are therefore able to see beneath the superficial to the beauty of a mellow soul. (Sang, 1993, p. 504)

The Absence (or Presence) of Children

The majority of LGBs who are currently at midlife do not have children. The psychological consequences of this are many. These individuals have experienced neither the joys nor the traumas of raising children, and so their experience does not mesh with that of their heterosexual counterparts (nor of their LGB peers who have raised children). A corollary of this is that they do not see their lives reflected in common cultural portrayals of midlife, which depict heterosexual families with children.

Another impact of growing older without children is that life lacks many of the events that mark major transitions for those with children. A life built around raising children is very much structured by transitions in the children's lives: first word, first step, kindergarten, puberty, graduation, marriage, grandchildren, and so on. These events mark the passage of time, the process of the parents' growing older. Without such mileposts, life may be experienced as more continuous, less demarcated into stages. This phenomenon is reinforced by the absence of parental obligations, which allows one to continue to enjoy throughout adulthood the freedom common to young adults prior to parenthood. Thus, those without children might not think of themselves as growing older, may still have a sense of themselves as young adults even as they pass through midlife (Friend, 1991; Kehoe, 1986b; Kimmel, 1978).

Some LGBs of course, do have children. For those who are presently at midlife, most children come from previous heterosexual marriages. Indeed, most women who first come out at midlife have children (Sang, 1993), most of whom remain with their mothers, and almost all midlife LGB parents are lesbians. For these individuals, raising children has been a complicated process, involving not only the usual difficulties and pleasure of child care, but also the struggle to deal with LGB identity in the context of one's role as mother or father (Sang, 1992). In chapter 7, we will discuss LGB parenting and its impact on children, as well as the impact of children on the lives of LGB parents. For now, it is important to point out the increased stress on the parent of having to come to terms with a stigmatized identity in the midst of life's other challenges, and to cope with the question of how to address that issue with one's children.

Relationships

Relationships among lesbians. The relationship experiences of midlife lesbians are widely varied. Most of those studied are in partnerships, and many of these relationships are of considerable duration (Johnson, 1990; Kimmel & Sang, 1995). However, many midlife lesbians are single, and many who are in relationships nevertheless live alone; overall, lesbians are nearly twice as likely to live alone as are women in the general population (Bradford & Ryan, 1987). In some cases, this may reflect fear of revealing one's lesbianism by living openly with another woman. Also, some single midlife lesbians only want an intimate relationship if it "fits" without unduly disrupting the balance already achieved among life's elements. Many no longer expect to find the one, perfect relationship, and some are interested in alternative forms of living arrangements, such as lesbian communities, which may or may not involve sexual intimacy (Kimmel & Sang, 1995; Raphael & Robinson, 1984). Across these variations in relationship styles, a dominant theme for midlife lesbians appears to be the struggle to find a balance among important aspects of their lives: work, intimate relationships, and friendships (Kimmel & Sang, 1995; Sang, 1993).

Friendships are extremely important to midlife lesbians, who derive the majority of their support from extended "chosen families," which often include former lovers. For a variety of reasons (including cohort effects and a sense that the community is not attuned to their needs), women in this age group are often not connected with broader LGB communities, so that such friendship networks may provide the major source of social interaction (Sang, 1992).

Gay male relationships. Little research has explored the nature of gay male relationships at midlife. However, early research found that gay men place greater emphasis on intimate relationships than do heterosexual men of the same age, a finding that might point to the gender balance discussed above—gay men can focus more on the relationship and less on achievement than their heterosexual counterparts without fear of violating prescribed gender norms. Friendship networks are also of central importance to gay men, as they turn for support more to friends than to biological family (Kimmel & Sang, 1995).

A major issue in any consideration of relationships among gay men is the impact of AIDS. Most gay men now at midlife, living in the height of the epidemic, have experienced multiple losses as lovers and friends have died from complications of AIDS. At any point in time, many others are likely to be in various stages of the disease. The consequences of the epidemic for gay men's relationships are bound to be lasting and profound. We will return to this issue when we consider LGB relationships (chapter 7) and LGB communities (chapter 8).

Sexuality
Most gay men and lesbians remain sexually active during midlife, and many report that their sex lives are more satisfying than ever before (Pope & Schulz, 1991; Raphael & Robinson, 1984; Sang, 1993). For women, the physical changes of menopause do not appear to detract from sexual experiences;

rather, because the focus for women tends to be more on the relationship than on sexuality per se, changes in sexual functioning are not seen as crucial (Cole & Rothblum, 1991). For gay men, physiological changes of midlife may lessen the focus on orgasm, allowing for greater attention to generalized sexual pleasure that may actually enhance midlife sexuality (Kimmel & Sang, 1995).

In contrast, gay men must deal with the fear of losing their attractiveness— and thereby, their competitive edge in the search for relationships. This fear is reflected in gay men's sense of "accelerated aging," that is, the sense that the loss of youthful attractiveness will diminish their appeal in the gay community (Bennett & Thompson, 1991; Friend, 1987; Kimmel & Sang, 1995). Finally, it is clear that HIV/AIDS is bound to have an impact on the sexual behavior and experience of midlife gay and bisexual men; although unfortunately no research has yet documented the nature of these effects as they relate specifically to this group (Kimmel & Sang, 1995).

Employment Issues
For those midlife lesbians who came out in adolescence or early adulthood, work has always been a central focus of their lives; indeed, it appears that lesbians without children who have never married are comparable to men in their commitment to work. This is not surprising, as they have always known that they would not rely on a husband and would support themselves. However, these women express less dissatisfaction about their work than do men, evaluating their work in terms of its contribution to a sense of balance in their lives. Lesbians who came out at midlife are now self-supporting, and work plays a more significant part in their self-identity than is true for heterosexual women, even if those women are employed (Kimmel & Sang, 1995; Sang, 1993).

Research indicates that gay men at midlife place a great deal of emphasis on work-related achievements, with their sense of self closely tied to economic success. However, this finding may reflect sample bias, as most research has tapped well-educated and affluent populations. Even for these highly achievement-oriented men, the risk of their gay identity's being discovered and experiences with discrimination and harassment often keep them from full achievement in the business world. Many may avoid this discomfort and frustration by opting out of the corporate world and choosing self-employment (Kimmel & Sang, 1995).

Midlife Crises
Although the term "midlife crisis" derives from models of heterosexual development, it represents a meaningful concept for many LGBs. Nearly half of the lesbians interviewed by Sang (1993) said that they were presently in the midst of or had been through such a crisis. Often the crisis revolved around major

changes or losses—illness, the end of a relationship, a new awareness of one's limitations, or a reevaluation of life goals. For most, the crisis was seen as a catalyst or an opportunity to move in new directions.

It is likely that gay men, too, experience crises at midlife, precipitated both by common life events and by distinctive aspects of gay midlife: concerns about family lineage, loss of "sexual prowess," work issues related to gay identity, a search for personal meaning in a heterosexist society. Such crises, however, can be well met by individuals already practiced in crisis management by virtue of a lifetime of dealing with heterosexism (Kimmel, 1978; Kimmel & Sang, 1995).

Common Issues, Differing Contexts

Most of the issues that LGB individuals face at midlife are the same as those faced by heterosexuals. Midlife individuals are concerned about their health, about financial security and retirement, about aging parents. All deal with potential "mid-life crises": the loss of relationships, the demise of youthful dreams. For all, these crises may lead them to reevaluate their lives and embark on new directions. All strive to find a balance among the pieces of their lives— family, work, friends, interests.

The stresses of midlife are mediated for heterosexual individuals by a host of social support systems, but LGBs do not have such supports available and they confront instead homonegative attitudes and discriminatory practices. In the face of such homonegativity, midlife LGBs must struggle with managing stigma as well as the tasks of midlife. Particularly for those who are relatively closeted, the need to hide their identity may isolate them from those resources that are available and may complicate their managing life transitions where LGB identity is salient.

Here is one place where social change may transform individual experience. As the LGB community becomes more visible and more effective in initiating social programs that are responsive to the needs of LGB individuals, perhaps this situation will improve. Perhaps by the time today's youth are in midlife, they will find sufficient support so that the costs of being lesbian, gay, or bisexual will be minimized and the strengths of LGB midlife can be turned toward positive ends.

Joys of LGB Midlife

Despite these stresses, LGB midlife has its beauties. As far as we can tell from the existing research, most midlife LGBs find their lives satisfying and productive; indeed, many are more satisfied with themselves than at any time in their lives. They are less concerned about others' opinions, feel able to stand up for their beliefs, are open to new experiences, are able to let go of painful past experiences, and at the same time relish reconnecting with former friends and reengaging old interests.

A smattering of quotations from Sang's (1993) lesbian sample suggests the rich flavor of LGB midlife: "I quite like it; each year seems to get better despite some of the seemingly endless struggles. Generally, I feel better about myself and my life than I ever have ... more focused yet more diverse in my interests and activities" (p. 505); "I passed a serious crisis at forty to forty two—had to let go of all hopes and dreams and finally accept myself as an average person regarding set values and goals" (p. 507); "I seem to have less bravado and more feeling of real stature and accomplishment" (p. 505); "My philosophy revolves around the concept of *balance* between inner and outer forces, work and play, and so forth. It also includes a notion of integrating aspects of self previously compartmentalized. I think positive action comes from integration and balance for myself" (p. 511); "I have no idea of what will unfold for me but I have an abiding trust based on my experience so far that my life will always delight me and bring me richness of all sorts" (p. 515).

Aging and LGB Experience

Nowhere is the problem of gathering a representative sample more obvious than with now-old[8] LGBs. A profound cohort effect makes LGBs over the age of sixty even more difficult to reach than their younger counterparts. These people came of age in an extremely repressive era when homophilia was regarded in the most negative terms. They grew up knowing only this under-standing of themselves and living with the realistic fear that exposure would be devastating to their lives. Early in their lives, there was no community to provide any sense of shared experience, and they are likely to have grown up feeling alone and isolated, perhaps sinful, mentally ill, almost certainly ashamed of their feelings. These early lessons are not simply set aside with changing social beliefs; they are deeply imbedded in people's sense of them-selves and of their safety in the world, and these people are likely to have lived a life of hiding. Accordingly, now-old LGBs tend to be deeply closeted and therefore difficult to include in research. In addition, this age group is likely to be less open in general—and especially about sexuality—than are later cohorts, further diminishing their willingness to talk about their personal experience. For these reasons, those who are open enough to be identified and to partici-pate in research may be extremely atypical.

---

8. Cruikshank (1991) reports an increasing preference for the straightforward use of the word "old" rather than euphemisms such as elderly, older, senior, and so forth. The argument is that such euphemisms only serve to point up our discomfort with the fact of age, and thereby patronize and diminish the experience of those who are, in fact, old. "Old" is not a negative quality, but rather one of many descriptors that tells us something about people.

We also find the same problems of selectivity we have encountered with other research on LGB experience. Most studies explore the experience of old LGBs who are not only unusually open, but also who are almost entirely white, middle class, and well educated. The role of gender remains almost totally unexplored, and the literature includes no systematic information regarding the distinctive experiences of various ethnic groups (Reid, 1995).

"Old" is itself a term that disguises considerable diversity. Old age encompasses a period of perhaps four decades—the sixties through the nineties—and is sometimes divided into "young old," "old old," and "oldest old" (Reid, 1995). The experiences of people at various ages in this period are clearly different, both because of developmental changes and because of cohort effects. However, the literature usually does not make such distinctions by age, so we are unable to differentiate responses from these various groups. Finally, old LGBs show tremendous individual diversity; in fact, with increasing age, individual variation actually increases (D'Augelli, 1994; Reid, 1995). For all these reasons, we cannot begin to draw generalizations about old LGBs from the research that is currently available. Still, the experiences of these limited samples can provide some glimpse into the process of growing older as a lesbian, gay man, or bisexual person—even if only as experienced by a segment of that population.

Mental Health and Marginality

The stereotype of the lonely, aging gay man or lesbian is not supported by research. On the contrary, the literature indicates that there are no differences between old LGBs and their heterosexual counterparts in psychological adjustment. Rather, research depicts both groups as psychologically well adjusted, generally self-accepting, and adapting well to aging (Adelman, 1991; Berger, 1980; Friend, 1991; Reid, 1995).

On the other hand, LGB identity does complicate the process of aging. In this youth-oriented society, old age bears a stigma and is a source of discrimination and oppression. For aging LGBs, homophilic identity makes for double stigmatization and oppression. For old lesbians, the stigma and discrimination are triple, as they must deal with sexism as well (Kehoe, 1986a). It is apparent that this circumstance is similar in many respects to that faced by (other) minorities. Old LGBs are marginalized, fully accepted neither in the community of the old (whose homonegative attitudes were formed in their own early years) nor by the LGB community (whose members hold ageist attitudes).

Two issues point to the ageism of the LGB community. First is the work on accelerated aging, discussed previously, which points to the youth-oriented nature of the community—at least for gay men. Second, the extreme differences between the historical experiences of now-old and now-young LGBs create a division between the generations. Many young LGBs reject their elders as assimilationist, closeted, and apolitical; old LGBs see the actions of young LGBs as inappropriate and dangerous. Martin and Lyon quote a lesbian couple who wrote:

> We are looking for companions, friendship, and support, but in the lesbian organizations we've contacted we find only badge-wearing, drum-beating, foot-stomping social reformers. They consider our conservative life "oppressed," and we think of their way of life as "flagrant." (1992, p. 106)

The role of mentor previously available to old LGBs, who introduced young LGBs into the community, has been dissolved as the community has become more visible and accessible. Accordingly, older LGBs are without a role in the evolving community, and are actively rejected by many of its members (Friend, 1991; Grube, 1991; Lee, 1988).

Some argue that this generation gap is not as great for women as for men. First of all, physical appearance is not as important to women, so that the loss of youthful attractiveness does not result in the devaluation of older lesbians. And second, the feminist movement provides a link across generations (Cruikshank, 1991; Lee, 1988; Adelman, 1986). Others, however, argue that ageism persists, even among feminists (Copper, 1988; MacDonald & Rich, 1991), so that old lesbians are surely not free of its impact.

This marginality and the dual (or triple, for old lesbians) oppression it reflects creates special problems for old LGBs. At the same time, it may stimulate the development of unique coping mechanisms.

Special Problems

Old LGBs face many of the same life changes as do heterosexuals during this life period, but they do not have the same resources and social support systems for dealing with them. Overt discrimination, heterosexist institutions, neglect by social service agencies, policies insensitive to LGB experience, and the persistent fear of disclosure combine to preclude old LGBs from finding adequate resources to deal most effectively with the demands of aging.

True, such exclusion from common support systems is a phenomenon shared by LGBs at all ages; however, it is particularly salient here because old LGBs are likely to be so deeply closeted. Many now-old LGBs have told almost no one about their sexual orientation; for some, the topic has never been discussed even with close friends. Added to that, many are estranged from their families because of their LGB identity, and years of hiding make it difficult to seek out new connections (Kehoe, 1991). Finally, because they have been so closeted, they have no connection to the LGB community, which might otherwise moderate some of this isolation. Under these circumstances, difficult life events take on added poignancy. It is impossible to grieve, to share feelings, to seek assistance or support—for to do so would risk revealing one's identity.

Health Care

Ordinary health care issues that accompany aging raise problems directly related to heterosexist attitudes (Friend, 1987; Kimmel, 1978). An LGB individual may be kept from visiting or caring for a sick partner, participating in medical decisions, getting information from doctors, accompanying the ill partner to examinations and treatments, and so forth. Such exclusion may occur even if the nature of the relationship is known, thereby reflecting the persistent homonegativity of the health care system. Such exclusionary treatment is effectively assured if the nature of the relationship is not known; if medical personnel believe the partner to be just a "friend" or "roommate," they are almost certain to exclude her or him from much of the health care process.

In more subtle ways, too, ideal health care is compromised by negative attitudes toward homophilia. Staff may be rude or inattentive so that patients receive less adequate care and are less likely to request the care they need. Fearful of expressing affection or neediness toward their partners, LGBs may feel—and in fact, be—isolated from their major course of support and well-being. Fear of exposure may prevent them from seeking or accepting needed services, such as home care, where they fear exposure of their identity.

Maintaining secrecy about one's sexual orientation might put one at increased health risk, as it might interfere with the LGB individual's obtaining adequate health care information. Also, closeted LGBs might be afraid to report health problems related to their sexual orientation, and thus receive inadequate attention to their health care needs (Reid, 1995).

Many aging LGBs fear that they will be separated from loved ones in hospital or nursing home care. While cohabitation and extensive visiting privileges are now routine for heterosexual couples in extended care, homonegative attitudes prevent such opportunities for LGB partners in many facilities. If the nature of the couple's relationship is unknown, there is no hope that such closeness will be possible for them.

While no specific figures are available regarding the incidence of HIV/AIDS among old LGBs, about 10 percent of all people with AIDS are over sixty, suggesting that a number of LGBs are affected (Reid, 1995). Many old gay men may be at greater risk because their secretive lives preclude their taking advantage of educational and other preventative resources. For those who are closeted, an AIDS diagnosis may force disclosure, an event that might be extremely traumatizing to the individual whose identity has been secret for decades and who deeply fears exposure. A diagnosis of HIV/AIDS adds another layer of stigma to an already vilified identity; the consequences for the psychological well-being of old LGBs remains to be investigated.

Bereavement

Perhaps the most difficult transition of aging is dealing with the illness and death of loved ones. Among gay men, this painful experience has become all too frequent, as many have lost lovers and friends to HIV/AIDS. In the case of very closeted LGBs, the loss of a partner or close friend is as painful as for anyone, but it cannot be acknowledged or grieved. In the extreme, there is literally no place to go, as no one knows the nature of the relationship. In less extreme cases, a few close friends might help one to deal with the loss, but it must still be hidden in everyday interactions for fear that the secret will be exposed.

Practical issues arise from the death of a partner, as well. Where the relationship is not acknowledged (either because it is unknown or because it is taken as not "real" by a heterosexist society), no practical support is provided—assistance with funeral arrangements and estate management, for instance. In fact, a surviving partner may not be allowed to participate in decision making around death—final health care, burial or cremation arrangements, memorial services, and so forth. In the absence of a legally sanctioned relationship, the partner is often not recognized as a legitimate heir to the possessions of the deceased—even to those things that belonged to them jointly.

Legal and Financial Issues

A third class of concerns involves legal and financial arrangements (Kimmel, 1978; Reid, 1995). For LGBs attempting to plan for the eventuality of their death, estate planning is hampered by their inability to portray their life honestly. Even for those who are out, estate laws are designed for heterosexual couples and often leave no leeway for uncomplicated distributions to same-sex partners. Often the biological family automatically takes precedence if there is no heterosexual spouse, and family members may contest a will that favors a same-sex partner.

Other inequities may exist, as well. For example, retirement benefits, routinely paid to the surviving spouse of a heterosexual couple, are not available to a surviving LGB partner. This situation is even more difficult for lesbians; because women earn far less than men, women's financial resources are likely to be much more limited than those of men. The inability to receive survivor benefits with the death of a partner means that one's standard of living is likely to decrease drastically.

Consider how disturbing these events must be when confronted in addition to the loss of a partner. At a moment when life is already extremely painful, one cannot participate in the last moments of the life of a loved one, cannot participate in decisions about what will happen to her or his remains, cannot retain shared possessions and financial resources, and is discounted and made invisible by a system designed to deal with heterosexual marriages. This is a poignant illustration of the personal costs of heterosexism.

Special Strengths

As counterpoint to the stereotypic portrayal of aging LGBs as victims of dual stigma, we can once again appeal to D'Augelli's (1994) affirmation assumption, and view LGB aging in terms of the distinctive capacities conferred by a lifetime of coping with stigma. Recent gerontological research centers on the notion of "successful aging," identifying processes that make for optimal development in late life. Reid (1995) applies this perspective to a review of literature on LGB aging, suggesting that coming out marks a major life transition that restructures the life experience of LGB individuals.

The transition to a positive LGB identity requires that the individual adapt to the alienation that LGB identity portends, forging a positive sense of self in the face of heterosexism. Calling upon the notion of "crisis competence" (Friend, 1990; Kimmel, 1978), Reid argues that the process of LGB identity development results in psychological well-being and self-respect, as well as coping skills and interpersonal relationships that provide distinctive resources for successful aging. Indeed, the development of a positive LGB identity "places the individual at a distinct advantage for continuing adaptation to the challenges of aging" (Reid, 1995, p. 221).

Dunker's reflections as an old lesbian depict this process:

> Old lesbians, out or closeted, have had to develop certain skills and character traits in order to survive, as do other oppressed minorities. . . . We've had to develop a degree of stubborn self-confidence and courage. These qualities depend on a clear and pervasive sense of self worth. We have *had* to be autonomous and in charge of our own lives. These skills are even more necessary to minority women . . . [who] have had to deal with the double oppression of race and sex. (1987, p. 76)

In addition to this crisis competence, old LGBs may arrive at old age with other advantages. The gender flexibility discussed previously as an asset at midlife allows LGBs to approach old age with a variety of skills and interests that reaches far beyond those typically developed in the context of traditional roles. Their long-held assumption that they would be self-reliant rather than dependent on their biological family is likely to have prepared them for a life alone, as well as encouraged the development of friendship networks that now sustain them in old age. And for those whose lives have not been demarcated by the rites of passage that characterize traditional family life, old age may have a very different flavor—not an ending but rather a continuation of what one's life has been. This continuity can include a sense of remaining young, including maintaining earlier interests and activities, and extending one's friendship circle to incorporate young people (Adelman, 1991; Kehoe, 1986a; Kimmel, 1978; Reid, 1995).

Styles of Aging

Friend (1991) has outlined a model for LGB aging that is compatible with this affirmative view. Basic to this model is the realization that, in their pasts, now-old LGBs feared arrest, rejection by their families, loss of jobs and housing, perhaps even institutionalization for their "illness." Various responses to this intense homonegativism shape how individuals form and express LGB identity.

Some now-old LGBs were overwhelmed by the stigmatization and oppression first encountered in their youth and internalized these negative attitudes. These people, whom Friend refers to as *stereotypic* old LGBs, live very isolated existences, constantly fearing exposure, often left with intense self-loathing. Because people who responded this way have remained very closeted, they are unlikely to have made contact with other LGBs or with the LGB community, leaving their own negative stereotypes and self-abnegation unchallenged. From this position, they cannot establish the crisis competence that derives from successfully managing stigma and achieving a positive LGB identity.

Another response to homonegative attitudes is reflected in attempts to keep one's identity hidden. Friend refers to those who respond in this manner as *passing* old LGBs, invoking a stigma management technique we have considered in detail previously. Those who pass have largely accepted society's negative evaluation of homophilia, and strive to make themselves as acceptable as possible. Thus, they may disguise their own feelings, even entering into heterosexual marriage to assure legitimacy. Many LGBs who come out at midlife may have married heterosexually in an attempt to pass. Those who live a gay or lesbian life often work to distance themselves from anything that might be construed as LGB-related. Thus, they are not involved in LGB politics or community activities, eschew associations with people who are openly LGB, and in other ways avoid any actions that might imply an association with LGB issues or identity. Anxiety over exposure interferes with their forming meaningful relationships, and results in a life that is often fragmented and compartmentalized. The tenuous quality of their self-acceptance prevents these individuals from overcoming their own internalized homophobia and constructing a truly affirmative LGB identity. This, in turn, prevents them from benefiting from the crisis competence that derives from a successful completion of that process.

The third and most positive response to homonegativity is seen among *affirmative* old LGBs, who have managed to transcend heterosexist beliefs and to construct for themselves positive LGB identities. These are the individuals who manifest crisis competence; they have established high self-esteem and excellent psychological adjustment in spite of the hostile environment and repressive historical times they have endured. For some, this positive sense of LGB identity leads to active involvement in social action and in the LGB community. One old gay man wrote:

> The candle of being an activist was lit and I am very grateful for it. . . . And I hope I will be around to fight for a longer time. I will fight for any minority discrimination, whether it be Black or Jewish, elderly or gay/ lesbian. I will always fight. As long as I live, I hope I have the spirit to fight. (Friend, 1990, p. 253–54)

For others, it becomes the foundation for a quietly contented life. In either case, the life these individuals lead is not possible for those who have been unable to shed society's condemnation of them.

For the most part, research supports Friend's perspective on various styles of aging for LGBs. For example, Adelman (1991) found that, in general, those who have internalized negative attitudes about homophilia (stereotypic LGBs) are characterized in old age by relatively poor psychological adjustment, whereas those who have rejected such judgments and developed a positive sense of LGB identity show good overall adjustment. Positive LGB identity, defined as being "very satisfied with being LGB," is related to high life satisfaction, high self-acceptance, and few psychosomatic symptoms. Responses reflecting that one is less than very satisfied with LGB identity are correlated with the opposite characteristics (Adelman, 1991; Berger, 1982; Morin & Schultz, 1978).

This research clearly indicates that it is not LGB identity per se but how one responds to social stigma that determines adjustment among old LGBs. The words of a sixty-year-old gay man, who describes himself as less than very satisfied with his gay identity, express this point: "I don't feel very (satisfied) because of the disadvantages. Because of the loneliness and intolerance of other people. You cannot just live your life" (Adelman, 1991, pp. 21–22).

An intriguing additional finding is that involvement with the LGB community may not have the same meaning for now-old LGBs as it does for younger individuals. As we have discussed previously, most research with younger LGBs shows that involvement with the LGB community and disclosure of one's homophilia are closely related to self-esteem and life satisfaction. For now-old LGBs, on the other hand, it appears that high life satisfaction is related to low levels of disclosure and to little involvement with the LGB community. Among Adelman's (1991) subjects, psychological adjustment was unrelated to being out, although older LGBs expressed frustration and anger at the necessity of being closeted and at the discrimination they encounter when they are out.

The fact that disclosure is not related to psychological adjustment in older LGBs when it so clearly appears to be in younger LGBs may be a direct result of the extreme homophobia in which now-old LGBs grew up. Given that disclosure was extremely risky, skills at information management were developed as a necessity. Life satisfaction may well have come from success in this endeavor rather than from openly declaring one's sexual orientation.

In keeping with this interpretation, Lee (1987) suggests that successful aging among LGBs does not necessarily reflect a negotiation of the tensions of coming out and growing old. Rather, Lee's longitudinal study of older gay men led him to conclude that "happy homosexual old age may be more a matter of steering clear of storms, rather than weathering them" (p. 57). His work found that successful aging for these men had to do with avoiding stressors, including the stress of coming out. Again, among this cohort, nondisclosure may have been the most adaptive possible stance.[9]

Relationships and Sexuality

Given the selective nature of samples in this research, it is impossible to make generalizations about the relationship patterns of old LGBs. However, the few available findings are of interest. Some research indicates that old men are more likely to live alone than their younger counterparts, and to have sex less frequently. However, they also report that sex is still important to them, and as satisfying as when they were younger. The quality of sexual expression appears to have changed, with greater focus on the total experience rather than on sexual release alone (Kimmel, 1978; Reid, 1995).

Similarly, most older lesbians do not feel lonely; although many live alone, they often prefer this arrangement (Kehoe, 1986b). Most report a lifetime pattern of relationships that might be described as "serial monogamy," although a variety of relationship patterns characterize lesbians' past and present lives (Raphael & Robinson, 1984). Nearly half of the lesbians in Kehoe's study (1986b) had been heterosexually married prior to coming to lesbian identity; they described their relationships with women as more "emotional, caring, sharing, spiritual, gentle, sensitive, understanding, sympathetic,

---

9. This work raises an important question: to what extent might findings of a relationship between satisfaction and affirmative identity reflect sample bias? Perhaps it is only affirmative LGBs who come to the attention of researchers, and many passing or stereotypic LGBs are also content with life but not represented in research samples.

thoughtful, unselfish, desirable, with easier communication and less role-playing" than previous relationships with men (Kehoe, 1986b, p. 145).

Sex is still important and enjoyable for many lesbians, but it has also assumed less centrality in their lives. Some lesbians are celibate, often for quite some time; in many cases, this is a result of absence of a partner. Even single lesbians remain interested in sex and have expectations for future sexual relationships (Raphael & Robinson, 1984). Among Kehoe's subjects who had been previously heterosexually married, sexual relationships with women were described as "less sexually demanding, less hurried, less mechanical, and more affectionate, intimate, and natural with greater reciprocity on all levels" than had been true in their sexual relations with men (Kehoe, 1986b, p. 146).

Friendships

Friendships are extremely important to old gay men and lesbians, especially since many of them are estranged from their biological families (Adelman, 1991; Raphael & Robinson, 1984). It is probably the fear of such estrangement that has kept many old LGBs from revealing their sexual orientation to their families. Those who have disclosed to their families often pay a price; Adelman (1991) found that self-criticism was higher among old LGBs who had disclosed to their families, most of whom had met with rejection. Rejection is not inevitable, however. Friend (1990) reported that although gay men expect to be shunned by their families, many are not; the result is often a broad base of support that includes both friends and biological family.

Although friendships outside one's primary relationship are important to coupled lesbians, single lesbians tend to have more friends than do those who are in a couple—in part because members of lesbian couples tend to be best friends and confidantes, as well as romantic partners. Some lesbians also have close heterosexual friends, but their primary reference group is typically other lesbians. This does not necessarily translate into participation in lesbian organizations, as now-old LGBs tend to be relatively isolated from contemporary homophile political and social activities (Grube, 1991; Kehoe, 1986b). However, a segment of the old lesbian population is involved in lesbian and/or feminist activities. Such involvement brings them in contact with younger lesbians, a connection that bridges the oft-impugned generation gap within LGB communities.

Present and Future Promise

As is true for LGB teens, a burgeoning movement promises an increasingly positive world for future generations of old LGBs. The LGB community is progressively aware of and responsive to the special needs of old people, and programs that respond to these needs are fast becoming a staple of LGB community efforts. A growing scholarly literature addresses the particular experiences of LGBs, and a number of anthologies provide us with telling glimpses into the personal lives of old gay men and lesbians (e.g., Adelman, 1986; Johnson, 1990; Nardi, Sanders, & Marmor, 1994; Vacha, 1985).

Many now-old LGBs are not able to avail themselves of this progress, for their own experience precludes the openness and engagement required to tap into these resources. Although we might bemoan this fact, we must recall that these individuals have managed to find a comfortable and affirming place in a homophobic world. Reid (1995) suggested that successful aging involves selecting those environments and actions that people feel optimize their life experience. For some, that means remaining closeted. Perhaps in the future the community will be more sensitive to the needs of old LGBs, more active in advocacy for those needs, and more welcoming of the individuals who are old and lesbian, gay, or bisexual. Subsequent generations, having grown up in a less hostile environment, will be in a position better to avail themselves of this progress.

In the interim, we all—LGB and straight, old and young—have much to gain from old LGBs, as well. Friend (1990) pointed out that those who have managed so stigmatized an identity with such success can serve as models for others. Affirmative older LGBs provide living examples of crisis competence, of the benefits of gender flexibility, of affirmative challenges to "isms"— heterosexism, ageism, sexism—and of the possibilities for living a fulfilling life even in a hostile world. A sixty-nine-year-old lesbian says:

> For many years, homosexuals, men and women, had to live in a hetero-sexual world and absorb the guilt and the shame and the stereotyping that was foisted upon us.... But after a while ... I began to dispel all that internalization and realize that I was a human being. I was a moral woman and I had raised a wonderful family. My children and my grandchildren loved me and respected me. And there must be a reason for that. Because I'm a respectable and respectful citizen, living my life the best way I could. And I developed a very strong identity of who I was—I'm a lesbian woman and I live like one. I defy anyone to pass judgement on the way I live. (Friend, 1990, p. 254)

PART III

Lesbian/Gay/Bisexual Relationships

CHAPTER SEVEN

LESBIAN/GAY/BISEXUAL FAMILIES
Partners and Children

CONTEMPORARY DISCUSSIONS of family—couched in terms such as "family values" and "disintegration of the family"—refer explicitly and nearly exclusively to the heterosexual family; "family" is defined by heterosexual marriage, reproduction, and parenting. If we rely on the image of family portrayed in everyday discourse, we might assume that LGB individuals do not have families. Of course, this is not the case. LGB individuals come from families, almost always from heterosexual families. LGB people form their own families, which may include partners and/or children. They often reproduce and parent, having natural, adoptive, and foster children, as well as children conceived through alternative insemination or surrogacy. And they create friendship networks that serve as extended families. These networks are often referred to as "families of choice," to distinguish them from biological families, which are often not available to and supportive of LGBs. In this chapter we will explore the first level of LGB families, the intimate relationships among partners and children.

Understanding LGB relationships requires that we suspend well-learned biases about the nature of families, of love, and of parenting—all of which are grounded in heterosexual models. It requires also that we consider the impact of heterosexism on the lives of LGB people and how that persistent stress might affect the formation and the viability of intimate relationships and of family systems that incorporate children. While we will find that, in many ways, LGB relationships and LGB parenting are no different from heterosexual partnerships and parenting, behind such superficial similarities lurks the inescapable reality that LGB individuals must build their families against a background of prejudice and, often, in an atmosphere of secrecy.

177

As has been true for other topics we have addressed, most research on LGB families has used very limited samples, drawn almost entirely from white, middle-class, well-educated groups, who are further distinguished by sufficient openness to allow their participation in research projects. While such research offers a glimpse of some LGB families, it certainly cannot provide an adequate depiction of all LGB families. Given what we know about the profound impact of cultural diversity and cohort, for instance, it is clear that we cannot generalize from these limited samples to the experience of minority or now-old LGBs.

LGB Relationships

As we have discussed previously, one of the potential advantages to LGB identity is the opportunity to transcend traditional roles and the relationship patterns they prescribe. In the abstract, LGBs are free to explore alternative forms of relationships and can modify such arrangements at will. On a more concrete level, in the absence of prescriptive norms applicable to their lives, LGB individuals often adopt the model readily available to them: traditional coupling. Given the wide variation possible between these two very disparate models—normative creativity (Brown, 1989) and traditional partnerships—a broad array of relationship patterns can be found in the LGB community.

That said, most of the research on LGB relationships has focused on those who have formed partnerships reflecting traditional norms. These are individuals who have formed couple relationships, who view and present themselves as a couple, commonly live together, and share their social lives and often their financial resources. Many have formalized their commitment in some manner; indeed, participation in much of the research requires that couples live together, that they have been together for a specified period of time, and often that they meet other criteria that identify them as a "real" couple.

This selectivity is in part a response to the sorts of questions that have been asked. Much of the research has been addressed toward comparisons between same-sex and heterosexual couples; in order to make such comparisons valid, it is reasoned, the couples must be comparable along such dimensions as cohabitation. While such comparisons surely address some crucial questions, they also limit our understanding by dealing with the experience of only a limited segment of the LGB community—in this case, only those whose relationships match in fundamental ways those of heterosexual couples. Ironically, research intended to be LGB-affirming may here act to reinscribe the heterosexist norm for what "real" relationships look like, and thereby distract from the vast potential for creative relationship formation accessible to LGB individuals.

A picture of the typical couple that might be found in this sort of research can be gleaned from a recent nationwide survey of 1,749 individuals, representing 506 gay and 706 lesbian couples (Bryant & Demian, 1994). Because these subjects were recruited through LGB organizations and publications, the sample is limited to those who read and/or participate in openly LGB publications. Additionally, these people actively chose to participate in research about lesbian and gay couples, and this process of self-selection probably excludes both people in nontraditional relationships (that is, those who would not define their relationship pattern as "a couple"), and those who are unwilling to discuss their relationships—as would be likely, for instance, if the relationship were troubled. Further limitations lie in the fact that the subjects were overwhelmingly white (95 percent), well educated (averaging 16.8 years of education), not old (mean age of thirty-five), middle class as defined by income, and urban dwelling. What follows is a description of the relationships described by this particular sample.

About two-thirds of these respondents had had at least one previous major gay or lesbian relationship or had been heterosexually married. More women (27 percent) than men (19 percent) had been heterosexually married; these figures are compatible with Blumenstein and Schwartz's (1983) finding that 22 percent of lesbian and 15 percent of gay male respondents had been married previously. As would be expected, among those in Bryant and Demian's sample who identified as bisexual (7 percent of men, 3 percent of women), previous marriage was more common than it was for those who identified as gay or lesbian. Overall, women had been in more previous major relationships than had men, and their relationships appeared to have been shorter in duration than had the men's.

Men and women differed in how they first met their partners. Lesbians were more likely than gay men to have met through friends; other research indicates that many lesbians meet through feminist or lesbian activities. As in other research, men in the Bryant and Demian sample were more likely to have met in a bar than in any other place, and were far more likely to have met this way than were lesbians. Over a third of men had met through anonymous or public sexually related venues (bars, baths, classified ads, etc.), whereas less than a tenth of women did (see also Berger, 1990; B. Murphy, 1994).

Some research indicates that lesbians and gay men tend to have relatively short "courtships" before taking some action to confirm their relationship. For example, Berger (1990) found that almost a fourth of his sample of gay male couples moved in together within one month of their first meeting; the median time before moving in together was under four months, with a range of less than a week to six years. Mendola (1980) reported that almost half of the couples she studied moved in together within six months of meeting. This rapid move to cohabitation may be an attempt to lend external validation to relationships that enjoy no affirmation from traditional social norms.

Returning to the Bryant and Demian sample, current relationships averaged almost six years in length, with men's current partnerships having lasted significantly longer than women's. More than one hundred couples had been together for more than fifteen years, and four relationships had lasted forty years or longer. Over 90 percent were committed to remaining in this relationship for life or "for a long time."

Many of these couples had made some symbolic commitment to the relationship, with women more likely than men to have exchanged rings or engaged in some form of commitment ceremony. Such ceremonies appear to be growing increasingly common in the LGB community, and recent publications offer ideas and illustrations of their variety (B. Butler, 1990; Ulrig, 1984). While these ceremonies may appear to replicate heterosexual unions and their popularity therefore suggests a concession to heterosexual norms, research has found that most lesbians and gay men studied would not choose to be legally married, even if it were possible. Such reluctance stems, especially for lesbians, from the patriarchal underpinnings of heterosexual marriage, and from the implications of "ownership" that accompany marriage (Berger, 1990; Mendola, 1980; Murphy, 1994).

One practical consequence of the lack of validation of LGB relationships is that there is no clear terminology by which one refers to one's partner. The two terms currently most common are "lover" and "partner" or "life partner," with others (significant other, boyfriend/girlfriend, friend, roommate, spouse, etc.) enjoying far less common usage. For many LGBs, the term "lover" carries purely sexual connotations; on the other hand, partner may be too broad a term (bridge partner, business partner, etc.) to do justice to the deep attachment of love relationships. Among Bryant and Demian's couples, most referred to their partners as "lover" or as "partner or life partner," with men more likely to use the former and women the latter. In his research with gay couples, Berger (1990) also found that a large majority of gay men prefer the term "lover," with a smaller group selecting "partner."

Most of the couples in Bryant and Demian's research lived together at least part-time, with about 90 percent reporting at least some degree of cohabitation during the previous year. Women were slightly more likely to live apart at least part of the time than men. This difference may reflect, in part, complications resulting from child care and/or custody issues, which disproportionately affect women. Respondents had experienced a great deal of discrimination based on their sexual orientation—for example in housing, child custody, application for foster or adoptive care—with 71 percent reporting at least one form of discrimination and 39 percent reporting three or more forms. Women had experienced more discrimination than men, probably due to the added factor of discrimination against women in general. Over three-fourths of these couples shared all or part of their finances; less than 5 percent were covered by any part of their partner's employment benefits.

Few of these couples had children; about 21 percent of female couples and 9 percent of male couples reported caring for children. Although most of these children were from previous heterosexual marriages, 13 percent of lesbians reported taking care of children conceived through alternative insemination. Nearly a third of all respondents under age thirty-five were considering or actively planning to have children (or more children). One in ten women and about 4 percent of men planned to have children in the future.

This, then, is a sketch of lesbian and gay couples who have responded to a request for participation in research. It is reasonable to speculate that the couples described here are quite similar to those participating in the bulk of research dealing with LGB relationships. As we review this research, it is important to keep in mind the limitations of generalizability implied by this depiction; in those few instances where the sample in question is explicitly different from this portrait, that fact will be noted.

We now turn to a consideration of literature that depicts some of the dynamics of selected LGB couples. A useful means of organizing this research is to ask how it relates to stereotypes of LGB relationships (Pepleau, 1991).

Desire for Enduring Relationships

A common belief is that LGBs are uninterested in long-term relationships, preferring instead to engage in short-lived sexual encounters. This image is belied by numerous studies that have explored both the wish for and commitment to enduring intimate partnerships, which consistently demonstrates that lesbians and gay men very much hope for long-term relationships, and are successful in establishing them. Various studies report that between 40 percent and 80 percent of lesbians are in a steady relationship at any given time, with about 75 percent being the modal frequency. Among gay men, between 40 percent and 60 percent are in a committed relationship. These figures probably underestimate the proportions of gay men and lesbians in such relationships, as researchers have less access to those who are not active in the social scene, such as long-term and (especially) older couples (Kurdek, 1995b; Pepleau, 1991).

Research also challenges the notion that LGB relationships are short-lived. Although most research has sampled young adults, who, by definition, cannot have been in a relationship for long, the scant data on older LGBs reveals that relationships of twenty years or more are common (Bryant & Demian, 1994; Pepleau, 1991). In one of the few longitudinal studies on the topic, Blumenstein and Schwartz (1983) followed lesbian, gay, heterosexually married, and heterosexual cohabiting couples over an eighteen-month period. Among all groups, couples who had been together for ten years were rarely separated eighteen months later; 6 percent of lesbian, 4 percent of gay men, and 4 percent of married couples had separated (no cohabiting heterosexual couples had been together for ten years). Of those who had been together for less than ten years, only minor differences in break-up rates were found: 22 percent of lesbians, 16 percent of gay couples, 17 percent of heterosexual cohabiting, and 4 percent of married couples.

These data raise some interesting issues. First, these results show far greater stability in gay and lesbian relationships than myth would have it, although the minor differences between these and heterosexual couples are worth exploring; we will return to this topic. Second, both this research and Bryant and Demian's (1994) survey results, discussed above, suggest that lesbian relationships are less enduring than are gay men's. This finding stands in contrast to the common assumption that lesbians' relationships are more enduring than are gay men's. One possible explanation for this discrepancy is that gay men may indeed have numerous uncommitted relationships, but that once they enter into a couple relationship, they remain. Women, however, may be more likely to form partnerships, but may do so prematurely because of gender socialization that makes relationships paramount in women's identity. Also, these particular samples may not accurately represent relationship patterns across the LGB community. Or, it may be that gay men do indeed form more enduring relationships, but this fact has been missed because of pervasive stereotypes to the contrary.

A final piece to the issue of gay men's and lesbians' apparent commitment to enduring relationships is found in the data on cohabitation. It appears that a substantial percentage of lesbians and gay men do not live with their partners full-time. In fact, Jay and Young (1979) estimated that about half of gay male partners do not live together. Bryant and Demian (1994) found substantially lower percentages than this, but nevertheless reported that about 25 percent of lesbians and about 18 percent of men did not live together full time. This number was considerably higher among those who had been together for less than a year, but about 4 percent of those who had been together for more than ten years still did not live together.

A number of factors might contribute to this phenomenon; some point to the impact of heterosexism on gay and lesbian couples. For instance, partners may live apart as a stigma management technique, to avoid being seen as gay or lesbian; this might occur to protect employment, to prevent custody battles, to avoid families' becoming aware of the nature of the relationship, or simply as a reflection of partners' fears of disclosure. Alternatively, rejection of the "marriage" model, resistance to sharing finances, job demands, desire for a sexually open relationship, or other factors may lead gay men and lesbians who identify as couples to live apart.

The Health of LGB Relationships

Another stereotype about gay and lesbian relationships is that they are pathological, unfulfilling, less loving, and less healthy than heterosexual relationships. This myth probably derives from the stereotype that portrays LGBs —particularly gay men—as preoccupied with sex, and their relationships as purely sexual liaisons rather than broad-based personal commitments. This stereotype, too, has been found erroneous by research measuring relationship satisfaction, attachment, and love in lesbian and gay couples.

For example, Pepleau and her colleagues (Pepleau, 1991; Pepleau & Cochran, 1990) have summarized research comparing same-sex and heterosexual couples. Overall, lesbian and gay couples are as much in love with their partners and as satisfied with their relationships as are heterosexual couples. Furthermore, lesbian and gay couples are indistinguishable from heterosexual couples on measures of couple adjustment. Specifically, lesbian and gay couples express strong feelings of attachment, caring, and intimacy, and score high on measures of "liking," which reflect respect and affection toward their partners. When asked to indicate what are the "best things" and the "worst things" about their relationships, same-sex and heterosexual couples give virtually identical responses—so much so that independent judges were unable to distinguish the responses of homophilic from those of heterosexual couples.

This is not to say that lesbian and gay partnerships are universally healthy, but only that they evidence no less attachment and satisfaction on average than do heterosexual relationships. It is unfortunately true that some lesbian and gay relationships suffer difficulties—sometimes severe—as do some heterosexual ones. For instance, a growing literature addresses violence in same-sex couples (e.g., Island & Letellier, 1991; Lobel, 1986; Renzetti, 1992). As is true in heterosexual relationships, violent interactions may involve verbal, emotional, sexual, or physical abuse. In both cases, women are less likely to use physical aggression than are men.

We might expect that the possibility of alternative relationship scripts and the striving for equality that characterizes gay and lesbian partnerships might minimize such abusive interactions. However, in fact some gay and lesbian individuals have the same dysfunctional coping styles and the same relational deficits as do some heterosexual individuals. Further, certain aspects of the LGB experience might underpin relationship violence. For instance, violence toward one's partner might reflect one's own internalized homophobia, so that the partner becomes victim to one's own hostility toward LGB identity. Extreme dependency might also lead to violence, as one strives to assert independence by controlling the partner. For lesbians, dependency may represent the passive "femininity" expected in heterosexual relationships; for men, dependency is a violation of expectations for masculinity. In addition, violence between lesbians might reflect internalized misogyny. Among gay men, violence could reflect an element of socialized masculinity, and its accepted use in conflict management elsewhere may be mirrored in gay relationships.

Gender Roles in LGB Couples

Many people believe that members of gay and lesbian couples assume traditional gender roles, with one acting as the "wife" and the other as "husband."

This stereotype clearly reflects heterosexist assumptions, suggesting that "real" relationships must have these two distinct roles, and that gays and lesbians trying to form relationships will mimic heterosexual role differentiation.

There have been historical periods when such clear role differentiation was common. In the 1950s many lesbians assumed "butch" and "femme" roles; this was especially true among working-class lesbians active in the bar culture. However, these roles have diminished drastically, in part in response to the emergent feminist movement and criticisms of the sexism (and heterosexism) implied by such roles (Faderman, 1991). Recently, there has been some resurgence of butch and femme identities among lesbians, importantly, these identities do not match traditional male-female gender roles. Members of couples who identify as butch-femme do not divide activities traditionally seen as "masculine" and "feminine" (Faderman, 1992).[1]

In general, research indicates that most lesbians and gay men reject traditional gender roles in their relationships. In most couples, both members are employed and self-supporting, so neither plays the role of provider and both share in domestic tasks. In the absence of gender-based norms to structure roles, gay men and lesbians are free to arrange activities within their relationships as they choose. Social obligations, household duties, decision making, and other tasks are typically divided according to individual skills and interests, rather than along lines of traditional gender roles (Blumenstein & Schwartz, 1983; Kurdek, 1995b; Pepleau, 1991).

In contrast to traditional heterosexual relationships, both lesbians and gay men strive for equality of power in their relationships, and both are more satisfied with their relationships when they perceive them to be egalitarian. Lesbians appear to be more likely than either gay or heterosexual couples to endorse and attain this "ethic of equality." This relationship script has often been described as most closely approximating a friendship, rather than a marriage, as stereotypes would have it (Kurdek, 1995a, 92; see also Eldridge & Gilbert, 1990; Kurdek, 1995b; Pepleau, Cochran, Rook, & Padesky, 1978; Pepleau, Padesky, & Hamilton, 1983; Scrivner & Eldridge, 1995).

Support Networks

LGB individuals are frequently portrayed as lonely and isolated, and gay and lesbian couples as without meaningful support systems. This belief derives, once again, from heterosexist assumptions that presume that the only support possible for couples is the (heterosexual, biological) family, so that LGBs estranged from this family will be left alone. Indeed, LGB adolescents do

---

1. These identities now carry very different meanings than in the past. See, for example, Nestle, 1992.

frequently face social isolation, as do many old LGBs. However, it appears that young adult and midlife gay and lesbian couples enjoy a level of social support comparable to heterosexual couples. The difference lies in its source.

Research indicates that lesbians and gay men place as much importance on social support systems as do heterosexuals, and find similar levels of support. Some studies indicate that gay and lesbian couples regard family members—especially mothers and sisters—as significant sources of support (Kurdek, 1988, 1993), and Berger (1990) reported that a majority of gay male couples in his sample found their families "polite and friendly." Also, lesbian mothers are as likely as are heterosexual mothers to turn to their parents or other family members for assistance and support (Pepleau, 1991).

However, other research indicates that gay and lesbian couples rely more on friends and perceive more emotional support from them than from biological family, whereas heterosexual couples perceive more support from family (Kurdek & Schmitt, 1987). Bryant and Demian's (1994) subjects reported low levels of support from all types of relatives—even less than they received from coworkers. In fact, participants rated families as among the greatest stressors in their relationships, with lesbians facing greater challenges from relatives than did gay men. These couples turned instead to LGB friends and community institutions. Of particular importance for Berger's (1990) gay male subjects were other gay or lesbian couples.

Correlates of Relationship Satisfaction

The correlates of relationship satisfaction appear to be the same for lesbian as for gay couples. These include a high degree of attachment between partners, perceived equality of power and shared decision making, equality of investment in and commitment to the relationships, and similarity in attitudes and backgrounds. In addition, having at least one emotionally expressive partner and few dysfunctional beliefs regarding the relationship (e.g., that disagreements are destructive) make for greater relationship satisfaction. Finally, satisfaction is related to the perception of high rewards and low costs from the relationship (Blumenstein & Schwartz, 1983; Eldridge & Gilbert, 1990; Kurdek, 1994, 1995b; Pepleau & Cochran, 1990). These variables are similar to those found to correlate with relationship satisfaction among heterosexual couples, providing a basis for applying traditional relationship theory to gay and lesbian couples.

Why Relationships Last, Why They Don't

As Pepleau and Cochran pointed out, "love is no guarantee that a relationship will endure" (1990, p. 335), and the question of what makes a relationship last is as compelling for gay and lesbian couples as for heterosexual partnerships. Some researchers suggest that social exchange theory is valuable in understanding why gay and lesbian relationships last—or don't—as well as the ways in which they differ from heterosexual partnerships (Caldwell & Pepleau, 1984; Duffy & Rusbult, 1986; Kurdek, 1995b; Pepleau, 1991; Pepleau & Cochran, 1990).

One set of questions in social exchange theory deals with commitment and permanence in relationships, which depend on two major factors: (1) the strength of positive attractions that keep one in the relationship; and (2) the presence and salience of barriers that prevent or inhibit one's leaving the relationship. Included among the attractions is the degree of affection one feels for a partner, as well as the level of relationship satisfaction one experiences. As we have seen, lesbian and gay couples are characterized by the same level of affection, caring, and satisfaction as are heterosexual couples.

It is in the area of perceived barriers that lesbian and gay partnerships have been demonstrated to differ from heterosexual relationships. Such barriers can include practical difficulties that make ending a relationship costly, and the investment one has made in the relationship, as well as a dearth of perceived alternatives to the relationship—if this relationship seems the best available, one is unlikely to end it. For heterosexually married couples, barriers are created by marriage, such as the monetary cost of divorce, joint investments, concerns about children, social condemnation of divorce, and so forth. In contrast, gay and lesbian couples face relatively few barriers, other than the emotional costs that are common to any relationship's end. This may lie at the heart of the slightly higher rates of relationship dissolution for gay and lesbian couples.

Lesbians and married couples perceive the fewest alternatives to the current relationship. Gay men perceive more, and unmarried heterosexual couples perceive the greatest range of alternatives. As would be predicted from exchange theory, commitment to a relationship is correlated for all groups with relationship satisfaction, a high degree of perceived investment, and fewer alternatives.

The usefulness of this model in predicting the course of a relationship was explored by Kurdek (1995a), who investigated attachment and autonomy in lesbian and gay couples. Kurdek found that commitment to the relationship declines when the level of equality falls below one's ideal and when the relative importance of autonomy over attachment increases. Thus, commitment is effected by both benefits internal to the relationship (equality) and by attractions outside (a greater desire for autonomy).

Stages of Relationship Development

While lesbian and gay couples show the same range of diversity as do heterosexual couples, some have suggested that the course of relationships can be described in terms of a sequence of typical stages through which most couples move. It is important to keep in mind that these models are premised on limited samples that are, as their authors pointed out, biased toward the experience of a particular group—namely, the very group that has been represented in most research and theory discussed here. The evolution of relationships might be strikingly different for poor, rural, or minority couples, for different cohorts, or for those who are not open enough about their lives to participate in research.

All stage models are problematic because they tend to homogenize the experience of extremely diverse individuals. While they may be helpful in providing broad hints about human processes, they also distract us from the rich variety of those processes. For instance, the level of attachment experienced by couples will surely affect the course of relationship development, and this attachment might be influenced by numerous factors. Indeed, Pepleau and Cochran (1982) demonstrated that attachment in gay couples was consistently related to important features of their lives and relationships—how they met their partners, their attitudes toward sexuality, how much time they spent together, their predictions for the future, and how they respond to the dissolution of relationships. Without taking into account such variations in experience and their impact on attachment, we cannot expect to understand the progress of a given relationship. With these cautions in mind, we consider two models of relationship development.

McWirther and Mattison (1984) presented a six-stage model for the evolution of gay male partnerships, roughly associated with the duration of the relationship. In this scheme, the first year is characterized by *blending,* which entails intense closeness or merging, limerence (preoccupation with the partner, longing to be together, etc.), extensive shared activities, and frequent sexual relations. The second stage, *nesting,* typically covers the second and third years. During this stage, the couple settles into homemaking, limerence declines, and some ambivalence about the relationship emerges. During the fourth and fifth years, termed *maintaining,* members of the couple begin to reassert their independence and individuality, conflict management strategies evolve, and traditions are established. In the *building* stage, which encompasses years six through ten, partners move further toward individual productivity while also developing collaborative efforts. The ability to rely on one's partner is a central theme of this stage.

The fifth stage, *releasing,* covers the period from ten to twenty years, and is marked by a more taken-for-granted attitude. Trust between partners becomes implicit, finances and possessions are merged, individual and relationship priorities are evaluated. Finally, after the couple has been together for more than twenty years, they experience *renewing* of their commitment. Having achieved financial and emotional security, the couple deals together with the tasks of later life, reminisces about the partnership's history, and renews the romance of earlier years.

Clunis and Green's (1988) model of lesbian couple development begins with a *prerelationship* stage, when women decide whether to invest the time and energy necessary to build a relationship. The duration of this stage varies widely among couples, and subsequent stages are similarly variable in length. The second stage, dubbed *romance,* is quite similar to McWirther and Mattison's first stage and is characterized by limerence, merging, and an intense focus on the relationship and the partner. The *conflict* stage is similar to McWirther and Mattison's maintaining stage, and entails a shift away from the profound involvement of the earlier stage and the emergence of conflict as partners begin to reestablish independence. *Acceptance* reflects an awareness of the faults of the partner and a sense of stability and security in the relationship. During the *commitment* stage, the partners negotiate a balance between their respective needs and come to a sense of implicit trust in each other. Finally, during the *collaboration* stage, partners work together toward shared goals that extend beyond the relationship itself.

We must keep in mind that stage models are *descriptive* of a particular sample, and not *prescriptive* for the course of LGB relationships. The fact that particular couples tend to follow the patterns described here does not mean that couples *should* follow this sequence, nor that to do so is in any sense more correct or healthy. Even in arguing for an orderly process of relationship development among their sample, McWirther and Mattison caution that "characteristics from one stage also are present in other stages, and they overlap. . . . Not all male couples fit this model" (1984, p. 16). Clunis and Green similarly warn us that "not every couple starts with the first stage. Some couples never go through all the stages, and certainly not in the order they are presented" (1988, p. 10).

Very little research has addressed the validity of these models to date. Kurdek and Schmitt (1986) applied the McWirther and Mattison model to an analysis of relationship quality in lesbian, gay, heterosexually married, and heterosexual cohabiting couples. Their findings support the notion that the second and third years of a relationship ("nesting," in this scheme) were marked by greater disillusionment and greater relationship stress. Couples in this period reported fewer shared activities and lower relationship satisfaction than did couples who had been together for either a shorter or a longer period of time. This same pattern characterized all four types of couple, indicating that relationship evolution is similar for same-sex as for heterosexual couples.

Gender Differences

We have discussed previously the impact of gender on all of our experience; the power of gender is strikingly apparent in any consideration of same-sex couples, where the effects of gender socialization are multiplied. We have already noted a few ways in which gender influences such relationships; in particular, the absence of prescribed roles allows for creative variation in relationship patterns and task distribution for both lesbian and gay male couples. In addition, research with lesbian and gay couples reveals many differences between them, suggesting that gender socialization shapes the experience of these couples.

Power and Persuasion

All couples experience conflict at some time, and strategies evolve by which the couple resolves these conflicts. Research has shown that, in heterosexual relationships, men tend to use "strong" tactics such as bargaining, domination, and interruption to win a point. Women in heterosexual relationships, on the other hand, are more likely to rely on appeals to emotion, withdrawal, supplication, and manipulation. This apparent gender difference raises the question of how same-sex couples resolve disagreements.

Pepleau (1991) summarized research indicating that it is not gender, per se, that leads one to use particular tactics, but the balance of power in the relationship. That is, women tend to use "weak" strategies because they have less power, and men use "strong" tactics because they have more. In same-sex couples, where gender does not control power, other factors operate. Partners who perceive themselves as more powerful are likely to use interruption, bargaining and persuasion; the partner perceived as less powerful is likely to use emotion and withdrawal.

We might well ask what grants greater power to one partner than the other, if not gender. Research exploring the role of power in gay and lesbian relationships is unclear in its conclusions. Some research indicates that a difference in income is a major determinant of power differences in both heterosexual and gay men's relationships, but does not translate into power differentials in lesbian relationships (Pepleau, 1991; Berger, 1990). Similarly, age differences often structure power in gay men's relationships, but appear not to have the same impact in lesbian ones (Kurdek, 1995b; Pepleau, 1991). However, other research indicates that among lesbians, the partner with greater education and/or higher income appears to hold greater power in the relationship (Caldwell & Pepleau, 1984).

Relationship Satisfaction

On global measures of relationship satisfaction, no differences have been found between lesbians and gay men. However, when the value of the relationship and perceived rewards are measured specifically, lesbians report greater relationship satisfaction than do gay men (Kurdek, 1994, 1995b). This phenomenon may be attributable to gender socialization, which leads women to focus on relationships as definitive of themselves, whereas men are taught to attend more to their independent achievements. As a result, a lesbian relationship may be characterized by a great deal of attention to and investment in the health of the relationship.

Gender-based Patterns of Relating
A very extensive literature has explored the implications for same-sex partnerships of the fact that both partners have been socialized to a particular manner of relating. Thus, lesbian and gay relationships might be expected to magnify gender socialization, making for dynamics very different from those found in heterosexual partnerships.

Lesbian relationships. Since women are socialized to focus on relationships even to the point of self-sacrifice, it has been argued that lesbian relationships are likely to be intense and at risk of merger or fusion—the loss of independent identity, a feeling of oneness, and a sense that "we," the couple, is core to one's identity. The resultant emotional intensity and closeness may hamper individual autonomy. In addition to reflecting women's gender socialization, such merger might provide a sense of protection and solidarity in the face of a sexist and heterosexist world. Some research indicates that lesbian couples show greater "dyadic attachment," or close attachment within the couple, than do gay or heterosexual couples (Krestan & Bepko, 1980; Lewis, Kozac, Milardo, & Grosnick, 1981; B. Murphy, 1994; Pearlman, 1989; Pepleau, Cochran, Rook, & Padesky, 1978; Renzetti, 1992).

Although some characterize such fusion as problematic, others argue that the degree of connection possible in lesbian relationships is not intrinsically a problem, as is indicated by the high degree of relationship satisfaction found in lesbian couples. Rather, the tendency to employ skills of emotional expressiveness and connection might make for more nurturing relationships, a model that might well be emulated by gay and heterosexual couples, as well (Burch, 1993; Green, 1990; Scrivner & Eldridge, 1995). Further, fusion is not a simple phenomenon; sharing extensive time together is quite different from sharing possessions, which is different from sharing professional relationships such as with a therapist. While the latter two may be problematic in many cases, some research indicates that the first typically is not (Causby, Lockhard, White, & Green, 1995).

Finally, there is some question as to whether lesbians actually face particular problems with fusion (Causby, Lockhart, White, & Green, 1995; Kurdek, 1995b). According to Clunis and Green (1988), this state is "both the goal and the reality" early on in lesbian relationships, but couples move beyond fusion to reestablish their autonomy and individuality in later stages.

Thus, the presumption that lesbian relationships might be problematic as a result of the magnification of gender socialization has found mixed support, and some question whether close bonding and emotional expressiveness is a problem, in any case. Rather, such a negative assumption may reflect traditionally masculine understandings of health as grounded in separation and individuality rather than in relatedness.

Gay male relationships. In contrast to this portrait of lesbian relationships, gay couples are composed of individuals who are socialized to be independent and competitive, to avoid expressions of affection, and to expect caretaking from others. Also, male socialization identifies masculinity with sexuality, and the ability to "score" sexually is a primary criterion of one's success as a man. Anonymous or uncommitted sexual relationships are acceptable, as they offer evidence of masculinity without the complications of connection and emotion. Because men are not allowed to express closeness in other ways, sex may become the sole means for achieving connection to others. This tendency toward emotionally disconnected sexual liaisons may be aggravated by the norms of the gay community, which values sexual expressiveness as a rejection of traditionally conservative heterosexual norms and an affirmation of gay liberation. For gay males, accordingly, the issue may be difficulties in attaining intimacy, because that requires emotional expressiveness, interdependence, and caregiving (Elise, 1986; Scrivner & Eldridge, 1995).

Sexuality

The most consistent findings regarding differences among relationships lie in the area of sexuality. The frequency of a couple's sexual relations is sharply influenced by gender: gay male couples report the greatest frequency, lesbian couples the lowest, and heterosexual couples fall in between (Blumenstein & Schwartz, 1983; Pepleau & Cochran, 1990; Pepleau, 1991). For all groups, sex is most frequent early in the relationship, declining with relationship duration and, to a degree, with age. At all stages of the relationship, lesbians report less frequent sex than do gay men or heterosexual couples.[2] In all groups, some couples do not have sexual relationships with each other, although one or both may do so with other people (Rothblum & Brehony, 1993; Shernoff, 1995).

It appears from these findings that women's behavior is modified toward more frequent sexual activity by the presence of a man in the couple (or men's, toward less frequent activity by the presence of a woman). Some writers explain this phenomenon by an appeal to women's socialization, arguing that women are not encouraged to be sexual and therefore suppress sexual urges, or

---

2. Although numerous studies report this pattern, sample limitations preclude our drawing conclusions about all groups from these data. For instance, Bell and Weinberg (1978) analyzed data for African American gay and lesbian participants, and found no difference between the two groups in sexual interest. Clearly, not only gender but other variables affect the nature of sexual experience.

that women's socialization to sexual passivity interferes with their initiating sexual relations.

However, other considerations are important, as well. Women engage in more hugging, kissing, cuddling, and other forms of nongenital physical expression than do men (Murphy, 1994). In light of this fact, it is difficult to know how to tabulate sexual frequency; although counting genital sexual contacts that lead to orgasm may represent men's sexuality fairly accurately, it may badly misrepresent women's. The level of women's sexuality may not reflect "suppression" at all, but different means of expression. Given that heterosexual couples, lesbians, and gay men are equally satisfied with the level of sexual activity in their relationship, variations in level of genital sexuality needn't be explained away. Less genital sex clearly does not necessarily mean a less satisfying sexual life.

Another area of gender difference in sexual experience has to do with sexual exclusivity. Unfortunately, nearly all of the research on this topic predates the HIV/AIDS epidemic, so that its precise impact on sexual behavior cannot be documented. This research documented that gay men had more permissive attitudes toward sex outside of the primary relationship than did either heterosexual or lesbian couples. Blumenstein and Schwartz (1983) found that in heterosexual couples, about two-thirds of men and over three-fourths of women saw exclusivity as important; among same-sex couples, only about one-third of gay men but about three-fourths of lesbians regarded sexual exclusivity as important.

In this pre-AIDS research, the widespread acceptance of nonmonogamy among gay men was reflected in their behavior, as well. Blumenstein and Schwartz (1983) found that, among couples together for less than two years, about two-thirds of gay men were nonmonogamous, compared to about 15 percent of lesbians and heterosexual men and women. For couples who had been together for ten or more years, 94 percent of gay men reported at least one sexual experience outside the relationship, as compared with about 22 percent of wives, 30 percent of husbands, and 43 percent of lesbians. After ten years or more together, gay couples had sex together less often than heterosexual couples, but had frequently made explicit arrangements for sex outside the relationship.

Nonmonogamy may take many forms; what is considered "infidelity" may vary significantly among couples. For instance, Shernoff (1995) has differentiated between acknowledged and unacknowledged nonmonogamy among gay men, and points to the very different dynamics underlying these. Early research addressing the impact of nonmonogamy indicated that it was not intrinsically threatening to gay men's relationships, as nonmonogamous couples reported relationship satisfaction equal to that of monogamous pairs. Rather, what appeared to be important was whether the partners had reached an agreement about the level of exclusivity (Kurdek, 1995b; Pepleau & Cochran, 1990).

A number of explanations have been offered for this pattern of higher rates of sexual behavior and nonmonogamy among gay men. Among these are the equation of sexuality with masculinity and the need for gay men to assert their masculinity in the face of cultural assumptions that they are effeminate; the tendency for men to separate sex from emotional commitment; norms of the gay male community, which stress sexual freedom; and the availability of many opportunities for casual sex in the gay men's community. Conversely, sex is more closely linked to love and emotion for lesbians than for gay men, thereby leading to fewer uncommitted sexual liaisons (Kurdek, 1995b; Leigh, 1992; Pepleau, 1991; Pepleau & Gordon, 1983).

One avenue to a clearer view of the impact of gender on sexuality is to explore the experiences of people who identify as bisexual. Weinberg, Williams, and Pryor (1994) found that bisexually-identified women and men both describe sex with women as more caring, person-centered, tender, and emotionally satisfying; sex with men was described as more impersonal and mechanical. These descriptions are entirely in keeping with socially constructed understandings of differences in sexuality, and appear to have little impact on partner choice. Thus, both men and women reported selecting partners for qualities independent of gender—personality, appearance, and so forth—rather than for a particular quality of sexual relations.

The Impact of AIDS

There is emerging information that the HIV/AIDS epidemic has altered these patterns, with recent research reporting higher rates of monogamy among gay and bisexual men. Kurdek (1988), for example, reported that, in his sample of gay couples from 22 states, 26 percent of couples who had been together for ten years or more were monogamous. Berger (1990), using a sample of men who belonged to a couples network, found that over 96 percent were currently monogamous, and over two-thirds of Berger's subjects reported that AIDS had had a significant impact on their sexual behavior, in terms of greater exclusivity, safer sex practices, or both. Weinberg, Williams, and Pryor (1994) reported increasing monogamy among bisexual men and women over recent years, often expressly related to AIDS. These samples may be highly selective, but all three were also conducted post-AIDS, while the Blumenstein and Schwartz findings were pre-AIDS.

In a study commendable for its inclusion of culturally diverse participants, Remien, Carballo-Dieguez, and Wagner (1995) looked at the behaviors of couples where one partner is HIV positive and the other is negative, and reported a range of behavioral adjustments intended to decrease risk. Similarly, Weinberg, Williams, and Pryor (1994) found a greater emphasis on safe sex among bisexual men and women. While many of the changes in behavior reported by these subjects were ill-informed and may be ineffective in preventing the transmission of HIV, they nevertheless demonstrate that the epidemic is reshaping sexual attitudes and activities.

Other research has also suggested a decline in unsafe sex and sexual nonexclusivity among gay men and bisexual individuals (Bryant & Demian, 1994; Kurdek, 1995b; Meyer, 1990; Pepleau & Cochran, 1990), and some facilities that earlier provided easy access to casual sex (such as the baths) have closed or changed their focus in response to the epidemic. Many argue that there is growing pressure in the gay male community toward coupling, rather than unrestricted sex, and toward monogamy (Berger, 1990). However, there are also some indications of recent returns to unsafe sex among many gay men. This shift may be in part a response to a sense of futility in the battle against HIV/AIDS, as well as resentment of restrictions on sexual freedom. Exactly what long-term impact HIV/AIDS will have on gay men's relationship patterns remains to be seen.

Bisexuality and Relationships

The most thorough recent information on the formation of intimate relationships among bisexually identified men and women comes from an extensive longitudinal study by Weinberg, Williams, and Pryor (1994). Similar to heterosexual, gay, and lesbian couples, bisexual individuals in this sample anticipated that their current relationship would be long lasting. Indeed, follow-up research five years after the initial contact found that these relationships were more enduring than were lesbian or gay partnerships, although less so than heterosexual ones.

While bisexual individuals shared an attraction to both men and women, they varied widely in the balance of preferences. Some, described as *homosexual leaning,* preferred same-sex relationships, while others, *heterosexual leaning,* were more attracted to members of the other sex. Among those who had had relationships with both sexes, both women and men reported important differences between these. Men and women both reported greater ease of expression with women partners than with men. Both women and men indicated that power issues arose in their relationships, particularly in heterosexual relationships, where the major difficulty was women's dissatisfaction with the power differential favoring men in heterosexual partnerships. And both men and women indicated that they formed stronger bonds of intimacy with same-sex partners, with whom they shared common experiences.

Mixed Relationships: LGBs in Heterosexual Marriages

As mentioned previously, some individuals identify as LGB prior to and others only after they have entered into heterosexual relationships. Most commonly, the disclosure of this identity in the context of heterosexual marriage leads to separation or divorce. However, some couples are able to remain married, often restructuring the relationship to accommodate the LGB partner's same-sex attractions. Such arrangements appear to be more common with gay or bisexual men and heterosexual wives, as marriages that include lesbians and bisexual women are more likely to be terminated soon after the revelation (Coleman, 1985a, 1985b). A substantial literature has evolved that addresses the process by which couples negotiate this issue and the variety of adaptations they might make (Brownfain, 1985; Buxton, 1991; Coleman, 1985b; Eichberg, 1990; Gochros, 1989; Matteson, 1985; Ross, 1983). Although a thorough discussion of this phenomenon is beyond the scope of this book, it is intriguing in that it further dismantles common assumptions—that is, socially constructed beliefs—about sexual orientation and about intimate relationships. For people to be heterosexually married while identifying as LGB suggests that our usual categories are inadequate to the variety and complexity of identity.

Unique Stresses

LGB partnerships face some stresses that are unique either by virtue of their quality as same-sex relationships or because of the high need to manage stigma. For example, where one member of the couple is a member of a minority group, the couple must deal not only with heterosexism but also with racism— within the couple as well as from the external world. The dynamics generated by such a relationship are complicated and require unique adaptations (Clunis & Green, 1988; Garcia, Kennedy, Pearlman, & Perez, 1987; Lockman, 1984; Sang, 1984).

Another distinctive feature of lesbian and gay partnerships has to do with friendships outside the relationship. In heterosexual couples, each partner is able to have close same-sex friendships; in fact, gender-based customs and institutions explicitly support such relationships. For same-sex couples, however, these friendships constitute a potential threat to the partnership. Accordingly, one task that lesbian and gay couples must address is negotiating agreements that support each partner's pursuing close friendships without their being perceived as threatening.

An additional issue concerns partners' decisions about being out. Where one member of the couple is more open than the other, conflict may arise if the second partner feels threatened by the activities of the first. Conversely, the individual who is more out may feel restricted in her or his actions by the need to protect a partner's more secretive position, and may feel that such nondisclosure reflects a devaluation of or lack of commitment to the relationship.

In recent years, the HIV/AIDS epidemic has added another layer to the stigma of LGB identity. The public conflation of AIDS with gay and bisexual identity has served further to demean homophilic relationships, disrupting whatever sense of acceptance had begun to emerge in the more progressive pre-AIDS era. In this atmosphere, men's (and, to a lesser degree, women's) same-sex relations are increasingly condemned, internalized homophobia is fed by the added stigma, and the wish for intimacy is increasingly fraught with the threat of illness and death. The need to invent means for coping with this epidemic while maintaining the ability to form loving relationships is an enormous challenge.

Finally, perhaps the most pervasive, persistent, and profound stressor for lesbian and gay partnerships is the persistent denial of their legitimacy. No matter how long a couple has been together, no matter how deep their personal commitment, they are constantly faced with the societal erasure of their relationship. They may be viewed as friends or roommates, as single adults who never "had a family," as unfortunate "old maids," as eccentric and fundamentally lonely bachelors. Slater and Mencher (1991) provide these illustrations:

> "My mother invited me home for the weekend," my client reported angrily. "Me—that's who she invited. It's like I never came out to her at all. It's like Andrea doesn't even exist."

> The obituary read, "Joan Reynolds is survived by two sisters, Helen Jenkins and Rhona Stewart, her brother, John Reynolds, and one nephew." My eyes searched in vain for mention of her partner of 36 years. (p. 376)

In the face of this near-total withholding of relationship status, the validation of the partnership's existence relies almost completely on the couple themselves. It is here that the broader community—the family of choice—may be crucial in granting legitimacy to gay and lesbian couples.

Summary

In sum, gay and lesbian relationships are in many ways strikingly similar to heterosexual ones. Old myths about unhappy, transient, and loveless unions are clearly false; gay men and lesbians form loving, lasting, richly satisfying partnerships. They also face relationship problems, as do heterosexual couples. But in other respects, lesbian and gay relationships are quite different from heterosexual ones. Same-sex relationships face unique stresses and embody remarkable promise. The absence of prescribed gender roles and partnership

scripts grants a range of flexibility that allows for tremendous creativity in the   *197*
formation and conduct of relationships.

Lesbian and Gay Parents and Their Children

While the terms "lesbian mother" or "gay father" might seem paradoxical in our heterosexist society, in fact many of the families of gay and lesbian people include children. The fact that an identity as a parent may conflict, psychologically and socially, with a lesbian or gay identity makes the task of synthesizing the two a difficult one for many gay and lesbian parents (Bozett, 1987, 1989). Some avoid the dilemma by not having children or resolve it by relinquishing custody of children born before the parent came to a homophilic identity. Others choose to integrate the two identities and to live both as gay or lesbian and as parents.

At this point in time, the majority of children with lesbian or gay parents come from prior heterosexual marriages, but there is a growing trend toward lesbian and, to a lesser extent, gay individuals or couples bringing children into their lives. Some of these children are conceived through alternative insemination or surrogacy; others are adoptive or foster children (Crawford, 1987; Patterson, 1995b; Pies, 1985, 1990; Ricketts & Achtenberg, 1990). This trend may reflect changing social values that celebrate family, commensurate with greater openness regarding homophilia and growing support systems for gay and lesbian parents. It may also reflect a growing emphasis on commitment by gay men in reaction to the HIV/AIDS epidemic (Green & Bozett, 1991).

Future research will need to explore differences between parents with children from previous heterosexual relationships and those who choose to parent after they come out. For instance, it is important to learn what impact it has on parenting styles and on children's development when parents have experienced no social pressure to parent and must, in fact, negotiate a number of barriers to parenthood. Repeated attempts at alternative insemination or surrogacy, prolonged efforts to be approved for adoption or foster parenting—the persistence such undertakings represent are testimony to how much these children are wanted. Research on these families is just beginning, but promises to be a fruitful source of new understandings of families (Crawford, 1987; Patterson, 1994; Pies, 1990).

Gay and lesbian parents differ along many other dimensions, in addition to how they became parents. Where there are children from a previous heterosexual relationship, the lesbian or gay parent may or may not have custody of the child(ren.) Because of heterosexist attitudes on the part of courts and social service agencies, a disproportionate number of lesbian and gay parents have been refused or have lost custody because of their sexual orientation, and are therefore noncustodial parents.

For the gay or lesbian parent who has custody, there may or may not be a partner who may or may not live with the family. If there is a live-in partner, she or he may or may not assume a coparenting role with the children. If the partner also has children, step-sibling relationships add to the complexity of family dynamics. We would also expect the experience of lesbian or gay parents and of their children to be influenced by race/ethnicity, income, education, and culture.

Thus, it is meaningless to speak of a typical gay or lesbian parenting situation, as it is meaningless to describe a typical heterosexual one. It is also impossible to know the number of such families, in part because many gay or lesbian parents carefully avoid revealing their identity, precisely because they might lose custody or visiting rights. However, recent estimates suggest that there are at least 2 million and perhaps as many as 8 million gay and lesbian parents in the United States; estimates of the number of children of gay and lesbian parents range from 4 million to 14 million (Patterson, 1995b).

Lesbian and Gay Parents

We might first ask who are the lesbians and gay men who are parents, and what are the effects on them and their relationships of the presence of children in their lives. A large number of studies have focused on the psychological status of lesbian mothers, because issues of their mental health and maternal abilities are so often raised in custody battles. This research consistently demonstrates that lesbian mothers are at least as well adjusted as their heterosexual counterparts, do not differ in "gender-appropriate" behavior, and are as warm toward children and as committed to child rearing as are heterosexual mothers. Some differences have been noted, including that lesbian mothers are more confident and assertive, more likely to be involved in feminist activities, and less likely to choose sex-typed toys for their children than their heterosexual peers. In addition, some research describes lesbian mothers as more child centered in their parenting techniques, more flexible about rules, and more likely to hold nontraditional expectations for their daughters (Falk, 1989; Patterson, 1995c). Working with African American lesbian and heterosexual mothers, Hill (1987) found similar results, in that the lesbian mothers held less rigid gender role expectations, were more flexible about rules, and were more tolerant overall than were heterosexual mothers.

No comparable research has assessed the psychological adjustment of gay as compared to heterosexual fathers, perhaps because the impetus of custody battles has not driven such research. Indeed, only a small percentage of gay fathers have been reported to live with their children (Patterson, 1995b). However, some research has explored the parenting attitudes and behaviors of gay fathers. Bigner and Jacobsen (1989, 1992) found that gay fathers hold similar motivations for becoming parents as do heterosexual fathers, and that their

self-reported interactions with their children were similar to those of heterosexual fathers in terms of intimacy and involvement. However, gay fathers'
characterizations of their parenting revealed greater responsiveness, reasoning,
and limit setting than did heterosexual fathers. There are some indications that
gay fathers work harder at being sensitive, attentive, and responsive, perhaps
in an attempt to dispel negative stereotypes about their ability as fathers.

For both lesbian and gay parents, the role of the parent's partner appears to
be important. Lesbian mothers have been found to be more likely than
divorced heterosexual mothers to be living with a romantic partner. As with
heterosexual families, the presence of a step-parent can be a source of both
strength and stress. Kirkpatrick (1987) noted that lesbian mothers who lived
with a partner as well as with children had more economic and emotional
resources than did those living without a partner. Similarly, inclusion of gay
fathers' partners and the quality of partners' relationships with children were
found to be predictive of happiness with family life (Crosbie-Burnett &
Helmbrecht, 1993). However, conflicts over parenting styles, resentment about
shared time and attention, and problems within the adult relationship can
complicate the task of parenting, as they can in any family.

The Impact of Children

Gay men and lesbians choosing to enter into parenthood after coming out
face a plethora of health care, legal, financial, social and emotional hurdles.
Most of these must be negotiated without the benefit of formalized support
systems that assist heterosexual couples toward parenthood. Indeed, individuals or couples choosing parenthood may lose much of the support of their
circle of LGB friends, for whom parenthood does not structure life (Bigner &
Bozett, 1990; Crawford, 1987; Patterson, 1994, 1995b; Pies, 1990; Ricketts &
Achtenberg, 1990).

When a couple makes a decision to be parents, their own relationship must
accommodate to the presence of a child. Some research shows that couples
tend to shift away from more egalitarian roles when a child enters, such that
the biological parent assumes more child-care activities and is likely to work
less than full-time, while the nonbiological parent assumes more tasks of the
provider role. Even with this shift, gay and lesbian relationships are still far
more egalitarian than are heterosexual marriages, with nonbiological gay and
lesbian parents significantly more involved in child care than heterosexual
fathers. Furthermore, gay and lesbian couples report greater satisfaction with a
more egalitarian division of child care tasks (Patterson, 1995a; 1995b).

Despite these adjustments, the arrival of a child brings new stressors for the
relationship. For gay or lesbian—as for heterosexual—families, the presence of
a child results in less freedom, less time alone for the couple, and often a
decrease in sexual relations. An additional difficulty for lesbian and gay couples

stems from the absence of social validation for their parenting arrangement. For instance, Stiglitz (1990), in a comparison of lesbian and heterosexual parents, found that the arrival of a child made heterosexual mothers feel more integrated into the community and more satisfied with the emotional support they received from family. Lesbian mothers, in contrast, felt more isolated, more like a "separate family." Because the LGB community is not structured around children as the heterosexual community is, and because the broader society validates neither gay and lesbian couples nor their right to raise children, there is no clear community of support for gay and lesbian parents. Fortunately, such support systems are beginning to evolve, in large part as a result of the increase in lesbian and gay couples who choose to parent (Pies, 1990; Scrivner & Eldridge, 1995).

Children of Gay and Lesbian Parents

A large body of research is now available, exploring the impact on children of parents' identifying as lesbian or gay (for reviews, see Bozett, 1987, 1989; Falk, 1989; Gibbs, 1988; Gottman, 1990; Green & Bozett, 1991; Patterson, 1992, 1995b). The bulk of this research deals with the children of lesbian mothers, who have been the primary focus of court decisions and who also comprise the large majority of primary parents among lesbians and gay men.

Sexual Identity, Gender, and Sexual Orientation

One of the major concerns expressed by opponents of gay and lesbian parenting has been the belief that the parent's sexual orientation would adversely affect the children's development. This concern has many components, which we will consider in turn.

First, the fear that children's *sexual identity* or *gender identity*—the sense of being male or female—would be distorted has found no support. Numerous studies have found no difference in sexual or gender identity between the children of lesbian mothers and those of heterosexual divorced mothers.

Second, concerns about *gender role* behavior have also proven unfounded. In most research, toy preferences, vocational aspirations, activity preferences, and other measures of gender roles are no different among these two groups of children, nor have differences been found among adult children of lesbian mothers vis-à-vis those of heterosexual mothers. However, these findings are not necessarily unabashedly positive. Given the detrimental impacts of traditional gender roles, we might hope that adherence to those roles in any group—in heterosexual or in gay and lesbian families—would be cause for concern. The fact that LGB identity offers an opportunity for greater role flexibility would seem to suggest that lesbian and gay parents might provide their offspring with more flexible options for behavior, in which case we might find

less gender role adherence among their children. The fact that this research
shows no such difference might thus be taken as an indication of a problem
rather than as reassuring.

Finally, despite assumptions that gay or lesbian parents may influence their
children's *sexual orientation,* research has found no greater incidence of LGB
identity among the children of gay and lesbian parents than in the population
as a whole (although estimating either population is extremely difficult, as we
have discussed). It appears that many children with lesbian mothers do worry
about their own sexual orientation, wondering whether they will be lesbian or
gay and whether their peers might think they are. However, such worries dissi-
pate as children begin dating, and some children report that they feel more
clear about and comfortable with their own heterosexual orientation because of
having considered the alternatives (O'Connell, 1993).

It is important to consider the underlying meaning of this line of research—
more specifically, of the very question it asks. The presumption underlying
this work is that it would be a serious problem if the children of lesbian and
gay parents were more likely to be gay or lesbian themselves. While research
demonstrating that this is not the case may be calming to those steeped in
heterosexist norms, the fact that it is important demonstrates the depth and
pervasiveness of homonegative attitudes in our society. If LGB identity were
not condemned, no one would worry if we produced more LGB children.
Thus, this research, intended to be LGB affirmative, betrays homonegative
cultural biases.

Psychological Adjustment

Another assumption implicit in both social judgments and judicial decisions is
that children will be harmed by living with a gay or lesbian parent and will
suffer in terms of psychological adjustment. Again, this assumption is not
upheld by the data. On the contrary, children with lesbian and gay parents are
indistinguishable from children reared in heterosexual families on measures of
self-esteem, personality, locus of control, moral judgment, intelligence, and
behavior problems. Some research indicates that children of lesbians experience more stress than do children of heterosexual parents, but also express a
greater sense of well-being (Patterson, 1994, 1995c).

Social Relations

The courts—and lay people, as well—often express concern that children of
gay or lesbian parents will face taunting and rejection from peers, with con-
sequent damage to their emotional health. However, research exploring relations with peers has consistently found that the quality of these relationships
is good, as described both by the children's parents and by independent
observers. Children of lesbian and gay parents do not differ from children of

heterosexual families in peer group relations, popularity, or social adjustment (Falk, 1989; Patterson, 1995c). In fact, some research indicates that children of lesbian parents may have an advantage in social skills. Steckel (1987) found that children of heterosexual parents saw themselves as more aggressive, and were described by parents and teachers as more bossy, domineering, and negativistic than were children of lesbian parents. In contrast, children of lesbian parents described themselves as more lovable, and their teachers and parents saw them as more responsive, affectionate, and protective toward younger children.

First-person accounts do indicate that children are concerned about possible stigmatization and often work to keep their parent's sexual orientation a secret (O'Connell, 1993; Rafkin, 1990). However, there is no indication that this has a negative effect on their relationships or development. In reality, children face teasing for many things, and most they handle adequately. It may be that lesbian and gay parents who are comfortable with their own identity can help children to deal with this experience, much as minority parents help their children to deal with prejudice and stigma.

Children of lesbian mothers also have good relationships with adults; if the parents are divorced, the children are more likely than the children of divorced heterosexual mothers to have regular contact with their fathers, and lesbian mothers are more concerned than their heterosexual counterparts that their children have positive interactions with adult men in general. Because the social circles of lesbian mothers have been shown to include both women and men, it appears that their children have opportunities for a wide range of relationships with adults of both sexes.

The topic of children's relationships with their parents' friends often raises concerns about the potential for sexual abuse. The presumption that contact with gay and lesbian adults will expose the child to greater risk is a belief grounded in the stereotype of gay men and lesbians as child molesters. This belief is patently false. The vast majority of adults who molest children are males, and their victims are usually girls. A recent study found that 82 percent of sexually abused children were molested by the heterosexual partner of a close relative of the child; less than 1 percent of abusers were gay or lesbian (Jenny, Roesler, & Poyer, 1994). Thus, the likelihood of a child's being molested by a lesbian or a gay male is extremely small (see also Finkelhor, 1986; Patterson, 1995b).

Finally, we can consider children's relations with the world at large. Here, the children of gay and lesbian parents may be at an advantage, as both mothers' reports and children's own observations indicate that children raised by lesbian mothers are more tolerant and have a better understanding of prejudice and its damaging effects. Not only have they experienced the consequences of prejudice in their own families, but they also report seeing their mothers as unusually open and more tolerant than other mothers, a model certainly worth emulating. Although they may be aware of problems related to their mother's identity, they clearly recognize that the fault lies with prejudicial beliefs and not with their mother (Falk, 1989; O'Connell, 1993; Rafkin, 1990).

We can see that the developmental difficulties experienced by children of gay and lesbian parents derive from social attitudes and the need to manage stigma. Children worry whether their friends might think that they are gay or lesbian and perhaps shun them for it. They keep their parents' identity a secret to protect themselves or their parents from prejudice or to protect others from the embarrassment of having to deal with it. Such secrecy may be modeled by their parents, particularly if—as is often the case—a lesbian mother risks losing custody if her identity is known. The problem is not gay and lesbian parents; the problem is heterosexism (see also Raymond, 1992).

Family Variations: Impact on Children

A number of factors intrinsic to particular families have an impact on children in gay and lesbian families. For example, Patterson (1995a) reported that the children of lesbian couples are better adjusted if their mothers divide child-care tasks equally. Since lesbian couples also report greater relationship satisfaction with egalitarian division of child care, such arrangements appear beneficial to all members of the family. Similar research with heterosexual and male gay couples might provide valuable insights into optimal family functioning.

A second—and intriguing—set of variables has to do with the impact on children of lesbian mothers' degree of openness. The mother's own psychological well-being is related to the extent of her openness about her sexual orientation with employers, exhusbands, and her own children. Children whose fathers are acceptant of their mother's lesbianism have higher self-esteem than do those whose fathers reject this aspect of her identity. Finally, the daughters of lesbians have been found to have higher self-esteem when their mother's partner lives with the family. It may be that these findings in combination reveal an atmosphere that encourages positive adjustment for all family members. Given research indicating a relationship between the mother's adjustment and that of her children, perhaps the mother's satisfaction with her identity—as reflected in an open partnership, disclosure to others in her life, and acceptance by people important to the children—fosters positive self-esteem in her children.

Another family variation with implications for children's well-being has to do with whether and when the parent's sexual orientation is disclosed to children. In general, it appears that honesty in this realm is crucial to positive parent-child relationships, despite the difficulties involved in the disclosure. Coming out to children is more difficult for gay fathers than it is for lesbian mothers, and children are likely to respond more negatively to fathers' revelations than to mothers' (Bozett, 1989)—a finding completely in keeping with evidence that, in society as a whole, greater hostility is expressed toward gay men than toward lesbians. Bozett (1980) and Clunis and Green (1988) offer guidelines for parents who are addressing the question of whether, when, and how to come out to their children.

While some research suggests that children generally respond positively to a parent's coming out regardless of the child's age or the means of disclosure, other work indicates that children who are told in childhood or late adolescence have an easier time coping with the news than do children told in early or middle adolescence. There is some suggestion that children who learn this news in childhood have higher self-esteem than do those who are told later. In all cases, the effects of disclosure are often difficult to separate from the impact of divorce, which often accompanies the parent's coming out (Bozett, 1987, 1989; O'Connell, 1993; Patterson, 1995b).

Children's ability to adapt is remarkable. O'Connell found that, although they wished for more support and greater openness about the topic, adolescent children of lesbians were deeply affectionate toward and loyal to their mothers and able to place the issue in perspective. One daughter insisted:

> I think people should understand it's not going to affect you adversely. I mean, it's not world news. People's ideas about what's important are weird. Bombs and alcoholism and violence are world news. So is hunger and homelessness. My mother's being a lesbian is definitely not news. (O'Connell, 1993, p. 293)

CHAPTER EIGHT

LESBIAN/GAY/BISEXUAL COMMUNITIES

LESBIAN, GAY, AND BISEXUAL INDIVIDUALS share with other people the wish to belong to social groups that support and validate their worth and that provide opportunities for meaningful interactions with others. Because of the heterosexism intrinsic to mainstream society, however, LGBs do not have ready access to such supportive environments; instead, they must create their own. This chapter will consider the formal and informal social networks constructed by LGBs. Broadly, this topic addresses LGB communities; more specifically, it includes two levels of community. At one level are the relatively small and informal friendship networks comprised of one's own immediate family and close friends. This group is often referred to as the family of choice, as contrasted with blood or biological families. At another level, community refers to the broader, more nebulous LGB community, including both formal and informal groupings, whose existence derives from and acts as an antidote to personal isolation and political oppression. These two levels of community are often intertwined, as close friends may also share organizational or cultural involvements, and activity in the broader community may engender close friendships.

Families of Choice

LGB individuals frequently feel estranged from their biological families. In the extreme, this alienation may result from the family's active rejection of an LGB member, where family ties are not actually severed, LGBs may still sense a lack of complete validation for their lives; and even where families are entirely supportive, a degree of distance may persist because of the inescapable discrepancies between heterosexual and LGB experience. In any case, a wish for a supportive circle of intimate others commonly leads LGB individuals to create families or kinship networks to whom their ties are emotional rather than biological.

Weston (1991) depicts families of choice as a challenge to the traditional notion that the assumption of LGB identity necessarily means "exile from kinship." Rather, LGB individuals have established distinctive forms of family—and the word "family" and other kinship terms are often invoked to describe the nature of these relationships—that evolve from friendship networks, and family ties are characterized by mutuality of caring and commitment. This sort of intimacy between same-sex peers is not in keeping with traditional gender socialization for men, which equates such intimacy with homosexuality. Indeed, research indicates that gay men are more able to create and sustain close friendships with other men than are heterosexual men (Nardi, 1992). This discrepancy in openness to same-sex friendship highlights yet another way in which homophobia/heterosexism limits the experience of heterosexual as well as LGB individuals.

LGB individuals embrace as family those with whom they have had long-standing relationships; those with whom they exchange emotional support and material services; and those with whom a reciprocal commitment has outlived conflict, who have "worked through" difficulties and disagreements and still find each other to be close friends. The duration of these connections and the willingness of family members to "be there for" each other serve as testimony to their authenticity as kinship systems.

> Some of my friends I've known for fifteen years. You get attached. You stay in one place long enough, you go through seasons and years together, it's like they're part of you, you're part of them. You have fights, you get over them.... It's just unconditional love coming through to people that you didn't grow up with. (Weston, 1991, p. 115)

Unlike biological families, families of choice have very fluid boundaries; family composition may change over time or with geographic mobility. However, in some cases, although considerable time or distance has come between family members, they still consider each other family based on the certainty of reciprocal support and assistance.

Because biological bonds are not relevant here, individuals can freely choose who is to be included in family. Nuclear families—partners and possibly children—may participate in several, sometimes overlapping extended families. Each partner may identify individuals as part of her or his family that would not be so identified by the other, as well as their both designating some people as shared family.

Often these extended families include one or more former lovers. While the inclusion of former romantic partners into heterosexual social circles is relatively rare, it appears to be common among LGBs—particularly among women, a reflection of the fact that women's relationships tend to be more grounded in emotional than in sexual attachment (Becker, 1988; Nardi, 1992; Pearlman, 1987; Weston, 1991). Several dynamics underlie this phenomenon, among them the powerful bonds that are formed through the shared experience of oppression. Men and women in same-sex relationships inevitably struggle together against a host of difficulties; such struggles create a shared history that frequently survives the dissolution of a partnership. In addition, the ability to maintain connections with former lovers testifies to the validity of relationships that are often denigrated, and challenges stereotypes of LGB relationships as superficial and transient. And, because former partners are likely to know one another better than anyone else, they provide an especially valuable resource in coming to terms with a stigmatized identity. For women, sexism adds an additional layer of shared oppression that may forge closer ties between former lovers than is the case with heterosexual (or gay male) relationships.

Families of choice that include former lovers are sometimes parodied as the residue of "musical beds." However, the richness that they afford is illustrated in the following true scenario:

> Many years ago, a group of women built a cabin in the mountains. Among those women were Ann and Barb, who were partners at the time. Some years later, Ann and Barb broke up, and Ann entered into a relationship with Cathy. Cathy, who had previously been in a romantic but nonsexual relationship with Diane, knew that both Barb and Diane enjoyed hiking, and so introduced the two. Barb and Diane subsequently entered into a relationship that is now over twenty years in duration. For the winter holidays, they snowshoe into the cabin, which is now owned by Ann and her current partner, sometimes inviting other friends on the excursion. Both Ann and Cathy and the partners of each are included among Barb and Diane's extended "family."

The friendships among this group of women have evolved and been sustained over a period of two decades, providing them all with a rich source of companionship, support, and pleasure.

We might ask whether families of choice are substitutes for biological family. Weston (1991) argues that, although some LGBs express their own experience in such terms, this is an inadequate explanation for or description of these families and their role in LGBs' lives. First, unlike biological families, families of choice are not intergenerational. That is, although they may include children, there is no attempt to replace parental figures or the role they might have served. Families of choice are comprised of peers, and the kinship language used is that of brothers and sisters. In addition, even those LGB people who have good relationships with their biological families create families of choice, demonstrating that chosen kinships have a unique role and purpose of their own, rather than substituting for biological relations.

Some LGB individuals do not accept this portrayal of friendship networks as family. Particularly among minority LGBs, for whom the biological family may represent the primary bastion against racism, the biological family remains the true family, despite the importance and value of friends.

> As a Latin woman, the bonds that I got with my family are irreplaceable. They can't be replaced. They cannot. So my family is my family, my friends are my friends. My friends can be *more important* than my family, but that doesn't mean that they are my family.... They didn't have the same connection. They didn't go through what you did.... If I talk to my friends, they will understand me, but they will never feel the same. (Weston, 1991, p. 36)

Not all minority LGBs dissent from the notion of chosen families, however. Indeed, in some instances the nature of minority experience might support an understanding of extended families that needn't involve blood relationships (Weston, 1991).

Whereas heterosexual people report that their primary source of emotional and material assistance is biological family (including both nuclear and extended families), LGBs receive greater support from friends, that is, from families of choice (D'Augelli & Garnets, 1995; Kurdek, 1988; Kurdek & Schmitt, 1987; Weston, 1991). The role played by these families is much the same as that played by biological families under other circumstances. It includes pragmatic help ranging from babysitting and borrowing vehicles to financial assistance. And it includes emotional support ranging from listening to daily woes through informal relationship counseling to a supportive presence during crisis and bereavement.

The nature and structure of these kinship networks is yet another area where the impact of HIV/AIDS has been profound. Most LGB individuals have lost lovers and/or friends to the disease, disrupting most and decimating many families of choice. As people are lost to the epidemic, it becomes increasingly difficult to maintain existing and form new friendship networks, both because the social sphere continues to shrink and because the risk of yet another loss may inhibit the emergence of new friendships. On the other hand, the need for friends becomes ever greater as people deal with illness, loss, and the added stigma brought on by AIDS. It is the family of choice that often provides sole or major support and assistance during the progression of AIDS and through the bereavement that follows the death of a loved one (Dworkin & Kaufer, 1995; Paul, Hays, & Coates, 1995).

Thus, families of choice are paradoxically more crucial and more vulnerable than ever. One response to this paradox has been the emergence of more formal opportunities for the establishment of friendships. For instance, AIDS "buddy" programs, usually staffed by volunteers, provide close one-on-one support for people living with AIDS; many community centers offer self-help groups that address the need for forming relationships that do not center on sexuality (Kayal, 1994; Nardi, 1992; Omoto & Crain, 1996).

The close link between friendship and family that characterizes these kinship networks provides the underpinning for the emergence of LGB communities that extend beyond friendship networks. Such relationships provided the seeds for the establishment of a community based on shared sexual orientation (Weston, 1991).

LGB Communities

In the past, community referred to a geographically defined location, but it has recently come to mean a group of people joined by a sense of shared experience and identification with a social category or group. In some cases, LGB communities do indeed inhabit specific geographic locales, since LGB individuals are disproportionately found in large cities, to which people often migrate with the express intent of locating LGB community. Within such cities, it is often possible to identify specific neighborhoods where LGB individuals live and where many business, agencies, and services are LGB owned and/or operated. As used here, the term, "LGB community," refers more broadly to the sense of connection to a social category defined by sexual orientation, whether or not it is identified with a particular geographic location.

The LGB community differs from many other communities in that it is not grounded in experiences with family and peers in early life—as is true, for example, for minority communities, religious communities, and so forth. Rather, the LGB community is constituted by adults who voluntarily participate in a network of social relationships and institutions. A number of recent commentaries have chronicled the evolution of LGB communities over recent decades (e.g., Berube, 1990; Cruikshank, 1992; D'Augelli & Garnets, 1995; D'Emilio, 1983; Esterberg, 1996; Faderman, 1991; Weston, 1991). A brief review of this information will provide the basis for discussion of contemporary LGB communities.

World War II and The Emergence of Community

As we discussed briefly in chapter 1, the LGB community is a product of sociohistorical context. While there were some inklings of community prior to World War II, it was the events surrounding that war that kindled the emergence of active and self-conscious community. Prior to this, industrialization had diminished the importance of the nuclear family as the primary economic unit, freeing young adults to leave the family and move to the cities. This shift, in turn, allowed for increased independence and the anonymity necessary for the emergence of associations based on discreditable, stigmatized identity.

Against this background of urbanization, World War II brought together large numbers of people in sex-segregated environments. Both men and women entered the military in unprecedented numbers, and many women assumed positions in industrial settings that were largely sex segregated. These circumstances allowed those with same-sex feelings to find each other, which in turn diminished their sense of isolation while affording opportunities for the development of same-sex relationships. At war's end, many of these people remained in the cities where they had gone to work or where they had disembarked upon return to the United States. Military personnel who had been dishonorably discharged because of their sexual orientation were unlikely to return to their homes and took up residence in the cities, as well. The result was high concentrations of LGB-identified people in several large cities, especially along the coasts.

Aware now that they were not alone, these people began the process of establishing an identity as members of a definable minority. This process was aided by the publication in 1948 and 1953 of Kinsey's landmark works on human sexuality. Kinsey's demonstration that there are large numbers of nonheterosexual people in the United States was frightening to some, who saw in these data indications of the moral decay of the nation. At the same time, it provided further impetus for the formation of the LGB community, because it indicated to LGBs that their numbers were larger than they had previously had reason to believe.

This increased visibility had paradoxical effects. On the one hand, it supported the evolution of community; on the other, it stirred up the homophobic attitudes that had lain dormant in an era when the topic of sexuality, much less homosexuality, was largely taboo. The first formal LGB organizations, termed homophile organizations, emerged in the early 1950s. The Mattachine Society was established by a group of gay men in Los Angeles in 1951, and The Daughters of Bilitis (DOB) was founded in San Francisco in 1955 to serve homophile women. The two organizations were entirely independent of each other.

Although the Mattachine Society originally evolved from Marxist roots, both organizations soon assumed a less radical, more assimilationist stance, with the aim of helping homophile individuals to adapt to society and of educating the public as a means of decreasing discrimination and violence against LGBs. This philosophy of accommodation was reflected in the groups' urging homophile people to dress and act as much as possible in accord with mainstream standards and to avoid disrupting the status quo through overt displays of identity. It was hoped that such behavior, accom-

panied by the normalizing implications of the Kinsey reports, might yield a
degree of acceptance.[1]

Despite attempts by these groups to normalize homophilia, the same visibility that helped LGBs find each other also brought homophilic identity to public attention. Rather than reaping acceptance through quiet organizing and compliant demeanor, the early homophile movement stood as further evidence of the homosexual menace. It was an era of political conservatism, when public rhetoric and governmental programs supported a national movement toward establishing the nuclear, heterosexual family with well-defined roles as the epitome of American society. Further, Kinsey's work notwithstanding, homosexuality was still regarded as a psychiatric disorder and was illegal in all states. In this atmosphere, homophilia was clearly anathema.

When Senator Joseph McCarthy enlisted the House Un-American Activities Committee to rout out communists, it was an easy step to depicting homosexuals as equally dangerous to the state—indeed, the two were often linked, as in references to "communist perverts." In the resultant purge, anyone suspected of being either a communist sympathizer or a homosexual was at risk for loss of job, family, housing, and future earning potential. Homosexuals were excluded from positions with the federal government, and similar prohibitions were enacted by state and local governments and by uncounted businesses and institutions. In the absence of any protective countermeasures, explicit discrimination against LGBs became routine, and legal harassment by police and other authorities was not only unchecked but condoned.

Even in this hostile environment, small groups of LGBs continued to organize, educate, and to a degree, resist. Chapters of Mattachine, DOB, and One, Inc. (another early homophile organization) appeared in major population centers across the country, and their publications reached many LGBs elsewhere through an informal distribution network that generated an expanding mailing list.

For most lesbians and gay men, the center of social life was the bars. Several men's bars could be found in large cities, as well as some women's bars; some bars catered to a mixed clientele. Police raids on these establishments were commonplace, and often involved sexual and physical as well as verbal abuse of bar patrons. Those who were arrested were usually taken in, held over night, and released without formal charges. Their names were often listed in the newspaper, and their employers notified of their arrest. They were unable to

---

1.   The accommodationist position of the early homophile movement has frequently been criticized by those who assumed a more activist stance in the later LGB rights movement. However, it is important to recognize that these groups' very public stances in support of gay and lesbian identity and rights was extremely courageous, given the political climate of the day. Despite the subsequent change in the political tone of the movement, it had its beginnings in the fortitude of these people.

report abuse, because to do so would risk further exposure and would surely be futile in the face of official hostility toward homophilia.

Thus, the danger inherent in making contact with other LGBs was enormous. Most bar clients, especially among women, were working-class LGBs; those of higher social status rarely risked the consequences of arrest. Middle- and upper-class LGBs remained largely invisible, making social contacts primarily through friendship networks and homophile organizations. DOB and its newspaper, *The Ladder,* actively discouraged their largely white, middle-class audience from participation in the butch-femme roles that dominated the bar culture, urging instead "feminine" behavior acceptable to mainstream society.

During the 1960s, inspired by the civil rights movement, some lesbian and gay groups moved toward a more activist stance, protesting against discrimination and harassment. The emerging argument that oppression rather than homophilia was the problem underscored the parallel between this and other human rights movements. In the end, this refusal to persist in the assimilationist position that gay men and lesbians should adapt themselves to a prejudiced society triggered the events that thoroughly altered the landscape of LGB communities.

Stonewall: The Beginning of "Gay Rights"

If World War II constituted a milestone on the road to the current LGB community, a second occurred on the night of June 27–28, 1969 when New York City police conducted a routine raid on a gay bar in Greenwich Village, The Stonewall Inn. This night, at this bar, lesbian and gay patrons did not meekly submit to arrest. Rather, someone—stories vary as to who it was— refused to climb into the paddy wagon police had backed up to the door. Others followed this lead, and soon a full-blown riot ensued. For several nights afterward, ever-increasing numbers of gay men and lesbians appeared at Stonewall and battled with police. Among the slogans painted on walls was "Gay Pride"; it became the rallying cry of the new "Gay Liberation Movement" born from that initial act of defiance. Far from the assimilationist messages of the early homophile movement, the new gay rights movement was assertive and unapologetic.

Stonewall launched a remarkable movement, as LGB organizations proliferated across the country. Before 1969, there were fewer than 50 such organizations in the United States; by 1973, there were over 700 (D'Emilio, 1983). Stonewall marked the beginning of a new era in LGB community, one characterized by political activism as well as social cohesion. Coming out, which had previously been a private act undertaken with considerable trepidation and at great risk, now became a political statement. Not only did it affirm the individual's sense of positive homophilic identity; just as importantly, it provided models who challenged demeaning stereotypes. Coming out helped lesbians and gay men to find each other, and served as a rite of passage into the emerging, self-conscious community.

The gay rights movement that grew up in the wake of Stonewall was born into a nation whose consciousness had been raised by civil rights activism, lending hope that LGBs would indeed find acceptance and support. It took its inspiration and its tactics from the civil rights and women's movements, which had already achieved significant gains. LGB individuals began to see themselves as members of a collective, joined together by common oppression. The notion of LGBs as a minority community emerged, along with arguments that discrimination against LGBs was as wrong as other forms of discrimination and should be resisted with the same fervor.

The 1970s witnessed the rapid growth of this newly politicized community, now far more visible than it had been previously. During this era of heightened social tolerance and advocacy for personal and sexual freedom, the LGB community took on a new identity. For some, political activity defined the nature of the community, and organized striving to attain civil rights was core to their sense of LGB identity. For the majority of LGB people, however, identity and community were personal and social rather than political phenomena. Increased visibility made it possible to find others like themselves, and the concept of gay liberation was taken to mean greater freedom to pursue experiences that defined their LGB identity. There were marked gender differences here.

Gay Men's Post-Stonewall Community
Herdt and Boxer (1992) pointed to the radical impact of Stonewall on gay male culture, differentiating between the early "homosexual" culture, which focused on bar life and secrecy, and the post-Stonewall "gay" culture based on more public identity and a sense of shared community. For men, gay liberation meant sexual freedom and an end to harassment. The new gay identity was expressed by a celebration of gay male sexuality, a reaction against the previously unquestioned denigration of homosexuality. The gay male community encouraged sexual license, a rejection of heterosexual norms regarding monogamy and intimacy, and the formation of institutions that supported this sexualized culture. Ironically, the politicization promised by Stonewall found only limited expression, and activists bemoaned gay men's immersion in this highly sexualized culture in preference to political activity.

The term "clone" has been used to describe the prescribed appearance and style of gay men in the 70s—especially young, urban, white gay men. The image of masculine, sexually available gay men, which may have been a reaction to the demeaning effeminate portrayals of gay men so common in the pre-Stonewall era, served to shape the behavior and identity of many gay men; it also served to deny the reality of those men who didn't fit the image (Esterberg, 1996; Paul, Hays, & Coates, 1995).

Lesbians and Post-Stonewall Community
In contrast to men's celebration of sexual freedom, for women, liberation meant freedom from the constraints of heterosexist expectations and provided the opportunity to establish and find validation for new forms of relationships. The emergent feminist movement played a significant role in the formation of lesbian communities, providing the political and philosophical critique that undergirded women's relationships with women. In addition, experiences of sexism within the gay rights movement turned many women with political interests away from that movement, fostering the development of separate lesbian feminist communities.

Lesbian feminism revealed the extent to which lesbians and gay men held different agendas for liberation. In its liberal form, lesbian feminism urged a feminist analysis of women's roles and an embrace of lesbianism as an expression of feminist solidarity; in the extreme, lesbian feminist separatists rejected interaction with any males, including gay males. The sexism and preoccupation with sex that characterized the gay male community stood in stark contrast to the ideals of lesbian feminism.

Feminism also created strains within the lesbian community itself. As was the case for gay men, the modes of being prescribed by 1970s lesbian feminism, which was rooted in a rejection of heterosexuality and of traditional gender roles, proved exclusionary. These dictates discounted the experience of lesbians who chose to enact butch and femme roles in their relationships, of lesbians who were not feminist or who held a less doctrinaire approach to feminism, and also of feminists who were not lesbian. In addition, feminist analysis inspired the widespread adoption of lesbian identity by previously heterosexual women, a phenomenon that many primary lesbians found offensive and trivializing of their lifelong struggle. On the positive side, feminist political activities provided lesbians with social contacts outside the bar scene, as well as a sense of political involvement that transcended specifically lesbian issues (Esterberg, 1996; Golden, 1996; Pearlman, 1987; Weston, 1991).

Thus, gay men and lesbians held very discrepant perspectives on the nature of LGB identity, community, and experience. For men, the focus was on sexual expression and freedom from harassment; for women it was on political analysis and new forms of relationships. Not surprisingly, lesbians and gay men took very different paths in the 1970s and the early 1980s. In an impor-

tant sense, it is erroneous to speak of an LGB community during this era, as
gay men and lesbians pursued separate cultures and no identifiable bisexual
community had as yet emerged.

"Community" as Construct

It is not only the 1970s' versions of community that are open to question.
Indeed, some have critiqued the very notion of "community," suggesting that
it has served to disguise fault lines within the LGB population and to glorify
those individuals and groups with the power and visibility to define the public
agenda of this fictive community. The very concept of an LGB community
presumes the existence of a somewhat homogenous collective comprised of
individuals who identify with each other and with the collective. In the case of
the LGB community, this presumption has focused on shared sexual orientation and on the oppression experienced by virtue of nonheterosexist orientation. However, it is crucial to recognize that this depiction of community is not
without its problems.

First, note that community in this sense includes the entire population of
lesbian, gay, and bisexual individuals without regard for their self-identification and without acknowledgement of the wide variations in their involvement with that collective. Such a definition also destroys any element of
choice; everyone who is lesbian, gay, or bisexual is a member of "the"
community. While the language of family is often invoked to describe this
image of community—people speak of "sisters" and "brothers" and "family"
as meaning any and all LGBs—this is not the family of choice portrayed
above (Weston, 1991).

This depiction of the community as an egalitarian collective serves to
disguise diversity among LGBs. This was abundantly clear in the 1970s—the
era of gay male "clones" and lesbian feminist doctrine. The motive behind this
homogenization may have come from the need to pull together, to identify as a
monolithic entity standing against the attacks of a heterosexist society.
Ironically, in striving to have LGB identity affirmed as a valid variation in
human experience, the mainstream LGB community disregarded the wide
diversity found among LGBs. Indeed, since Stonewall, the LGB community
has faced tremendous division from within, as various of its presumed
members have challenged the homogenizing implications of the very notion of
the community. In this process, the mainstream LGB community has been
indicted as being (at minimum) sexist, racist, classist, ageist, and biphobic.

Among lesbians and among gay men, of course, there are many communities. Gay and lesbian identity are further refined by age and cohort, by race and
ethnicity, by rural or urban location, and by numerous other demographic

variables. While such variation was often disregarded in the community's early years, recently there has been a concerted effort to address these issues and to create communities that celebrate diversity.

As illustrative of the variations that can be found within communities, Grube (1991) discussed contrasts between the experiences of older and younger gay men, and how those differences shape their sense of community. Grube used the analogy of natives and settlers, arguing that older gay men already had a community, which he termed the "traditional gay community," before the territory of gay life was colonized by the new "organized gay community." Because the former culture was grounded in secrecy and accommodation, older gay men have been offended by the flagrant manner of the younger community; members of the new organized community, in turn, reject their predecessors as too closeted. Roles that were valued in the traditional community are now demeaned, especially the role of mentor, where an older man introduced a younger one into the community; correlatively, the new role of activist leader is meaningless to older gay men. Thus, within the gay male community there are at least two identifiable communities, one based on old models and comprised largely of older gay men, the other based on new perspectives and comprised of younger men. Comparable divisions can undoubtedly be identified across other demographic and political variables.

There are multiple lesbian identities, as well, and lesbian communities have been particularly self-conscious in their analysis of the meaning of lesbian identity and the implications of variations in that meaning. In addition to struggling with issues of demographic variability, lesbian communities have been characterized by ongoing debates about the politics of feminist and lesbian identity. Among these has been the perennial question of the association between lesbianism and feminism.

Lesbians were among the most involved of early feminist activists, and feminist political analysis supported lesbianism as a critique of heterosexism. However, the feminist movement grew wary of lesbians' strong presence, fearing that feminism's aims would be jeopardized by accusations of rampant lesbianism. Feminist leaders succumbed to the homophobia intrinsic in such attacks, actively rejecting open lesbian involvement in the movement. The feminist movement split along lines of sexual orientation, paving the way for lesbian separatism as a radical political stance that rejected not only traditional gender roles but also the liberal and assimilationist politics of mainstream (heterosexual) feminism (Pearlman, 1987; Wolf, 1979). Yet, while lesbian feminism has arguably been the most vocal political position in lesbian communities, it is not the predominant form of lesbian identity, as many lesbians do not identify as feminists (Whisman, 1993). Correlatively, although some have argued that all bonds among women can be understood as points along a lesbian "continuum" (Rich, 1980), most feminists clearly do not identify as lesbian.

Lesbians have also engaged in debates regarding who is a "true" lesbian. As we have seen, sexual orientation appears to be fluid for many women, and some women specifically assert that their lesbianism is a conscious choice. To those who experience their lesbianism as a given, an essence, these other forms of lesbian identity may be condemned as false, as fad, or as duplicitous. Divisions along lines such as these fragment the lesbian community into many very diverse communities, whose criteria for belonging differ widely. Zita (1981) pointed to the divisiveness of attempts to define who is truly lesbian and who belongs in the lesbian community, referring to these debates as the "lesbian olympics."

Another persistent controversy in lesbian communities has addressed the importance of sexuality in defining lesbian identity. As mentioned previously, for most women, identity appears to be less grounded in sexuality per se than is the case for gay men. It even appears that many women identify as lesbian despite an absence of sexual involvement with women (e.g., Rothblum & Brehony, 1993). However, some have argued that this disjunction between sexuality and lesbian identity reflects not any intrinsic quality of lesbian experience but the historic suppression of women's sexuality by patriarchy. While the denial of the fundamentally sexual nature of lesbianism may serve to calm the fears of an erotophobic public, this argument goes, it denies to women the full expression of their sexuality (e.g., Golden, 1996). Whisman (1993) has drawn a distinction between lesbian feminists of the 1970s who defined their lesbianism in terms of its social and political meaning, and the "new lesbians" of the 1980s and 1990s, who are more likely to align with gay men, identifying as "queer" and defining their lesbianism in more sexual terms.

Critiques such as those sketched here have underlain the gradual acknowl-edgment of a wide range of communi*ties* that strive not only to affirm LGB experience but also to speak to the diverse realities of their own constituents. However, the desire for a community that transcends diversity persists,and we may now be witnessing its beginnings in a certain rapprochement between gay and lesbian communities in recent years. The so-called lesbian sex wars of the '80s fostered a more openly sexual lesbian social scene and also highlighted the diversity of lesbian identities previously masked by lesbian feminism. Simultaneously, the HIV/AIDS epidemic forced a dual shift in gay male iden-tity, away from unrestrained sexuality because of the risks it entailed, and toward greater caring and nurturance as lovers and friends grew ill and died (Adam, 1992). This shift toward more similar grounding for gay and lesbian identity coincided with increased right-wing political attacks against LGBs beginning in the late 1970s. The confrontation with this common enemy encouraged cooperation between gay men and lesbians, rendering a joint community increasingly a reality rather than a slogan. Finally, in addition to forging changes in gay men's identity, the HIV/AIDS epidemic brought changes within LGB communities that have acted to unite lesbians and gay men. We will return to discuss the profound impact of AIDS on LGB communities later in this chapter.

Bisexual Communities

Very little has been written about bisexual communities, perhaps because the biphobia found in both lesbian and gay as well as heterosexual communities has precluded their evolution. In addition, the motivation for community may be less urgent among those who identify as bisexual. Klein (1993) argued that bisexually identified people may not require their own community in the same way that lesbians and gay men do, because they already have two communities in which they are comfortable—namely, heterosexual and lesbian or gay.

> A male operating freely in both homosexual and the heterosexual world can choose to define himself as bisexual and not need to form his own subculture.... He can live in both communities, moving back and forth as his needs or desires dictate.... [H]e does not necessarily need to belong to a community of bisexuals. He is among his kind when he is among *human beings*. (Klein, 1993, p. 107)

However, this position does not address the fact that bisexual individuals are not fully integrated into either heterosexual or lesbian/gay communities precisely because, as Klein also noted, their identity violates the presumed exclusiveness of one or another orientation. Accordingly, the need for a bisexual community is based on the need for acceptance and validation of one's identity, an experience unlikely anywhere but in a bisexual community.

With the burgeoning awareness that bisexuality does indeed define an identity embraced by large numbers of people, bisexual communities are beginning to emerge. Often, they appear as subgroups within existing lesbian and gay communities; thus, many community centers now incorporate "bisexual" in their title, community agencies have begun offering bisexual support and discussion groups, and so forth. Other bisexually identified people feel more at home in organizations that are explicitly inclusive of a wide range of variations in sex and gender, such as Queer Nation. And others have worked to form bisexual communities independent of connections with other groups (D'Augelli & Garnets, 1995; Esterberg, 1996; Klein, 1993).

Contemporary LGB Communities

Contemporary LGB communities have a rich complexity that reflects the diversity of their members and the wide range of motives for their involvement. Political action dominates some segments of community life, locally,

nationally, and even internationally. Political agendas range from advocating
for nondiscrimination legislation through securing partner benefits and legal-
izing same-sex unions to the radical activism of ACT-UP (AIDS Coalition to
Unleash Power) and Queer Nation. However, most LGB individuals are not
actively involved in political endeavors; for many of them, community has
other meanings.

For some, community means culture. Lesbian community, in particular, has
long been characterized by a striving to create a distinctive women's culture,
including music, literature, theater, dance, film, and other cultural forms.
While gay male culture has meant bars and bath houses, gay men are increasingly working to shift toward a less sexualized and more broadly defined
community that includes a range of cultural activities. The larger LGB
community, also, has evolved its own culture to include coffee houses and
bookstores as well as choruses and bands; fiction and poetry as well as dance
and theater.

For some, community means opportunities to establish contacts with other
LGBs. Whereas the primary locales for such contacts previously were
comprised of bars, bath houses (for men), athletic teams (for women), and
friendship circles, contemporary LGB communities are rich with organizations, community centers, support groups, educational programs, libraries,
coming out groups, choruses, professional associations, square dancing clubs,
and innumerable other vehicles for meeting other LGBs in supportive settings
that also connect one to the broader community (Bronski, 1992; Cruikshank,
1992; D'Augelli & Garnets, 1995; Esterberg, 1996; Podolsky, 1992).

One important function served by a community is the provision of a social
support system that persists even as relationships change. Partners and friends
may come and go, but LGB individuals are able to avoid the isolation that
might otherwise result from stigma by their connection to an ongoing if fluid
and ill-defined LGB community. Indeed, one of the first acts of many LGBs
upon moving to a new city is to tap into a local community.

Complex communities are now common in major cities. They tend to be
highly visible and easily accessible, and they serve as the primary vehicle for
the socialization of newly out LGBs into the customs, mores, and culture of
LGB life. In addition, they provide support for the task of coming to a positive
LGB identity and serve as an antidote to feelings of isolation that commonly
accompany that process. The role of community in buttressing LGBs' psychological well-being is illustrated by Russell's (1995) work (discussed in chapter
2), which investigated the psychological impact of anti-LGB legislation.
Russell found that being out, being integrated into the LGB community, and
having a positive sense of LGB identity were all related to more positive
outcomes following this experience of "institutionalized trauma."

Regrettably, nearly all research has dealt with LGB communities in
major metropolitan areas, and we know very little about other forms. It is

clear, however, that such communities, with all their rich resources and psychological benefits, are not available to all LGBs. Those who live in rural areas, for instance, typically have difficulty locating each other and form only small—and usually very secretive—networks. These can reduce the sense of isolation, but they cannot provide the range of opportunities and support possible in the vast communities of large urban areas.

Even within major cities, many people may be unable to access LGB communities because of language or cultural differences that make them inaccessible or irrelevant to their particular needs. Also, one must be somewhat out in order to dare entering into an LGB community; thus, many people who might benefit from supportive communities may be unable to take the steps necessary to participate for fear that their sexual orientation will be revealed.

AIDS and Community

It has been argued that in the history of LGB communities in this country, "the point dividing the world 'pre-AIDS' and 'post-AIDS' seems likely to eclipse the significance of the so-called Stonewall riots" (Paul, Hays, & Coates, 1995, pp. 347–48). The community's reaction to the appearance of HIV/AIDS in the early 1980s demonstrated how far the community had come since Stonewall in establishing a rich and viable web of organizations and resources that undergirded the community's concerted response to the epidemic. When it became clear in the early 1980s that AIDS was disproportionately concentrated in the gay male community, a transformation began that has reshaped the entire LGB community, even as it profoundly altered the lives and identities of gay and bisexual men.

Cases of AIDS began to appear in the late 1970s, although the Centers for Disease Control did not report the first officially diagnosed case until 1981. In 1984, the HIV virus was identified as the cause of AIDS. AIDS is not itself lethal; rather, it suppresses the immune system, leaving the individual susceptible to opportunistic infections—that is, infections that would not normally be dangerous but that "take advantage" of the weakened immune system. Because of the nature of the disease, the progression from infection to illness and from illness to death is often slow, making for a prolonged period of psychological and physical distress.[2]

HIV/AIDS appeared in the gay male community at the height of the bar and bath-house culture, which celebrated homoeroticism and sexual freedom.

---

2. When one becomes infected with HIV, the resultant condition is referred to as HIV positive, or HIV+. The shift to HIV+ status is termed seroconversion—that is, conversion from HIV− to HIV+ status. The AIDS disease occurs some time later, often after many years, and is diagnosed when certain designated symptoms appear. An individual who has developed full-blown AIDS may continue to live for many years, often with generally good health until the late stages of the disease.

This culture had been a topic of debate within the gay male community prior to AIDS, and was always a core element in mainstream society's hostility toward LGB identity. The introduction of AIDS served to heighten both the debate and the stigma.

Impact on Individuals

Behavior change. The most obvious and widespread consequence for gay and bisexual males has been the undeniable need to change behaviors. In this matter, the community has proven invaluable. Among the outcomes of early community activism in education and social services was what has been described as the greatest change in health-related behavior ever documented. Dramatic reductions in unsafe sex practices were accompanied by increasing support for monogamy and celibacy, and substance use accompanying sexual activity decreased significantly. Social norms supporting safer sex evolved in and were supported by community educational programs and agencies, providing a basis for long-term changes in behavior. These changes were most obvious in major metropolitan areas where existing community structures could be diverted to deal with the epidemic. It was in these areas where sexual freedom had been most avowed, so that changing behaviors here had a major impact on the rate of the spread of HIV. Changes have been less pronounced outside these centers, as well as among younger, minority, and substance-abusing men (Morin, 1988; Paul, Hays, & Coates, 1995).

Despite promising initial changes in behavior, many men appear to "relapse," returning to earlier patterns of unsafe behavior. This may reflect, in part, despair born of the fact that the epidemic has gone on so long with no end in sight. Also, many younger gay men perceive AIDS as a disease of older men and do not see pressures toward safer sex as applying to them. These attitudes point up the need to develop programs that support continuing change and that speak to the specific experiences of subgroups of the gay population (Paul, Hays, & Coates, 1995).

It is crucial to recognize that changes in sexual activity are not simply a matter of behavioral adaptations based on information about their importance. These behaviors also have implications for personal identity and the meaning of intimacy, and may be difficult to sustain where those motives urge unsafe sex. For instance, to the degree that gay men's identity is defined by particular forms of sexual activity with other men, changing those behaviors amounts to a denial of one's sense of self. A belief that safer sex is less intimate and more artificial may preclude safer sex practices in situations where intimacy is particularly desired (Gonsiorek & Shernoff, 1991; Paul, Hays, & Coates, 1995; Risman & Schwartz, 1988).

Psychological impact. Individuals who learn that they have been infected with the HIV virus are faced with tremendous psychological tasks. Paul, Hays, and Coates (1995) identified three primary categories of adaptation. First, these individuals must deal with the probability that their lifespan will be curtailed. This confrontation with mortality is made more difficult by the fact that these men are commonly young and, were it not for AIDS, would not be facing decisions raised by impending illness and potential early death. Not surprisingly, depression and anxiety are common, as is increased suicide risk. Second, these men must address the question of how to manage the added stigma; they must decide whom to tell and how. In some cases this revelation also means coming out to loved ones for the first time, which compounds the stress of coping with HIV/AIDS. Feelings of shame are common, along with renewed internalized homophobia, as individuals wrestle with the thought that they are being punished for their gay identity. Third, people infected with HIV must develop strategies for maintaining physical and emotional health. Those who become ill experience multiple personal losses—of general health, of work and financial stability, of physical attractiveness, of bodily functions, and of social roles— that call for further assistance and support from the community. It is in these last areas, especially—the need to maintain psychological and physical health and to deal with loss—that the community serves a crucial role by providing information, networking, and social and material support.

For those who are not ill, the impact of the epidemic is also great and is reflected in elevated rates of psychological distress among noninfected members of the community. Most have been involved to a greater or lesser degree in caring for friends and/or lovers; indeed, unlike other illnesses, friends and partners are almost always the primary caregivers for HIV/AIDS patients, and most LGB people have experienced the deaths of many—often people their own age or even younger. Both caregiving and bereavement are continuing and repeated stresses, so that people do not have time to recover from one round before another comes upon them. Finally, healthy men are likely to experience "survivor guilt," the sense that it could as easily have been them who was ill or who died, and that their health is somehow a betrayal of others (Dworkin & Kaufer, 1995; Paul, Hays, & Coates, 1995).

Impact on Relationships
As mentioned in chapter 7, the HIV/AIDS epidemic has had major consequences for gay men's relationships. The greater emphasis on monogamy and on forming long-term partnerships is at least in part a response to the epidemic. However, there is some question about whether this shift in attitudes in reflected in actual behavior changes. Surveys conducted since the late 1960s have found that the rate of men reporting that they are in primary relationships has remained stable over that time period. But, while a large majority

of men agreed that monogamy is best, less than 10 percent were monogamous   *223*
in most of these surveys (Paul, Hays, & Coates, 1995).

Equally unfortunate is the fact that many gay men do not routinely discuss
HIV status with potential partners, and many HIV+ men do not reveal their
status to one or more of their sexual partners (Paul, Hays, & Coates, 1995).
Here again, what may appear to be a need for simple behavioral changes actually disguises complex feelings and motives, and points to future needs in
education and support.

Impact on Community Systems
Kayal (1994) argues that the only way to deal effectively with the profound
despair created by HIV/AIDS has been for people to create "intensive
personal linkages with one another," coming together as a community. Indeed,
the hope that has emerged from the tragedy of AIDS lies in "communalization," the coming together of individuals and friendship networks to forge a
closely interlinked collective. This community has proven invaluable. Research
indicates that gay men rely primarily on friends and community support
systems in their efforts to cope with HIV/AIDS. Regardless of their HIV
status, gay men find their peers more helpful than any other source of support,
and close connections with friends and community are related to lower levels
of anxiety and depression. Conversely, those who experience inadequate
support are more likely to evidence greater mood disturbance, depression, and
lower quality of life (Paul, Hays, & Coates, 1995).

Unfortunately, since many individuals have already been lost to AIDS,
friendship networks are depleted. Those who remain are often drained by
repeated caretaking and loss, so that the resources available among friends
grow ever more meager. It is here that the broader community has assumed a
central role, and the process has significantly altered the community.

Renewed activism. Although the creation of a new LGB community that resulted
from Stonewall was a profoundly political event, most LGB individuals had not
been actively involved in political activity. The AIDS crisis, however, changed
that. The government and other public agencies were extremely slow to
respond to the epidemic (Shilts, 1987). Realizing this, the community began to
organize to demand greater attention to the crisis and better care for its
members. The result was new levels of political activity in the LGB community. The most visible manifestation of this trend has been the confrontational
actions of ACT-UP, an organization dedicated specifically to actions that bring
attention to AIDS. Other, less radical, and equally important groups have
worked to address the HIV/AIDS crisis at local and national levels.

The politicization of the community stimulated by the AIDS crisis has
expanded to address other issues, as well. Following the lead of ACT-UP,

Queer Nation uses similar tactics to confront other issues affecting the LGB community, such as hate crimes. In recent years, membership has swelled in national and local organizations that address a range of political issues, from gays in the military to local political battles over LGB rights (D'Augelli & Garnets, 1995; Paul, Hays & Coates, 1995).

Community-based organizations. The development that may represent the clearest expression of "community" is the emergence of organizations in the LGB community whose intent is to serve its own members. The HIV/AIDS epidemic generated enormous demands for a wide range of services, including education, health care, and support services that were not met by governmental or other existent agencies, so the community established its own grass-roots agencies. Staffed largely by volunteers, these agencies have become the primary support system for people living with AIDS, their friends and family, and the entire community as it struggles to deal with this crisis.

They also serve important roles for those involved, who find in this work an opportunity to serve the community while also gaining a sense of control over a frightening situation. An additional benefit of community-based organizations is that they provide social contacts, thereby assisting in the formation of new social networks to supplement diminished families of choice (Omoto & Crain, 1996).

Community Support and Psychological Well-Being

The massive involvement of community in the AIDS crisis has had an enormous impact on the well-being of its members. Political activism has succeeded in bringing greater government attention and increased funding to AIDS-related issues. Many community-based organizations, which have provided front-line care and support to community members for over a decade, have established unprecedented connections with governmental, private, and public agencies outside the community. Additionally, community-based initiatives have clearly served the aim of undergirding psychological health of those they reach. Research indicates that people living with AIDS as well as LGBs coping with anxiety, depression, and multiple loss fare better as they tap into community resources (Adam, 1992; Dworkin & Kaufer, 1995; Paul, Hays, & Coates, 1995; Remien & Rabkin, 1996).

Hope Arising from Loss

The community has succeeded in creating many good things from the fundamental tragedy of this epidemic. One of these has been the improved relations between lesbians and gay men. Lesbians have been visibly involved in community agencies and volunteer work as well as in the personal care of friends who are ill and support of those suffering the loss of loved ones. This has brought

LGB men and women far closer, making it today more accurate to speak of a 225 true LGB community than was possible in the past. Wolverton reflected on her experience in this regard. "By the mid-eighties I began to see how insulated I had become, sequestered in a world of women. An epidemic was ravaging the gay community, men were dying by the thousands, but *I didn't know them....* [I]t felt obscene to me, like standing by and passively watching while someone gets beaten to death" (1992, p. 228). Her own subsequent involvement in community projects related to AIDS gave her a new perspective:

> These men seem to possess an astonishing level of self-awareness, a depth of feeling quite unlike the men I turned my back on a decade earlier. Although I was tempted at first to attribute those qualities to the illness these men are facing, I've also witnessed the same capacities in uninfected men who've nursed friends through sickness and watched lovers die, those who've been touched by the consequences of AIDS. The epidemic has spawned a change within the gay community, and for all the terrible loss, it seems gay men have discovered a courage and level of compassion previously unexplored. (p. 229)

Some women express concern over women's assuming the traditional role of caretaker; and, pointing to the relative lack of concern about women's health care issues, such as breast cancer, some doubt that gay men would respond with the same degree of caring had the epidemic affected primarily lesbians. Others argue that gay men have, by necessity, learned to be more nurturant than their socialization would ordinarily ensure, and that, having witnessed women's involvement on their behalf, reciprocity is now far more likely. Thus, a second benefit is revealed here as well: the unfolding in gay men of a new level of sensitivity and caring.

A third hopeful outcome of the epidemic is that it has made lesbian, gay, and bisexual concerns more visible than ever before. As has been true in the past, this heightened visibility has mixed consequences. On the one hand, it arouses the hostility of those with strong homonegative attitudes, fueling the anti-LGB movement. On the other hand, it affords opportunities to address LGB issues in the public forum and thereby to diminish the potential for distortions of LGB experience and demonization of LGB identity.

Finally, HIV/AIDS has personalized LGB identity. As more and more respected public figures and everyday people reveal that they are HIV+ or have AIDS, the demonic portrayals of homophilia lose credibility. It is hard to think of Rock Hudson or one's congenial neighbor as suddenly evil. Also, many heterosexual people have come into contact with LGBs through the provision of medical and social services or through volunteer work in community agencies. These people come to know LGBs in a new and personalized light. As we discussed in chapter 2, the single best predictor of nonhomonegative attitudes is contact with LGB individuals; what better circumstance for this to occur than to work alongside LGBs caring for their families of choice.

The HIV Community

The benefits of this newly flourishing LGB community extend beyond its own members. Although HIV/AIDS has been associated in public discourse with homophilia, in fact it affects many people who are not LGB-identified and many who do not engage in same-sex sex. It is not identity but particular acts that transmit HIV, and a growing proportion of those infected are not gay or bisexual. Yet, the vast majority of community programs designed to cope with HIV/AIDS have emerged from the LGB community; as a result, many non-LGB people have sought out these organizations for support and assistance. Remien and Rabkin (1996) share the words of a woman who turned to the gay community when she learned she was HIV+:

> I made a lot of gay friends since this all started, because most of the men in the groups are gay. The first time I was really involved was a weekend meeting, with primarily gay men and a couple of women and they just embraced me. They made sure I wasn't left out.... I think back and wonder, who would I have turned to if it weren't for them? ... So I feel indebted to the gay community because, no questions asked, they just took me right in. (p. 183)

The positive legacy of the HIV/AIDS epidemic is this open, embracing community that has eased the way not only for its own but for others through the nightmare that is AIDS.

COMING TO TERMS

OVER THE COURSE OF THIS BOOK, we have examined various aspects of the process of coming to terms. We began by exploring the very concept of sexual orientation and the terms to which we have come to name the categories and delineate the experiences that we include under the rubric, "sexual orientation." Subsequently, we surveyed various aspects of the process of coming to terms with an identity defined by one or another of these categories. These two inquiries have been intertwined: it is apparent that coming to terms with a particular identity is profoundly influenced by the categories available and the meanings given to them. In this Conclusion, we will further close this circle, returning to the questions raised earlier regarding the relationship between essentialist and constructionist views of sexual orientation.

The goal is to explore where we might go from here: what questions linger, what are their implications for LGB experience, and what role might psychology play in addressing these questions? We will address three major themes: the implications of constructionism for psychological practice, potential challenges to heterosexual normativity, and the primacy of gender in considerations of sexual orientation.

Constructionism and Psychological Practice

As you recall, the social constructionist position argues that what we take as knowledge is, in fact, interpretation and is inevitably shaped by the context in which it is formed. The meaning of events is not intrinsic to the events themselves, but is constructed, imposed upon phenomena, by the sociohistorical and political surround in which they occur. Thus, understanding is "situated," and what is taken as self-evidently true depends on existing sociohistorical forces that define the nature of knowledge.

A growing literature addresses the implications of constructionism for psychology, with two major (and overlapping) classes of work. One area of discussion entails critiques of theory and research addressing LGB experience; the other has to do with the practice of psychotherapy.

The Issue of Categories

The most fundamental critique of psychological work dealing with sexual orientation challenges the reification of categories—that is, the assumption that our conceptual categories actually exist as real phenomena. As we have seen, psychological theory and research persistently presume that it is possible to sort individuals into clearly defined and mutually exclusive and stable categories, designated by labels that identify their sexual orientation. Psychology's attachment to this position has been demonstrated throughout this book; it is particularly clear in the literature on identity formation. With a few exceptions, this literature portrays LGB identity as a quality intrinsic to the individual, one that is discovered and then gradually acknowledged in the process of coming out.

Deconstructing Categories
This essentialist view of sexual orientation is not supported by the literature, especially that outside of psychology. A constructionist analysis reveals that this position ignores, first, the evidence of history; second, the findings of cross-cultural research; and, third, the experience of many individuals. The first two demonstrate that what we take as a free-standing phenomenon, sexual orientation, is in fact a culturally and historically situated meaning. The last reveals that the categories we employ do not do justice to all individuals' experiences, despite the strong cultural pressure to assume the identities described by those categories. This issue is particularly relevant for psychology, whose aim is to understand the subjective experience of individuals.

As an illustration of this debate, we can consider the arguments of Epstein (1992), who urged an intermediate stance. Among his arguments was that if we take constructionism literally, there would be an enormous number of possible identities. If each of the many components (he suggested five elements) of sexual orientation can vary independently and each might take any of three values (feminine, masculine, or neither/both), then there would be 243 possible sexual orientation identities. No culture, he argued, has ever demonstrated this many variations in identity.

Actually, he may underestimate; there could be even more identities than Epstein suggested—"neither" is not the same as "both," feminine and masculine are not discrete and exhaustive categories, and there may more dimensions than the five mentioned by Epstein (for example, Klein identified seven).

Nonetheless, whether it is 243 or many more identities, Epstein's point exactly demonstrates the constructionist argument. No culture has *named* this many variations in identity, but this does not mean that no society has included individuals whose personal experience did in fact reflect this vast range of variation. Indeed, looking at just two of the possible dimensions that define sexual orientation—self-identification and sexual behavior—Golden (1987, 1996) found among her subjects all possible combinations of these two variables. Women who identified as heterosexual or as lesbian or as bisexual might have exclusively heterosexual sexual relationships, both same-sex and heterosexual relations, exclusively lesbian relationships, might be celibate while maintaining any of these identities, or might have had no actual sexual experience at all and yet hold any of these identities. If we were to include the many other dimensions subsumed under sexual orientation and expand the population to include men, we might indeed find Epstein's 243 separate identities—or more.

In fact, this is precisely the point made by constructionism: this incredibly rich variety is erased by the meanings imposed by circumscribed categories.

Psychological Essentialism

At the same time, it appears that most people do, indeed, experience their sexual orientation as intrinsic, and many (perhaps most) experience it as fixed and permanent. This phenomenon offers a telling illustration of how cultural truths are translated into psychological realities. Guided by societal understandings in assuming an identity, people self-identify using the limited labels provided them. Given the cultural understanding that sexual orientation is fixed, an individual experiences her or his own identity accordingly. This point brings us to a consideration of the importance of constructionism for psychological practice.

Implications for Psychotherapy

Traditionally, LGB-affirmative counseling or therapy has been geared toward helping LGB or questioning individuals come to terms with their sexual orientation, and to establish a positive sense of self that incorporates this aspect of identity. This approach assumes that sexual orientation is a core trait to be discovered, acknowledged, and accepted. Hesitancy to adopt a lesbian or gay identity might be seen as a reflection of internalized homophobia—as might bisexual identity, for many therapists. Fluctuation between identities might be interpreted as a resistance to accepting a stigmatized label or as a sign of unfinished work where sexual orientation is concerned.

230   However, a recognition of the inadequacy of available categories and of the potential fluidity of sexual orientation necessarily changes this focus.[1] Not only would a bisexual identity be seen as perfectly legitimate, but so would an ill-defined, diffuse, and flexible pattern of self-identification. Far from a sign of internalized homophobia, "resistance" to adopting an unequivocal lesbian or gay identity would be seen as a healthy acceptance of the reality of fluidity in human sexual and affectional connections. The task of the therapist here is not to help clients arrive at a firm and fixed identity, but to support an awareness of their own flexibility and to affirm that as a healthy identity in its own right.

Still, socially constructed categories have a persuasive effect on individuals' understandings. In a culture that sees sexual orientation as permanent and essential, people seek a stable identity for themselves. Indeed, people may enter therapy precisely with the hope of discovering and/or coming to accept who they "really are." The distress accompanying this search is not made easier by arguments that it doesn't matter, that the categories are not real. Thus, the therapeutic task is complicated by the intersection between what might (or might not) be genuine and healthy fluidity and the individual's need to construct a personal understanding that matches cultural understandings (even if those diminish the potential richness of her or his identity). In Plummer's words, "to label too soon may prematurely close possibilities, and to label too late may add to the weight of suffering....In the short run, labels are comforting; in the long run, they are destructive" (1981a, pp. 108–109).

One circumstance where this dilemma becomes clear is in working with adolescents who are questioning their sexual orientation. Urging them to accept an LGB identity might have unintended consequences. First, if they believe that sexual orientation is permanent, pressure to assume a stigmatized identity might make the process of exploration more anxiety ridden, whereas an awareness that it is often fluid may allow them to examine their own experience more freely.[2] However, it is not helpful to define as "just a phase" the deeply felt self-identification of some gay and lesbian adolescents. Here, the struggle that precedes that identity must be acknowledged by a parallel argument that sexual orientation may be fixed as well as flexible. The experiences

---

1. Several writers have examined the impact on psychological practice of constructionist analyses of sexual orientation (e.g., Golden, 1987, 1996; Kitzinger, 1995; Plummer, 1981a; Richardson, 1987; Schippers, 1987).

2. Notice that this is a very different proposition from one urging that LGB identity *ought* to be resisted or changed. The point here is not the imposition of a coerced adaptation to moral injunctions from others, but the freedom to choose fluidity where it reflects changes in the individual's needs.

that lead one individual to identify as LGB might be very different from those that bring another to the same identity; the meaning of this identity in an individual's life might change over time; and the role it plays in total identity might fluctuate, as well. The complexity these variables add to questions of sexual orientation identity hints at how profoundly psychological practice would be altered by the adoption of a constructionist stance.

On a personal level, a paradox is raised for those who are intellectually convinced of the merits of constructionism but whose personal identity and political stance are grounded in an essentialist view of LGB identity:

> Society calls me a lesbian because it has a controlling stake in underlining the fact that my life partner is a woman. But I call myself a lesbian as a very personal expression of my opposition to those societal forces. . . . In the absence of repression, there would be no need for such an identity. In the presence of it, however, my identity as a lesbian is a vital part of how I give meaning to my life and acquire the strength to survive and surmount social difficulties. (Martin, 1994, p. 14)

Here, too, lies the potential for psychology to contribute significantly to an understanding of LGB experience. Identity research provides an excellent opportunity for psychology to explore the dialectic between individual and society, the question of how socially constructed truths become individually experienced realities. For instance, to borrow from Martin's comments above, how does resisting an essentialist identity serve as an expression of opposition? How does employing such an identity give meaning to life and provide one with strength? How do people resolve, psychologically, the apparent discrepancy between the two? Or, looking to how the fluidity of identity challenges essentialist renditions of sexual orientation, how do people who identify as heterosexual but have same-sex relationships process that discrepancy— intellectually, affectively, and socially? How is it that some people manage to retain a sense of their identity as flexible in the absence of socially constructed and culturally sanctioned understandings to justify their personal experience? In general, how do the terms of social discourse mediate the terms of individual identity?

Challenging the Heterosexual Norm

The paradox entailed in our accepting both constructionist and essentialist depictions of sexual orientation leads us to another quandary that is yet to be addressed by most psychological examinations of LGB experience. One of the persistent themes in psychological research dealing with LGB experience has been a tacit acceptance of the heterosexual norm. Thus, we find research demonstrating that LGB partnerships are much the same as heterosexual ones, and that LGB parenting is similar to heterosexual parenting. In each case, the yardstick is heterosexuality, a phenomenon reminiscent of the insistence by 1950s homophile organizations that LGBs are "just like everyone else."

Research such as this has proven affirming and may be valuable in garnering acceptance in mainstream circles. But this position can also be regarded as ultimately self-defeating and the favor it reaps as patronizing. LGBs might instead seek acceptance in their own right and for their own experience, whether or not it is just like heterosexual experience. This stance raises intriguing possibilities that, if taken seriously by psychology, would suggest a new paradigm that might transform the discipline. Brown (1989), in one of the first articles to place such a challenge before psychology, argued that certain aspects of LGB experience could, if they were taken as normative, grant an entirely different perspective on human experience in general.

The first such quality is *biculturalism*. LGB people must of necessity participate in two cultures: the mainstream culture where they conduct the majority of their daily lives, and LGB culture where stigmatized identity finds acceptance and support. In this circumstance, LGB experience is simultaneously both mainstream and separate; thus the individual's identity has intrinsic elements of difference. This experience of being "both/and" breaks down dichotomous thinking, fostering an ability to live with ambiguity, along with the openness to alternative perspectives that this allows. These qualities may be invisible to current psychological models, because they are characteristic of the experience of a discredited group. However, if the potential for flexibility and ingenuity were to be taken as normative, psychology's focus might shift to exploring conditions that enhance these strengths.

Marginality is a second aspect of LGB experience that suggests a new paradigm for psychology. Regardless of their participation in mainstream society, LGB individuals are, in fact, estranged from that society. This position on the margin provides a distinctive perspective. Already alienated and having less at stake, LGBs are able to challenge the dominant, heterosexist values of society in ways that others are not. For example, LGBs have established patterns of living that directly counter traditional beliefs about what constitutes healthy families; we see this in the strengths found in families of choice and in the successful practice of LGB parenting. If these patterns were taken as paradigmatic rather than as deviant, psychology might learn a great deal about the possibilities for human relationships.

Finally, proposing a concept that perhaps embraces the others, Brown suggested that LGB experience is characterized by *normative creativity*. Given the absence of role models and the lack of rules for how one lives as a lesbian, gay, or bisexual person, LGBs have the opportunity to create their own motifs for living. In Brown's words, "*being* lesbian or gay has been something we have had to invent for ourselves" (1989, p. 452). Consider the shift in psychology if such creativity were taken as normative not only for LGBs but for all, if it were accepted that people have both the opportunity and the obligation to construct their own life patterns rather than acceding to preexisting social norms. Consider the challenge this raises to traditional gender roles, for example, or to theories that presume the necessity of male and female parents. In short, the normative creativity that characterizes LGB experience raises questions that need to be asked about human experience in general.

As we consider the potential impact of such a paradigm shift, we are able to see more clearly how even research addressing questions of LGB experience has been limited by the dominant paradigm, rather than by using homophilia as a medium for nourishing a new one. For example, given the absence of clear norms for LGB life, the possibilities for how individuals might establish and pursue relationships are virtually limitless. Yet, nearly all research has investigated coupled relationships, often defined by other criteria that parallel heterosexual partnering—such as living together as a family unit. This is in part a product of the nature of psychological research, which requires comparable comparison groups, and it is in part because of our accession to the heterosexual norm. If our goal were to enrich our understanding of human experience using the insights provided by regarding LGB life as normative, we would need to investigate other forms of relationships, as well. Surely there is much to learn about human potential from exploring the varieties of relationships we might form when exercising normative creativity.

The Primacy of Gender

A final area of analysis points to the crucial role of gender in considerations of sexual orientation. We have seen that gender is a more significant determinant of behavior and experience than is sexual orientation. Gender role socialization appears to result in gay men's being more like straight men and lesbians more like straight women than gays and lesbians are like each other. We have seen this in the research on developmental tasks, on relationships, on sexuality, on the nature of community. It is especially evident in research demonstrating that many women have chosen lesbian identities as personal expressions of feminist challenges to patriarchy and to women's place in heterosexual relationships. It is a profound commentary on the oppressive nature of heterosexuality and the gender roles that undergird it that people would choose an identity that is so pervasively denigrated rather than accede to heterosexist norms. Put differently, heterosexist norms support relationships that are so much less fulfilling to women that they are abdicated in favor of more satisfying—albeit stigmatized—lesbian relationships.

In all these areas, the profound impact of gender is highlighted, and new directions for psychology emerge from the shadows. It is not sexual orientation per se that represents so great a challenge to established systems, but the coercive weight of socially constructed notions of gender. It is toward this coercion that psychology might well direct its energies, for it appears that gender rather than sexual orientation is the culprit. Except for issues of gender, many questions we now ask regarding sexual orientation would be moot.

It appears that in all this, sexual orientation is fundamentally a vehicle for incursions of gender. Were we less concerned about issues of gender propriety, variations in the sex of one's partner might well be deemed irrelevant. The very terms we use to designate sexual orientation (including that term itself) might disappear, to be replaced by others that depict some other aspect of human individuality as crucial. In a playful version of this argument, Martin also points to a core issue: our preoccupation with sexuality.

> I am inclined to believe that if we could someday remove the restricting effects of sexual orientation categories, and all traces of heterosexist bias, there still would be some people who report that from as early as they can remember they had exclusive attractions to one sex or the other and never for a moment experienced any variation in that. And under those circumstances it might perhaps be interesting to ask some of the research questions we now ask, like what makes those with exclusively homosexual attractions different from those with exclusively heterosexual attractions, in the same way we might research what makes someone love or loath asparagus. *But we have to be very careful if we think that it is more important to do research on questions of sex than of asparagus.* We need to ask ourselves why we think so, what would it mean to us, and what conclusions we might want to draw from the data. Because the answers to these last questions have *less to do with science and more to do with politics.* (1994, p. 14; italics added)

In the end, questions regarding the origin and nature of homophilia are the wrong questions. This is so not simply because the categories are nebulous, permeable, and changing, not only because cross-cultural and historical variation render the very notion of sexual orientation problematic. They are the wrong questions because they distract us from the more crucial issue, which is that oppression is unjust and it does psychological damage to both oppressor and oppressed.

At base, the questions we must ask are social psychological ones; they are questions about how social meanings translate to individual experience, and how those meanings can be made more humane. In the end, the twofold aim of

this book, the dual meaning of "coming to terms," reveals yet a third. It   *235*
remains to be seen how we as a society will come to terms with the growing
visibility of experiences that we term lesbian, gay, and bisexual. My hope is
that this book will facilitate understanding and stimulate thoughtful reflection
so that this third coming to terms is a transformative process.

REFERENCES

Abelove, H. (1993). Freud, male homosexuality, and the Americans. In H. Abelove, M. A. Barale, & D. M. Halperin (Eds.), *The lesbian and gay studies reader* (pp. 381–393). New York: Routledge.

Adam, B. S. (1986). Age, structure, and sexuality: Reflections on the anthropological evidence on homosexual relations. In E. Blackwood (Ed.), *The many faces of homosexuality: Anthropological approaches to homosexual behavior* (pp. 19–34). New York: Harrington Park.

Adam, B. S. (1992). Sex and caring among men: Impact of AIDS on gay people. In K. Plummer (Ed.), *Modern homosexualities: Fragments of lesbian and gay experience* (pp. 175–183). London: Routledge.

Adelman, M. (1986). *Long time passing: Lives of older lesbians.* Boston: Alyson.

Adelman, M. (1991). Stigma, gay lifestyles, and adjustment to aging: A study of later-life gay men and lesbians. *Journal of Homosexuality, 20,* 7–32.

Adorno, T. W., Frenkel-Brunswik, E., Levinson, D. J., & Sanford, R. N. (1950). *The authoritarian personality.* New York: Harper & Row.

Allen, P. G. (1984). Beloved women: The lesbian in American Indian culture. In T. Darty & S. Potter (Eds.), *Women-identified women* (pp. 83–96). Palo Alto, CA: Mayfield.

Allen, P. G. (1986). "Hwame," "Koshkalaka," and the rest: Lesbians in American Indian cultures. In *The sacred hoop* (pp. 245–261). Boston: Beacon.

Allen, P. G. (1989). Lesbians in American Indian cultures. In M. Duberman, M. Vicinus, & G. Chauncey (Eds.), *Hidden from history* (pp. 106–117). New York: New American Library

Allport, G. (1954). *The nature of prejudice.* Reading, MA: Addison-Wesley.

Almaguer, T. (1993). Chicano men: A cartography of homosexual identity and behavior. In H. Abelove, M. A. Barale, & D. M. Halperin (Eds.), *The lesbian and gay studies reader* (pp. 255–273). New York: Routledge.

Altman, D., Vance, C., Vicinus, M., & Weeks, J. (1987). *Homosexuality, which homosexuality? International conference on gay and lesbian studies.* Amsterdam: Dekker.

Altmeyer, B. (1988). *Enemies of freedom: Understanding right-wing authoritarianism.* San Francisco: Jossey-Bass.

Atkinson, D. R., Morten, G., & Sue, D. W. (1979). *Counseling American minorities: A cross-cultural perspective.* Dubuque, IA: William C. Brown.

Bailey, J. M. (1995). Biological perspectives on sexual orientation. In A. R. D'Augelli & C. J. Patterson (Eds.), *Lesbian, gay, and bisexual identities over the lifespan* (pp. 102–135). New York: Oxford University Press.

References

238   Bailey, J. M., & Pillard, R. C. (1991). A genetic study of male sexual orientation. *Archives of General Psychiatry, 48*, 1089–1096.

Bailey, J. M., Pillard, R. C., Neale, M. C., & Agyei, Y. (1993). Heritable factors influence female sexual orientation. *Archives of General Psychiatry, 50*, 217–223.

Bailey, J. M., & Zucker, K. J. (1995). Childhood sex-typed behavior and sexual orientation: A conceptual analysis and quantitative review. *Developmental Psychology, 31*, 43–55.

Bart, P. (1993). Protean woman: The liquidity of female sexuality and the tenacity of lesbian identity. In S. Wilkinson & C. Kitzinger (Eds.), *Heterosexuality: A "Feminism and Psychology" reader* (pp. 246–252). London: Sage.

Baumrind, D. (1995). Commentary on sexual orientation: Research and social policy implications. *Developmental Psychology, 31*, 130–136.

Bayer, R. (1981). *Homosexuality and American psychology: The politics of diagnosis.* New York: Basic Books.

Becker, C. (1988). *Unbroken ties: Lesbian ex-lovers.* Boston: Alyson.

Begelman, D. A. (1977). Homosexuality and the ethics of behavioral intervention. *Journal of Homosexuality, 2*(3), 213–219.

Bell, A. P., & Weinberg, M. S. (1978). *Homosexualities: A study of diversity among men and women.* London: Mitchell Beazley.

Bell, A. P., Weinberg, M. S., & Hammersmith, S. K. (1981). *Sexual preference: Its development in men and women.* Bloomington: Indiana University Press.

Bem, D. J. (in press). Exotic becomes erotic: A developmental theory of sexual orientation. *Psychological Review.*

Bem, S. L. (1993a). On the inadequacy of our sexual categories: A personal perspective. In S. Wilkinson & C. Kitzinger (Eds.), *Heterosexuality: A "Feminism and Psychology" reader* (pp. 50–51). London: Sage.

Bem, S. L. (1993b). *The lenses of gender: Transforming the debate on sexual inequality.* New Haven, CT: Yale University Press.

Bem, S. L. (1995, March). *Dismantling gender polarization: Shall we turn the volume up or down?* Paper presented at the annual convention of the Association for Women in Psychology, Indianapolis, IN.

Bennett, K. C., & Thompson, N. L. (1991). Accelerated aging and male homosexuality: Australian evidence in a continuing debate. *Journal of Homosexuality, 20*, 65–75.

Berenbaum, S. A., & Snyder, E. (1995). Early hormonal influences on childhood sex-typed activity and playmate preferences: Implications for the development of sexual orientation. *Developmental Psychology, 31*, 31–42.

Berger, P. L., & Luckmann, T. (1967). *The social construction of reality.* New York: Doubleday.

Berger, R. (1980). Psychological adaptation of the older male homosexual. *Journal of Homosexuality, 5*, 161–175.

Berger, R. (1982). *Gay and gray.* Champaign: University of Illinois Press.

Berger, R. (1990). Men together: Understanding the gay couple. *Journal of Homosexuality, 19*, 31–49.

Berk, R. A., Boyd, E. A., & Hamner, K. M. (1992). Thinking more clearly about hate-motivated crimes. In G. M. Herek & K. T. Berrill (Eds.), *Hate crimes: Confronting violence against lesbians and gay men* (pp. 123–143). London: Sage.

Berrill, K. T. (1992). Anti-gay violence and victimization in the United States: An overview. In G. M. Herek & K. T. Berrill (Eds.), *Hate crimes: Confronting violence against lesbians and gay men* (pp. 19–40). London: Sage.

Bersoff, D. N. & Ogden, D. W. (1991). APA amicus curiae briefs: Furthering lesbian and gay male civil rights. *American Psychologist, 46*, 950–956.

Berube, A. (1990). *Coming out under fire: The history of gay men and women in World War II.* New York: Free Press.

Bickelhaupt, E. E. (1995). Alcoholism and drug abuse in gay and lesbian persons: A review of incidence studies. *Journal of Gay and Lesbian Social Services, 2,* 5–14.

Bieber, I., Dain, H. J., Dince, P. R., Drellich, M. G., Grand, H. G., Grundlach, R. H., Kremer, M. W., Rifkin, A. H., Wilbur, C. B., & Bieber, T. B. (1962). *Homosexuality: A psychoanalytic study.* New York: Basic Books.

Bierly, M. M. (1985). Prejudice toward contemporary outgroups as a generalized attitude. *Journal of Applied Social Psychology, 15,* 189–199.

Bigner, J. J., & Bozett, F. W. (1990). Parenting by gay fathers. *Marriage and Family Review, 14,* 155–175.

Bigner, J. J., & Jacobsen, R. B. (1989). Parenting behaviors of homosexual and heterosexual fathers. *Marriage and Family Review, 14,* 173–186.

Bigner, J. J., & Jacobsen, R. B. (1992). Adult responses to child behavior and attitudes toward fathering: Gay and non-gay fathers. *Journal of Homosexuality, 23,* 99–112.

Blackwood, E. (1984). Sexuality and gender in certain Native American tribes: The case of cross-gender females. *Signs: Journal of Women in Culture and Society, 19,* 27–42.

Blackwood, E. (1986a). Breaking the mirror: The construction of lesbianism and the anthropological discourse on homosexuality. In E. Blackwood (Ed.), *The many faces of homosexuality: Anthropological approaches to homosexual behavior* (pp. 1–18). New York: Harrington Park.

Blackwood, E. (Ed.). (1986b). *The many faces of homosexuality: Anthropological approaches to homosexual behavior.* New York: Harrington Park.

Blair, R. (1982). *Ex-Gay.* New York: Homosexual Counseling Center.

Bleich, D. (1989). Homophobia and sexism as popular values. *Feminist Teacher, 4*(2/3), 21–28.

Bleier, R. (1984). *Science and gender: A critique of biology and its theories on women.* New York: Pergamon.

Blumenfeld, W., & Raymond, D. (1993). *Looking at gay and lesbian life* (2d ed.). Boston: Beacon.

Blumenstein, P., & Schwartz, P. (1977). Bisexuality: Some social psychological issues. *Journal of Social Issues, 33,* 30–45.

Blumenstein, P., & Schwartz, P. (1983). *American couples: Money, work, and sex.* New York: William Morrow.

Blumenstein, P., & Schwartz, P. (1990). Intimate relationships and the creation of sexuality. In D. P. McWirther, S. A. Sanders, & J. M. Reinisch (Eds.), *Homosexuality/heterosexuality: The Kinsey scale and current research* (pp. 307–320). New York: Oxford University Press.

Bohan, J. S. (1993). Regarding gender: Essentialism, constructionism, and feminist psychology. *Psychology of Women Quarterly, 17,* 5–21.

Bonilla, L., & Porter, J. (1990). A comparison of Latino, Black, and non-Hispanic White attitudes toward homosexuality. *Hispanic Journal of Behavioral Sciences, 12,* 437–452.

Borhek, M. V. (1988). Helping gay and lesbian adolescents and their families: A mother's perspective. *Journal of Adolescent Health Care, 9,* 123–128.

Boxer, A. M., & Cohler. B. J. (1989). The life course of gay and lesbian adolescents: An immodest proposal for the study of lives. *Journal of Homosexuality, 17,* 317–355.

Bozett, F. W. (1980). Gay fathers: How and why they disclose their homosexuality to their children. *Family Relations, 29,* 173–179.

Bozett, F. W. (1981). Gay fathers: Evolution of the gay father identity. *American Journal of Orthopsychiatry, 51,* 552–559

Bozett, F. W. (1982). Heterogeneous couples in heterosexual marriage: Gay men and straight women. *Journal of Marital and Family Therapy, 8,* 81–89.

Bozett, F. W. (1987). *Gay and lesbian parents.* New York: Praeger.

240   Bozett, F. W. (1989). Gay fathers: A review of the literature. *Journal of Homosexuality, 18,* 137–162.

Bradford, J., & Ryan, C. (1987). *National lesbian health care survey: Mental health implications.* Washington, DC: National Gay and Lesbian Health Foundation.

Bronski, M. (1992). The changing world of gay men. In B. Berzon (Ed.), *Positively gay* (pp. 32–37). Berkeley, CA: Celestial Arts.

Brown, L. S. (1986). Confronting internalized oppression. *Journal of Homosexuality, 12,* 99–107.

Brown, L. S. (1988). Lesbians, gay men and their families: Common clinical issues. *Journal of Gay and Lesbian Psychotherapy, 1,* 65–77.

Brown, L. S. (1989). New voices, new visions: Toward a lesbian/gay paradigm for psychology. *Psychology of Women Quarterly, 13,* 445–458.

Brown, L. S. (1995). Lesbian identities: Concepts and issues. In A. R. D'Augelli & C. J. Patterson (Eds.), *Lesbian, gay, and bisexual identities over the lifespan* (pp. 3–23). New York: Oxford University Press.

Brownfain, J. J. (1985). A study of the married bisexual male: Paradox and resolution. *Journal of Homosexuality, 11,* 173–188.

Bryant, S. S., & Demian. (1994). Relationship characteristics of American gay and lesbian couples: Findings from a national survey. *Journal of Gay and Lesbian Social Services, 1,* 101–117.

Burch, B. (1993). *On intimate terms: Psychological differences in lesbian relationships.* Urbana: University of Illinois Press.

Butler, B. (1990). *Ceremonies of the heart.* Seattle, WA: Seal Press.

Butler, J. (1990). *Gender trouble: Feminism and the subversion of identity.* New York: Routledge.

Butler, J. (1992). Imitation and gender insubordination. In H. Abelove, M. A. Barale, & D. M. Halperin (Eds.), *The lesbian and gay studies reader* (pp. 307–320). New York: Routledge.

Butler, J. (1993). *Bodies that matter: On the discursive limits of "sex."* New York: Routledge.

Buxton, A. O. (1991). *The other side of the closet: The coming out crisis for straight spouses.* New York: Wiley.

Byne, W. (1994). The biological evidence challenged. *Scientific American,* May, 50–55.

Byne, W. (1995). Science and belief: Psychobiological research and sexual orientation. *Journal of Homosexuality, 28,* 303–344.

Byne, W., & Parsons, B. (1993). Human sexual orientation: The biologic theories reappraised. *Archives of General Psychiatry, 50,* 228–239.

Cain, R. (1991). Stigma management and gay identity development. *Social Work, 36,* 67–73.

Caldwell, M. A., & Pepleau, L. A. (1984). The balance of power in lesbian relationships. *Sex Roles, 10,* 587–599.

Carballo-Dieguez, A. (1995). The sexual identity and behavior of Puerto Rican men who have sex with men. In B. Greene & G. M. Herek (Eds.), *AIDS, identity and community* (pp. 105–114). Thousand Oaks, CA: Sage.

Carballo-Dieguez, A., & Dolezal, C. (1994). Contrasting types of Puerto Rican men who have sex with men (msm). *Journal of Psychology and Human Sexuality, 6,* 41–67.

Carrier, J. (1976). Cultural factors affecting urban Mexican male homosexual behavior. *Archives of Sexual Behavior, 5,* 103–124.

Carrier, J. (1985). Mexican male bisexuality. *Journal of Homosexuality, 11,* 75–85.

Carrier, J. (1989). Gay liberation and coming out in Mexico. *Journal of Homosexuality, 17,* 225–252.

Carrier, J. (1992). Miguel: Sexual life history of a gay Mexican American. In G. Herdt (Ed.), *Gay culture in America* (pp. 202–224). Boston: Beacon.

Cass, V. C. (1979). Homosexual identity formation: A theoretical model. *Journal of Homosexuality, 4*, 219–235.

Cass, V. C. (1984). Homosexual identity: A concept in need of definition. *Journal of Homosexuality, 4*, 105–126.

Cass, V. C. (1990). The implications of homosexual identity formation for the Kinsey model and scale of sexual preference. In D. P. McWirther, S. A. Sanders, & J. M. Reinisch (Eds.), *Homosexuality/heterosexuality: The Kinsey scale and current research* (pp. 239–266). New York: Oxford University Press.

Causby, V., Lockhart, L., White, B., & Greene, K. (1995). Fusion and conflict resolution in lesbian relationships. *Journal of Gay and Lesbian Social Services, 3*, 67–82.

Chan, C. (1987). Asian lesbians: Psychological issues in the "coming out" process. *Asian Psychological Association Journal, 12*, 16–18.

Chan, C. (1989). Issues of identity development among Asian-American lesbians and gay men. *Journal of Counseling and Development, 68*, 16–20.

Chan, C. (1992). Cultural considerations in counseling Asian American lesbians and gay men. In S. Dworkin & F. Gutierrez (Eds.), *Counseling gay men and lesbians* (pp. 115–124). Alexandria, VA: American Association of Counseling and Development.

Chapman, L. J., & Chapman, J. P. (1969). Illusory correlation as an obstacle to the valid use of psychodiagnostic signs. *Journal of Abnormal Psychology, 74*, 271–280.

Chodorow, N. (1978). *The reproduction of mothering.* Berkeley: University of California Press.

Choi, K., Salazar, N., Lew, S., & Coates, T. J. (1995). AIDS risk, dual identity, and community among gay Asian and Pacific Islander men in San Francisco. In B. Greene & G. M. Herek (Eds.), *AIDS, identity and community* (pp. 115–134). Thousand Oaks, CA: Sage.

Clarke, C. (1983). The failure to transform: Homophobia in the Black community. In B. Smith (Ed.), *Homegirls* (pp. 197–208). New York: Kitchen Table Press.

Clunis, D. M., & Green, G. D. (1988). *Lesbian couples.* Seattle, WA: Seal Press.

Cole, E., & Rothblum, E. (1991). Lesbian sex after menopause: As good as or better than ever. In B. Sang, J. Warshow, & A. Smith (Eds.), *Lesbians at midlife: The creative transition* (pp. 184–193). San Francisco: Spinsters.

Coleman, E. (1978). Toward a new model of treatment of homosexuality: A review. *Journal of Homosexuality, 3*, 345–359.

Coleman, E. (1982a). Bisexual and gay men in heterosexual marriage: Conflicts and resolutions in therapy. In J. C. Gonsiorek (Ed.), *A guide to psychotherapy with gay and lesbian clients* (pp. 93–103). New York: Haworth.

Coleman, E. (1982b). Developmental stages of the coming out process. In J. C. Gonsiorek (Ed.), *Homosexuality and psychotherapy: A practitioner's handbook of affirmative methods* (pp. 31–34). New York: Haworth.

Coleman, E. (1985a). Bisexual women in marriage. *Journal of Homosexuality, 11*, 87–99.

Coleman, E. (1985b). Integration of male bisexuality and marriage. *Journal of Homosexuality, 11*, 189–207.

Coleman, E. (1987). Assessment of sexual orientation. *Journal of Homosexuality, 14*, 9–24.

Coleman, E. (1990). Toward a synthetic understanding of sexual orientation. In D. P. McWirther, S. A. Sanders, & J. M. Reinisch (Eds.), *Homosexuality/heterosexuality: The Kinsey scale and current research.* New York: Oxford University Press.

Collins, M. (1992). The gay bashers. In G. M. Herek & K. T. Berrill (Eds.), *Hate crimes: Confronting violence against lesbians and gay men* (pp. 19–40). London: Sage.

Committee on Lesbian and Gay Concerns (1991a). *American Psychological Association policy statements on lesbian and gay issues.* Washington, DC: American Psychological Association.

242 Committee on Lesbian and Gay Concerns. (1991b). *A selected bibliography of lesbian and gay concerns in psychology: An affirmative perspective.* Washington, DC: American Psychological Association.

Committee on Lesbian and Gay Concerns. (1991c). *Avoiding heterosexist bias in language.* Washington, DC: American Psychological Association.

Committee on Lesbian and Gay Concerns. (1991d). *Bias in psychotherapy with lesbians and gay men.* Washington, DC: American Psychological Association.

Comstock, D. (1991). *Violence against lesbians and gay men.* New York: Columbia University Press.

Conger, J. (1975). Proceedings of the American Psychological Association, Incorporated, for the year 1974: Minutes of the annual meetings of Council of Representatives. *American Psychologist, 46,* 964–972.

Copper, B. (1988). *Over the hill: Reflections on ageism between women.* Freedom, CA: Crossing Press.

Crawford, S. (1987). Lesbian families: Psychosocial stress and the family-building process. In Boston Lesbian Psychologies Collective (Eds.), *Lesbian psychologies* (pp. 195–214). Urbana: University of Illinois Press.

Crosbie-Burnett, M., & Helmbrecht, L. (1993). A descriptive empirical study of gay male step-families. *Family Relations, 42,* 256–262.

Cruikshank, M. (1991). Lavender and gray: A brief survey of lesbian and gay aging studies. *Journal of Homosexuality, 20,* 77–87.

Cruikshank, M. (1992). *The gay and lesbian liberation movement.* New York: Routledge.

D'Augelli, A. R. (1991). Gay men in college: Identity processes and adaptations. *Journal of College Student Development, 32,* 140–146.

D'Augelli, A. R. (1993). Preventing mental health problems among lesbian and gay college students. *Journal of Primary Prevention, 13,* 1–17.

D'Augelli, A. R. (1994). Lesbian and gay male development: Steps toward an analysis of lesbians' and gay men's lives. In B. Greene & G. M. Herek (Eds.), *Lesbian and gay psychology: Theory, research, and clinical applications* (pp. 118–132). Thousand Oaks, CA: Sage.

D'Augelli, A. R., & Garnets, L. (1995). Lesbian, gay, and bisexual communities. In A. R. D'Augelli & C. J. Patterson (Eds.), *Lesbian, gay, and bisexual identities over the lifespan* (pp. 293–320). New York: Oxford University Press.

D'Augelli, A. R., & Hershberger, S. L. (1993). Lesbian, gay, and bisexual youth in community settings: Personal challenges and mental health problems. *American Journal of Community Psychology, 21,* 421–448.

Davies, P. (1992). The role of disclosure in coming out among gay men. In K. Plummer (Ed.), *Modern homosexualities: Fragments of lesbian and gay experience* (pp. 75–83). London: Routledge.

Davison, G. C. (1991). Constructionism and morality in therapy for homosexuality. In J. C. Gonsiorek & J. D. Weinrich (Eds.), *Homosexuality: Research implications for public policy* (pp. 137–148). Newbury Park, CA: Sage.

DeCecco, J. P. (1985). Bisexualities: Theory and research [special issue]. *Journal of Homosexuality, 11*(1/2).

DeCecco, J. P., & Parker, D. A. (Eds.). (1995). Sex, cells, and same-sex desire: The biology of sexual preference [special issue]. *Journal of Homosexuality, 28.*

DeCrescenzo. T. (1985). Homophobia: A study of attitudes of mental health professionals toward homosexuality. In R. Schoenberg, R. Goldberg, & D. Shore (Eds.), *With compassion toward some: Homosexuality and social work in America* (pp. 115–136). New York: Harrington Park.

DeCrescenzo, T. (Ed.) (1994). *Helping gay and lesbian youth: New policies, new programs, new practice.* New York: Haworth.

D'Emilio, J. (1983). *Sexual politics, sexual communities: The making of a homosexual minority in the United States, 1940–1970.* Chicago: University of Chicago Press.

D'Emilio, J. (1992) . *Making trouble: Essays on history, politics, and the university.* New York: Routledge.

D'Emilio, J., & Freedman, E. B. (1988). *Intimate matters: A history of sexuality in America.* New York: Harper & Row.

de Monteflores, C. (1986). Notes on the management of difference. In T. S. Stein & C. J. Cohen (Eds.), *Contemporary perspectives on psychotherapy with lesbians and gay men* (pp. 73–101). New York: Plenum.

DeVine, J. L. (1985). A systematic inspection of affectional preference and the family of origin. In R. Schoenberg, R. S. Goldberg, & D. A. Shore (Eds.), *With compassion toward some: homosexuality and social work in America* (pp. 9–17). New York: Haworth.

Diamond, M. (1993). Some genetic considerations in the development of sexual orientation. In M. Haug, R. E. Whalen, C. Aron, & K. L. Olsen (Eds.), *The development of sex differences and similarities in behavior* (pp. 291–309). Dordrecht, the Netherlands: Kluwer.

Doell, R. G. (1995). Sexuality in the brain. *Journal of Homosexuality, 28,* 345–354.

Dollard, J., Doob, L. W., Miller, N. E., Mowrer, O. H., & Sears, R. R. (1939). *Frustration and aggression.* New Haven, CT: Yale University Press.

Doucette, J. (1989). Redefining difference: Disabled lesbians resist. *Resources for Feminist Research, 18*(2), 17–21.

Duberman, M., Vicinus, M., & Chauncey, G. (1989). *Hidden from history: Reclaiming the gay and lesbian past.* New York: New American Library.

Duffy, S. M., & Rusbult, C. E. (1986). Satisfaction and commitment in homosexual and heterosexual couples. *Journal of Homosexuality, 12,* 1–23.

Dunker, B. (1987). Aging lesbians: Observations and speculations. In Boston Lesbian Psychologies Collective (Eds.), *Lesbian psychologies* (pp.72–82). Urbana: University of Illinois Press.

Durby, D. D. (1994). Gay, lesbian, and bisexual youth. *Journal of Gay and Lesbian Social Services, 1,* 1–37.

Dworkin, S., & Gutierrez, F. (1992). *Counseling gay men and lesbians: Journey to the end of the rainbow.* Alexandria, VA: American Association of Counseling and Development.

Dworkin, J., & Kaufer, D. (1995). Social services and bereavement in the lesbian and gay community. *Journal of Gay and Lesbian Social Services, 2,* 41–60.

Ehrlich, H. J. (1992). The ecology of anti-gay violence. In G. M. Herek & K. T. Berrill (Eds.), *Hate crimes: Confronting violence against lesbians and gay men* (pp. 105–111). London: Sage.

Eichberg, R. (1990). *Coming out: An act of love.* New York: Dutton.

Eldridge, N. S., & Gilbert, L. A. (1990). Correlates of relationship satisfaction in lesbian couples. *Psychology of Women Quarterly, 14,* 43–62.

Eliason, M. (1995). Attitudes toward lesbians and gay men: A review and implications for social service training. *Journal of Gay and Lesbian Social Services, 2,* 73–90.

Elise, D. (1986). Lesbian couples: The implications of sex differences in separation-individuation. *Psychotherapy, 23,* 305–310.

Epstein, S. (1992). Gay politics, ethnic identity: The limits of social constructionism. In E. Stein (Ed.), *Forms of desire: Sexual orientation and the social constructionist controversy* (pp. 239–293). New York: Garland.

Ernst, F., Francis, R., Nevels, H., & Lemeh, C. (1991). Condemnation of homosexuality in the Black culture: A gender-specific phenomenon? *Archives of Sexual Behavior, 20,* 579–585.

244   Espin, O. M. (1984). Cultural and historical influences on sexuality in Hispanic/Latin women: Implications for psychotherapy. In C. Vance (Ed.), *Pleasure and danger* (pp. 149–163). London: Routledge and Kegan Paul.

Espin, O. M. (1987). Issues of identity in the psychology of Latina lesbians. In Boston Lesbian Psychologies Collective (Eds.), *Lesbian psychologies* (pp. 33–51). Urbana: University of Illinois Press.

Espin, O. M. (1994). Crossing borders and boundaries: The life narratives of immigrant lesbians. *Division 44 Newsletter, 10*(3), 18–27.

Esterberg, K. G. (1996). Gay cultures, gay communities: The social organization of lesbians, gay men, and bisexuals. In R. C. Savin-Williams (Ed.), *The lives of lesbians, gay men, and bisexuals* (pp. 377–91). Ft Worth, TX: Harcourt Brace.

Faderman, L. (1981). *Surpassing the love of men: Romantic friendships and love between women from the Renaissance to the present.* New York: William Morrow.

Faderman, L. (1991). *Odd girls and twilight lovers: A history of lesbian life in twentieth-century America.* New York: Columbia University Press.

Faderman, L. (1992). The return of butch and femme: A phenomenon of lesbian sexuality of the 1980s and 1990s. *Journal of the History of Sexuality, 2*, 578–596.

Faderman, L. (1994, August). *The social constructionism of lesbianism.* Paper presented at the annual convention of the American Psychological Association, Los Angeles, CA.

Falk, P. J. (1989). Lesbian mothers: Psychosocial assumptions in family law. *American Psychologist, 46*, 941–947.

Fausto-Sterling, A. (1992). *Myths of gender: Biological theories about women and men.* New York: Basic Books.

Fausto-Sterling, A. (1995). Animal models for the development of human sexuality: A critical evaluation. *Journal of Homosexuality, 28*, 217–236.

Feldman, D. A. (1989). Gay youth and AIDS. *Journal of Homosexuality, 17*, 185–193.

Finkelhor, D. (1986). *A sourcebook on child sexual abuse.* Newbury Park, CA: Sage.

Folayan, A. (1992). African American issues: The soul of it. In B. Berzon (Ed.), *Positively gay* (pp. 235–239). Berkeley, CA: Celestial Arts.

Foucault, M. (1979). *The history of sexuality.* London: Allen Lane.

Fox, R. C. (1995). Bisexual identities. In A. R. D'Augelli & C. J. Patterson (Eds.), *Lesbian, gay, and bisexual identities over the lifespan* (pp. 48–86). New York: Oxford University Press.

Franke, R., & Leary, M. R. (1991). Disclosure of sexual orientation by lesbians and gay men: A comparison of public and private processes. *Journal of Social and Clinical Psychology, 10*, 262–269.

French, M. (1992). Loves, sexualities, and marriages: Strategies and adjustments. In K. Plummer (Ed.), *Modern homosexualities* (pp. 87–97). London: Routledge.

Fricke, A. (1981). *Reflections of a rock lobster.* Boston: Alyson.

Friend, R. (1987). The individual and social psychology of aging: Clinical implications for lesbians and gay men. *Journal of Homosexuality, 14*, 307–331.

Friend, R. (1990). Older lesbian and gay people: Responding to homophobia. *Marriage and Family Review, 14*, 241–265.

Friend, R. (1991). Older lesbian and gay people: A theory of successful aging. *Journal of Homosexuality, 20*, 99–118.

Fry, P. (1986). Male homosexuality and spirit possession in Brazil. In H. Blackwood (Ed.), *The many faces of homosexuality: Anthropological approaches to homosexual behavior* (pp. 137–153). New York: Harrington.

Garcia, N., Kennedy, C., Pearlman, S. F., & Perez, J. (1987). The impact of race and culture differences: Challenges to intimacy in lesbian relationships. In Boston Lesbian Psychologies Collective (Eds.), *Lesbian psychologies* (pp. 142–160. Urbana: University of Illinois Press.

Garnets, L., Hancock, K. A., Cochran, S. D., Goodchilds, J., & Peplau, L. A. (1991). Issues in   *245* psychotherapy with lesbians and gay men. *American Psychologist, 46*, 964–972.

Garnets, L., Herek, G. M., & Levy, B. (1992). Violence and victimization of lesbians and gay men: Mental health consequences. In G. M. Herek & K. T. Berrill (Eds.), *Hate crimes: Confronting violence against lesbians and gay men* (pp. 207–226). London: Sage.

Garnets, L., & Kimmel, D. C. (1993). Lesbian and gay male dimensions in the psychological study of human diversity. In *Psychological perspectives on lesbian and gay male experiences* (pp. 1–51). New York: Columbia University Press.

Gay, J. (1986). "Mummies and babies" and friends and lovers in Lesotho. In E. Blackwood (Ed.), *The many faces of homosexuality: Anthropological approaches to homosexual behavior* (pp. 97–116). New York: Harrington Park.

Geller, T. (1990). *Bisexuality: A reader and sourcebook.* Ojai, CA: Times Change Press.

George, S. (1993). *Women and bisexuality.* London: Scarlet.

Gergen, K. J. (1985). The social constructionist movement in modern psychology. *American Psychologist, 40*, 266–75.

Gibbs, E. D. (1988). Psychosocial development of children raised by lesbian mothers: A review of research. *Women and Therapy, 8*, 65–75.

Gibson, P. (1989). Gay male and lesbian youth suicide. In *Report of the Secretary's Task Force on Youth Suicide, Vol. 3: Prevention and Intervention in Youth Suicide* (pp. 110–142). Washington, DC: USDHHS.

Gladue, B. A. (1993). The psychobiology of sexual orientation. In M. Haug, R. E. Whalen, C. Aron, & K. L. Olsen (Eds.), *The development of sex differences and similarities in behavior* (pp. 437–455). Dordrecht, the Netherlands: Kluwer.

Gladue, B. A., & Bailey, M. (1995). Aggressiveness, competitiveness, and human sexual orientation. *Psychoneuroendocrinology, 20*, 478–485.

Gochros, J. S. (1985). Wive's reactions to learning that their husbands are bisexual. *Journal of Homosexuality, 11*, 101–113.

Gochros, J.S. (1989). *When husbands come out of the closet.* New York: Haworth.

Gock, T. (1992). Asian-Pacific Islander issues: Identity integration and pride. In B. Berzon (Ed.), *Positively gay* (pp. 247–252). Berkeley, CA: Celestial Arts.

Goffman, E. (1963). *Stigma: Notes on the management of spoiled identity.* Englewood Cliffs, NJ: Prentice-Hall.

Golden, C. (1987). Diversity and variability in women's sexual identities. In Boston Women's Psychologies Collective (Eds.), *Lesbian psychologies: Explorations and challenges* (pp. 19–34). Urbana: University of Illinois Press.

Golden, C. (1994). Our politics, our choices: The feminist movement and sexual orientation. In B. Greene & G. M. Herek (Eds.), *Lesbian and gay psychology: Theory, research, and clinical applications* (pp. 54–70). Thousand Oaks, CA: Sage.

Golden, C. (1996). What's in a name? Sexual self-identity among women. In R. C. Savin-Williams (Ed.), *The lives of lesbians, gay men, and bisexuals* (pp. 227–249). Ft. Worth, TX: Harcourt Brace.

Gomez, J., & Smith, B. (1990). Taking the home out of homophobia: Black lesbian mental health. In E. C. White (Ed.), *The Black women's health book: Speaking for ourselves* (pp. 198–213). Seattle, WA: Seal.

Gonsiorek, J. C. (1988). Mental health issues of gay and lesbian adolescents. *Journal of Adolescent Health Care, 9*, 114–22.

Gonsiorek, J. C. (1991). The empirical basis for the demise of the illness model of homosexuality. In J. C. Gonsiorek & J. D. Weinrich (Eds.), *Homosexuality: Research implications for public policy* (pp. 115–136). Newbury Park, CA: Sage.

Gonsiorek, J. C. (1995). Gay male identities: Concepts and issues. In A. R. D'Augelli & C. J.

246   Patterson (Eds.), *Lesbian, gay, and bisexual identities over the lifespan* (pp. 24–47). New York: Oxford University Press.

Gonsiorek, J. C., & Shernoff, M. (1991). AIDS prevention and public policy: The experience of gay men. In J. C. Gonsiorek & J. D. Weinrich (Eds.), *Homosexuality: Research implications for public policy* (pp. 230–243). Newbury Park, CA: Sage.

Gonsiorek, J. C., & Weinrich, J. D. (1991). *Homosexuality: Research implications for public policy*. Newbury Park, CA: Sage.

Gooren, L. J. G. (1995). Biomedical concepts of homosexuality: Folk belief in a white coat. *Journal of Homosexuality, 28*, 237–246.

Gottman, J. S. (1990). Children of gay and lesbian parents. *Marriage and Family Review, 14*, 177–196.

Grahn, J. (1986). Strange country this: Lesbianism and North American Indian tribes. *Journal of Homosexuality, 12*, 43–57.

Green, G. D. (1990). Is separation really so great? *Women and Therapy, 9*, 87–104.

Green, G. D., & Bozett, F. W. (1991). Lesbian mothers and gay fathers. In J. C. Gonsiorek & J. D. Weinrich (Eds.), *Homosexuality: Research implications for public policy* (pp. 197–214). Newbury Park, CA: Sage.

Greenberg, D. E. (1988). *The construction of homosexuality*. Chicago: University of Chicago Press.

Greene, B. (1994a). Ethnic minority lesbians and gay men: Mental health and treatment issues. *Journal of Consulting and Clinical Psychology, 62*, 243–251.

Greene, B. (1994b). Lesbian women of color: Triple jeopardy. In L. Comas-Diaz & B. Greene (Eds.), *Women of color: Integrating ethnic and gender identities in psychotherapy* (pp. 389–427). New York: Guilford.

Grube, J. (1991). Natives and settlers: An ethnographic note on early interaction of older homosexual men with younger gay liberationists. *Journal of Homosexuality, 20*, 119–35.

Gutierrez, E. (1992). Latino issues: Gay and lesbians claiming *La Raza*. In B. Berzon (Ed.), *Positively gay* (pp. 240–246). Berkeley: Celestial Arts.

Gutierrez, F., & Dworkin, S. (1992). Gay, lesbian, and African American: Managing the integration of identities. In S. Dworkin & E. Gutierrez (Eds.), *Counseling gay men and lesbians* (pp. 141–156). Alexandria, VA: American Association of Counseling and Development.

Haldeman, D. C. (1991). Sexual orientation conversion therapy for gay men and lesbians: A scientific examination. In J. C. Gonsiorek & J. D. Weinrich (Eds.), *Homosexuality: Research implications for public policy* (pp. 149–160). Newbury Park, CA: Sage.

Haldeman, D. C. (1994). The practice and ethics of sexual orientation conversion therapy. *Journal of Consulting and Clinical Psychology, 62*, 221–227.

Halleck, S. L. (1971). *The politics of therapy*. New York: Science House.

Halperin, D. M. (1989). Sex before sexuality: Pederasty, politics and power in classical Athens. In M. Duberman, M. Vicinus, & G. Chauncey (Eds.), *Hidden from history: Reclaiming the gay and lesbian past* (pp. 37–53). New York: New American Library.

Halperin, D. M. (1993). Is there a history of sexuality? In H. Abelove, M. A. Barale, & D. M. Halperin (Eds.), *The lesbian and gay studies reader* (pp. 416–431). New York: Routledge.

Hamer, D. H., Hu, S., Magnuson, V. L., Hu, N., & Pattatucci, A. (1993). A linkage between DNA markers on the X chromosome and male sexual orientation. *Science, 261*, 321–327.

Hare-Mustin, R., & Marecek, J. (1988). The meaning of difference: Gender theory, postmodernism, and psychology. *American Psychologist, 43*, 455–464.

Hare-Mustin, R., & Marecek, J. (1990). *Making a difference: Psychology and the construction of gender*. New Haven, CT: Yale University Press.

Harry, J. (1992). Conceptualizing anti-gay violence. In G. M. Herek & K. T. Berrill (Eds.), *Hate crimes: Confronting violence against lesbians and gay men* (pp. 113–122). London: Sage.

Haumann, G. (1995). Homosexuality, biology, and ideology. *Journal of Homosexuality, 28,* 57–77.

Henley, N. M., & Pincus, F. (1978). Interrelationship of sexist, racist, and antihomosexual attitudes. *Psychological Reports, 42,* 83–90.

Herdt, G. (1984). *Ritualized homosexuality in Melanesia.* Berkeley: University of California Press.

Herdt, G. (1989b). Introduction: Gay and lesbian youth, emergent identities, and cultural scenes at home and abroad. In *Gay and lesbian youth* (pp. 1–42). New York: Haworth.

Herdt, G. (1992). Coming out as a rite of passage: A Chicago study. In *Gay culture in America* (pp. 29–68). Boston: Beacon.

Herdt, G. (Ed.). (1989a). *Gay and lesbian youth.* New York: Haworth.

Herdt, G., & Boxer, A. (1992). Introduction: Culture, history, and lifecourse of gay men. In G. Herdt (Ed.), *Gay culture in America: Essays from the field* (pp. 1–28). Boston: Alyson.

Herek, G. M. (1984). Beyond "homophobia": A social psychological perspective on attitudes toward lesbians and gay men. *Journal of Homosexuality, 10,* 1–21.

Herek, G. M. (1986). On heterosexual masculinity: Some psychical consequences of the social construction of gender and sexuality. *American Behavioral Scientist, 29*(5), 563–577.

Herek, G. M. (1988). Heterosexuals' attitudes toward lesbians and gay men: Correlates and gender differences. *Journal of Sex Research, 25,* 451–477.

Herek, G. M. (1990). The context of anti-gay violence: Notes on cultural and psychological heterosexism. *Journal of Interpersonal Violence, 5* (3), 316–333.

Herek, G. M. (1992). Psychological heterosexism and anti-gay violence: The social psychology of bigotry and bashing. In G. M. Herek & K. T. Berrill (Eds.), *Hate crimes: Confronting violence against lesbians and gay men* (pp. 149–169). Newbury Park, CA: Sage.

Herek, G. M. (1995). Psychological heterosexism in the United States. In A. R. D'Augelli & C. J. Patterson (Eds.), *Lesbian, gay, and bisexual identities over the lifespan* (pp. 320–346). New York: Oxford University Press.

Herek, G. M., & Berrill, K. T. (1992). Introduction. In G. M. Herek & K. T. Berrill (Eds.), *Hate crimes: Confronting violence against lesbians and gay men* (pp. 1–10). Newbury Park, CA: Sage.

Herek, G. M., & Glunt, E. K. (1993). Interpersonal contact and heterosexuals' attitudes toward gay men: Results from a national survey. *The Journal of Sex Research, 30,* 239–244.

Herek, G. M., Kimmel, D. C., Amaro, H., & Melton, G. B. (1991). Avoiding heterosexist bias in psychological research. *American Psychologist, 46,* 957–963.

Hershberger, S. L., & D'Augelli, A. R. (1995). The impact of victimization on the mental health and suicidality of lesbian, gay, and bisexual youths. *Developmental Psychology, 31,* 65–74.

Hetrick, E. S., & Martin, A. D. (1987). Developmental issues and their resolution for gay and lesbian adolescents. *Journal of Homosexuality, 14,* 25–42.

Hidalgo, H. (1984). The Puerto Rican lesbian in the United States. In T. Darty & S. Potter (Eds.), *Women-identified women* (pp. 105–115). Palo Alto, CA: Mayfield.

Hidalgo, H. (Ed.) (1995). Lesbians of color: Social and human services [special edition]. *Journal of Gay and Lesbian Social Services, 3* (2).

Hill, M. (1987). Child-rearing attitudes of Black lesbian mothers. In Boston Lesbian Psychologies Collective (Eds.), *Lesbian Psychologies* (pp. 215–226). Urbana: University of Illinois Press.

Hooker, E. A. (1957). The adjustment of the male overt homosexual. *Journal of Projective Techniques, 21,* 17–31.

hooks, b. (1989). Homophobia in Black communities. In *Talking back* (pp. 120–126). Boston, MA: South End.

Hu, S., Pattatucci, A. M. L., Patterson, C., Li, L., Fulker, D. W., Cherny, S. S., Kuglyak, L., & Hamer, D. (1995). Linkage between sexual orientation and chromosome Xq28 in males but not in females. *Nature Genetics, 11,* 248–256.

Hunter, A. (1993). Same door, different closet: A heterosexual sissy's coming out party. In S. Wilkinson & C. Kitzinger (Eds.), *Heterosexuality: A "Feminism and Psychology" reader* (pp. 150–168). London: Sage.

Hutchins, L., & Kaahumanu, L. (1991). *Bi any other name: Bisexual people speak out.* Boston: Alyson.

Icard, L. (1986). Black gay men and conflicting social identities: Sexual orientation versus racial identity. *Journal of Social Work and Human Sexuality, 4,* 83–93.

Island, D., & Letellier, P. (1991). *Men who beat the men who love them.* New York: Haworth.

Jackson, D., & Sullivan, R. (1994). Developmental implications of homophobia for lesbian and gay adolescents: Issues in policy and practice. *Journal of Gay and Lesbian Social Services, 1,* 93–109.

Jay, K., & Young, A. (1979). *The gay report.* New York: Summit Books.

Jayakar, K. (1994). Women of the Indian subcontinent. In L. Comas-Diaz & B. Greene (Eds.), *Women of color* (pp. 161–181). New York: Guilford.

Jeffreys, S. (1993). *The lesbian heresy: A feminist perspective on the lesbian sexual revolution.* N. Melbourne: Spinifex.

Jennes, V. (1992). Coming out: Lesbian identity and the categorization problem. In K. Plummer (Ed.), *Modern homosexualities: Fragments of lesbian and gay experience* (pp. 64–74). London: Routledge.

Jenny, C., Roesler, T. A., & Poyer, K. L. (1994). Are children at risk for sexual abuse by homosexuals? *Pediatrics, 94,* 41–46.

Johnson, S. E. (1990). *Staying Power: Long term lesbian couples.* Tallahassee, FL: Naiad.

Jones, E. (1965). *The life and work of Sigmund Freud.* New York: Basic Books.

Jordan, J., Kaplan, A. G., Miller, J. B., Stiver, I., & Surrey, J. (1992). *Women's growth in connection: Writings from the Stone Center.* New York: Guilford.

Katz, J. (1992). *Gay American history: Lesbians and gay men in the USA* (2d ed.). New York: Meridian.

Kayal, P. M. (1994). Communalization and homophile organization membership: Gay volunteerism before and during AIDS. *Journal of Gay and Lesbian Social Services, 1,* 33–57.

Kehoe, M. (1986a). A portrait of older lesbians. *Journal of Homosexuality, 12,* 157–61.

Kehoe, M. (1986b). Lesbians over 65: A triply invisible minority. *Journal of Homosexuality, 12,* 139–152.

Kehoe, M. (1991). *Lesbians over 60 speak for themselves.* New York: Haworth.

Kennedy, H. C. (1980). The "third sex" theory of Karl Heinrich Ulrichs. *Journal of Homosexuality, 6,* 103–111.

Kessler, S., & McKenna, W. (1978). *Gender: An ethnomethodological approach.* New York: Wiley.

Kimmel, D. C. (1978). Adult development and aging: A gay perspective. *Journal of Social Issues, 34,* 113–130.

Kimmel, D. C., & Sang, B. E. (1995). Lesbians and gay men in midlife. In A. R. D'Augelli & C. J. Patterson (Eds.), *Lesbian, gay, and bisexual identities over the lifespan* (pp. 190–214). New York: Oxford University Press.

Kinsey, A. C., Pomeroy, W. B., & Martin, C. E. (1948). *Sexual behavior in the human male.* Philadelphia: W. B. Saunders.

Kinsey, A. C., Pomeroy, W. B., Martin, C. E., & Gebhard, P. H. (1953). *Sexual behavior in the human female.* Philadelphia: W. B. Saunders.

Kirk, K. (1987). Hetiquette (A plain man's guide to passing for straight). In G. Hanscombe & M. Humphries (Eds.), *Heterosexuality* (pp. 26–33). London: GMP.

Kirkpatrick, M. (1987). Clinical implications of lesbian mother studies. *Journal of Homosexuality, 13,* 201–211.

Kirsch, J. A. W., & Weinrich, J. D. (1991). Homosexuality, nature, and biology: Is homosexuality natural? Does it matter? In J. C. Gonsiorek & J. D. Weinrich (Eds.), *Homosexuality: Research implications for public policy* (pp. 13–31). Newbury Park, CA: Sage.

Kite, M. E. (1994). When perceptions meet reality: Individual differences in reactions to lesbians and gay men. In B. Greene & G. M. Herek (Eds.), *Lesbian and gay psychology: Theory, research, and clinical applications* (pp. 25–53). London: Sage.

Kite, M. E., & Deaux, K. (1986). Attitudes toward homosexuality: Assessment and behavioral consequences. *Basic and Applied Social Psychology, 7,* 137–162.

Kite, M. E., & Deaux, K. (1987). Gender belief systems: Homosexuality and the implicit inversion theory. *Psychology of Women Quarterly, 11,* 83–96.

Kitzinger, C. (1987). *The social construction of lesbianism.* London: Sage.

Kitzinger, C. (1991). Lesbians and gay men in the workplace: Psychological issues. In M. J. Davison & J. Earnshaw (Eds.), *Vulnerable workers: Psychosocial and legal issues* (pp. 233–240). Chichester, England: Wiley

Kitzinger, C. (1995). Social constructionism: Implications for gay and lesbian psychology. In A. R. D'Augelli & C. J. Patterson (Eds.), *Lesbian, gay, and bisexual identities over the lifespan* (pp. 136–161). New York: Oxford University Press.

Kitzinger, C., & Wilkinson, S. (1995). Transitions from heterosexuality to lesbianism: The discursive production of lesbian identities. *Developmental Psychology, 31,* 95–104.

Klein, F. (1993). *The bisexual option* (2d Ed.). New York: Harrington Park.

Klein, F., Sepekoff, B., & Wolf, T. J. (1985). Sexual orientation: A multivariable dynamic process. *Journal of Homosexuality, 11,* 35–49.

Klein, F., & Wolf, T. J. (1986). *Bisexualities: Theory and research.* New York: Haworth.

Kokopeli, B., & Lakey, G. (1992). More power than we want: Masculine sexuality and violence. In M. L. Anderson & P. H. Collins (Eds.), *Race, class, and gender: An anthology* (pp.443–449). Belmont, CA: Wadsworth.

Kominars, S. B. (1995). Homophobia: The heart of darkness. *Journal of Gay and Lesbian Social Services, 2,* 29–39.

Kourany, R. F. C. (1987). Suicide among homosexual adolescents. *Journal of Homosexuality, 13,* 111–117.

Krestan, J., & Bepko, C. 1980). The problem of fusion in lesbian relationships. *Family Processes, 19,* 277–289.

Kurdek, L. A. (1988). Perceived social support in gays and lesbians in cohabiting couples. *Journal of Personality and Social Psychology, 54,* 504–509.

Kurdek, L. A. (1993). The allocation of household labor in homosexual and heterosexual cohabiting couples. *Journal of Homosexuality, 15,* 93–118.

Kurdek, L. A. (1994). The nature and correlates of relationship quality in gay, lesbian, and heterosexual cohabiting couples: A test of individual difference, interdependence, and discrepancy models. In B. Greene & G. M. Herek (Eds.), *Lesbian and gay psychology* (pp. 133–155). Thousand Oaks, CA: Sage.

Kurdek, L. A. (1995a). Developmental changes in relationship quality in gay and lesbian cohabiting couples. *Developmental Psychology, 31,* 86–94.

Kurdek, L. A. (1995b). Lesbian and gay couples. In A. R. D'Augelli & C. J. Patterson (Eds.), *Lesbian, gay, and bisexual identities over the lifespan* (pp. 244–261). New York: Oxford University Press.

Kurdek, L. A., & Schmitt, J. P. (1987). Relationship quality of partners in heterosexual married, heterosexual cohabiting, and gay and lesbian relationships. *Journal of Personality and Social Psychology, 51,* 711–720.

Kurdek, L. A., & Schmitt, J. P. (1987). Perceived emotional support from family and friends in members of homosexual, married, and heterosexual cohabiting couples. *Journal of Homosexuality, 14,* 57–69.

Laumann, E. O., Gagnon, J. H., Michael, R. T., & Michaels, S. (1994). *The social organization of sexuality: Sexual practices in the United States.* Chicago: University of Chicago Press.

Lee, J. A. (1987). What can gay aging studies contribute to theories of aging? *Journal of Homosexuality, 13,* 43–71.

Lee, J. A. (1988). Invisible lives of Canada's gray gays. In V. Marshall (Ed.), *Aging in Canada* (pp. 138–155). Toronto: Fitzhenry & Whiteside.

Leigh, B. C. (1992). Reasons for having and avoiding sex: Gender, sexual orientation, and relationship to sexual behavior. In N. J. Kenney, M. D. Brot, K. E. Moe, & K. Dahl (Eds.), *The complexities of women* (pp. 108–115). Dubuque, IA: Kendall/Hunt.

LeVay, S. (1991). A difference in hypothalamic structure between heterosexual and homosexual men. *Science, 253,* 1034–1037.

Lewes, K. (1988). *The psychoanalytic theory of male homosexuality.* New York: New American Library.

Lewis, R. A., Kozac, E. B., Milardo, R. M., & Grosnick, W. A. (1981). Commitment in same-sex relationships. *Alternative Lifestyles, 4,* 22–42.

Lobel, Kerry (Ed.). (1986). *Naming the violence: Speaking out about lesbian battering.* Seattle, WA: Seal.

Lockman, P. T. (1984). Ebony and ivory: The interracial gay male couple. *Lifestyles, 7,* 44–55.

Loiacano, D. K. (1989). Gay identity issues among Black Americans: Racism, homophobia, and the need for validation. *Journal of Counseling and Development, 68,* 21–25.

Lorde, A. (1983). There is no hierarchy of oppression. *Interracial Books for Children Bulletin, 14,* 7.

Lorde, A. (1984). *Sister/outsider.* Freedom, CA: Crossing.

MacDonald, B., & Rich, S. (1991). *Look me in the eye: On women, aging and ageism.* Minneapolis, MN: Spinster.

Malyon, A. K. (1981). The homosexual adolescent: Developmental issues and social bias. *Child Welfare, 60,* 321–330.

Malyon, A. K. (1982). Psychotherapeutic implications of internalized homophobia in gay men. In J. C. Gonsiorek (Ed.), *Homosexuality and psychotherapy: A practitioner's handbook of affirmative methods* (pp. 59–69). New York: Haworth.

Margolies, L., Becker, M., & Jackson-Brewer, K. (1987). Internalized homophobia: Identifying and treating the oppressor within. In Boston Lesbian Psychologies Collective (Eds.), *Lesbian psychologies* (pp. 229–241). Urbana: University of Illinois Press.

Martin, A. (1994). Fruit, nuts, and chocolate: The politics of sexual identity. *Harvard gay and lesbian review,* Winter, 10–14.

Martin, A. D. (1984). The emperor's new clothes: Modern attempts to change sexual orientation. In E. S. Hetrick & T. S. Stein (Eds.), *Innovations in psychotherapy with homosexuals.* Washington, DC: American Psychiatric Association.

Martin, A. D. (1982). Learning to hide: The socialization of the gay adolescent. *Adolescent Psychiatry, 10,* 52–65.

Martin, A. D., & Hetrick, E. (1988). The stigmatization of the gay and lesbian adolescent. *Journal of Homosexuality, 15,* 163–184.

Martin, D., & Lyon, P. (1992). The older lesbian. In B. Berzon (Ed.), *Positively gay* (pp. 111–120). Berkeley, CA: Celestial Arts.

Masters, W., & Johnson, V. (1979). *Homosexuality in perspective.* Boston: Little Brown.

Matteson, D. R. (1985). Bisexual men in marriage: Is a positive homosexual identity and stable marriage possible? *Journal of Homosexuality, 11,* 149–173.

Mays, V., & Cochran, S. (1988). The Black women's relationship project: A national survey of Black lesbians. In M. Shernoff & W. Scott (Eds.), *The sourcebook on lesbian/gay health care* (2d Ed.), (pp. 54–62). Washington, DC: National Lesbian and Gay Health Foundation, Inc.

Mays, V., Cochran, S., & Rhue, S. (in press). The impact of perceived discrimination on the intimate relationships of Black lesbians. *Journal of Homosexuality.*

McGuire, T. R. (1995). Is homosexuality genetic? A critical review. *Journal of Homosexuality, 28*, 115–145.

McIntosh, M. (1968). The homosexual role. *Social Problems, 16*, 182–192.

McWirther, D., & Mattison, A. (1984). *The male couple.* Englewood Cliffs, NJ: Prentice Hall.

Melton, G. B. (1989). Public policy and private prejudice: Psychology and law on gay rights. *American Psychologist, 44*, 933–940.

Mendola, M. (1980). *The Mendola report.* New York: Crown.

Meyer, J. (1990). Guess who's coming to dinner this time? A study of gay intimate relationships and the support for those relationships. *Marriage and Family Review, 14*, 59–82.

Meyer-Bahlburg, H. (1984). Psychoendocrine research on sexual orientation: Current status and future options. In G. J. De Vries, J. P. C. De Bruin, H. M. B. Uylings, & M. A. Corner, (Eds.), *Progress in brain research* (vol. 61, pp. 375–398). Amsterdam: Elsevier.

Meyer-Bahlburg, H. (1995). Psychoneuroendocrinology and sexual pleasure: The aspect of sexual orientation. In P. R. Abramson & S. D. Pinkerton (Eds.), *Sexual nature/sexual culture* (pp. 135–153). Chicago: University of Chicago Press.

Meyer-Bahlburg, H., Ehrhardt, A. A., Rosen, L. R., Gruen, R. S., Veridiano, N. P., Vann, F. H., & Newwalder, H. F. (1995). Prenatal estrogens and the development of homosexual orientation. *Developmental Psychology, 31*, 12–21.

Miller, N. (1995). *Out of the past: Gay and lesbian history from 1869 to the present.* New York: Random House.

Money, J. (1987). Sin, sickness, or status: Homosexual gender identity and psychoneuroendocrinology. *American Psychologist, 42*, 384–399.

Money, J. (1988). *Gay, straight, and in between: The sexology of erotic orientation.* New York: Oxford University Press.

Morales, E. S. (1990). Ethnic minority families and minority gays and lesbians. *Marriage and Family Review, 14*, 217–239

Morales, E. S. (1992). Latino gays and Latina lesbians. In S. Dworkin & F. Gutierrez (Eds.), *Counseling gay men and lesbians* (pp. 125–139). Alexandria, VA: American Association of Counseling and Development.

Morgan, K. S., & Nerison, R. M. (1993). Homosexuality and psychopolitics: An historical overview. *Psychotherapy, 30*, 133–140.

Morin, S. F. (1988). AIDS: The challenge to psychology. *American Psychologist, 43*, 838–842.

Morin, S. F., & Charles, K. A. (1983). Heterosexual bias in psychotherapy. In J. Murray & P. R. Abramson (Eds.), *Bias in psychotherapy* (pp. 309–338). New York: Praeger.

Morin, S. F., & Rothblum, E. (1991). Removing the stigma: Fifteen years of progress. *American Psychologist, 46*, 947–949.

Morin, S. F., & Schultz, S.J. (1978). The gay movement and the rights of children. *Journal of Social Issues, 34*, 137–148.

Murphy, B. C. (1994). Difference and diversity: Gay and lesbian couples. *Journal of Gay and Lesbian Social Services, 1*, 5–31.

Murphy, T. F. (1992). Redirecting sexual orientation: Techniques and justifications. *Journal of Sex Research, 29*, 501–523.

Nardi, P. M. (1992). That's what friends are for: Friends as family in the gay and lesbian community. In K. Plummer (Ed.), *Modern homosexualities: Fragments of gay and lesbian experience* (pp. 108–120). London: Routledge.

Nardi, P. M., Sanders, F., & Marmor, J. (1994). *Growing up before stonewall.* New York: Routledge.

National Gay and Lesbian Health Foundation. (1987). National lesbian heath care survey: Mental health implications. Unpublished report. Atlanta: Author.

252

Nestle, J. (1992). *The persistent desire: A femme-butch reader.* Boston: Alyson.

Nicolosi, J. (1991). *Reparative therapy of the male homosexual: A new clinical approach.* Northvale, NJ: Aronson.

O'Connell, A. (1993). Voices from the heart: The developmental impact of a mother's lesbianism on her adolescent children. *Smith College Studies in Social Work, 63,* 281–299.

Omoto, A. M., & Crain, A. L. (1996). AIDS volunteerism: Lesbian and gay community-based responses to HIV. In G. M. Herek & B. Greene (Eds.), *AIDS, identity, and community* (pp. 187–209). Thousand Oaks, CA: Sage.

Ortner, S. B., & Whitehead, H. (Eds.). (1981). *Sexual meanings: The cultural construction of gender and sexuality.* Cambridge: Cambridge University Press.

Padgug, R. (1989). Sexual matters: Rethinking sexuality in history. In M. Duberman, M. Vicinus, & G. Chauncey (Eds.), *Hidden from history: Reclaiming the lesbian and gay past* (pp. 54–64). New York: New American Library.

Parker, D. A., & DeCecco, J. P. (1995). Sexual expression: A global perspective. *Journal of Homosexuality, 28,* 427–430.

Parker, R. (1986). Masculinity, femininity, and homosexuality: On the anthropological interpretation of sexual meanings in Brazil. In E. Blackwood (Ed.), *The many faces of homosexuality: Anthropological approaches to homosexual behavior* (pp. 155–164). New York: Harrington Park.

Pattatucci, A. (1992). *On the quest for the elusive gay gene: Looking within and beyond determinism* (unpublished manuscript). Bethesda, MD: National Institutes of Health.

Pattatucci, A. M. L., & Hamer, D. (1995). Development and familiality of sexual orientation in females. *Behavior Genetics, 25,* 407–420.

Patterson, C. J. (1992). Children of lesbian and gay parents. *Child Development, 63,* 1025–1042.

Patterson, C. J. (1994). Children of the lesbian baby boom: Behavioral adjustments, self concepts, and sex role identity. In B. Greene & G. Herek (Eds.), *Lesbian and gay psychology* (pp. 156–175). Thousand Oaks, CA: Sage.

Patterson, C. J. (1995a). Families of the lesbian baby boom: Parents' division of labor and children's adjustment. *Developmental Psychology, 31,* 115–123.

Patterson, C. J. (1995b). Lesbian mothers, gay fathers, and their children. In A. R. D'Augelli & C. J. Patterson (Eds.), *Lesbian, gay, and bisexual development over the lifespan* (pp. 262–290). New York: Oxford University Press.

Patterson, C. J. (1995c). Sexual orientation and human development: An overview. *Developmental Psychology, 31,* 3–11.

Pattison, E. M., & Pattison, M. (1980). Ex-gays: Religiously mediated change in homosexuals. *American Journal of Psychiatry, 137,* 1553–1562.

Paul, J. P., Hays, R. P., & Coates, T. J. (1995). The impact of the HIV epidemic on U.S. gay male communities. In A. R. D'Augelli & C. J. Patterson (Eds.), *Lesbian, gay, and bisexual identities over the lifespan* (pp. 347–397). New York: Oxford.

Pearlman, S. F. (1987). The saga of continuing clash in lesbian community, or Will an army of ex-lovers fail? Boston Lesbian Psychologies Collective (Eds.), *Lesbian psychologies* (pp. 313–326). Urbana: University of Illinois Press.

Pearlman, S. F. (1989). Distancing and connectedness: Impact on couple formation in lesbian relationships. *Women and Therapy, 8,* 77–88.

Pederson, W. B. (1994). HIV risk in gay and lesbian adolescents. *Journal of Gay and Lesbian Social Services, 1,* 131–147.

Penelope, J. (1993). Heterosexual identity: Out of the closets. In S. Wilkinson & C. Kitzinger (Eds.), *Heterosexuality: A "Feminism and Psychology" reader* (pp. 261–265). London: Sage.

Pepleau, L. A. (1991). Lesbian and gay relationships. In J. C. Gonsiorek & J. D. Weinrich (Eds.), *Homosexuality: Research implications for public policy* (pp. 177–196). Newbury Park, CA: Sage.

Pepleau, L. A., & Cochran, S. D. (1982). Value orientations in the intimate relationships of gay men. *Journal of Homosexuality, 6,* 1–19.

Pepleau, L. A., & Cochran, S. D. (1990). A relationship perspective on homosexuality. In D. P. McWirther, S. A. Sanders, & J. M. Reinisch (Eds.), *Homosexuality/heterosexuality* (pp. 321–349). New York: Oxford University Press.

Pepleau, L. A., Cochran, S. D., Rook, K., & Padesky, C. (1978). Loving women: Attachment and autonomy in lesbian relationships. *Journal of Social Issues, 3,* 7–27.

Pepleau, L. A., & Gordon, S. L. (1983). The intimate relationships of lesbians and gay men. In E. R. Allgeier & N. B. McCormick (Eds.), *The changing boundaries: Gender roles and sexual behavior* (pp. 226–244). Palo Alto, CA: Mayfield.

Pepleau, L. A., Padesky, C., & Hamilton, M. (1983). Satisfaction in lesbian relationships. *Journal of Homosexuality, 8,* 23–35.

Peterson, J. L. (1995). AIDS-related risks and same-sex behaviors among African American men. In B. Greene & G. M. Herek (Eds.), *AIDS, identity, and community* (pp. 85–104). Thousand Oaks, CA: Sage.

Pharr, S. (1988). *Homophobia as a weapon of sexism.* Inverness, CA: Chadron.

Pies, C. (1985). *Considering parenthood.* San Francisco: Aunt Lute.

Pies, C. (1990). Lesbians and the choice to parent. *Marriage and Family Review, 14,* 137–154.

Pillard, R. C. (1991). Masculinity and femininity in homosexuality: "Inversion" revisited. In J. C. Gonsiorek & J. D. Weinrich (Eds.), *Homosexuality: Research implications for public policy* (pp. 32–43). London: Sage.

Plummer, K. (1981a). Going gay: Identity, life cycles and life styles in the male gay world. In J. Hart & D. Richardson (Eds.), *The theory and practice of homosexuality* (pp. 93–110). London: Routledge and Kegan Paul.

Plummer, K. (1981b). *The making of the modern homosexual.* London: Hutchinson.

Podolsky, R. (1992). The changing lesbian social scene. In B. Berzon (Ed.), *Positively gay* (pp. 26–31). Berkeley, CA: Celestial Arts.

Ponse, B. (1978). *Identities in the lesbian world: Social constructions of self.* Westport, CT: Greenwood.

Pope, R. L., & Schulz, R. (1991). Sexual attitudes and behaviors in midlife and aging homosexual males. *Journal of Homosexuality, 20,* 169–177.

Rafkin, L. (Ed.). (1990). *Different mothers: Sons and daughters of lesbians.* Pittsburgh: Clei Press.

Raphael, S., & Robinson, M. (1984). The older lesbian: Love relationships and friendship patterns. In T. Darty & S. Potter (Eds.), *Women-identified women* (pp. 67–82). Palo Alto, CA: Mayfield.

Ratner, E. F. (1988). Treatment issues for chemically dependent lesbians and gay men. In. M. Shernoff & W. A. Scott (Eds.), *The sourcebook on lesbian/gay healthcare* (pp. 162–168). Washington, DC: National Lesbian and Gay Health Foundation.

Ratti, R. (1993). Introduction. *A lotus of another color: An unfolding of South Asian gay and lesbian experience.* Boston: Alyson.

Raymond, D. (1992). "In the best interests of the child": Thoughts on homophobia and parenting. In W. Blumenfeld (Ed.), *Homophobia: How we all pay the price* (pp. 114–130). Boston: Beacon.

Reid, J. (1976). *The best little boy in the world.* New York: Ballantine.

Reid, J. (1995). Development in late life: Older lesbian and gay lives. In A. R. D'Augelli & C. J. Patterson (Eds.), *Lesbian, gay, and bisexual identities over the lifespan* (pp. 215–240). New York: Oxford University Press.

254   Remafedi, G. (1987a). Homosexual youth: A challenge to contemporary society. *Journal of the American Medical Association, 258,* 222–225.

Remafedi, G. (1987b). Male homosexuality: The adolescent's perspective. *Pediatrics, 79,* 326–330.

Remafedi, G., Farrow, J. A., & Deisher, R. W. (1991). Risk factors for attempted suicide in gay and bisexual youth. *Pediatrics, 87,* 869–875.

Remien, R. H., Carballo-Dieguez, A., & Wagner, G. (1995). Intimacy and sexual risk behaviour in serodiscordant male couples. *AIDS Care, 7,* 429–438.

Remien, R. H., & Rabkin, J. G. (1996). Long-term survival with AIDS and the role of community. In G. M. Herek & B. Greene (Eds.), *AIDS, identity, and community* (pp. 169–186). Thousand Oaks, CA: Sage.

Renzetti, Claire M. (1992). *Violent betrayal: Partner abuse in lesbian relationships.* Newbury Park, CA: Sage.

Rich, A. (1980). Compulsory heterosexuality and lesbian existence. *Signs, 5,* 631–660.

Richardson, D. (1981). Theoretical perspectives on homosexuality. In J. Hart & D. Richardson (Eds.), *The theory and practice of homosexuality* (pp. 5–37). London: Routledge and Kegan Paul.

Richardson, D. (1987). Recent challenges to traditional assumptions about homosexuality: Some implications for practice. *Journal of Homosexuality, 13,* 1–12.

Ricketts, W., & Achtenberg, R. (1990). Adoption and foster parenting for lesbians and gay men: Creating new traditions in family. *Marriage and Family Review, 14,* 83–118.

Risman, B., & Schwartz, P. (1988). Sociological research on male and female homosexuality. *Annual Review of Sociology, 14,* 125–147.

Robinson, B. E., Walters, L. H., & Skeen, P. (1989). Responses of parents to learning that their child is homosexual and concern over AIDS: A national study. *Journal of Homosexuality, 18,* 59–80.

Rofes, E. (1982). *I thought people like that killed themselves: Lesbians, gay men, and suicide.* San Francisco: Grey Fox.

Rofes, E. (1989). Opening up the classroom closet: Responding to the needs of gay and lesbian youth. *Harvard Educational Review, 59,* 444–453.

Roscoe, W. (1987). Bibliography of "berdache" and alternative gender roles among North American Indians. *Journal of Homosexuality, 14,* 81–171.

Ross, M. W. (1983). *The married homosexual man.* Boston: Routledge.

Ross, M. W. (1985a). Femininity, masculinity, and sexual orientation: Some cross-cultural comparisons. In M. W. Ross (Ed.), *Homosexuality, masculinity and femininity* (pp. 27–36). New York: Harrington Park.

Ross, M. W. (1985b). Introduction: Homosexuality and social sex roles: A re-evaluation. In M. W. Ross (Ed.), *Homosexuality, masculinity and femininity* (pp. 1–6). New York: Harrington Park.

Ross, M. W. (1991). A taxonomy of global behavior. In R. A. P. Tielman, M. Carballo, & A. C. Hendriks (Eds.), *Bisexuality and HIV/AIDS: A global perspective* (pp. 21–26). Buffalo, NY: Prometheus.

Ross, M. W., & Paul, J. P. (1992). Beyond gender: The basis of sexual attraction in bisexual men and women. *Psychological Reports, 92,* 1283–1290.

Rothblum, E. (1993). Gay and lesbian faculty face issues in academia. *APA Monitor,* September, p. 4.

Rothblum, E. (1994). Transforming lesbian sexuality. *Psychology of Women Quarterly, 18,* 627–641.

Rothblum, E., & Brehony, K. A. (1993). *Boston marriages: Romantic but asexual relationships among contemporary lesbians.* Amherst: University of Massachusetts Press.

Rudolph, J. (1988). Counselors' attitudes toward homosexuality: A selective review of the literature. *Journal of Counseling and Development, 67,* 165–168.

Russell, G. M. (1995). The psychological effects of Amendment 2 on lesbians, gay men, and bisexuals in Colorado. Unpublished manuscript.

Rust, P. C. (1992). The politics of sexual identity: Sexual attraction and behavior among lesbian and bisexual women. *Social Problems, 39*, 366–386.

Rust, P. C. (1993). "Coming out" in the age of social constructionism: Sexual identity formation among lesbian and bisexual women. *Gender and Society, 7*, 50–77.

Sampson, E. E. (1993). Identity politics: Challenges to psychology's understandings. *American Psychologist, 48*, 1219–1230.

Sang, B. (1984). Lesbian relationships: A struggle toward partner equality. In T. Darty & S. Potter (Eds.), *Women-identified women* (pp. 51–65). Palo Alto, CA: Mayfield.

Sang, B. (1992). Counseling and psychotherapy with midlife and older lesbians. In S. Dworkin & F. Gutierrez (Eds.), *Counseling gay men and lesbians: Journey to the end of the rainbow* (pp. 35–48). Alexandria, VA: American Association for Counseling and Development.

Sang, B. (1993). Some existential issues of midlife lesbians. In L. Garnets & D. Kimmel (Eds.), *Psychological perspectives on lesbian and gay male experiences* (pp. 500–516). New York: Columbia University Press.

Sankar, A. (1986). Sisters and brothers, lovers and enemies: Marriage resistance in southern Kwangtung. In E. Blackwood (Ed.), *The many faces of homosexuality: Anthropological approaches to homosexual behavior* (pp. 69–95). New York: Harrington Park.

Saunders, J. M., & Valente, S. M. (1987). Suicide risk among gay men and lesbians: A review. *Death Studies, 11*, 1–23.

Savin-Williams, R. (1989). Coming out to parents and self-esteem among gay and lesbian youths. *Journal of Homosexuality, 18*, 1–35.

Savin-Williams, R. (1990). Gay and lesbian adolescents. *Marriage and Family Review, 14*, 197–216.

Savin-Williams, R. (1994). Verbal and physical abuse as stressors in the lives of lesbian, gay male, and bisexual youths: Associations with school problems, running away, substance abuse, prostitution, and suicide. *Journal of Consulting and Clinical Psychology, 62*, 261–269.

Savin-Williams, R. (1995). Lesbian, gay male, and bisexual adolescents. In A. R. D'Augelli & C. J. Patterson (Eds.), *Lesbian, gay, and bisexual identities over the lifespan* (pp. 165–189). New York: Oxford University Press.

Savin-Williams, R. C., & Rodriguez, R. G. (1993). A developmental, clinical perspective on lesbian, gay male, and bisexual youths. In T. P. Gullotta, G. R. Adams, & R. Montemayor (Eds.), *Advances in adolescent development* (Vol. 5) (pp. 77–101). Newbury Park, CA: Sage.

Schippers, J. (1987). Homosexual identity, essentialism, and constructionism. In D. Altman, C. Vance, M. Vicinus, & J. Weeks (Eds.), *Homosexuality, which homosexuality?* (pp. 139–147). Amsterdam: Dekker.

Schneider, M. (1989). Sappho was a right on adolescent: Growing up lesbian. *Journal of Homosexuality, 17*, 111–130.

Scrivner, R., & Eldridge, N. S. (1995). Lesbian and gay family psychology. In R. H. Mikesell, D. D. Lusterman, & S. H. McDaniel (Eds.), *Family psychology and systems therapy: A handbook*. Washington, DC: American Psychological Association.

Sears, J. T. (1989). The impact of gender and race on growing up lesbian and gay in the South. *National Women's Studies Association Journal, 1*, 422–457.

Shernoff, M. (1995). Male couples and their relationship styles. *Journal of Gay and Lesbian Social Services, 2*, 43–57.

Shidlo, A. (1994). Internalized homophobia: Conceptual and empirical issues in measurement. In B. Greene & G. M. Herek (Eds.), *Lesbian and gay psychology: Theory, research, and clinical applications* (pp. 176–205). Thousand Oaks, CA: Sage.

256   Shields, S. A. (1975). Functionalism, Darwinism and the psychology of women: A study in social myth. *American psychologist, 30*, 739–753.

Shields, S. A., & Harriman, R. E. (1985). Fear of male homosexuality: Cardiac responses of low and high homonegative males. In J. P. DeCecco (Ed.), *Baiters, bashers, & bigots: Homophobia in American society* (pp. 53–67). New York: Harrington Park.

Shilts, R. (1987). *And the band played on: Politics, people, and the AIDS epidemic.* New York: St. Martin's.

Shively, M. G., & DeCecco, J. P. (1977). Components of sexual identity. *Journal of Homosexuality, 3*, 41–48.

Siegelman, M. (1972a). Adjustment of homosexual and heterosexual women. *Archives of British Psychiatry, 120*, 477–481.

Siegelman, M. (1972b). Adjustment of male homosexuals and heterosexuals. *Archives of Sexual Behavior, 2*, 9–25.

Silvera, M. (1991). *Piece of my heart: A lesbian of color anthology.* Toronto: Sister Vision.

Silverstein, C. (1991). Psychological and medical treatments of homosexuality. In J. C. Gonsiorek & J. D. Weinrich (Eds.), *Homosexuality: Research implications for public policy* (pp 101–114). Newbury Park, CA: Sage.

Slater, B. R., (1988). Essential issues in working with lesbian and gay male youths. *Professional Psychology: Research and Practice, 19*, 226–235.

Slater, S., & Mencher, J. (1991). The lesbian family life cycle: A contextual approach. *American Journal of Orthopsychiatry, 6*, 372–382.

Smith, B. (1993). Homophobia: Why bring it up? In H. Abelove, M. Barale, & D. Halperin (Eds.), *The lesbian and gay studies reader* (pp. 99–102). New York: Routledge.

Smith-Rosenberg, C. (1975). The female world of love and ritual: Relations between women in nineteenth century America. *Signs: The Journal of Women in Culture and Society, 1*, 1–29.

Smith-Rosenberg, C. (1985). *Disorderly conduct: Visions of gender in Victorian America.* New York: Alfred A. Knopf.

Socarides, C. W. (1975). *Beyond sexual freedom.* New York: Quadrangle.

Socarides, C. W. (1978). *Homosexuality.* New York: Jason Aronson.

Sophie, J. (1986). A critical examination of stage theories of lesbian identity development. *Journal of Homosexuality, 12*, 39–51.

Sophie, J. (1987). Internalized homophobia and lesbian identity. *Journal of Homosexuality, 14*, 53–66.

Steckel, A. (1987). Psychosocial development of children of lesbian mothers. In F. W. Bozett (Ed.), *Gay and lesbian parents* (pp. 75–85). New York: Praeger.

Stein, E. (Ed.). (1992). *Forms of desire: Sexual orientation and the social constructionist controversy.* New York: Routledge.

Stiglitz, E. (1990). Caught between two worlds: The impact of a child on a lesbian couple's relationship. *Women and Therapy, 19*, 99–116.

Storms, M. (1980). Theories of sexual orientation. *Journal of Personality and Social Psychology, 38*, 783–92.

Strommen, E. F. (1989). "You're a what?": Family members' reactions to the disclosure of homosexuality. *Journal of Homosexuality, 18*, 35–78.

Suppe, F. (1984). In defense of a multidimensional approach to sexual identity. *Journal of Homosexuality, 10*, 7–14.

Swaab, D. F., Gooren, L. J. G., & Hofman, M. A. (1995). Brain research, gender, and sexual orientation. *Journal of Homosexuality, 28*, 283–301.

Tafoya, T. (1992). Native gay and lesbian issues: The two-spirited. In B. Berzon (Ed.), *Positively gay* (pp. 253–260). Berkeley, CA: Celestial Arts.

Tafoya, T., & Rowell, R. (1988). Counseling Native American lesbians and gays: In M. Shernoff & W. A. Scott (Eds.), *The sourcebook for lesbian/gay health care* (pp. 63–67). Washington, DC: National Lesbian and Gay Health Foundation.

Taylor, C. L. (1986). Mexican male homosexual interaction in public contexts. In E. Blackwood (Ed.), *The many faces of homosexuality: Anthropological approaches to homosexual behavior* (pp. 117–136). New York: Harrington Park.

Terman, L. M., & Miles, C. C. (1936). *Sex and personality: Studies in masculinity and femininity.* New York: McGraw-Hill.

Thompson, N. L., McCandless, B. R., & Strickland, B. (1971). Personal adjustment of male and female homosexuals and heterosexuals. *Journal of Abnormal Psychology, 78,* 237–240.

Tiefer, L. (1987). Social constructionism and the study of human sexuality. In P. Shaver & C. Hendrick (Eds.), *Sex and gender: Review of personality and social psychology* (vol. 7, pp. 70–94). Beverly Hills, CA: Sage.

Tiefer, L. (1991). Historical, scientific, clinical, and feminist criticisms of "The Human Response Cycle" model. *Annual Review of Sex Research, 2,* 1–23.

Tremble, B., Schneider, M., & Appathurai, C. (1989). Growing up gay or lesbian in a multicultural context. *Journal of Homosexuality, 17,* 243–267.

Troiden, R. R. (1989). The formation of homosexual identities. *Journal of Homosexuality, 17,* 43–73.

Ulrig, L. (1984). *The two of us: Affirming, celebrating and symbolizing gay and lesbian relationships.* Boston: Alyson.

Unger, R. K. (1979). Toward a redefinition of sex and gender. *American Psychologist, 34,* 1085–1094.

Unks, G. (Ed.). (1995). *The gay teen: Educational practice and theory for lesbian, gay, and bisexual adolescents.* New York: Routledge.

Vacha, K. (1985). *Quiet fire: Memoirs of older gay men.* Trumansburg, NY: Crossing Press.

Vasey, P. L. (1995). Homosexual behavior in primates: A review of evidence and theory. *International Journal of Primatology, 16*(2), 173–204.

Vicinus, M. (1988). "They wonder to which sex I belong": The historical roots of modern lesbian identity. In D. Altman, C. Vance, M. Vicinus, & J. Weeks (Eds.), *Homosexuality, which homosexuality?* (pp. 171–198). Amsterdam: Dekker.

von Schulthess, B. (1992). Violence in the streets: Anti-lesbian assault and harassment in San Francisco. In G. M. Herek & K. T. Berrill (Eds.), *Hate crimes: Confronting violence against lesbians and gay men* (pp. 65–75). Newbury Park, CA: Sage.

Weeks, J. (1977). *Coming out: Homosexual politics in Britain from the nineteenth century to the present.* London: Quartet.

Weeks, J. (1981). Discourse, desire and sexual deviance: Some problems in a history of homosexuality. In K. Plummer (Ed.), *The making of the modern homosexual* (pp. 76–111). London: Hutchinson.

Weeks, J. (1985). *Sexuality and its discontents.* London: Routledge & Kegan Paul.

Weeks, J. (1989). *Sex, politics, and society: The regulation of sexuality since 1800* (2d ed.). London: Longman.

Weinberg, G. (1972). *Society and the healthy homosexual.* New York: St. Martin's.

Weinberg, M. S., Williams, C. J., & Pryor, D. W. (1994). *Dual attraction: Understanding bisexuality.* New York: Oxford University Press.

Weinberg, T. S. (1983). *Gay men, gay selves: The social construction of homosexual identities.* New York: Irvington.

Weinrich, J. D., & Williams, W. L. (1991) Strange customs, familiar lives: Homosexualities in other cultures. In J. C. Gonsiorek & J. D. Weinrich (Eds.), *Homosexuality: Research implications for public policy* (pp. 44–59). Newbury Park, CA: Sage.

258 Weise, E. R. (1992). *Closer to home: Bisexuality and feminism.* Seattle, WA: Seal.

Weissman, E. (1978). Kids who attack gays. *Christopher Street,* August, pp. 9–13.

West, C., & Zimmerman, D. H. (1987). Doing gender. *Gender and Society, 1,* 125–151.

Weston, K. (1991). *Families we choose: Lesbians, gays, and kinship.* New York: Columbia University Press.

Whisman, V. (1993). Identity crises: Who is lesbian, anyway. In A. Stern (Ed.), *Sisters, sexperts, and queers: Beyond the Lesbian Nation* (pp. 47–60). New York: Penguin.

Whitehead, H. (1981). The bow and the burdenstrap: A new look at institutionalized homosexuality in native North America. In S. Ortner & H. Whitehead (Eds.), *Sexual meanings: The cultural construction of gender and sexuality* (pp. 80–115). Cambridge: Cambridge University Press.

Wieringa, S. (1987). An anthropological critique of constructionism: Berdaches and butches. In D. Altman, C. Vance, M. Vicinus, & J. Weeks (Eds.), *Homosexuality, which homosexuality?* (pp. 215–238). Amsterdam: Dekker.

Williams, W. (1986a). Persistence and change in the Berdache tradition among contemporary Lakota Indians. *Journal of Homosexuality, 11,* 191–200.

Williams, W. (1986b). *The spirit and the flesh: Sexual diversity in American Indian culture.* Boston: Beacon.

Wirth, S. (1983). Coming out close to home: Principles for psychotherapy with families of lesbians and gay men. In S. Bergstrom & L. Cruz (Eds.), *Counseling lesbian and gay male youth* (pp. 8–20). New York: National Network of Runaway and Youth Services, Inc.

Wolf, D. (1979). *The lesbian community.* Berkeley: University of California Press.

Wolverton, T. (1992). Reunification: Changing relationships between gay men and lesbians coping with AIDS. In B. Berzon (Ed.), *Positively gay* (pp. 226–231). Berkeley, CA: Celestial Arts.

Wooden, W. S., Kawasaki, H., & Mayeda, R. (1983). Lifestyles and identity among gay Japanese-American males. *Alternative Lifestyles, 5,* 236–243.

Zinik, G. (1985). Identity conflict or adaptive flexibility? Bisexuality reconsidered. *Journal of Homosexuality, 11,* 7–19.

Zita, J. (1981). Historical amnesia and the lesbian continuum. *Signs, 7,* 172–187.

INDEX

acceptance, 98, 103, 118

accommodation, 210–11

ACT-UP, 219, 223–24

Adelman, M., 170–73

adolescence, LGB: coming out in, 144–45, 153, 154–55; and identity, 146–50; isolation during, 147–48; and LGB experience, 141–42; risks during, 150–54; self-identification in, 142–44; violence in, 150–51

Adorno, Frenkel-Brunswik, Levinson, and Sanford, 47

adult hormonal imbalance, 68

affectional attraction, 25

African American LBGs, 129–32

Afrocentrism, 129–30

ageism in LGB communities, 166, 215

aging: perception of, 160, 162; problems of, 164–70; styles of, 170–74

AIDS/HIV: and African Americans, 130, 131–32; and brain structures, 73–74; and coming out, 112, 116; and families of choice, 208–209; and Hispanic Americans, 136; and identity formation, 109, 111; impact of, 222–23; LGB communities and, 23, 208–209, 217, 220–26; and lesbian/gay male relations, 224–26; and midlife, 157; psychology and, 23; and relationships, 193–96; and sexuality, 192–94; and stereotypes, 48; and violence, 54; and teens, 145, 151

Allport, G., 43

Amendment 2, Colorado, 56

American Psychological Association (APA), 3, 18, 19, 20

androgen, 69, 70

anticipatory socialization, 146

anti-Semitism, 46, 47, 126

Asian American LBGs, 132–35

assimilation, 96

Atkinson, Morten, and Sue, 123

attitudes: altering, 57–59; function of, 50–52

authoritarian personality, the, 47, 52

autonomy vs. commitment, 186

aversion therapy, 18

bars as social centers, 210–11, 214

Bart, P., 86

behavior change post-AIDS, 221–22

behaviorism, 78–82

Bem, Sandra, 35

benefits, access to by same-sex partners, 168–69, 180, 218–19

berdache, the, 15–16

bereavement, 168, 208

Berger, R., 193

biculturalism, 232

Bieber, I., et al., 77
Bigner and Jacobsen, 198
biological explanations of sexual
    orientation, 65–75, 89–90
biphobia, 39, 42, 95, 113, 218
bisexuality: among African Americans,
    131–32; authenticity of, 104; emerging
    community of, 214, 218; complex
    models of, 28; gay, lesbian attitudes on,
    39, 42; identity development models,
    104–109; origins of, 83; relationships
    in, 194; as unclear category, 25
Blumenstein and Schwartz, 107, 108, 179,
    192, 193
Bonilla and Porter, 129
"Boston marriages," 16
Bozett, F. W., 120, 203
brain organization: and sex differences,
    69–71; and sexual orientation,
    71–75
Brown, L. S., 93, 232
Bryant and Demian, 179–80, 181, 182
butch-femme roles, 212, 214
Byne, W., 75
Byne and Parsons, 82–83

capitulation, 99
Cass's identity development model, 87,
    102–103
categorizations: deconstructing, 228–31;
    problems of, 25, 29–30, 228; as
    stereotyping, 46–48, 105
Centers for Disease Control, 220
children: of LBG parents, 160–61, 180–81,
    196–204; as life-structuring, 160
Chodorow, N., 77
choice, 84–88, 90–91, 121
chromosomal sex, 66–68
classism, 126
"clone" style, 213–14, 215
Clunis and Green's model of lesbian
    couple development, 188, 190, 203
cognitive dissonance reduction, 46
cognitive sources of prejudice, 44–46
cohabitation, 182
collusion as difference management, 97

coming out: by bisexuals, 112–13; to
    children, 203; and cohort effects,
    110–12; to family, 116–19, 145; and
    identity development, 110; as political,
    22–23, 212–13; reasons for and against,
    114–16; to spouses, 119–21; stages in,
    113–14, 117–19; and suicide, 153; by
    teens, 144–45, 153, 154–55
"coming to terms," 5–10, 147–50, 227–35
communities, LBG: and AIDS, 23,
    208–209, 217, 220–26; diversity in,
    215–18; emergence of, 21–23, 209–15;
    families of choice in, 205–209;
    generation gap in, 173, 215–16;
    intersection with other communities,
    122–39; in midlife, 161; in old age,
    170–72; post—World War II changes,
    21–22, 209–12; present day, 218–26;
    racism in, 126–27, 215; after Stonewall,
    212–15
"community" as construct, 215–18
compartmentalization, 97
concordance, genetic, 66
confrontation as difference management,
    97
constructionism: and psychology, 8–10, 21,
    227–31; and sexual orientation, 6–8,
    228
"contagion" hypothesis, 81
conversion therapies, 19–20
correlates of homonegativity, 48–50
courtship, 179
covering and blending as stigma
    management, 100
cross-gender behavior as predictive, 71–73,
    81, 153
cross-sex: behavior, 64, 70; brain
    organization, 69, 74
cultural scripts, 146

Darwin, Charles, 17
D'Augelli's "affirmative assumption," 100,
    110, 129, 155, 69
Daughters of Bilitis, 210–12
Davies, P., 97
denial, 98, 117, 49

depression and LGB teens, 152–54
detypification, 86–87
DeVine, J. L., 117
Diagnostic and Statistical Manual (DSM), 18–19, 23
difference: eroticization of, 83–84; of lesbians vs. gay males, 30, 161, 179–80, 188–94, 214, 233–34; management of, 95–97; among older LGBs, 172; and prejudice, 43–48; "qualifying," 94
disclosure: by adolescents, 142; in marriage, 120; reasons for, 114–15; and well-being, 110
discredited identity, 124–25
diversity within LBG identities, 122–39
DNA, 67–68
dominance: eroticization of, 35; as masculine, 34, 72
Doucette, J., 124
Dunker, B., 169

ego-defensive function of attitude, 51, 54
"egodystonic homosexuality," 19
elective lesbianism, 84–88, 121, 214
Eliason, M., 49
Ellis, Havelock, 17
environmental explanations for sexual orientation, 75–82, 90
Epstein, S., 228–29
eroticization: of difference, 83–84; of dominance, 35
Espin, O. M., 137
essentialism: in feminism, 78; and views of lesbian identity, 85; in psychology, 8–10, 88, 111, 228–31; and sexual orientation, 5–6
experience-altered neurological structures, 74
experiential function of attitude, 50–51

Faderman, Lillian, 34
"familial clustering," 68
families: assault within, 55; of choice, 205–209; coming out to, 116–19, 143, 145; of LGB teens, 143, 145; LGB, 177–202, 215; in minority cultures,

127–39; as origin of homphilia, 77; support by for LBGs, 55–56, 184–85
femininity: as dependent, 183; as relational, 78, 188; as submissive, 34–35, 135
feminism: and aging, 166; and identity development, 111; lesbian, 34, 84–88, 157, 214, 215–17; and psychoanalytic theory, 77–78
Freud, Sigmund, 17, 76
friendship networks, 207–209
Friend's model for LGB aging, 170–71, 174
frustration/aggression hypothesis, 47
fundamental attribution error, 45

gay gene, 24
gay rights movement, 18, 19, 22–23, 157, 212–15, 218–19
gender: in Asian/Pacific Island cultures, 132–33, 134; in bisexual identity, 108; among children of LGB parents, 200–201; compliance, 35–36, 64–65; cultural variations in, 37, 132–38; deviance, 81; display, 3–4; and heterosexual assumption, 33–36; and attitudes, 51–52, 54, 59; in Hispanic culture, 135–36; and homosexuality, 36–38; importance of, 233–35; and LGB parents, 198, 199–200; in LGB relationships, 183–84, 188–94; among midlife LGBs, 159–60; in Native American culture, 137–38; politics of, 34; and prediction of gay identity, 71–72; in relationships, 183–84, 188–94, 198, 199–200; and research assumptions, 64; roles, 3–4, 35–36, 59; in sex, 191–93
generation gap in LGB communities, 173, 215–16
genetic explanations of sexual orientation, 66–68
ghettoization, 96–97
Goffman, E., 124–25
Golden, C., 85–86
Gooren, L. J. G., 74–75
Greece, ancient, 16

group alignment, 99
Grube, J., 216

Herdt and Boxer, 213
Herek, Gregory, 34–35, 49, 50–52, 54
heterophobia, 79
heterosexism: 24; and gender roles, 37–38;
    vs. homophobia, 38–39;
    institutionalized, 49; and prejudice,
    42–48; as privilege, 39–42; as
    projection, 51–52; psychological
    correlates of, 48–50; and religious
    beliefs, 51, 131; trauma caused by,
    56–57; and violence, 52–56
heterosexuality: vs. homosexuality, as
    model, 24–25; as norm, 31–36, 39, 64,
    231–33; and sexual abuse, 79–80, 202
Hirschfield, Magnus, 17
Hispanic or Latin American LBGs,
    135–37
homophile organizations, 22–23, 210–12
homophobia: vs. heterosexism, 24, 38–39;
    institutionalized, 39; internalized,
    19–20, 94–95, 113, 183, 229; research
    on, 48–50
homosexuality: as acts, 16–17, 33;
    biological treatments for, 18; and
    heterosexuality, 24–29, 32–36; as
    identity, 17, 33: as narcissism, 76; as
    pathology, 17–21, 22, 23, 32, 63, 76–77,
    211; as sin, 16, 24, 76, 91, 113
Hooker, Evelyn, 18
hormonal explanations of sexual
    orientation, 64, 68–75
Hudson, Rock, 225
Hunter, Alan, 35
hypothalamus, the, 70, 73–75

identity: vs. acts, 16–17, 33; in
    adolescence, 146–50; and biology,
    89–90; and culture, 88–89; development
    models, 101–11; discredited, 124–25;
    homosexuality as, 17, 33; as individual,
    121; intersecting, 124–39; lesbian,
    84–88, 121; and lifespan development,
    140–74; minority, 123–24; narratives of,

9–10, 86; prediction of, 71–72; sexual,
    4; sexual activity as, 221; women's,
    78
illusory correlation, 45
Illustrated Medical Encyclopedia, 32
in-groups, 44, 47
interactionist explanations of sexual
    orientation, 82–84, 91
interstitial nuclei of the anterior
    hypothalamus (INAH), 73–75
isolation, forms of, 147–48

Jennes, V., 86–87
just world phenomenon, 45–46

Kehoe (researcher), 172–73
Kimmel and Sang, 158
Kinsey, A. C., 20, 25–29, 210–11
Kitzinger, C., 34
Kitzinger and Wilkinson, 86
Klein, F., 25–26, 27–29, 105, 106, 218
"knowledge," 6–7, 8, 57
Krafft-Ebbing, Richard, 17
Kurdek, L. A., 186
Kurdek and Schmitt, 190

Ladder, The, 212
Lee, J. A., 172
"lesbian continuum, the," 34
lesbian feminism, 34, 84–88, 157, 214,
    215–17
lesbian/gay relations in AIDS crisis,
    224–26
LeVay, S., 73–74
LGB experience as normative, 232–33
lifespan development, 140–74
Lorde, Audre, 125–26
lordosis, 70
"lovemap," 82
low self-esteem and prejudice, 46–47

McCarthy era, 22, 112, 211
machismo/marianismo, 135
McWirther and Mattison model of gay
    male partnerships, 187–88
marginality, 232

marriage, hetero: in Asian/Pacific Island cultures, 134; coming out within, 119–21: as heterosexual privilege, 40; LGBs in, 194–95
Martin, A. D., 149, 234
Martin and Hetrick, 148
"masculine" role in intercourse, 136
masculinity: as dominance, 34–35, 72; and ego-defensive attitudes, 51–52, 54, 58–59; as hormonal, 69–73; as independence, 78; as sexuality, 192–93
Masters and Johnson, 19–20
Mendola, M., 179
mental illness, homosexuality as, 18–20, 22, 63, 76, 211
midlife LGB experience: cohort effects in, 156–58; developmental issues in, 158–64; relationships and sexuality in, 161–62
minority communities, homonegativity in, 127–28, 130–31, 132–35, 136–37, 138
Minority Identity Development Model, 123–24
minstrelization, 99, 149
models of identity development, 101–11
Money, J., 4, 72, 73, 82
monogamy, 172, 192–93, 221
mounting, 70
multiple oppression, 124–26, 166

narrative, 9–10, 86
National Gay and Lesbian Task Force, 53, 55
Native American LBGs, 137–39
"nature," 32–33
nature-nurture controversy, 75–76
nongenital physical expression, 191–92
normative creativity, 232–33

O'Connell, A., 204
old age among LGBs: community response, 174; problems of researching, 164–65; health care in, 167–68; mental health in, 165; relationships in, 172–73

out-groups: homogeneity effect, 44; projection onto, 46–47

parents, LBG, 160–61, 180–81, 196–204
"passing," 96, 98–99, 149, 170
"paternal transmission," 68
pathologizing of homosexuality, 17–21, 22, 23, 32, 63, 76–77, 211
Pattatucci, A., 63
Patterson, C. J., 203
Pattison and Pattison, 20
Paul, Hays, and Coates, 222
Pepleau, L. A., 183, 189
Pepleau and Cochran, 185–86, 187
Pharr, Suzanne, 35
political action, 218–19, 223–24
Ponse, B., 85
population, LBG, 28–29
power and gender in relationships, 189
pregnancy among lesbian teens, 151
prejudice: cognitive sources of, 42–48; personality correlates of, 46–48
privilege, heterosexual, 39–42
psychiatry, 17–21, 76–77
psychodynamic explanations of sexual orientation, 75–78
psychological risks to teens, 151–54
psychology: and AIDS, 23; bias in, 20; and constructionism, 8–10, 21, 227–31; and essentialism, 8–10; on gender, 36–37, 233–35; historic role, 17–21, 23, 36; and the individual, 92–93; LGB affirmative, 20–21, 23; on sexual orientation, 17–30
psychotherapy and constructionism, 229–31

"qualifying difference," 94
Queer Nation, 218, 219

racism: 44–46, 53; in LGB communities, 126–27, 131, 134; and teens, 153–54
reaction formation, 149–50
redefinition as stigma management, 98
Reid, J., 169, 174

relationships: in adolescence, 154; AIDS and, 222–23; endurance of, 185–86; gender roles in, 183–84, 188–94, 198, 199–200; in midlife, 161–62; and parenting, 199–200; patterns of, 178–83, 193–96; stages in, 186–88; stresses on, 195–96

religious beliefs and heterosexism, 51, 130. 135

Remien, Carballo-Dieguez, and Wagner, 193

repair as stigma management, 98

reparative therapies, 19–20, 24

research: on aging LGBs, 164–65, 169; anthropological, 14–16; on brain structures, 73–75; on children of LBG parents, 200–201; on choice, 84; on coping with AIDS, 223, 224; on disclosure, 114–16, 120–21; essentialist, 9–10; gender assumptions of, 64; on gender in sex, 192; genetic, 66–68; on homophobia/heterosexism, 48–58; on origins of homosexuality, 36–37; interpretation of, 71; on sources of prejudice, 42–48; on relationships, 178–96; on sexual orientation, 29–30, 63–92; on teen suicide, 152–53

Rich, Adrienne, 33–34, 35

"romantic friendships," 16

Russell, G. M., 219

Rust, P. C., 111

Savin-Williams, R., 141

scapegoating, 47

seduction or recruitment theory, 79–80

selective perception, 45

self-identification, 142–44

self-in-relation theory, 78

sex hormones, 68–75

sexology, 17–21

"sex role," 4

sex-typical behaviors, 69–70

sexual abuse, 79–80

sexuality: and aging, 172–73; and gender, 191–93; as personality, 17; vs. sexual orientation, 25, 27, 71, 78

sexualized culture, gay male, 213–14

sexually dimorphic nucleus, the (SDN), 70, 73–75

sexual orientation: biological explanations, 65–75, 89–90; brain organization and, 69–75; choice in, 84–88, 90–91; components of, 228–29; as continuum, 25–30, 105; cultural variations in, 12–16, 37; defined, 4–5; as dichotomous, 24–25, 91; and essentialism, 5–6, 8–10; as gender, 37–38, 52, 233–35; genetic explanations, 66–68; historical variations in, 16–23, 37; hormonal explanations, 68–75; as an inherent quality, 6, 7, 9, 10, 17; interactionist explanations, 82–84, 91; meaning of, 12–31; plasticity of, 109–10, 111, 230; psychodynamic explanations of, 75–78; in psychology, 9–10, 29–30, 227–31; vs. sexuality, 25, 27, 71, 78; social learning theory explanations for, 78–82; as socially constructed, 6–10, 228

Shively and DeCecco, 25

"sissy" role, 72, 82

social-exchange theory, 186

social-expressive function of attitude, 51, 58

social-identity function of attitude, 51, 54, 58

social learning theory explanations of sexual orientation, 78–82

stereotypes: of African Americans, 130; and aged LGBs, 170; of bisexuals, 105; of LGBs, 48; and prejudice, 42–43; as roles for teens, 144; sources of, 44–48

stigma: and children of LGB parents, 202; community and, 219; management, 95–101, 148–50; varieties of, 93–95

Stonewall, 22–23, 54, 112, 157, 212–13

Storms, M., 25

suicide, teen, 144, 150, 152–54

teens, LGB, 141–55

terminology of sex and gender, 2–5

testosterone, 74

"tomboy" role, 35, 73
Tremble, Schneider, and Appathurai, 130
Troiden, R. R.: identity development
    model, 103–104; on stigma
    management, 97–100, 149
"true" lesbianism debate, 216–17
twins, 66–68

unsafe sex, 133–34, 151, 193–94, 221
urbanization, 210

values and attitude-change, 58–59
verbal harassment, 53, 150
violence: consequences of, 55–56; by family
    members, 53, 150; and heterosexism,
    52–53; in LGB couples, 183;
    perpetrators of, 54–55; against teens,
    150–51
vivid cases, 44–45

volitional explanations of sexual
    orientation, 84–88, 90–91

Weinberg, George, 38
Weinberg, Williams, and Pryor, 107, 108,
    193
Weston, K., 206, 207
"white problem," homophilia as, 133
Williams, W., 15
wills for same-sex partners, 168
Winkte, the, 15
Wirth, Scott, 117
World War II shift in LBG life, 21–22,
    209–12

Xq28 chromosomal segment, 67–68, 88

Zinik, G., 106
Zita, J., 217